BTEC Level 3 National
Sport & Exercise Sciences
Third Edition

BTEC Level 3 National Sport & Exercise Sciences

Third Edition

Jennifer Stafford-Brown
and Simon Rea

Orders: please contact Bookpoint Ltd, 130 Milton Park, Abingdon, Oxon OX14 4SB. Telephone: (44) 01235 827720. Fax: (44) 01235 400454. Lines are open from 9.00 – 5.00, Monday to Saturday, with a 24-hour message answering service. You can also order through our website www.hoddereducation.co.uk.

British Library Cataloguing in Publication Data
A catalogue record for this title is available from the British Library

ISBN: 978 1 444 111 989

First Published 2010
Impression number   10 9 8 7 6 5 4 3 2 1
Year   2016 2015 2014 2013 2012 2011 2010

Copyright © 2010 Jennifer Stafford-Brown, Simon Rea

Cover photo © Aflo Foto Agency/Alamy
Typeset by Fakenham Photosetting, Fakenham, Norfolk

Printed in Italy for Hodder Education, an Hachette UK Company.

Contents

Mandatory units in **bold**

🖱 *If you see this icon next to a unit, you will be able to access it by logging onto Dynamic Learning Student Online.*

vi

Mandatory units in **bold**

If you see this icon next to a unit, you will be able to access it by logging onto Dynamic Learning Student Online.

vii

Mandatory units in **bold**

🖱 *If you see this icon next to a unit, you will be able to access it by logging onto Dynamic Learning Student Online.*

Mandatory units in **bold**

⌁ *If you see this icon next to a unit, you will be able to access it by logging onto Dynamic Learning Student Online.*

Acknowledgements

I would like to thank a number of people who have provided me with help in various different ways in researching and writing this book.

First of all, my thanks go out to my husband Matt and children Ellie and Alex for their patience and encouragement throughout the writing process, and to my parents, Ann and Brian, for all of their support and help over the years.

I would also like to say a big 'thank you!' to my friend and co-author, Simon, for all of his hard work, expertise and enthusiasm.

I would also like to thank Paul Butler for writing **Unit 13** *Current Issues in Sport*, which is available via Dynamic Learning.

Finally, I would also like to thank Lavinia Porter and Alison Walters and all of the people who have helped with the publication of this book.

JENNIFER STAFFORD-BROWN

Thank you to all the people who made this book possible: Lavinia Porter and Alison Walters at Hodder; my co-author, Jenny, for her continual support and enthusiasm; and to the additional authors for sharing their expertise.

Thank you to my parents, Tony and Pam, the Sewells and the Samways, for their interest, support and understanding and continuing the family's love of sport.

Above all, to Tanya, who gave me the time and space to get the writing done and who brought love, fun and happiness to my life.

SIMON REA

The authors and publishers wish to thank the following for their permission to reproduce their images:

Unit 1 introduction	Warren Little/Getty Images
1.29	David Rogers/Getty Images
Unit 2 introduction	Phimann/Mauritius/Photolibrary Group
2.1	www.purestockX.com
2.4	Jon Buckle/EMPICS Sport/Press Association Images
2.13	© PCN Photography/Corbis
Unit 3 introduction	David Davies/PA Wire/Press Association Images
3.2	Achim Scheidemann/DPA/Press Association Images
3.3	Glyn Kirk/Action Plus
Unit 4 introduction	BEN STANSALL/AFP/Getty Images
4.1	© Detail Nottingham/Alamy
Unit 5 introduction	© Tatyana Parfyonova—Fotolia.com
5.1	© Daniel Dempster Photography/Alamy
5.2	© Adrian Sherratt/Alamy
Unit 6 introduction	ADRIAN DENNIS/AFP/Getty Images
6.1	IAN STEWART/AFP/Getty Images
6.2	Matthew Ashton/EMPICS Sport/Press Association Images
6.5	Kevin Frayer/AP Photo/Press Association Images
6.6	Glyn Kirk/Action Plus
Unit 7 introduction	© Roy Morsch/Corbis
7.1	ARTHUR GLAUBERMAN/SCIENCE PHOTOLIBRARY
7.3	MARTIN M. ROTKER/SCIENCE PHOTOLIBRARY

Introduction

BTEC National Sport and Exercise Sciences for the Edexcel examination boards is a subject that helps to prepare you for work in the sports industry or for higher education within the fields of sport science and sport.

BTEC Level 3 National Sport and Exercise Sciences Third Edition is a comprehensive textbook that covers all mandatory units in the BTEC National Sport and Exercise Sciences qualifications that include:

- National Certificate in Sport and Exercise Sciences
- National Subsidiary Diploma in Sport and Exercise Sciences
- National Diploma in Sport and Exercise Sciences
- National Extended Diploma in Sport and Exercise Sciences

To ensure that you are following the correct pathway for your chosen qualification, please see the table in 'Pathways for BTEC National Sport and Exercise Sciences Qualifications'.

As well as all mandatory units, *BTEC Level 3 National Sport and Exercise Sciences Third Edition* contains many of the more popular optional units that you can take. Some optional units have been provided as PDFs for you to read online or download via Dynamic Learning. For details of these, look for the Dynamic Learning icon on the Contents page. For details about Dynamic Learning and how to access these online units, see the inside front cover of this book.

The BTEC National Sport and Exercise Sciences qualifications are all assessed through coursework. You will be given assignments that cover all of the grading criteria for each unit that you are studying. *BTEC Level 3 National Sport and Exercise Sciences Third Edition* will help to show you where you can find the information related to the grading criteria that you are working on, which will help to ensure that you are including the appropriate subject content in your coursework.

Success in this qualification is a combination of your teacher's expertise, your own motivation and ability as a student, and accessibility to the appropriate resources–including a relevant textbook! Written by senior external verifiers and experienced BTEC Sport and Exercise Sciences teachers, *BTEC Level 3 National Sport and Exercise Sciences Third Edition* is highly relevant to your qualification and provides you with resources that will not only support and help you prepare for your assessments, but which will also stretch and challenge you.

Within *BTEC Level 3 National Sport and Exercise Sciences Third Edition* you will find that each unit offers a wide range of learning resources, including:

- **Activities** related to each of the grading criteria to help you to practice assessment activities for your coursework. Each activity has a suggested time-frame so that you will have an idea of how long you need to spend on each.
- **Clear signposting throughout:** each section is clearly signposted with the relevant grading criteria
- **Quick quizzes:** at the end of each learning outcome are a number of short questions to help consolidate your knowledge before you move on to the next section.
- **Learning goals** are placed at the start of each unit to keep you on track with the requirements of the Edexcel BTEC National Sport and Exercise Sciences specification
- **Definition boxes** are provided throughout, giving you clear definitions of complex physiological and technical phrases without you having to look these up in a separate glossary section
- **Useful websites** are suggested at the end of each unit so that you can access these directly to top up your knowledge in important areas of unit content
- **Figures:** Lots of sports photographs and clear illustrations to help bring your learning to life.

BTEC Level 3 National Sport and Exercise Sciences Third Edition is written in a clear, highly readable way that will help you to understand and learn about Sport and Exercise Sciences and prepare you and provide information for your assessments in this course.

Pathways for BTEC National Sport and Exercise Sciences Qualifications

To ensure that you are following the correct pathway for the **Certificate**, **Subsidiary Diploma** or **Diploma** in BTEC Sport and Exercise Sciences, please see the table below.

Unit	Certificate	Subsidiary Diploma	Diploma
1 Anatomy for Sport & Exercise	✓	✓	✓
2 Sport & Exercise Physiology	✓	✓	✓
3 Sport & Exercise Psychology	✓	✓	✓
		Selection of **three** units from choices below	
4 Research Methods for Sport & Exercise Sciences		✓	✓
5 Research Project in Sport & Exercise Sciences		✓	✓
			Selection of **seven** units from choices below
6 Sports Biomechanics in Action		✓	✓
7 Exercise, Health & Lifestyle		✓	✓
8 Fitness Testing for Sport & Exercise		✓	✓
9 Fitness Training & Programming		✓	✓
10 Sport & Exercise Massage		✓	✓
11 Analysis of Sports Performance			✓
12 Sports Nutrition		✓	✓
13 Current Issues in Sport		✓	✓
14 Instructing Physical Activity & Exercise		✓	✓
15 Sports Injuries		✓	✓
16 Sports Coaching		✓	✓
17 & 18 Practical Individual & Team Sports		✓	✓
19 Outdoor and Adventurous Activities		✓	✓
20 Applied Sport & Exercise Psychology			
21 Applied Sport and Exercise Physiology			

Unit	Certificate	Subsidiary Diploma	Diploma
22 Exercise for Specific Groups			
23 Work Experience in Sport		✓	✓
24 Sports Facilities & Operational Management			
25 Research Investigation in Sport & Exercise Sciences			✓
26 Laboratory & Experimental Methods in Sport & Exercise Sciences			✓
27 Profiling Sports Performance			✓

Note: Units 17 & 18 are combined within the Edexcel specification

To ensure that you are following the correct pathway for the **Extended Diploma** in BTEC Sport and Exercise Sciences, please see the table below.

Unit	Extended Diploma
1 Anatomy for Sport & Exercise	✓
2 Sport & Exercise Physiology	✓
3 Sport & Exercise Psychology	✓
4 Research Methods for Sport & Exercise Sciences	✓
5 Research Project in Sport & Exercise Sciences	✓
8 Fitness Testing for Sport & Exercise	✓
	Choice of **twelve** units from the choices below
6 Sports Biomechanics in Action	✓
7 Exercise Health and Lifestyle	✓
9 Fitness Training & Programming	✓
10 Sport & Exercise Massage	✓
11 Analysis of Sports Performance	✓
12 Sports Nutrition	✓
13 Current Issues in Sport	✓
14 Instructing Physical Activity & Exercise	✓
15 Sports Injuries	✓
16 Sports Coaching	✓
17 & 18 Practical Individual & Team Sports	✓
19 Outdoor and Adventurous Activities	✓
20 Applied Sport & Exercise Psychology	✓
21 Applied Sport and Exercise Physiology	✓

Unit	Extended Diploma
22 Exercise for Specific Groups	✓
23 Work Experience in Sport	✓
24 Sports Facilities & Operational Management	✓
25 Research Investigation in Sport & Exercise Sciences	✓
26 Laboratory & Experimental Methods in Sport & Exercise Sciences	✓
27 Profiling Sports Performance	✓

Note: Units 17 & 18 are combined for the Edexcel specification

1: Anatomy for Sport & Exercise

1.1 Introduction

In order for us to take part in sport and exercise, our body has to be able to produce energy and movement. Our body is made up of many different systems that work together to allow us to take part in physical activity, such as sprinting over a short distance or running continually for many miles.

This unit explores the structure and function of the main body systems involved in human movement – these include the skeletal, the muscular, the cardiovascular, the respiratory and the energy systems. These systems are all very different; however, they all work together to produce movement.

By the end of this unit you should know the:

- structure and function of the skeletal system
- structure and function of the muscular system
- structure and function of the cardiovascular system
- structure and function of the respiratory system.

Assessment and grading criteria

To achieve a PASS grade the evidence must show that the learner is able to:	To achieve a MERIT grade the evidence must show that, in addition to the pass criteria, the learner is able to:	To achieve a DISTINCTION grade the evidence must show that, in addition to the pass and merit criteria, the learner is able to:
P1 describe the structure and function of the skeletal system		
P2 describe the different classifications of joints and the range of movement available at each	**M1** explain the different classification of joints and the range of movement available at each	**D1** compare and contrast the different classifications of joints and the range of movement available at each
P3 identify the location, function, origin and insertion of the major muscles		
P4 describe the different types of muscle and the fibre types	**M2** explain the properties of the different types of muscle and the different muscle types	**D2** compare and contrast the properties of the different types of muscle and the different muscle fibre types
P5 describe the process of muscular contraction and the different types of contraction	**M3** explain how muscles produce movement and the different types of contraction	
P6 describe the structure and function of the cardiovascular system	**M4** explain the function of the cardiovascular system	
P7 describe the structure and function of the respiratory system	**M5** explain the function of the respiratory system	

1.2 The Structure and Function of the Skeletal System

The skeleton is the central structure of the body and provides the framework for all the soft tissue to attach to, giving the body its defined shape. The skeleton is made up of bones, joints and cartilage and enables us to perform simple and complex movements such as walking and running.

Axial and Appendicular Skeleton

The axial skeleton (Fig 1.1) is the central core of the body or its axis. It consists of the skull, the vertebrae, the sternum and the ribs. It provides the core that the limbs hang from.

The appendicular skeleton (Fig 1.2) comprises the parts hanging off the axial skeleton. It consists of the shoulder girdle (scapula and clavicle), the pelvic girdle, upper and lower limbs.

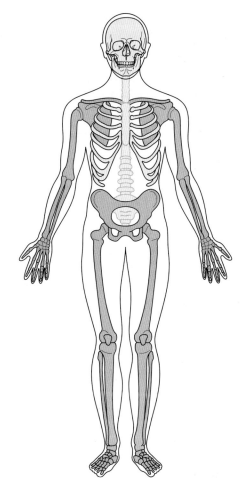

Fig 1.2 Appendicular skeleton

Types of Bone

The bones of the body fall into five general categories based on their shape.

- Long
- Short
- Flat
- Irregular
- Sesamoid.

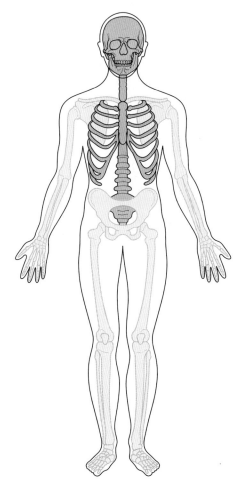

Fig 1.1 Axial skeleton

Type of bone	Example in body	Description
Long	Femur, tibia, humerus	Cylindrical in shape and found in the limbs. Main function is to act as a lever
Short	Carpals, calcaneum	Small and compact, often equal in length and width. Designed for strength and weight bearing
Flat	Sternum, cranium, pelvis	Protection for the internal organs of the body
Irregular bones	Vertebrae, face	Complex individual shapes. Variety of functions, including protection and muscle attachment
Sesamoid	Patella	Found in a tendon. Eases joint movement and resists friction and compression

Table 1.1 Different types of joint

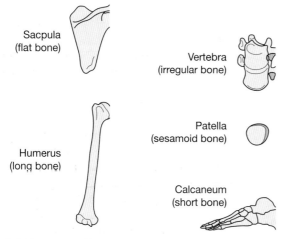

Sacpula (flat bone)

Vertebra (irregular bone)

Patella (sesamoid bone)

Humerus (long bone)

Calcaneum (short bone)

Fig 1.3 Five types of bone

Major Bones of the Body

The skeleton consists of 206 bones, over half of which are in the upper and lower limbs. Babies are born with around 300 bones and over time these fuse together to reduce the number.

Cranium

The cranium consists of eight bones fused together that act to protect your brain. There are 14 other facial bones, which form the face and jaw.

Sternum

This is the flat bone in the middle of the chest that is shaped like a dagger. It protects the heart and gives an attachment point for the ribs and the clavicles.

Ribs or Costals

Adults have 12 pairs of ribs, which run between the sternum and the thoracic vertebrae. The ribs are flat bones that form a protective cage around the heart and lungs. An individual will have seven pairs of ribs that attach to both the sternum and vertebrae

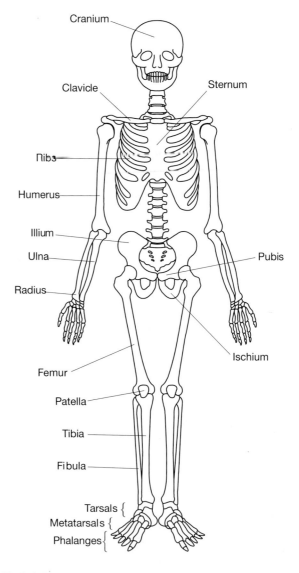

Cranium

Clavicle

Sternum

Ribs

Humerus

Illium

Ulna

Pubis

Radius

Ischium

Femur

Patella

Tibia

Fibula

Tarsals

Metatarsals

Phalanges

Fig 1.4 Anterior view of a skeleton

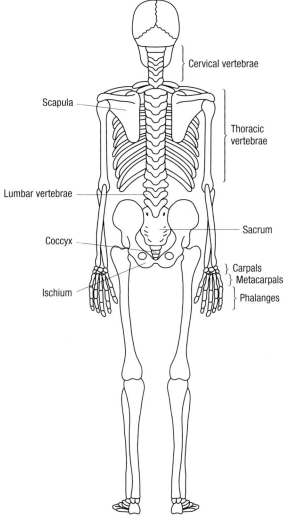

Fig 1.5 Posterior view of skeleton

Labels on figure: Cervical vertebrae, Scapula, Thoracic vertebrae, Lumbar vertebrae, Sacrum, Coccyx, Carpals, Metacarpals, Phalanges, Ischium

(true ribs), three that attach from the vertebrae to a cartilage attachment on the sternum, and two that attach on the vertebrae but are free as they have no second attachment (floating ribs).

Clavicle

This bone connects the upper arm to the trunk of the body. One end is connected to the sternum and the other is connected to the scapula. The role of the clavicle is to keep the scapula at the correct distance from the sternum.

Scapula

This bone is situated on the back of the body. The scapula provides points of attachment for many muscles of the upper back and arms.

Arm

This consists of three bones: the humerus (upper arm), the radius and the ulna (lower arm). The ulna forms the elbow joint with the humerus and runs in line with the little finger. The radius is positioned beside the ulna and runs in line with the thumb side. When the hand turns, the radius turns across the ulna.

Hand

The hand has three areas made up of different types of bones. First, the wrist is made up of eight carpals, which are small bones arranged in two rows of four; the five long bones between the wrist and fingers are the metacarpals and the bones of the fingers are called phalanges. There are 14 phalanges altogether with three in each finger and two in the thumb. There are a total of 30 bones in the upper limb.

Pelvis

The pelvis protects and supports the lower internal organs, including the bladder, the reproductive organs and also, in pregnant women, the developing foetus. The pelvis consists of three bones, the ilium, the pubis and the ischium, which have become fused together to form one area.

The Leg

The leg consists of four bones: the femur is the longest bone in the body and forms the knee joint with the tibia, which is the weight-bearing bone of the lower leg; the fibula is the non-weight bearing bone of the lower leg and helps form the ankle; the patella is the bone that floats over the knee, it lies within the patella tendon and smoothes the movement of the tendons over the knee joint.

Foot

Like the hand, the foot has three areas: the seven tarsals, which form the ankle; the five metatarsals, which travel from the ankle to the toes; and the 14 phalanges, which make up the toes. There are three phalanges in each toe, with only two in the big toe. Again, the lower limb has 30 bones; it has one less tarsal but makes up for it with the patella.

Vertebrae

The spine is made up of five areas:

- cervical – 7
- thoracic – 12
- lumbar – 5
- sacrum – 5
- coccyx – 4.

The seven cervical vertebrae make up the neck and run to the shoulders. The twelve thoracic vertebrae make up the chest area, and the five lumbar vertebrae make up the lower back. The sacrum consists of five vertebrae, which are fixed together and form joints with the pelvis, and the coccyx, which is four bones joined together – the remnants of when we had a tail.

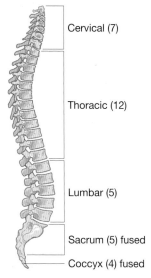

Cervical (7)

Thoracic (12)

Lumbar (5)

Sacrum (5) fused

Coccyx (4) fused

Fig 1.6 Structure of the vertebral column

Functions of the Skeleton

P1

The skeleton performs the following functions.

● Provides a bony framework for the body – the bones give the body a distinctive shape and a framework to which muscles and other soft tissue can attach. Without bones we would just be a big sac of muscles and fluids.

● Allows movement of the body as a whole and its individual parts – the bones act as levers, and by forming joints they allow muscles to pull on them and produce joint movements. This enables us to move in all directions and perform the functions we need on a daily basis.

● Offers protection to the organs found within the skeleton – the bones support and protect the vital organs they contain. For example, the skull protects the brain; the ribs offer protection to the heart and lungs; the vertebrae protect the spinal cord; and the pelvis offers protection to the sensitive reproductive organs.

● Production of blood cells – certain bones contain red bone marrow, and the bone marrow produces red blood cells, white blood cells and platelets. The bones that contain marrow are the pelvis, sternum, vertebrae, costals, cranial bones and clavicle.

● Storage of minerals and fats – the bones themselves are made of minerals stored within cartilage; therefore, they act as a mineral store for calcium, magnesium and phosphorous, which can

be given up if the body requires the minerals for other functions. The bones also store dietary fats (triglycerides) within the yellow bone marrow.

● Attachment of soft tissue – bones provide surfaces for the attachment of soft tissue such as muscles, tendons and ligaments. This is why they are often irregular shapes and have bony points and grooves to provide attachment points.

Structure of a Long Bone

● Epiphysis – this is the ends of the bone.
● Diaphysis – this is the long shaft of the bone.
● Hyaline cartilage – this is the thin layer of bluish cartilage covering each end of the bone.
● Periosteum – this is the thin outer layer of the bone. It contains nerves and blood vessels that feed the bone.
● Compact bone – this is hard and resistant to bending.
● Cancellous bone – this lies in layers within the compact bone. It has a honeycomb appearance and gives the bones their elastic strength.

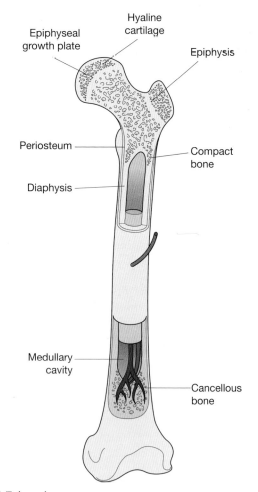

Fig 1.7 Long bone

● Medullary cavity – this is the hollow space down the middle of the compact bone and contains bone marrow. There are two types of bone marrow: red marrow, which produces blood cells, and yellow marrow, which stores fat.

Bone Growth

In a fetus, most of the skeleton consists of cartilage, which is a tough flexible tissue. As the fetus develops, minerals are laid down in the cartilage and the bones become harder and less flexible. This process is called ossification and it continues until we are adults. Bones keep growing until between the ages of 18 and 30, depending upon the bone and the body part. When a bone grows it occurs at the epiphyseal plate, which is an area just behind the head of the bone at each epiphysis; as a bone grows, its two ends are slowly pushed away from each other.

Bones are very much alive and full of activity. We know bones are living material because they can repair if they are damaged, grow when we are young and they produce blood cells. Bones contain blood vessels and nerves.

Bone is continually being broken down and replaced; this process is done by different cells, osteoblasts and osteoclasts:

● osteoblasts are cells that will build bone
● osteoclasts are cells that destroy or clean away old bone.

Osteoclasts and osteoblasts will replace around 10 per cent of bone every year; this means that no matter how old we are our skeleton is no older than ten years of age!

Key term

Ossification: The process of creating bone from cartilage.

Connective Tissue

There are connective tissues in the body to connect tissue and stabilise joints. There are three types of connective tissue:

● cartilage
● ligament
● tendon.

Cartilage is a dense and tough tissue that cushions joints. It comes in three types:

● hyaline (found at the ends of bones)
● fibro (thick chunks found in the knee and between vertebrae)
● elastic (gives shape to structures such as the ear and the nose).

Ligaments:

● attach bone to bone
● act to give stability to joints
● are tough, white and inelastic.

Tendons:

● attach muscle to bone
● carry the force from muscle contraction to the bone
● are tough, greyish and inelastic.

All these types of connective tissue have a very poor blood supply, hence their whitish colour, and will take a long time to repair if they become damaged.

Student activity 1.1 — 30 minutes — P1 M1 D1

Structure and function of the skeleton

Our skeleton is made up of 206 bones and has many different functions.

Task 1

Label a diagram of the skeleton to name all of the major bones.

Task 2

Draw a spider diagram that illustrates the different functions of the skeleton.

Task 3

Write a report that describes the structure and function of the different parts of the skeleton, including:

• the axial and appendicular skeletons
• the different types of bones
• the five main functions of the skeleton as a whole.

7

The place where two or more bones meet is called a joint or an articulation. A joint is held together by ligaments, which give the joints their stability.

Key term

Joint: Where two or more bones meet

Joints are put into one of three categories depending upon the amount of movement available.

1 Fixed joints/fibrous – these joints allow no movement. These types of joints can be found between the plates in the skull.

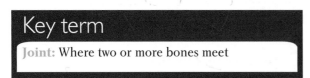
Suture in dome of skull

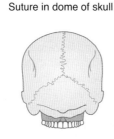
Fig 1.8 A fixed joint

2 Slightly moveable/cartilaginous – these joints allow a small amount of movement and are held in place by ligaments and cushioned by cartilage. These types of joints can be found between the vertebrae in the spine.

3 Moveable/synovial – these joints allow a wide range of movement and all have a similar joint structure.

Figure 1.10 shows the structure of a synovial joint, which is made up of the following components.

● Synovial capsule – keeps the contents of the synovial joint in place.
● Synovial membrane – releases synovial fluid onto the joint.
● Synovial fluid – a thick 'oil like' solution that lubricates the joint and allows free movement.
● Articular cartilage – a bluish-white covering of cartilage that prevents wear and tear on the bones.

There are six types of synovial joints and all allow varying degrees of movement. The six types of synovial joint are: hinge, ball and socket, pivot, condyloid, sliding, and saddle.

Hinge joint

These can be found in the elbow (ulna and humerus) and knee (femur and tibia). They allow flexion and

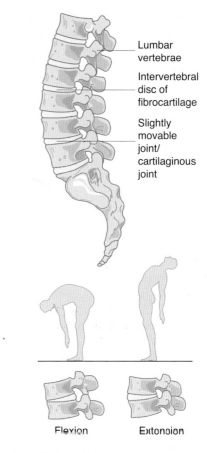

Lumbar vertebrae

Intervertebral disc of fibrocartilage

Slightly movable joint/ cartilaginous joint

Flexion   Extension

Fig 1.9 A cartilaginous joint

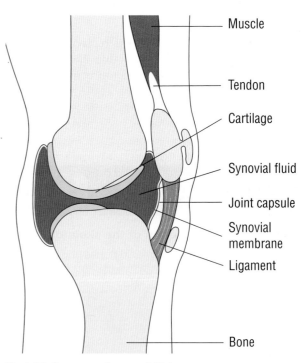

Muscle

Tendon

Cartilage

Synovial fluid

Joint capsule

Synovial membrane

Ligament

Bone

Fig 1.10 Structure of a synovial joint

extension of a joint. Hinge joints are like the hinges on a door, and allow you to move the elbow and knee in only one direction.

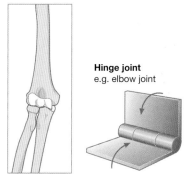

Hinge joint
e.g. elbow joint

Fig 1.11 Hinge joint

Ball and Socket Joint

These types of joint can be found at the shoulder (scapula and humerus) and hip (pelvis and femur) and allow movement in almost every direction. A ball and socket joint is made up of a round end of one bone that fits into a small cup-like area of another bone.

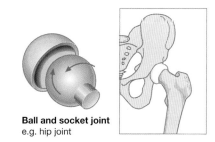

Ball and socket joint
e.g. hip joint

Fig 1.12 Ball and socket joint

Pivot Joint

This joint can be found in the neck between the top two vertebrae (atlas and axis). It allows only rotational movement – for example, it allows you to move your head from side to side as if you were saying 'no'.

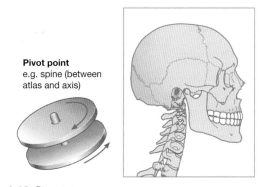

Pivot point
e.g. spine (between atlas and axis)

Fig 1.13 Pivot joint

Condyloid joint

This type of joint is found at the wrist. It allows movement in two planes; this is called biaxial. It allows you to bend and straighten the joint, and move it from side to side. The joints between the metacarpals and phalanges are also condyloid.

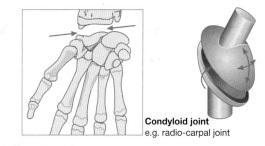

Condyloid joint
e.g. radio-carpal joint

Fig 1.14 Condyloid joint

Saddle Joint

This type of joint is found only in the thumbs. It allows the joint to move in three planes: backwards and forwards, and from side to side, and across. This is a joint specific to primates and gives us 'manual dexterity', enabling us to hold a cup and write, among other skills.

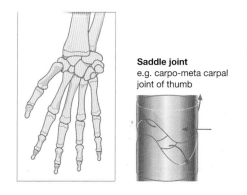

Saddle joint
e.g. carpo-meta carpal joint of thumb

Fig 1.15 Saddle joint

Gliding Joint

This type of joint can be found in the carpal bones of the hand. These types of joint occur between the surfaces of two flat bones. They allow very limited movement in a range of directions.

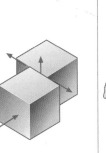

Gliding joint
e.g. carpals

Fig 1.16 Gliding joint

Types of Joint Movement

To enable us to understand sporting movements we need to be able to describe or label joint movements. Joint movements are given specific terms (see below).

General Movements

General movements apply to more than one joint.

● Flexion – this occurs when the angle of a joint decreases. For example, when you bend the elbow it decreases from 180 degrees to around 30 degrees.

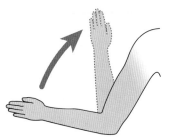

Fig 1.17 Flexion

● Extension – this occurs when the angle of a joint increases. For example, when you straighten the elbow it increases from 30 degrees to 180 degrees.

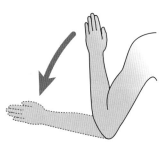

Fig 1.18 Extension

● Adduction – this means movement towards the midline of the body.

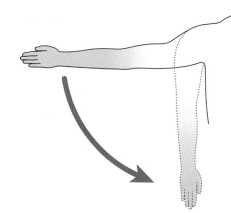

Fig 1.19 Adduction

● Abduction – this means movement away from the midline of the body. This occurs at the hip during a star jump.

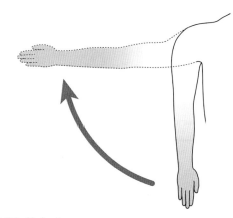

Fig 1.20 Abduction

● Circumduction – this means that the limb moves in a circle. This occurs at the shoulder joint during an overarm bowl in cricket.

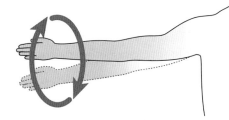

Fig 1.21 Circumduction

● Rotation – this means that the limb moves in a circular movement towards the middle of the body. This occurs in the hip in golf while performing a drive shot.

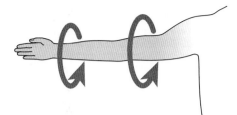

Fig 1.22 Rotation

Specific Movements

Specific movements apply to a specific joint.

- Pronation – this means when the hand is facing down while the elbow is flexed. Pronation occurs as the hand moves from facing up to facing down, and is the result of the movement of the pivot joint between the ulna and radius. This would happen when a spin bowler delivers the ball in cricket.

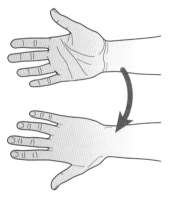

Fig 1.23 Pronation

- Supination – this means when the palm of the hand is facing up. Supination occurs as the hand moves from facing down to facing up, and is the result of the movement of the pivot joint between the ulna and radius. You can remember this by thinking that you carry a bowl of soup in a supinated position. Throwing a dart involves supination of the forearm.

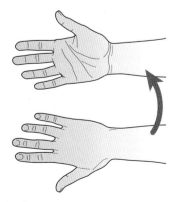

Fig 1.24 Supination

- Plantarflexion – this means that the foot moves away from the shin bone and you will be pointing your toes or raising onto your tiptoes. It is specific to your ankle joint and occurs when you walk.

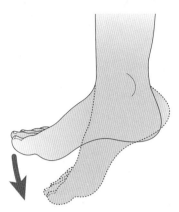

Fig 1.25 Plantarflexion

- Dorsiflexion – this means that the foot moves towards the shin as if you are pulling your toes up. It is specific to the ankle joint and occurs when you walk.

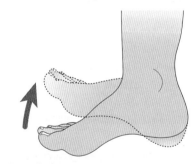

Fig 1.26 Dorsiflexion

- Inversion – this means that the soles of the feet are facing each other. It occurs at the gliding joints between the tarsals rather than at the ankle joint.

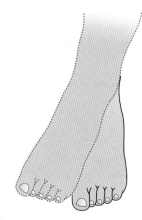

Fig 1.27 Inversion

11

● Eversion – this means that the soles of the feet are facing away from each other. It occurs at the gliding joints between the tarsals rather than at the ankle joint.

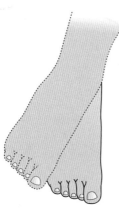

Fig 1.28 Eversion

● Hyperextension – this is the term given to an extreme or abnormal range of motion found within a joint – for example, at the knee or elbow.

Key learning points 1

● The functions of the skeleton are shape, movement, protection, blood production and mineral storage.
● Bones grow at their growth plates.
● There are three types of joint: fixed, slightly moveable and moveable/synovial.

Q Quick quiz 1

Ossification	Calcium	Flexion
Ribs	Abduction	Bone marrow
The leg	Bone marrow	
Immovable	Pivot	

Choose a word from the boxes above to answer each of the following questions.

1 What is the main mineral stored in bones?
2 Where are blood cells produced?
3 Which bones protect the heart and lungs?
4 Which limb consists of four bones?
5 What is the name given to the process of cartilage turning into bone?
6 The hinge joint allows only this type of movement and no other.
7 Which term describes movement away from the body?
8 This type of joint can be found in the neck.
9 This type of joint can be found in the skull.
10 This part of the bones produces new blood cells.

Student activity 1.2   30 minutes   P2   M1   D1

Different types of joints

The different joints in our body allow varying amounts of movement – some allow none, whereas others have a wide range of movement, which allows us to take part in sport and exercise activities.

Task 1

Describe, explain and compare and contrast the three different classifications of joints and give examples of each.

Task 2

Describe, explain and compare and contrast the six different types and range of synovial joint and the types and range of movements that each allow.

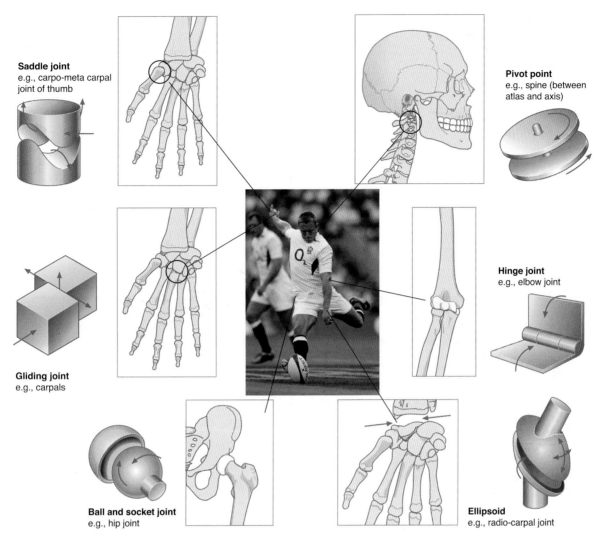

Saddle joint
e.g., carpo-meta carpal joint of thumb

Pivot point
e.g., spine (between atlas and axis)

Gliding joint
e.g., carpals

Hinge joint
e.g., elbow joint

Ball and socket joint
e.g., hip joint

Ellipsoid
e.g., radio-carpal joint

Fig 1.29 Synovial joints in action

1.3 The Structure and Function of the Muscular System

The muscular system will work in conjunction with the skeleton to produce movement of the limbs and body. The muscular system always has to work with the nervous system because it will produce a nervous impulse to initiate movement.

Major Muscles of the Body

There are three types of muscle tissue: smooth, cardiac and skeletal.

1 Smooth muscles – are also called involuntary muscles because they are out of our conscious control. They can be found in the digestive system (large and small intestine), the circulatory system (artery and vein walls) and the urinary system. Smooth muscles contract with a peristaltic action in that the muscle fibres contract consecutively rather than at the same time, and this produces a wavelike effect. For example, when food is passed through the digestive system it is slowly squeezed through the intestines.

2 Cardiac muscle – the heart has its own specialist muscle tissue, which is cardiac muscle. Cardiac muscle is also known as myocardium and is involuntary muscle. The heart has its own nerve supply via the sino-atrial node, and it works by sending a nervous impulse through consecutive cells. The heart will always contract fully – that is, all the fibres will contract – and contracts around 60–80 times a minute. The function of the myocardium is to pump blood around the body.

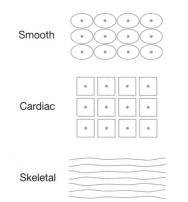

Smooth

Cardiac

Skeletal

Fig 1.30 Types of muscle fibre under the microscope

3 Skeletal muscle – muscle that is attached to the skeleton across joints. It is under voluntary control as we decide when to contract muscles and produce movement. Skeletal muscle is arranged in rows of fibres, and it is also called striated, or striped, on account of its appearance. The coordinated contractions of skeletal muscle allow us to move smoothly and produce sports skills. There are over 700 skeletal muscles in the human body, and they make up around 40 per cent of our body weight (slightly less for a female).

Some major muscles of the body have been provided for you in handout form. For details, see **BTEC National Sport & Exercise Sciences Dynamic Learning**.

Student activity 1.3   25 minutes   P3

Major muscles in the human body

There are lots of different muscles in the human body and you will need to know the names and locations of each so that you can go on to understand how they produced movements.

Task 1

Working in pairs, write the following muscle names on to some sticky labels:

- Biceps
- Biceps Brachii
- Biceps Femoris
- Deltoid
- Erector Spinae
- Gastrocnemius
- Gluteus Maximus
- Iliopsoas
- Latissimus Dorsi
- Obliques
- Pectoralis Major
- Rectus Abdominus

- Rectus Femoris
- Rhomboids
- Sartorius
- Semimembranosus
- Semitendinosus
- Soleus
- Teres Major
- Tibialis Anterior
- Trapezius
- Triceps
- Triceps Brachii
- Vastus Intermedius
- Vastus Lateralis
- Vastus Medialis

Task 2

One of you will be the anterior muscles and the other will be the posterior muscle groups. In your pairs, place the appropriate muscle labels over your partner's clothes to indicate where each major muscle is located.

Tendons are responsible for joining skeletal muscles to your skeleton. Skeletal muscles are held to the bones with the help of tendons.

Tendons are cords made of tough tissue; they work to connect muscle to bones. When the muscle contracts, it pulls on the tendon, which in turn pulls on the bone and makes the bone move.

When muscles contract they work as a group in that the muscle contracting is dependent on other muscles to enable it to do its job. A muscle can play one of four roles, as outlined below.

1 Agonist (or prime mover) – this muscle contracts to produce the desired movement.

2 Antagonist – this muscle relaxes to allow the agonist to contract.

3 Synergist – this muscle assists the agonist in producing the desired movement.

4 Fixator – these muscles will fix joints and the body in position to enable the desired movement to occur.

An antagonistic muscle pair comprises muscle that contracts to produce the movement and muscle that relaxes to produce the movement. For example, when you perform a bicep curl, the biceps brachii will be the agonist as it contracts to produce the movement, while the triceps brachii will be the antagonist as it relaxes to allow the movement to occur.

Sliding filament theory

Muscle contraction requires energy. We get tired after exercising because our muscles run out of energy.

So how does energy enable our muscles to contract? The contraction process occurs in four steps.

1 At rest, troponin and tropomyosin cover the actin and myosin filaments and prevent myosin from binding to actin. When we give the signal for our muscles to contract, calcium is released into the sarcoplasm. Calcium binds to troponin and takes it away from the myosin binding site. As it moves away, it moves the tropomyosin molecule with it. Therefore, as the troponin and tropomyosin bind to calcium, the myosin binding site is exposed.

2 The myosin heads bind to the actin filament and slide it across the myosin filament, which results in the sarcomere getting shorter.

3 Energy is used to break the attachment of the actin and myosin filaments. The myosin heads then re-attach at a site further up the actin filament, which results in further shortening of the sarcomere.

4 When the stimulus to the muscle ends, calcium ions are released from the troponin and are pumped out of the sarcoplasm. This causes the troponin and tropomyosin to bind to the myosin heads once again, which means they cannot bind to the actin molecule and contraction cannot occur.

The entire process is extremely fast and only takes a fraction of a second. The cycle then repeats itself until the muscle relaxes.

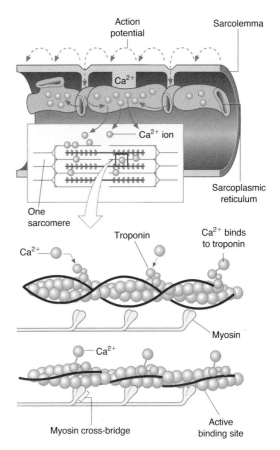

Fig 1.31 The structure of actin and myosin

Types of Muscle Movement

Muscles can contract or develop tension in three different ways.

1 **Concentric contraction** – involves the muscle shortening and developing tension. The origin and insertion of the muscle move closer together and the muscle becomes fatter. To produce a concentric contraction, a movement must occur against gravity.

2 **Eccentric contraction** – an eccentric contraction involves the muscle lengthening to develop tension. The origin and the insertion of the muscle move further away from each other. An eccentric contraction provides the control of a movement on the downward phase, and it works to resist the force of gravity.

If a person is performing a bench press, they will produce a concentric contraction to push the weight away from their body. However, on the downward phase they will produce an eccentric contraction to control the weight on the way down. If they did not, gravity would return their weight to the ground and they would be hurt in the process. The agonist muscle will produce

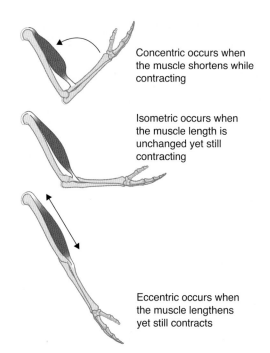

Concentric occurs when the muscle shortens while contracting

Isometric occurs when the muscle length is unchanged yet still contracting

Eccentric occurs when the muscle lengthens yet still contracts

Fig 1.32 Types of muscles contraction at the biceps brachii

concentric or eccentric contractions, while the antagonist muscle will always stay relaxed to allow the movement to occur.

3 **Isometric contraction** – if a muscle produces tension but stays the same length, then it will be an isometric contraction. This occurs when the body is fixed in one position; for example a gymnast on the rings in the crucifix position. Also, when we are standing up, our postural muscles produce isometric contractions

Muscle Fibre Types

Within our muscle we have two types of muscle fibre, which are called fast twitch and slow twitch fibres due to the speed at which they contract (see Table 1.2). If we look at the evolution of humans, we were originally hunters and gatherers; this meant that we had to walk long distances to find animals to eat and then, when we saw one, we would have to chase after it as fast as we could. Therefore, we adapted slow twitch muscle fibres to walk long distances and fast twitch muscle fibres to run quickly after our prey.

Slow Twitch Fibres (Type 1)

These will be red in colour as they have a good blood supply. They have a dense network of blood vessels, making them suited to endurance work and they are slow to fatigue. They also contain many mitochondria to make them more efficient at producing energy using oxygen.

Fast Twitch Fibres (Type 2)

Fast twitch fibres will contract twice as quickly as slow twitch fibres and are thicker in size. They have a poor blood supply, are whiter in appearance and, due to the lack of oxygen, they will fatigue fairly quickly. Their faster, harder contractions make them suitable for producing fast, powerful actions such as sprinting and lifting heavy weights.

Within the group of fast twitch fibres there are two types: 2A and 2B. The type that is used depends upon the intensity of the chosen activity. Type 2B fibres work when a person is working very close to their maximum intensity, while type 2A work at slightly lower intensities but at higher intensities than slow twitch fibres are capable of. For example, a 100-m runner would be using type 2B fibres, while a 400-m runner would be using type 2A fibres.

Slow twitch (Type 1)	Fast twitch (Type 2)
Red	White
Contract slowly	Contract rapidly
Aerobic	Anaerobic
Endurance based	Speed/strength based
Can contract repeatedly	Easily exhausted
Exert less force	Exert great forces

Table 1.2 Basic characteristics of fast twitch and slow twitch

Characteristics	Slow twitch (Type 1)	Fast oxidative glycolytic F.O.G. (Type 2A)	Fast twitch glycolytic F.T.G. (Type 2B)
Speed of contraction (ms)	Slow (110)	Fast (50)	Fast (50)
Force of contraction	Low	High	High
Size	Smaller	Large	Large
Mitochondrial density	High	Lower	Low
Myoglobin content	High	Lower	Low
Fatiguability	Fatigue resistant	Less resistant	Easily fatigued
Aerobic capacity	High	Medium	Low
Capillary density	High	High	Low
Anaerobic capacity	Low	Medium	High
Motor neuron size	Small	Large	Large
Fibres/motor neuron	10–180	300–800	300–800
Sarcoplasmic reticulum development	Low	High	High

Table 1.3 Structural characteristics of muscle fibres
Source: (Adapted from Sharkey *'Physiology of Fitness'*, Human Kinetics 1990).

Q Quick quiz 2

Answer the following questions about the muscular system.
1 Give three examples of where you may find smooth muscle.
2 Give five examples of skeletal muscles.
3 What is the name of the muscle that produces movement?
4 What is the name of the muscle that helps with the movement?
5 What is the name of the muscle that fixes the joint?
6 Look at the table below, then fill in the gaps:

Sporting action	Type of movement	Joint	Agonist	Antagonist	Fixator
Sit up – upwards phase	Flexion	Spine	Abdominals		
Press up – downwards phase	Flexion	Elbow		Triceps	
Football kick	Extension	Knee			
Chest press – upwards phase	Extension	Elbow			
Rugby conversion kick	Flexion	Hip			

(a) Name three athletes that would have mainly type 1 muscle fibres in their legs.
(b) Name three athletes that would have mainly type 2A muscle fibres in their legs.

Student activity 1.4   ⏱ 60 minutes   P5 M3

Muscular contraction

Our muscular system works by pulling on our skeleton to produce movement.

Task 1

Using hand-drawn illustrations, describe and explain the process of muscular contraction. Include in your answer:

- antagonistic muscle pairs
- fixator
- synergist
- different types of contraction.

Task 2

Write a report that describes and explains the process of the sliding filament theory. Include in your answer the following words:

- actin
- myosin
- sarcomere
- troponin
- tropomysosin
- calcium ions
- ATPase

Training effect on muscle fibres

Type 1 and 2B fibres always retain their distinctive features. However, type 2A fibres can take on characteristics of the type 1 or type 2B fibres depending upon the training involved. If you were to perform endurance training, the type 2A fibres would develop more endurance. If you were to perform speed training, they would develop more speed. They do not change their fibre type, but they do take on different characteristics.

Every muscle in the body contains a mixture of fast and slow twitch fibres depending upon its role in the body. Postural muscles, which keep us standing upright (e.g. the muscles in the legs, back and abdominal areas), will be predominantly slow twitch. For example, 90 per cent of the muscles in the back are slow twitch. Postural muscles need to produce low forces over a long period of time. The arms tend to be more fast twitch as they will need to move quickly, but over much shorter periods of time. The types of muscle found in the legs determine whether we are more suited to sprinting or endurance running. You will know which you have most of based on your own athletic performances.

1.4 The Cardiovascular System

P5 M2

18

The cardiovascular system is made up of three parts:

- heart
- blood vessels
- blood.

Close your hand into a fist and look at it. Your fist is approximately the same size as your heart, around 12 cm long, 9 cm wide and 6 cm thick. It is located behind the sternum and tilted to the left. The heart is made up mainly of cardiac muscle, which is also known as myocardium. The heart is a muscular pump that pumps the liquid, which is blood, through the pipes, which are the blood vessels.

The cardiovascular system is responsible for the following actions:

- delivering oxygen and nutrients to every part of the body
- carrying hormones to different parts of the body
- removing the waste products of energy production such as carbon dioxide and lactic acid
- maintaining body temperature by re-directing blood to the surface of the skin to dissipate heat.

Structure of the Heart

The heart is a large muscular pump that is made up of thick walls. The heart muscle is called the myocardium and is divided into two halves, which are separated by the septum. The right-hand side of the heart is responsible for pumping deoxygenated blood to the lungs, and the left-hand side pumps oxygenated blood around the body. Each side of the heart consists of two connected chambers. Each side will have an atrium and a ventricle. The top chambers – the atria (plural of atrium) – are where the blood collects when it enters the heart. The lower chambers are called the ventricles, and are the large pumps which send the blood up to the lungs or around the body. Once the blood has entered the heart from the veins it will be sucked into the ventricles as they relax, and there follows powerful contraction of the ventricles. The left

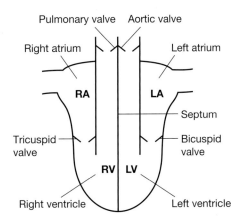

Fig 1.33 A simplified cross-section of the heart

ventricle is the largest and most muscular because it has to send the blood to the furthest destinations and thus has to produce the most pressure.

Valves of the heart

The heart uses valves to ensure the blood flows in the right direction. There are four main valves.

1 The right atrio-ventricular valve is called the tricuspid valve and opens up to allow blood to flow from the right atrium to the right ventricle. This valve consists of cusps made of muscle and fibrous tissues that are attached to several fine, tendinous cords called chordae tendinous, which prevent the valves being forced back into the atrium.

2 The left atrio-ventricular valve is called the mitral valve. It is similar to the tricuspid valve, although smaller, and acts to prevent the backflow of blood into the left atrium from the left ventricle as it contracts.

3 The aortic valve opens up to allow blood to flow from the left atrium into the aorta. The coronary arteries which supply the blood to the heart muscle (myocardium) are positioned just above the aortic valve.

4 The pulmonary valve allows blood to flow from the right ventricle into the pulmonary artery to take deoxygenated blood to the lungs.

Here is a summary of structures of the heart and their functions:

● **right atrium (RA)** – receives deoxygenated blood from the organs of the body
● **right ventricle (RV)** – pumps deoxygenated blood to the lungs
● **left atrium (LA)** – receives oxygenated blood from the lungs
● **left ventricle (LV)** – pumps oxygenated blood to

all organs of the body; it is larger and therefore stronger than the right ventricle as it has to pump the blood through the body
● **valves** – there are four one-way valves in the heart that open or close in response to pressure of blood flow
    (i) **bicuspid valve** – separates the left atrium from the left ventricle
    (ii) **tricuspid valve** – separates the right atrium from the right ventricle
    (iii) **aortic valve** – separates the left ventricle from the aorta
    (iv) **pulmonary valve** – separates the right ventricle from the pulmonary artery.

All these valves (1) ensure that blood flows in one direction and (2) prevent the backflow of blood into the ventricles.

The blood vessels leading to and from the heart are as follows.

● The **aorta** carries oxygenated blood out of the left ventricle to the body.
● The **superior vena cava** returns deoxygenated blood to the right atrium from the head and upper body; the **inferior vena cava** returns deoxygenated blood to the right atrium from the lower body.
● The **pulmonary vein** carries freshly oxygenated blood from the lungs to the left atrium.
● The **pulmonary artery** carries deoxygenated blood from the body to the lungs.

Blood Flow through the Heart

Blood flows through the heart and around the body in one direction. This one-way 'street' is maintained due to special valves placed within the heart and within the blood vessels leading from the heart.

The heart is sometimes called a 'double pump' because the right-hand side of the heart pumps blood to the lungs and the left-hand side of the heart pumps blood to the body.

Right-hand side

1. When the heart is relaxed, deoxygenated blood from the body enters the heart via the venae cavae.
2. Blood enters the right atrium.
3. The right atrium contracts and pushes blood down through the tricuspid valve and into the right ventricle.
4. The right ventricle contracts, the tricuspid valve closes, and blood is pushed up and out of the heart through the semilunar valve and into the pulmonary artery, which takes the blood to the lungs.

19

5. The heart relaxes and the semilunar valves close to prevent blood flowing back into the heart.
6. The blood flows to the lungs where it becomes oxygenated and ready to be returned to the heart for distribution around the body.

Left-hand side

1. When the heart is relaxed, oxygenated blood from the lungs enters via the pulmonary vein.
2. Blood enters the left atria.
3. The left atria contracts and pushes blood down through the bicuspid valve and into the left ventricle.
4. The left ventricle contracts; the bicuspid valve closes to prevent blood flowing back into the heart. Blood is then pushed up and out of the heart through the semilunar valve and into the aorta, which is the large artery leaving the heart, taking blood to the rest of the body.
5. The heart relaxes and the semilunar valves close to prevent blood flowing back into the heart.

Pulmonary circulation

The right ventricle pumps blood through the pulmonary artery to the lungs. Here, the blood 'picks up' oxygen and carbon dioxide is released into the lungs. From the lungs, oxygenated blood is carried to the left atrium. This short loop is called the 'pulmonary circulation'.

Systemic circulation

From the left atrium blood flows down to the left ventricle. The left ventricle pumps oxygenated blood through the aorta to all tissues of the body. Oxygen and nutrients are released from the blood to nourish cells, and carbon dioxide and other waste products are carried back to the heart via the two venae cavae. The blood enters the right atrium. Carbon dioxide is carried to the lungs and removed from the body.

Nervous control of the heart

The heart muscle has its own independent nerve supply via a specialised tissue called the sino-atrial node (the pacemaker of the heart), which is situated close to the point where the vena cava enters the right atrium. When a nervous impulse is produced it will pass through both atria to the atrio-ventricular node positioned in the septum where the atria and ventricles meet. The nervous impulse pauses slightly and then enters the walls of the ventricles through the atrio-ventricular bundles (Bundle of His), one into each ventricle. These bundles break up into specialist fibres, called purkinje fibres, which carry nervous impulses to all parts of the ventricles.

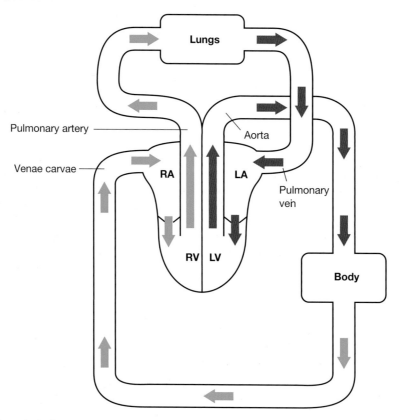

Fig 1.34 Blood flow through the heart

The heart is controlled by the autonomic nervous system. First, the vagus nerve which slows down the heart rate and decreases the power of ventricular contraction by delivering impulses through the sino-atrial node. Second, the sympathetic nerves increase the heart rate and the force of contraction of the ventricles. This innervation of the heart is controlled through the cardiac centre of the brain, which is positioned within the medulla oblongata

Blood Vessels

In order to make its journey around the body, blood is carried through five different types of blood vessels:

- arteries
- arterioles
- capillaries
- venules
- veins.

Arteries and Arterioles

Arteries are the large blood vessels that leave the heart. They have thick, muscular walls, which contract and relax to send blood to all parts of the body. The main artery leaving the heart is the aorta and it quickly splits up into smaller vessels, which are called the arterioles. Arterioles mean 'little arteries'. Artery walls contain elastic cartilage and smooth muscle. This flexible wall allows the vessels to expand and contract, which helps to push the blood along the length of the arteries. This action is called peristalsis and is how smooth muscle contracts.

Arteries do not contain any valves as they are not required and they predominantly carry oxygenated blood. The exception to this is the pulmonary artery, which carries deoxygenated blood away from the heart.

- Arteries carry blood away from the heart.
- Arteries have thick, muscular walls.
- Arteries carry predominantly oxygenated blood.
- Arterioles are the small branches of arteries.

Capillaries

Once the arteries and arterioles have divided, they will eventually feed blood into the smallest blood vessels, called capillaries. These are found in all parts of the body, especially the muscles, and are so tiny that their walls are only one cell thick. There are tiny spaces within these thin cell walls, which allow oxygen and other nutrients to pass through (a process called diffusion). The blood flows very slowly through the capillaries to allow for this process. In the capillaries the blood will also pick up the waste products of metabolism: carbon dioxide and lactic acid. There are more capillaries than any other type of blood vessel in the body.

- Capillaries are tiny blood vessels one cell thick.
- Small spaces in the thin walls of capillaries allow for diffusion.
- Oxygen and nutrients will diffuse into the cells.
- Carbon dioxide and lactic acid will flow from the cells into the capillaries.

Veins and Venules

The capillaries will eventually feed back into larger blood vessels called venules, which are the smallest veins, and they eventually become veins. The walls of these veins are thinner and less muscular than arteries, and they carry blood back to the heart. They also contain smooth muscle and contract to send the blood back to the heart. The veins are generally acting against gravity, so they contain non-return valves to prevent the blood flowing back once the smooth muscle has relaxed. These valves prevent the pooling of blood in the lower limbs. Veins predominantly carry deoxygenated blood, with the exception of the pulmonary vein, which carries oxygenated blood to the heart from the lungs.

- Veins always take blood towards the heart.
- Veins have thin, muscular walls.
- Veins have non-return valves to prevent backflow.
- Veins predominantly carry deoxygenated blood.
- Venules are smaller branches, which feed into veins.

Function of the cardiovascular system

The cells of the body need a steady and constant supply of oxygen. Blood is responsible for carrying and delivering oxygen to all the body's cells, and this blood is pumped around the body and to the lungs by the heart. The left-hand side of your heart pumps the oxygenated blood to the cells of the muscles, brain, kidneys, liver and all the other organs. The cells then take the oxygen out of the blood and use it to produce energy. This is called metabolism and it produces waste products, such as carbon dioxide. The deoxygenated blood then continues its journey back to the heart, enters the right-hand side and is pumped out of the right ventricle to the lungs. At the lungs, the blood becomes oxygenated and the waste product carbon dioxide is 'unloaded' and breathed out.

Blood

Blood is the medium in which all the cells are carried to transport nutrients and oxygen to the cells of the body. Among other things, blood will transport the following: oxygen, glucose, proteins, fats, vitamins, hormones, enzymes, platelets, carbon dioxide and electrolytes.

21

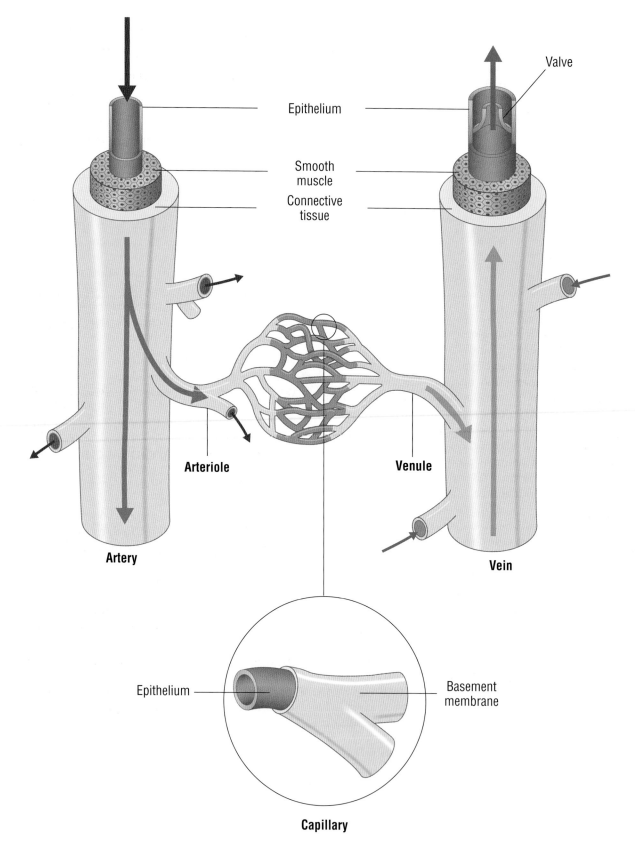

Epithelium

Valve

Smooth
muscle

Connective
tissue

Arteriole

Venule

Artery

Vein

Epithelium

Basement
membrane

Capillary

Fig 1.35 The five linked blood vessels

Blood is made up of four components:

- red blood cells
- white blood cells
- platelets
- plasma.

Blood can be described as a thick, gloopy substance due to the high concentration of solids it carries. Blood is made up of 55 per cent plasma and 45 per cent solids, which is a very high concentration.

Red Blood Cells

Of the blood cells in the body, around 99 per cent of them are red blood cells or erythrocytes. They are red in colour due to the presence of a red-coloured protein called haemoglobin. Haemoglobin has a massive attraction for oxygen, and thus the main role of the red blood cells is to take on and transport oxygen to the cells. There are many millions of red blood cells in the body; for example, there are 5 million red blood cells for 1 mm^3 volume of blood.

White Blood Cells

White blood cells are colourless or transparent and are far fewer in number (1:700 ratio of white to red blood cells). The role of white blood cells, or leucocytes, is to fight infection; they are part of the body's immune system. They destroy bacteria and other dangerous organisms and thus remove disease from the body.

Platelets

Platelets are not full cells but rather parts of cells; they act by stopping blood loss through clotting. They become sticky when in contact with the air to form the initial stage of repair to damaged tissue. Platelets also need a substance called factor 8 to enable them to clot. A haemophiliac is a person whose blood does not clot; this is not because they are short of platelets but rather factor 8, which enables the platelets to become active.

Plasma

Plasma is the liquid part of the blood, which is straw-coloured in appearance. It is the solution in which all the solids are carried.

Key learning points 3

- The heart has four chambers, two atria and two ventricles.
- The ventricles pump blood to the body and lungs.
- Valves in the heart make sure blood flows in one direction.
- Blood travels through five different types of blood vessesls, arteries, arterioles, capillaries, venules and veins.
- The heart adapts to aerobic training by becoming bigger and stronger.

Q Quick quiz 3

Structure of the heart

Fill in the blanks.

The heart is split into _____ sides and has _____ chambers. The top two chambers are called _____ and the bottom two chambers are called _____ . The heart is split into two separate sides by the _____ .

There are _____ valves that allow the blood to pass through the heart in one direction. The valve between the atrium and ventricle on the right side of the heart is called the _____ valve. The valve on the left side of the heart between the atrium and the ventricle is called the _____ valve. The valve between the pulmonary artery and right ventricle is called the _____ valve. The valve between the left ventricle and the aorta is called the _____ valve.

Student activity 1.5   🕐 60–90 mins   P6   M4

Structure and function of the cardiovascular system

Our cardiovascular system is responsible for supplying our body with blood, which contain nutrients and oxygen that provide our muscles with energy for movement.

Task 1

By hand, draw:

(a) the structure of the heart

(b) a diagram to illustrate how blood circulates through the heart, to the lungs and to the body.

(c) the cardiac cycle

Task 2

Describe and explain the structure of the cardiovascular system including:

- the heart
- the blood vessels.

Task 3

Describe and explain the function of the cardiovascular system.

1.5 The Respiratory System

P7   M5

The respiratory system is responsible for transporting the oxygen from the air we breathe into our body. Our body then uses this oxygen in combination with the food we have eaten to produce energy. This energy is then used to keep us alive by supplying our heart with energy to keep beating and pumping blood around the body, which in turn allows us to move and take part in sports and many more different types of activities. Each person has two lungs running the length of the ribcage; the right lung is slightly larger than the left lung. The left lung has to make space for the heart in an area called the cardiac notch.

Structure of the Respiratory System

The aim of the respiratory system is to provide contact between the outside and internal environments so that oxygen can be absorbed by the blood and carbon dioxide can be given up. It is made up of a system of tubes and muscles, which deliver the air into two lungs. The average person takes around 26,000 breaths a day to deliver the required amount of oxygen to the cells of the body.

Figure 1.36 shows the respiratory system in which the following processes occur.

1. Air enters the body through the mouth and nose.
2. It passes through the pharynx, which is the back of the throat area.
3. It then passes through the larynx, which is responsible for voice production.

4. Air passes over the epiglottis. The epiglottis closes over the trachea when we swallow food to stop the food going down 'the wrong way' into our trachea and down into our lungs.
5. The air enters the trachea, which is a membranous tube with horseshoe-shaped cartilage that keeps it open and delivers air to the lungs.
6. The trachea will divide into two bronchi, one into each lung.
7. The two main bronchi will divide into bronchioles, which will further subdivide 23 times and result in 8 million terminal bronchioles in each lung.
8. Around the bronchioles are groups of air sacs, called alveoli. There are around 600 million alveoli in each lung, and it is here that the exchange of gases (oxygen and carbon dioxide) occurs. Each alveolus is in contact with a capillary where the blood is present.

Respiratory Muscles

The respiratory system also includes two types of muscles that work to move air into and out of the lungs.

The diaphragm is a large dome-shaped muscle that covers the bottom of the ribcage. At rest it is dome-shaped, but when contracted it flattens and pushes the two sides of the ribcage away from each other.

The intercostal muscles attach between the ribs; when they contract they push the ribs up and out and increase the size of the chest cavity, drawing air in. If you put your hands on your ribs and breathe in, you will feel your ribs push up and out; this is the action of the intercostal muscles.

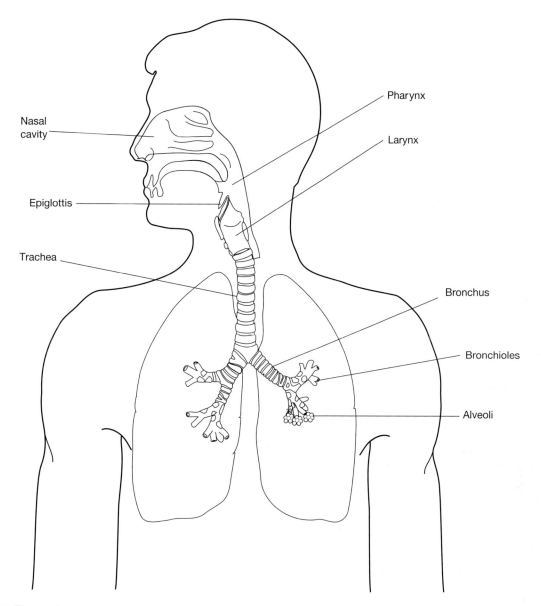

Pharynx

Larynx

Nasal
cavity

Epiglottis

Trachea

Bronchus

Bronchioles

Alveoli

Fig 1.36 The respiratory system

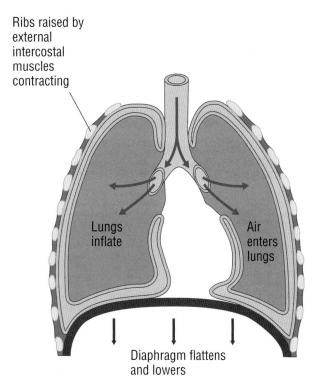

Ribs raised by external intercostal muscles contracting

Lungs inflate

Air enters lungs

Diaphragm flattens and lowers

Fig 1.37 Inhalation, diaphragm and intercostal muscles

Mechanisms of Breathing

Breathing is the term given to inhaling air into the lungs and then exhaling air out. The process basically works on the principle of making the thoracic cavity (chest) larger, which decreases the pressure of air within the lungs. The surrounding air is then at a higher pressure, which means that air is forced into the lungs. Then the thoracic cavity is returned to its original size, which forces air out of the lungs.

Breathing In (Inhalation)

At rest

The diaphragm contracts and moves downwards; this results in an increase in the sise of the thoracic cavity and air is forced into the lungs.

Exercise

During exercise, the diaphragm and intercostal muscles contract, which makes the ribs move upwards and outwards, and results in more air being taken into the lungs.

Breathing Out (Exhalation)

At rest

The diaphragm relaxes and returns upwards to a domed position. The thoracic cavity gets smaller, which results in an increase in air pressure within the lungs so that air is breathed out of the lungs.

Exercise

During exercise, the intercostal muscles contract to help decrease the size of the thoracic cavity, which results in a more forcible breath out.

Composition of Air

The air that is inspired is made up of a mixture of gasses; the air exhaled is different in its composition of gases (see Table 1.4).

Inhaled air	Gas	Exhaled air
79.04%	Nitrogen	79%
20.93%	Oxygen	17%
0.03%	Carbon dioxide	4%

Table 1.4 Composition of inhaled and exhaled air

Oxygen is extracted from the air and replaced by carbon dioxide. However, most of the oxygen stays in the air and this is why mouth-to-mouth resuscitation works, because there is still 17 per cent available to the casualty.

Functions of the Respiratory System

The aim of breathing is to get oxygen into the bloodstream where it can be delivered to the cells of the body. At the cells it enters the mitochondria where it combines with fats and carbohydrates to produce energy, with carbon dioxide and water produced as waste products. This energy is used to produce muscular contractions, among other things.

Fats/carbohydrates + oxygen = energy + carbon dioxide + water

It is important to say that when the body produces more energy, the amount of carbon dioxide increases in the body and which dissolves in the water in the body so that it becomes a weak acid. The body does not like the acidity of the blood to increase, so the respiratory centre in the brain speeds up the rate of breathing to get rid of the excess carbon dioxide. Therefore, the breathing rate increases because carbon dioxide levels rise, rather than as a result of the cells demanding more oxygen.

Diffusion of Gases

Key term

Diffusion: the movement of gas from an area of high concentration to an area of low concentration.

Gases will move around through a process of diffusion.

Diffusion is how gases move from one place to another. For example, if a person is wearing perfume, it will diffuse around a room so that everyone can smell it. This is because the person is in an area of high concentration of the perfume and the gas moves to areas of low concentration.

In the respiratory system diffusion takes place in the lungs and the muscles.

- Diffusion in the lungs – in the lungs we have a high concentration of oxygen, and in the muscles we have a high concentration of carbon dioxide, and they will diffuse across the semi-permeable membrane. Oxygen is attracted into the blood by the haemoglobin, which is a protein in the red blood cells, and it attaches to this haemoglobin.
- Diffusion in the muscles – in the muscles we have a high concentration of carbon dioxide and a low concentration of oxygen due to the process of energy production. As a result the oxygen diffuses into the muscles and is attracted by the myoglobin in the muscles and the carbon dioxide diffuses into the bloodstream. It is then taken to the lungs to be breathed out.

Key term

Myoglobin: oxygen store in muscle tissue

Control of respiration

Respiration is controlled through the respiratory centre in the brain, which is located in the medulla oblongata. As levels of carbon dioxide in the blood rise, the increase in acidity is sensed by specialised cells within the arteries. Messages are sent to the brain through the nerves to the respiratory centre. Messages are then delivered to the diaphragm and intercostal muscles by the phrenic nerves to increase the rate of respiration.

Respiratory Volumes

In order to assess an individual's lung function, we use a spirometer. An example of the readings given by a spirometer is shown in Fig 1.38.

An individual will have a lung capacity of around 5 litres, which is about the amount of air in a basketball. It will be slightly lower for a female and slightly higher for a male, due to the differing sizes of the male and female ribcages.

Tidal volume
This is the amount of air breathed in with each breath.

Inspiratory reserve volume
This is the amount of space that is available for air to be inhaled. If you breathe in and stop, and then try to breathe in more, this extra air inhaled is the inspiratory volume.

Expiratory reserve volume
This is the amount of air that could be exhaled after you have breathed out. If you exhale and then stop, and then try to exhale more, the air that comes out is the expiratory reserve volume.

Vital capacity
This is the maximum amount of air that can be breathed in and out during one breath. It is the tidal volume, plus the inspiratory reserve volume, plus the expiratory reserve volume.

Residual volume
This is the amount of air left in the lungs after a full exhalation. Around 1 litre will always remain, or else the lungs would deflate and breathing would stop.

Total lung volume
This is the vital capacity plus the residual volume, and measures the maximum amount of air that can be present in the lungs at any moment.

Breathing rate
This is the number of breaths taken per minute.

Respiratory volume
This is the amount of air that is moving through the lungs every minute:

Respiratory volume = breathing rate × tidal volume

For example, at rest a person may have a tidal volume of 0.5 litres per minute and a breathing rate of 12 breaths per minute. But during exercise both of these will rise, and at high exercise intensities tidal volume may rise to 3 litres per minute and breathing rate to 35 breaths per minute.

At rest respiratory volume:

0.5 litres × 12 = 6 litres/minute

During exercise respiratory volume:

3 litres × 35 = 105 litres/minute

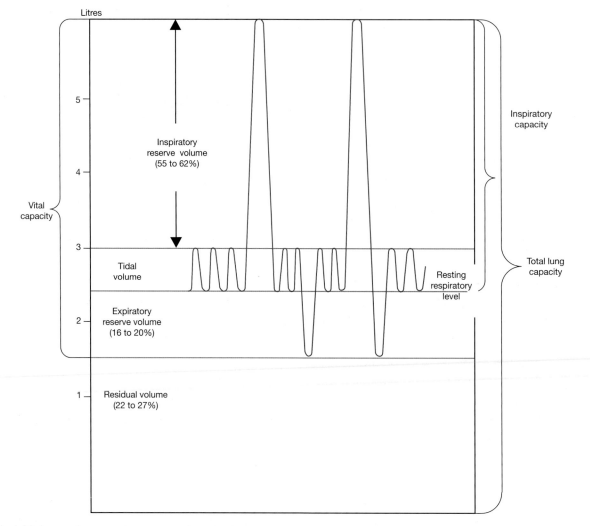

Fig 1.38 Lung volumes as shown on a spirometer trace

Key learning points 4

● Air travels into the body through the mouth and nose, down the trachea and into the bronchus. It then passes into the bronchioles and down into the alveoli. In the alveoli gaseous exchange takes place, which takes oxygen into the body and passes carbon dioxide out of the body.
● The diaphragm and intercostal muscles contract to allow you to breathe in and out.

Q Quick quiz 4

1 Describe which structures air flows through on its way from the mouth to the alveoli.
2 Explain the mechanics of breathing in and out.
3 What happens to tidal volume during exercise? Explain why this occurs.

Epiglottis	Diffusion	Trachea	Flattens	Inhalation
Carbon dioxide	Diaphragm	Oxygen	Gaseous exchange	Alveoli

4 Choose a word from the boxes above to answer the following.
  (a) This gas passes out of the blood stream and into the lungs.
  (b) When a person swallows, this closes over the trachea to prevent food going into the lungs.
  (c) This has horseshoe-shaped cartilage to help to keep it open.
  (d) The diaphragm does this during breathing in.
  (e) This is the process where gases move from a high to a low concentration.
  (f) This is the area in the lungs where gaseous exchange takes place.
  (g) When exhaling, this muscle relaxes and moves upwards into a domed position.
  (h) This is the name of the process in the lungs where oxygen is taken into the blood and carbon dioxide is breathed out.
  (i) All of our body cells need this gas to survive.
  (k) The name of the process for breathing in.

Student activity 1.6　　⏱ 45 minutes　P7　M5

The structure and function of the respiratory system

Task 1

By hand draw the structure of the respiratory system. Include in your diagram the following structures:

● nasal cavity
● epiglottis
● pharynx
● larynx
● trachea
● bronchus
● bronchioles
● lungs
● pleural membrane
● thoracic cavity
● visceral pleura
● pleural fluid
● alveoli
● diaphragm
● intercostals muscle – internal and external.

Task 2

Write a report that:
(a) Describes and explains the structure of each part of the respiratory system.
(b) Describes and explains the function of the respiratory system.

29

Further reading

Kapit, W. and Elson, L. (2001) *The Anatomy Coloring Book*, Benjamin Cummings.

Wesson, K., Wiggins-James, N., Thompson, G. and Hartigan, S. (2005) *Sport and PE: A Complete Guide to Advanced Level Study*, Hodder Arnold.

Useful websites

www.bhf.org.uk/research_health_professionals/resources.aspx

Guidance, statistics and information about research publications from the British Heart Foundation.

www.bhf.org.uk/keeping_your_heart_healthy/Default.aspx

Information for the general public on how to keep your heart healthy.

www.getbodysmart.com

An online examination of human anatomy and physiology that will help you to see the structure of the different body systems.

www.innerbody.com

Good information and diagrams of the different body systems.

www.instantanatomy.net

Useful anatomy pictures and information.

www.medtropolis.com/VBody.asp

A very good interactive website for anatomy with quizzes and tutorials.

2: Sport & Exercise Physiology

2.1 Introduction

Our body allows us to take part in a huge variety of sports and exercises. In order for us to carry out these activities, the body has to undergo a series of changes that provide us with the ability and the energy to carry out these actions.

This unit starts by exploring the responses of the cardiovascular, respiratory and energy systems to the anticipation and initial stress of exercise. There then follows a study of the response of the body after a period of around 20 minutes' exercise, when a steady state has been achieved. The mechanisms of fatigue are then explored, followed by the methods by which we recover from sports and exercise. A look at the ways in which the body adapts to repeated bouts of aerobic and anaerobic exercise completes the unit.

By the end of this unit you should:

- be able to investigate the initial responses of the body to exercise
- be able to investigate how the body responds to steady-state exercise
- know about fatigue and how the body recovers from exercise
- know how the body adapts to long-term exercise.

Assessment and grading criteria		
To achieve a PASS grade the evidence must show that the learner is able to:	To achieve a MERIT grade the evidence must show that, in addition to the pass criteria, the learner is able to:	To achieve a DISTINCTION grade the evidence must show that, in addition to the pass and merit criteria, the learner is able to:
P1 investigate the initial responses of the cardiovascular and respiratory systems to exercise	**M1** explain the initial responses of the cardiovascular, respiratory, neuromuscular and energy systems to exercise	**D1** analyse the initial responses of the cardiovascular, respiratory, neuromuscular and energy systems to exercise
P2 describe the initial responses of the neuromuscular and energy systems to exercise		
P3 investigate how the cardiovascular and respiratory systems respond to steady-state exercise	**M2** explain how the cardiovascular, respiratory, neuromuscular and energy systems respond to steady-state exercise	**D2** analyse the responses of the cardiovascular, respiratory, neuromuscular and energy systems to steady-state exercise
P4 describe how the neuromuscular and energy systems respond to steady-state exercise		
P5 describe fatigue and how the body recovers from exercise	**M3** explain fatigue, and how the body recovers from exercise	
P6 describe how the cardiovascular and respiratory systems adapt to long-term exercise	**M4** explain how the cardiovascular, respiratory, neuromuscular, energy and skeletal systems adapt to long-term exercise.	**D3** analyse how the cardiovascular, respiratory, neuromuscular, energy and skeletal systems adapt to long-term exercise.
P7 describe how the neuromuscular, energy and skeletal systems adapt to long-term exercise.		

2.2 The Initial Responses of the Body to Exercise

Exercise

There are two main classifications of the types of exercise that we take part in: aerobic and anaerobic.

- Aerobic exercises use oxygen in the process of supplying energy to the body. These types of exercises are low-intensity and will usually allow us to talk while taking part in them – for example, walking, jogging, cycling and swimming.
- Anaerobic exercises do not use oxygen in the process of supplying energy to the body. These types of exercises are of a high intensity, so we do not have 'the breath' to talk while participating – for example, sprinting, high jump, speed swimming and 400m running.

The Cardiovascular System's Initial Response to Exercise

The cardiovascular system consists of the heart and the blood vessels through which the heart pumps blood around the body. During exercise, a number of changes take place to the cardiovascular system to ensure that the muscles receive the required amounts of oxygen and nutrients. The structure of the cardio-vascular system is discussed in more detail in Unit 1: Anatomy for Sport and Exercise.

During exercise, the heart rate needs to be increased in order to ensure that the working muscles receive adequate amounts of nutrients and oxygen, and that waste products are removed. Before you even start exercising there is an increase in your heart rate, called the 'anticipatory rise', which occurs because when you think about exercising it stimulates the sympathetic nervous system to release adrenaline.

Key term

Adrenaline (also known as epinephrine): a hormone released during times of stress which gets the body ready for action, increasing blood pressure, heart rate, and so on.

One of the effects of adrenaline is to make the heart beat faster. Once exercise has started, there is an increase in carbon dioxide and lactic acid in the body, which is detected by chemoreceptors.

The chemoreceptors trigger the sympathetic nervous system to increase the release of adrenaline,

which further increases heart rate. In a trained athlete, the heart rate can increase by up to three times within one minute of starting exercise. As exercise continues, the body becomes warmer, which

Fig 2.1 A runner at the outset of exercise

Key term

Chemoreceptor: a group of cells that detect changes in the chemical environment around them and transmit this message to the brain so that the body can respond accordingly.

will also help to increase the heart rate because it increases the speed of the conduction of nerve impulses across the heart.

Cardiac Output

Cardiac output is the amount of blood pumped from the heart every minute and is the product of heart rate and stroke volume.

Cardiac output (litres per minute) = heart rate (bpm) × Stroke volume (litres)

33

The shorthand for this equation is:

$$Q = HR \times SV$$

The stroke volume is around 70 to 90 millilitres. It varies depending on a variety of factors. Generally, the fitter you are, the larger your stroke volume is and males tend to have larger stroke volumes than females. At rest, a person's cardiac output is approximately 5 litres per minute, while during exercise it can increase to as much as 30 litres per minute.

Blood Pressure

Blood pressure is necessary in order for blood to flow around the body. The pressure is a result of the heart contracting and forcing blood into the blood vessels. Two values are given when a person has their blood pressure taken.

A typical blood pressure for the average adult male is 120/80. The two values correspond to the systolic value (when the heart is contracting) and the diastolic value (when the heart is relaxing). The higher value is the systolic value and the lower is the diastolic value. Blood pressure is measured in milligrams of mercury: mmHg.

The value for a person's blood pressure is determined by the cardiac output (Q), which is a product of stroke volume and heart rate, and the resistance the blood encounters as it flows around the body. This can be put into an equation:

$$\text{Blood pressure} = Q \times R$$

where Q = cardiac output (stroke volume × heart rate) and R = resistance to flow.

Resistance to blood flow is caused both by the size of the blood vessels through which it travels (the smaller the blood vessel, the greater the resistance) and by the thickness of the blood (the thicker the blood, the greater the resistance).

Changing the resistance to blood flow can alter blood pressure. This is done by involuntary smooth muscles in the arterioles relaxing or contracting in order to alter the diameter of the arterioles. As the smooth muscle contracts, the diameter of the blood vessel gets smaller, so blood pressure is increased. As the smooth muscle relaxes, the diameter of the blood vessel is increased, which decreases the pressure of the blood flowing through it. The same principle can be applied to altering the diameter of water flow through a hose. If you place your finger over part of the opening of the hose, making the diameter smaller, the water will flow out quite forcibly because it is under higher pressure. However, if the water is left to flow unhindered through the end of the hose, it is under lower pressure, and will therefore not 'spurt' so far because there is less resistance.

A reduction in blood pressure is detected by baroreceptors in the aorta and the carotid artery.

Key term

Baroreceptor: a collection of cells that detect a change in blood pressure. They send signals to the brain so that the body can respond appropriately.

This detection is passed to the central nervous system (CNS), which then sends a nervous impulse to the arterioles to constrict. This increases the blood pressure and also has the effect of increasing the heart rate.

When blood pressure is increased, the baroreceptors detect this and signal the CNS, which makes the arterioles dilate and reduces blood pressure.

Changes to Blood Pressure During the Onset of Exercise

Exercise has the effect of increasing heart rate, which will result in an increased cardiac output, which will have the effect of increasing blood pressure. This can be seen from the equation:

$$BP = Q \times R$$

If cardiac output is increased and the resistance to blood flow does not change, then blood pressure will also automatically increase.

A typical blood pressure reading for a person at the onset of exercise would be around 120/80 mmHg.

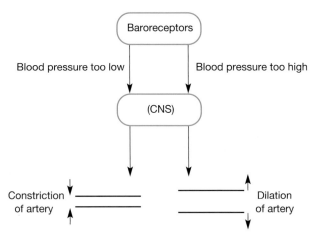

Fig 2.2 How baroreceptors initiate response to high blood pressure and low blood pressure

The Respiratory System's Initial Response to Exercise

The respiratory system is responsible for getting oxygen into the body and getting carbon dioxide out of the body. It is described in detail in Unit 1: Anatomy for Sport and Exercise. The oxygen is used to help produce energy while we take part in sporting activities. The process of creating energy also produces a waste product called carbon dioxide, which needs to be removed from the body.

Pulmonary Ventilation and Breathing Rate

The amount of air we breathe in and out per minute is called pulmonary ventilation and is given the symbol V_E.

Pulmonary ventilation can be worked out using the following equation:

$$V_E = \text{Frequency} \times \text{Tidal volume}$$

Frequency is the number of breaths per minute.

Tidal volume is the volume of air breathed in and out during one breath. At rest, the average breathing rate is around 12 breaths per minute. The average tidal volume is 0.5 litres (this will vary depending on the age, gender and size of a person).

Therefore, the average pulmonary ventilation at rest is:

$$V_E = 12 \times 0.5$$

$$V_E = 6 \text{ litres}$$

When you start to exercise, you need to take more oxygen into your body for it to be used to help produce energy. At the start of exercise, this increased oxygen demand occurs by breathing at a faster rate and breathing in more air and breathing out more air during each breath (i.e. tidal volume increases).

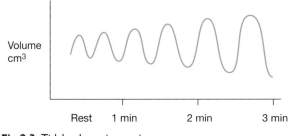

Fig 2.3 Tidal volume increasing

The intercostal muscles are used to aid breathing during exercise.

Key term

Intercostal muscles: located between the ribs, there are two types of intercostal muscle – internal and external. They help with inspiration and expiration during exercise.

The external intercostal muscles help with inspiration and the internal intercostal muscles help with expiration. As exercise becomes more strenuous, the abdominal muscles will also help aid expiration.

During anaerobic exercises, such as weightlifting, it is not uncommon for people to perform a Valsalva manoeuvre. This is basically the process of breathing out against a closed glottis or against a closed mouth and nose.

Fig 2.4 Weight lifting uses the Valsalva manoeuvre

The process of performing the Valsalva manoeuvre while lifting heavy weights helps to stabilise the shoulder girdle and torso. This helps the lifter to move the weight more efficiently. This process produces a marked increase in blood pressure and reduces blood flow to the thoracic cavity. Therefore, any person suffering with high blood pressure or heart problems should avoid this move.

Key term

Thoracic cavity: the part of the body that is enclosed by the ribcage and the diaphragm, containing the heart and the lungs.

Student activity 2.1 ⏱ 90–120 mins P1 M1 D1

In order to find out what happens to the cardio-vascular and respiratory systems during the initial stages of exercise, it is necessary to observe someone or take part in exercise and monitor the response of these systems.

Task 1

The aim of this activity is to examine what happens to heart rate before and during the onset of exercise. You will need the following equipment:

- Stopwatch or heart rate monitor
- Skipping rope
- Sports clothes
- Bench
- Pen and paper.

Follow the method set out below and record your results in the table; then answer the questions that follow.

- If you have a heart-rate monitor, place it around your chest. If not, find your pulse point, either on your neck or at your wrist.
- Sit quietly for five minutes, then take your resting heart rate. If you have a heart-rate monitor, write down the heart rate that appears on the monitor. If not, feel for your pulse point, then count your heart rate for 30 seconds. Double this figure and write it down.
- Think about what exercise you are about to perform for one minute.
- Record your heart rate after having thought about your exercise.

- Perform step-ups on to a bench for two minutes or skip for two minutes with a skipping rope.
- Immediately after you have finished your exercise, record your heart rate.

1. What happened to your heart rate immediately before you started exercising?

2. What caused this change in your heart rate and why is it necessary?

3. Explain and analyse why there is a difference between your resting heart rate, your pre-exercise heart rate and your post-exercise heart rate.

Task 2

- While sitting or lying down, count the number of breaths you breathe in during one minute – try to breathe as normally as possible. Write this number down and then work out your pulmonary ventilation using the equation: **VE = Frequency × Tidal volume**.

- Now take part in some form of exercise, such as skipping or step-ups, for three minutes.

- Immediately after completing your exercise, count the number of breaths you breathe in during one minute, then record your pulmonary ventilation.

- Explain and analyse why there is a difference between your resting pulmonary ventilation rate and your post-exercise pulmonary ventilation rate.

Resting heart rate (bpm)	Pre-exercise heart rate (bpm)	Post-exercise heart rate (bpm)

Initial Response of the Neuromuscular System

When we want to produce muscle movement, we have to get the message from our brain to our muscles. This communication between the brain and muscle is achieved through nerve impulses. A nerve impulse is an electrical current that runs from the central nervous system (CNS) through nerves and then to the muscle tissue, and results in muscle contraction. The term used to describe the signal travelling from the CNS to the muscle is called an action potential. Nerves that signal muscles to contract are called motor neurones.

Key terms

Central nervous system: consists of the brain and the spinal cord.

Motor neurone: a nerve that signals a muscle to contract.

The neuromuscular junction is the place at which the nerve and muscle meet. The nerve transmits its signal to make the muscle contract in the following manner:

● The pre-synaptic membrane reacts to the signal by its vesicles releasing acetylcholine.
● Acetylcholine diffuses across the gap between the nerve and the muscle (the synaptic cleft) and produces an electrical signal called the excitatory post-synaptic action potential.
● If the excitatory post-synaptic potential is big enough, it will make the muscle tissue contract.
● Once the muscle has carried out its desired movement, the enzyme cholinesterase breaks down the acetylcholine to leave the muscle ready to receive its next signal.

Motor Units

Key term

Motor unit: group of muscle fibres stimulated by one nerve.

As there are so many muscle fibres, a nerve stimulates more than just one fibre. In fact, it has a group of between 15 and 2000 muscle fibres, depending on the muscle it is connected to. This group of muscle fibres is called a motor unit.

When we want to produce muscle movements, we send signals from our CNS to the motor neurones. The strength of the signal determines whether the signal will reach the motor unit. This is called the all-or-nothing principle, which means that if the strength of the nerve signal is large enough, all of the motor unit will contract. And if the strength of the signal is not big enough, no part of the motor unit will contract. When we exercise, especially when we want to exert high levels of force, our motor units produce muscle contraction at different rates. Therefore, you will find that different parts of the muscle are contracting at slightly different times. This has the effect of producing smooth muscle contractions.

Muscle Spindles

A muscle spindle is an organ placed within the muscle which communicates with the CNS. The purpose of the muscle spindle is to detect when the muscle is in a state of contraction. When a muscle is contracted it changes the tension on the muscle spindle. This is relayed to the CNS and the CNS can deal with this information accordingly, by either increasing the contraction of the muscle or relaxing the muscle.

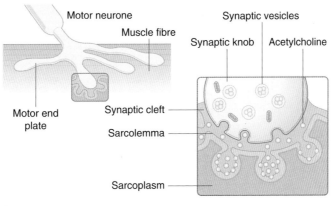

Fig 2.5 The neural transmission process

Initial Response of the Energy Systems

The function of energy systems is to produce adenosine triphosphate (ATP). ATP is used to make our muscles contract and therefore allows us to take part in exercise. It is basically a protein (adenosine) with three (tri) phosphates (phosphate) attached to it.

When chemical bonds are broken, energy is released. Therefore, when a phosphate is broken off the ATP to make ADP (adenosine diphosphate – di = two) energy is released, which is used to make the muscles contract.

Fig 2.6 Adenosine triphosphate (ATP)

ATP is not stored in large amounts in skeletal muscle and therefore has to be continually made from ADP for our muscles to continue contracting. There are three energy systems that the body uses to make ATP. They differ in the rate at which they make ATP. At the onset of exercise we will want ATP supplied very quickly. However, if we are on a long walk we do not need such a fast production of ATP, so the body uses a different energy system to make it.

Phosphocreatine Energy System

At the onset of exercise, the energy system that supplies the majority of ATP is the phosphocreatine system (also known as the creatine phosphate system). It supplies ATP much quicker than any other energy system. It produces ATP in the absence of oxygen, and is therefore an anaerobic energy system.

Phosphocreatine (PC) is made up of a phosphate and a creatine molecule. When the bond between the phosphate and the creatine is broken, energy is released which is then used to make the bond between ADP and a phosphate.

PC stores are used for rapid, high-intensity contractions, such as in sprinting or jumping. These stores only last for about ten seconds.

Lactic Acid Energy System

Once our PC stores have run out, we use the lactic acid system. This is also known as anaerobic glycolysis, which literally means the breakdown of glucose in the absence of oxygen. When glucose is broken down it is converted into a substance called pyruvate. When there is no oxygen present, the pyruvate is converted into lactic acid. This system produces ATP very quickly, but not as quickly as the PC system:

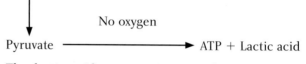

The lactic acid energy system is the one that is producing the majority of the ATP during high-intensity exercise lasting between 30 seconds and three minutes, such as an 800 m race.

Key learning points I

- At the onset of exercise, the various systems respond to try to increase oxygen delivery, energy production and carbon dioxide removal.
- Cardiovascular system: increased heart rate, increased blood pressure, increased cardiac output.
- Respiratory system: increased pulmonary ventilation, increased breathing rate, increased tidal volume.
- Neuromuscular system: increased number of nerve transmissions, skeletal muscular contraction.
- Energy system: ATP production through phosphocreatine energy system and lactic acid energy system.

Fig 2.7 Phosphocreatine energy system

Student activity 2.2   ⏱ 60–90 mins   P2 M1 D1

Task 1

Draw a spider diagram that illustrates the initial responses of the neuromuscular system and energy systems to exercise.

Task 2

Write a report that describes, explains and analyses

the initial responses of the neuromuscular system to exercise.

Task 3

Write a report that describes, explains and analyses the initial responses of the energy systems to exercise.

Ⓠ Quick quiz I

Choose the appropriate term from the following list to answer the questions below:

- Adrenaline
- Synovial fluid
- Pulmonary ventilation
- I2
- Electric current
- Micro-tears
- I20/80
- Valsalva manoeuvre
- Tidal volume
- Skeletal muscle.

1. This is the average number of breaths in and out for a person at rest.
2. This hormone is released before exercise to increase the heart rate.
3. A nerve impulse is an _____?
4. This is the technical term for breaths per minute.
5. This is released into the joints during a warm-up to help increase their range of movement.
6. This is an adult's average resting blood pressure.
7. The amount of air breathed in and out in one breath.
8. This is performed to help to stabilise the shoulder girdle and torso.
9. These occur in muscle tissue during resistance exercises.
10. Blood is directed here during exercise.

2.3 How the Body Responds to Steady-state Exercise

P3 P4 M2 D2

Once we have been performing continuous exercise for a period of around 20 minutes, our body reaches a 'steady state'. Continuous exercise includes all forms of exercise that have no stopping periods,

such as jogging, swimming or cycling. Examples of non-continuous exercise would be weightlifting, interval training and boxing.

Key term

Steady state: when the body is working at a steady state it means that lactic acid removal is occurring at the same pace as lactic acid production.

39

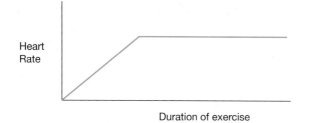

Fig 2.8 Heart rate response during continuous exercise

Various changes will have occurred in the body to allow this steady state to occur.

Cardiovascular:
● Heart rate levels off
● Increased stroke volume
● Vasodilation of blood vessels leading to working muscles
● Blood pressure levels off
● Thermoregulation.

Respiratory:
● Tidal volume levels off
● Breathing rate levels off
● Oxygen is unloaded from haemoglobin much more readily.

Neuromuscular:
● Increased pliability of muscles
● Increased speed of neural transmissions.

Energy:
● Aerobic ATP production.

Cardiovascular Response to Steady-state Exercise

Heart rate peaks during the first few minutes of exercise and then levels off.

Stroke Volume

While exercising, there is an increase in venous return.

> ## Key term
> **Venous return:** the amount of blood returned to the heart after circulating around the body.

This increased volume of blood has the effect of stretching the cardiac muscle to a greater degree than normal. This stretching has the effect of making the heart contract much more forcibly and thereby pumping out more blood during each contraction, so stroke volume is increased during exercise. This effect is known as Starling's law.

Blood Flow

The average cardiac output is around 5 litres per minute. When this blood is circulated around the body, some organs receive more blood than others. However, during exercise, the working muscles need a greater proportion of blood in order to supply them with energy. The body is able to redirect blood flow by constricting the blood vessels leading to organs that do not require such a large blood flow, and dilating the blood vessels feeding the muscles that do. The process of blood vessels constricting is called vasoconstriction and the process of blood vessels dilating is called vasodilation.

> ## Key term
> **Constriction:** becoming smaller.

> ## Key term
> **Dilation:** becoming larger.

Changes to Blood Pressure During Steady-state Exercise

Dilation of the blood vessels feeding the working muscle acts to reduce blood pressure, but this is counteracted by the increase in blood pressure caused by increased cardiac output.

Exercise raises systolic pressure, but there is only a slight change in diastolic pressure.

Immediately after exercise there is a fall in systolic pressure, as the skeletal muscular pump is no longer pumping blood from the muscles to the heart. This can lead to blood pooling in the muscles and cause the athlete to faint, as not enough blood is being pumped to the brain.

Thermoregulation

Thermoregulation is the process of maintaining a constant body core temperature. In humans this temperature is 37 °C. The skin temperature of the body can vary a great deal. If the core temperature is increased or decreased by 1 °C or more, this will affect an athlete's physical and mental performance. When exercising, we produce a great deal of excess heat. The cardiovascular system is vitally important in ensuring that we are able to lose this excess heat so that our core temperature does not increase. Excess heat is lost through sweating and dilatation of peripheral blood vessels, so that blood passes close to the surface of the skin. As the sweat evaporates, it cools down the skin surface. This has the effect of cooling the blood as it travels through the blood vessels that are close to the skin surface. When we are exercising at a high intensity in hot conditions, between 15 and 25 per cent of the cardiac output is directed to the skin.

Respiratory Responses

After having peaked in the first few minutes, if exercise remains at the same intensity, tidal volume and breathing rate level off and remain the same until exercise is terminated.

Oxygen Dissociation Curve

Only 1.5 per cent of oxygen is carried in the blood plasma. The majority of oxygen is transported in the blood by haemoglobin. Oxygen reacts with haemoglobin to make oxyhaemoglobin. The reaction of oxygen with haemoglobin is temporary and completely reversible. This means that oxygen can be unloaded from haemoglobin. The binding of oxygen to haemoglobin is dependent on the partial pressure of oxygen. Oxygen combines with haemoglobin in oxygen-rich situations, such as in the lungs.

Oxygen is released by haemoglobin in places where there is little oxygen, such as in exercising muscle.

The oxygen dissociation curve is an S-shaped curve that represents the ease with which haemoglobin releases oxygen when it is exposed to tissues of different concentrations of oxygen. The curve starts with a steep rise because haemoglobin has a high affinity for oxygen. This means that when there is a small rise in the partial pressure of oxygen, haemoglobin picks up and binds oxygen to it easily. Thus, in the lungs, the blood is rapidly saturated with oxygen. However, only a small drop in the partial pressure of oxygen results in a large drop in the percentage saturation of haemoglobin. Thus, in exercising muscles, where there is a low partial pressure of oxygen, the haemoglobin readily unloads the oxygen for use by the tissues.

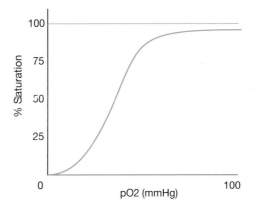

Fig 2.9 Oxygen dissociation curve

Changes in blood carbon dioxide level and hydrogen ion concentration (pH) cause shifts in the oxygen dissociation curve. These shifts enhance oxygen release in tissues and increase oxygen uptake in the lungs. This is known as the Bohr effect, named after the Danish physiologist, Christian Bohr, who discovered it. During exercise, the blood becomes more acidic because of the increased production of carbon dioxide.

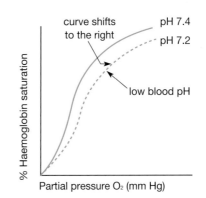

Fig 2.10 Shift in oxygen dissociation curve

41

This increase in carbon dioxide and decrease in pH shifts the dissociation curve to the right for a given partial pressure of oxygen, releasing more oxygen to the tissues.

In the lungs, there is a low partial pressure of carbon dioxide and low hydrogen ion concentration, which shifts the dissociation curve to the left for a given partial pressure of oxygen, and therefore enhances oxygen uptake.

As muscles exercise, they also increase in temperature. This has the effect of shifting the curve to the right, which means oxygen is released much more readily. Conversely, a decreased temperature shifts the curve to the left, which increases oxygen uptake.

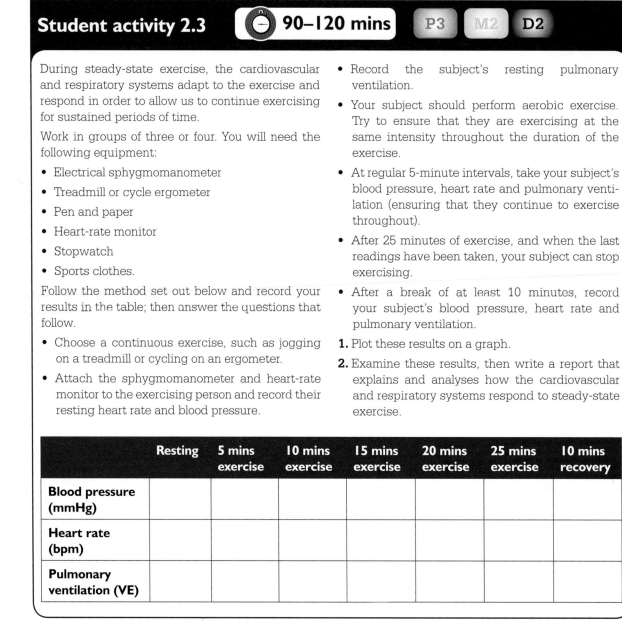

Student activity 2.3 ⏱ 90–120 mins P3 M2 D2

During steady-state exercise, the cardiovascular and respiratory systems adapt to the exercise and respond in order to allow us to continue exercising for sustained periods of time.

Work in groups of three or four. You will need the following equipment:

- Electrical sphygmomanometer
- Treadmill or cycle ergometer
- Pen and paper
- Heart-rate monitor
- Stopwatch
- Sports clothes.

Follow the method set out below and record your results in the table; then answer the questions that follow.

- Choose a continuous exercise, such as jogging on a treadmill or cycling on an ergometer.
- Attach the sphygmomanometer and heart-rate monitor to the exercising person and record their resting heart rate and blood pressure.

- Record the subject's resting pulmonary ventilation.
- Your subject should perform aerobic exercise. Try to ensure that they are exercising at the same intensity throughout the duration of the exercise.
- At regular 5-minute intervals, take your subject's blood pressure, heart rate and pulmonary ventilation (ensuring that they continue to exercise throughout).
- After 25 minutes of exercise, and when the last readings have been taken, your subject can stop exercising.
- After a break of at least 10 minutes, record your subject's blood pressure, heart rate and pulmonary ventilation.

1. Plot these results on a graph.
2. Examine these results, then write a report that explains and analyses how the cardiovascular and respiratory systems respond to steady-state exercise.

	Resting	5 mins exercise	10 mins exercise	15 mins exercise	20 mins exercise	25 mins exercise	10 mins recovery
Blood pressure (mmHg)							
Heart rate (bpm)							
Pulmonary ventilation (VE)							

Neuromuscular Response

As more blood is pumped through the muscles and excess heat is generated through exercising, muscle tissue warms up. The warmer the muscle tissue becomes, the more pliable it is.

Key term

Pliable: able to be stretched, shaped or bent.

This means that the muscle tissue is able to stretch to greater lengths without tearing. You can apply this principle to plasticine. If you take a piece of plasticine out of its container and pull it outwards with two hands, the plasticine will quickly break in two. But if you were to warm up the plasticine by rolling it in your hands, and then pull it apart, you would find that it is able to stretch much further without breaking.

As the muscle tissue warms up, the rate at which nervous impulses are sent and received is increased as the heat increases the speed of transmission.

Energy System's Response

The aerobic energy system provides ATP at a slower rate than the previous two energy systems discussed. It is responsible for producing the majority of our energy while our bodies are at rest or taking part in low-intensity exercise such as jogging. It uses a series of reactions, the first being aerobic glycolysis, as it occurs when oxygen is available to break down glucose. As in the anaerobic energy system, glucose is broken down into pyruvate. Because oxygen is present, pyruvate is not turned into lactic acid, but continues to be broken down through a series of chemical reactions, which include:

● The Krebs Cycle – pyruvate from aerobic glycolysis combines with Coenzyme A (CoA) to form acetyl CoA, which combines and reacts with a number of different compounds to produce ATP, hydrogen and carbon dioxide
● The Electron Transport Chain – the hydrogen atoms produced from the Krebs Cycle enter this chain and are passed along a chain of electron carriers, eventually combining with oxygen to form ATP and water.

Both the Krebs Cycle and the Electron Transport Chain take place in organelles called mitochondria.

The majority of ATP is produced in these organelles, so they are very important for energy production. They are rod-shaped and have an inner and outer membrane. The inner membrane is arranged into

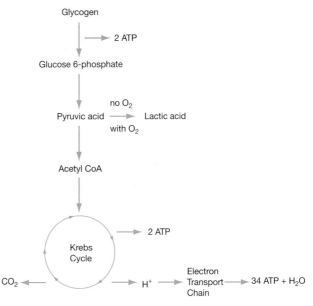

Fig 2.11 Aerobic energy system

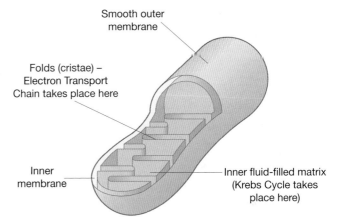

Fig 2.12 Mitochondrion

many folds that project inwards. These folds are called cristae and provide a large surface area for energy production to take place.

Key learning points 2

When exercising at a steady state, the body undergoes the following responses:
● Cardiovascular responses: HR levels off, increased stroke volume, vasodilation of blood vessels leading to working muscles, BP levels off.
● Respiratory responses: tidal volume levels off, breathing rate levels off, oxygen is unloaded from haemoglobin much more readily.
● Neuromuscular responses: increased pliability of muscles, increased speed of neural transmissions.
● Energy system responses: aerobic ATP production.

43

Student activity 2.4 ⏱ **60–90 mins** P4 M2 D2

Write a report that describes, explains and analyses the responses of the neuromuscular and energy systems to steady-state exercise.

Ⓠ Quick quiz 2

1. Give three examples of steady-state exercise.
2. Give two responses from the following body systems to show how they adapt to steady-state exercise:
3. (a) Cardiovascular system.
   (b) Respiratory system.
   (c) Neuromuscular system.
4. Draw a graph to illustrate how heart rate responds to steady-state exercise.
5. Describe Starling's law.
6. Explain the oxygen dissociation curve.
7. Which energy system is used during steady-state exercise?
8. In which organelle is the majority of ATP produced during steady-state exercise?

2.4 Fatigue and How the Body Recovers from Exercise

P5 M3

We cannot continue to exercise indefinitely because we will eventually fatigue.

Key term

Fatigue: tiredness from physical exertion.

Fatigue occurs as a result of a number of factors, including:

● Depletion of energy sources, such as reduced quantities of phosphocreatine, glucose and glycogen
● Effects of waste products, such as increased production of lactic acid and carbon dioxide
● Neuromuscular fatigue, such as depletion of acetylcholine and reduced calcium ion release.

As a result, it is necessary to rest in order to recover and return the body to its pre-exercise state.

Depletion of Energy Sources

In order to exercise, we must break down the energy stored in our body and turn it into ATP. Sources of energy include phosphocreatine, glucose and glycogen. We have only enough phosphocreatine to last us for ten seconds of maximal exercise. We then switch to glucose for energy production. We have around 15 to 20 g of glucose in our bloodstream, around 345 g of glycogen in our muscles, and 90 to 110 g of glycogen stored in our liver. When our blood sugar levels are low, the liver converts either its store of glycogen into glucose or the skeletal muscles' store of glycogen into glucose. We have only enough glycogen stores to last us for around two hours. So once the body's stores of glucose and glycogen are used up, we become fatigued and/or have to exercise at a lower intensity.

Effects of Waste Products

Lactic acid is the main by-product of anaerobic glycolysis. Blood always contains a small amount of lactic acid, and during high-intensity exercise this increases greatly. The increased production of lactic acid results in the pH of the blood decreasing. A blood pH of 6.4 or lower affects muscle and neural function and eventually prevents continued exercise.

Onset of blood lactate accumulation (OBLA) is the point at which lactic acid begins to accumulate in the muscles. It is also known as the anaerobic threshold. OBLA is considered to occur at somewhere between 85 and 90 per cent of your maximum heart rate.

Neuromuscular Fatigue

Neuromuscular fatigue means that the muscles are either not able to receive signals from the CNS that stimulate the muscle to contract or that the muscle tissue is unable to function properly.

High-intensity exercise or exercise for long periods of time can eventually interfere with calcium release, which is required for muscle contraction. If no calcium ions are available, the muscle is unable to contract.

Alternatively, transmission of nerve impulses can be affected, as the availability of acetylcholine can be decreased, which prevents the nervous stimulation reaching the muscle tissue/motor unit.

Recovery Process

After taking part in any type of exercise, the body has to recover and return to its pre-exercise state.

Excess post-exercise oxygen consumption (EPOC) is also referred to as oxygen debt. EPOC is the total oxygen consumed after exercise in excess of pre-exercise levels. It occurs when the exercise performed is totally or partially anaerobic. As a result, energy is supplied by the anaerobic energy systems, which results in lactic acid production. When the person stops exercising, breathing rate remains elevated so that extra oxygen is breathed in to:

● Break down lactic acid to carbon dioxide and water
● Replenish ATP, phosphocreatine and glycogen
● Pay back any oxygen that has been borrowed from haemoglobin and myoglobin.

After a bout of vigorous exercise, five events must take place before the muscle can operate again:

1. ATP must be replaced.
2. PC stores must be replenished.
3. Lactic acid must be removed.
4. Myoglobin must be replenished with oxygen.
5. Glycogen stores must be replenished.

The replacement of ATP and PC takes around three minutes and the removal of lactic acid takes around 20 minutes after stopping exercise, but the oxygen replenishment of myoglobin and refilling the glycogen stores take between 24 and 48 hours. If the exercise bout was of a very high intensity, it will take longer to recover. However, the fitter you are, the faster you will recover. The faster the debt can be repaid, the sooner the performer can exercise again.

The oxygen debt consists of two separate components:

● Alactacid debt (fast component)
● Lactacid debt (slow component).

Alactacid Debt

Alactacid oxygen debt is the process of recovery that does not involve lactic acid. The aerobic energy system is used to produce the ATP required to replenish the PC stores and ATP stores in the body:

$$ADP + P + Oxygen = ATP$$

$$ATP + C + P = PC + ADP$$

Around 50 per cent of the replenishment occurs during the first 30 seconds, while full recovery occurs at about three minutes.

The alactacid oxygen debt ranges between 2 and 3.5 litres of oxygen. The fitter you are, the greater the debt, because training increases the PC content within the muscle cells. However, the recovery time of a fitter person is reduced because they have enhanced methods of oxygen delivery, such as increased capillarisation and an improved cardiorespiratory system. These increase the rate of ATP production from the aerobic energy system.

Lactacid Debt

The lactacid oxygen debt takes much longer to complete and can last for minutes or hours, depending on the severity of the exercise. The process involves oxygen, which is required to break down the lactic acid produced during anaerobic glycolysis into pyruvate. Pyruvate can then enter the aerobic energy system and eventually be broken down into carbon dioxide and water.

$$Lactic\ acid + Oxygen = Pyruvate$$

Lactic acid can also be converted in the liver to glycogen and stored either in the liver or in muscle tissue. Research has shown that an active recovery increases the rate of removal of lactic acid, so walking or slow jogging after a bout of exercise will help to decrease the time it takes to rid the body of lactic acid. An active recovery keeps the heart rate and breathing rate up, which has the effect of increasing the rate of delivery of oxygen to the working muscles. This then helps to rid the body of the lactic acid.

Therefore, a cool-down is very important after any form of activity in order to maximise recovery. Failure to cool down adequately means that the levels of lactic acid will remain elevated. It is thought that this acidity level affects the pain receptors and contributes to the muscle soreness which people may feel some time after having exercised. This muscle soreness, termed delayed onset of muscle soreness (DOMS), is at its most uncomfortable 36 to 48 hours after exercise has ceased.

Muscle glycogen stores must also be restored. This is attained through a high carbohydrate diet and rest. It can take several days to recover muscle glycogen stores, depending on the intensity of the exercise.

Key learning points 3

- Fatigue occurs because of:
  - Depletion of energy sources
  - Accumulation of waste products
  - Lack of calcium ion availability
  - Decreased availability of acetylcholine.
- Recovery after exercise involves taking in excess oxygen in order to return the body to its pre-exercise state.
- Alactic phase of recovery: ATP and PC production takes place in the first few minutes of recovery.
- Lactic phase of recovery: lactic acid is removed and turned into pyruvate and myoglobin; stores of oxygen are repleted and glycogen stores are repleted.
- An active recovery increases the rate of lactic acid removal.

Student activity 2.5   ⏱ 60–90 mins   P5   M3

- Place a heart-rate monitor around your chest or take your heart rate by pressing on a pulse point and counting your pulse for one minute. Stand against a wall, then bend your knees and slide down the wall so that your knees are at right angles – you will be in a 'ski squat' position'.
- After 30 seconds or one minute, count your pulse and remain in the ski squat position.
- You will no doubt feel that your legs are very sore and you cannot maintain this position for very long, but your heart rate has not reached maximal values. You have had to stop this exercise because you have experienced neuromuscular fatigue in your quadriceps muscles!

Task 1

Describe and explain the process involved when a person becomes fatigued through taking part in exercise.

Task 2

You will need the following equipment:

- Stopwatch
- Running track/gym
- Sports clothes.

Follow the method set out below and record your results in the table; then answer the questions that follow.

- Take your resting pulse rate and make a note of it in the results table.

- Take part in some form of intense exercise that lasts at least five minutes.
- Find your pulse, then record your pulse for a ten-second count every minute after the exercise until your heart rate returns to its original level.
- Convert your heart rate into beats per minute by multiplying by six.

	Beats per minute
Resting pulse rate	
Immediately after exercise	
I minute after exercise	
2 minutes after exercise	
3 minutes after exercise	
4 minutes after exercise	
5 minutes after exercise	

1. Explain why your heart rate was different from resting levels immediately after exercise had stopped.
2. Explain why your heart rate remained elevated after three minutes of rest.
3. Draw a graph to illustrate the fast and slow components of the recovery process.
4. Write a report that describes and explains the recovery process from exercise participation.

Quick quiz 3

1. List three reasons why fatigue can occur.
2. How much glucose do we have in our bloodstream?
3. What is the main by-product of anaerobic glycolysis?
4. At what blood pH is muscle and neural function affected?
5. Which ions are required for muscle contraction?
6. What does EPOC stand for?
7. After a bout of vigorous exercise, what five events must occur before a muscle can operate again?
8. What is alactacid debt?
9. What is lactacid debt?

2.5 How the Body Adapts to Long-term Exercise

Fig 2.13 The athlete's body has adapted to strength training

Long-term exercise is also known as chronic exercise and means that a person has been participating in regular exercise for long periods of time (a minimum of eight weeks). This regular participation affects the body in a number of ways that make it more able to cope with the stresses of the exercise. This results in the person being able to exercise at higher intensities and/or for longer periods of time. This process is called adaptation.

Cardiovascular Adaptations

The main adaptations that occur to the cardio-vascular system through endurance training are concerned with increasing the delivery of oxygen to the working muscles. If you were to dissect the heart of a top endurance athlete, you would find that the size of the walls of the left ventricle are markedly thicker than those of a person who does not perform endurance exercise. This adaptation is called cardiac hypertrophy.

Key term

Cardiac hypertrophy: the size of the heart wall becomes thicker and stronger.

Adaptation occurs in the same way that we increase the size of our skeletal muscles – the more we exercise our muscles, the larger or more toned they become. In the same way, the more we exercise our heart through aerobic training, the larger it will become. This will then have the effect of increasing the stroke volume, which is the amount of blood that the heart can pump out per beat. As the heart wall becomes bigger, it can pump more blood per beat, as the thicker wall can contract more forcibly. As the stroke volume is increased, the heart no longer needs to beat as often to get the same amount of blood around the body. This results in a decrease in heart rate which is known as bradycardia.

Key term

Bradycardia: decreased resting heart rate.

An average male adult's heart rate is 70 beats per minute (bpm). However, Lance Armstrong, a Tour de France champion, had a resting heart rate of 30 bpm! As stroke volume increases, cardiac output also increases, so an endurance athlete's heart can pump more blood per minute than other people's. However, resting values of cardiac output do not change. An endurance athlete has more capillaries, allowing more blood to travel through them. This process, called capillarisation, aids in the extraction of oxygen. An increase in haemoglobin due to an increase in the number of red blood cells (which contain the haemoglobin) further aids the transport of oxygen. Though haemoglobin content rises, the increase in blood plasma is greater, and consequently the blood haematocrit (ratio of red blood cell volume to total blood volume) is reduced, which lowers viscosity (thickness) and enables the blood to flow more easily.

Strength training produces very few adaptations to the cardiovascular system, as this training does not stress the heart or oxygen delivery and extraction systems for sustained periods of time.

Respiratory Adaptations

The respiratory system deals with taking oxygen into the body and also with helping to remove waste products associated with muscle metabolism. Training reduces the resting respiratory rate and the breathing rate during sub-maximal exercise. Endurance training can also provide a small increase in lung volumes: vital capacity increases slightly, as does tidal volume during maximal exercise. The increased strength of the respiratory muscles is partly responsible for this as it aids lung inflation.

Endurance training also increases the capillarisation around the alveoli in the lungs. This helps to increase the rate of gas exchange in the lungs and, therefore, increase the amount of oxygen entering the blood and the amount of carbon dioxide leaving the blood.

Strength training produces very few adaptations to the respiratory system, as this type of training uses the anaerobic energy systems, whereas the respiratory system is only really concerned with the aerobic energy system.

Neuromuscular and Energy Systems' adaptations

Endurance training results in an increase in the muscular stores of muscle glycogen. There is increased delivery of oxygen to the muscles through an increase in the concentration of myoglobin and increased capillary density through the muscle. The ability of skeletal muscle to consume oxygen is increased as a direct result of an increase in the number and size of the mitochondria and an increase in the activity and concentration of enzymes involved in the aerobic processes that take place in the mitochondria. As a result, there is greater scope to use glycogen and fat as fuels. Slow-twitch fibres can enlarge by up to 22 per cent, which gives greater potential for aerobic energy production. Hypertrophy of slow-twitch fibres means that there is a corresponding increase in the stores of glycogen and triglycerides. This ensures a continuous supply of energy, enabling exercise to be performed for longer.

These adaptations result in an increased maximal oxygen consumption (VO_2max) being obtained before the anaerobic threshold is reached and fatigue begins.

High-intensity training results in hypertrophy of fast-twitch fibres. There are increased levels of ATP and PC in the muscle and an increased capacity to generate ATP by the PC energy system. This is partly due to the increased activity of the enzymes which break down PC. ATP production by anaerobic glycolysis is increased as a result of enhanced activity of the glycolytic enzymes. There is also an increased ability to break down glycogen in the absence of oxygen.

As lactic acid accumulates, it decreases the pH levels of the blood, making it more acidic. This increased level of hydrogen ions will eventually prevent the glycolytic enzyme functioning. However, anaerobic training increases the buffering capacity of the body and enables it to work for longer in periods of high acidity.

Energy System Adaptation

Aerobic training will increase the number of mitochondria in slow-twitch muscle fibres. This will allow greater production of ATP through the aerobic energy system. Greater amounts of glycogen can be stored in the liver and skeletal muscle. Aerobic training results in an increase in the number of enzymes required for body fat to be broken down, and more body fat is stored in muscle tissue, which means that more fat can be used as an energy source.

Anaerobic or strength training predominantly uses the PC and lactic acid energy system. Chronic anaerobic/strength training increases the body's tolerance levels to low pH. This means more energy can be produced by the lactic acid energy system, and the increased production of lactic acid can be tolerated for longer.

Skeletal Adaptations

Our skeleton responds to aerobic weight-bearing exercise or resistance exercise by becoming stronger and more able to withstand impact, which means you are less likely to break a bone if you fall over.

Key term

Weight-bearing exercise: this is when we are using our body weight as a form of resistance (e.g. walking, running).

This occurs because the stimulation of exercise means the mineral content (calcium in particular) is increased, which makes bones harder and stronger. Exercise also has an effect on joints, by increasing the thickness of cartilage at the ends of the bones and increasing the production of synovial fluid. This will have the effect of making joints stronger and less prone to injury. Strength training increases the strength of muscle tendons, which again makes them less prone to injury. Lastly, the ligaments which hold our bones together are able to stretch to a greater degree, which helps to prevent injuries such as joint strains.

Key learning points 4

- Adaptations to aerobic exercise:
  - Cardiovascular system: cardiac hypertrophy, increased SV, decreased resting HR, increased number of capillaries, increased number of red blood cells, decreased haematocrit.
  - Respiratory system: decreased resting breathing rate, increased lung volume, increased vital capacity, increased tidal volume (in maximal exercise), increased strength of respiratory muscles, increased capillarisation around alveoli
  - Neuromuscular system: increased myoglobin content, increased number of capillaries, increased number of mitochondria, hypertrophy of slow-twitch muscle fibres, increased stores of glycogen, increased stores of fat.
  - Energy systems: increased number of aerobic enzymes, increased breakdown of fat.
- Adaptations to anaerobic exercise:
  - Cardiovascular system: no significant adaptations.
  - Respiratory system: no significant adaptations.
  - Neuromuscular: hypertrophy of fast-twitch muscle fibres, increased content of ATP, increased content of PC, increased tolerance to lactic acid.
  - Energy systems: increased number of anaerobic enzymes.
  - Skeletal system: increased strength of bones, increased strength of tendons, increased stretch of ligaments.

Student activity 2.6   60–90 mins   P6 P7 M4 D3

Taking part in long-term exercise programmes, such as four 30-minute jogging sessions per week for eight weeks, or a six-week resistance training programme, will produce stimulus to make the body adapt to the exercise so that it is able to perform the activity more readily, with less perceived effort.

Task 1

Draw a spider diagram that illustrates how each of the following systems adapts to long-term exercise:

- Cardiovascular

- Respiratory
- Skeletal
- Neuromuscular
- Energy.

Task 2

Write a report that describes, explains and analyses how the cardiovascular, respiratory, skeletal, neuromuscular and energy systems adapt to long-term exercise.

Q Quick quiz 4

1. Explain what cardiac hypertrophy is and how this can help an endurance athlete.
2. Explain how capillarisation around the lungs can increase the rate of gas exchange.
3. Explain how the skeletal system adapts to weight-bearing exercises.
4. Describe how the cardiovascular and respiratory system of Paula Radcliff will have adapted through endurance training.
5. Describe how the neuromuscular and skeletal system of Usain Bolt will have adapted through resistance training.

Further reading

Clegg, C. (1995) *Exercise Physiology*, Feltham Press.

Crisfield, P. (1996) *Coaching Sessions: A Guide to Planning and Goal-setting*, National Coaching Foundation.

Davis, R.J., Bull, C.R., Roscoe, J.V. and Roscoe, D.A. (2000) *Physical Education and the Study of Sport*, Mosby.

Dick, F. (1997) *Sports Training Principles*, London: A & C Black.

Foss, M. and Keteyian, S. (1998) *Fox's Physiological Basis for Exercise and Sport*, Maidenhead: McGraw-Hill.

Honeybourne, J., Hill, M. and Moors, H. (2000) *Advanced Physical Education and Sport for A Level*, Cheltenham: Stanley Thornes.

McArdle, W., Katch, F. and Katch, V. (2001) *Exercise Physiology: Energy, Nutrition and Human Performance*, London: WMS & Wilkins.

Wesson, K., Wiggins, N., Thompson, G. and Hartigan, S. (2000) *Sport and PE: A Complete Guide to Advanced Level Study*, London: Hodder Arnold.

Useful websites

www.getbodysmart.com
Free tutorials and quizzes from an American site that looks at human anatomy and physiology, helping you to see the structure of the different body systems.

www.innerbody.com
Free and informative diagrams of the different body systems, including respiratory, cardiovascular, skeletal and muscular

www.instantanatomy.net
Free useful anatomy pictures and information, mainly from a medical viewpoint

3: Sport & Exercise Psychology

3.1 Introduction

Success in sport is derived from a series of variable factors. The athlete must be prepared physically, have the correct nutritional strategy, and ensure that they are appropriately recovered and in a positive mental state. Sport psychology deals with ensuring that the performer has this correct mental state and is able to control this state during training and training periods.

Through the systematic research and study of individuals in sporting environments, it has been possible to gain an insight into what makes certain performers successful. By 'modelling' these effective techniques, it has been possible to improve their performance and gain an insight into excellence. Sport psychologists have developed a body of techniques to assist performers in improving their performances and developing consistency. These sport psychology techniques can be applied to all levels of athletes:

● From giving a beginner the confidence to jump the high-jump bar to helping a professional footballer score a penalty in the World Cup final
● Helping coaches to produce the best performances from their athletes and stay calm as they watch
● Helping fitness trainers to motivate their clients and ensure that they keep performing their training routines.

Literally speaking, psychology means the study of (*ology*) the human mind (*psyche*). The work of several coaches has shown the value of psychologically preparing athletes: **Bill Beswick** in football, **Stephen Bull** with the English cricket team during the successful 2005 Ashes series, and **Jos Vanstiphort** with golfers Ernie Els and Retief Goosen.

By the end of this unit you should know the:

● effects of personality, motivation and aggression on sports performance
● impact of arousal, stress and anxiety on sports performance
● psychology of group dynamics in sports environments
● psychological factors that affect people in exercise environments.

Assessment and grading criteria

To achieve a PASS grade the evidence must show that the learner is able to:	To achieve a MERIT grade the evidence must show that, in addition to the pass criteria, the learner is able to:	To achieve a DISTINCTION grade the evidence must show that, in addition to the pass and merit criteria, the learner is able to:
P1 describe personality and its effects on sports performance	**M1** explain personality and its effects on sports performance	**D1** analyse personality and its effects on sports performance
P2 describe motivation and the factors that affect the motivation of athletes		
P3 describe the types and causes of aggressive behaviour	**M2** explain the types and causes of aggressive behaviour	
P4 describe arousal and its effect on sports performance	**M3** explain it arousal and its effect on sports performance	**D2** analyse anusal and its effect on sports performance
P5 describe stress and anxiety and their symptoms and causes		
P6 identify four different factors which contribute to the psychology of group dynamics	**M4** explain four different factors which contributes to the psychology of group dynamics	
P7 identify three psychological factors that affect people in exercise environments.	**M5** explain three psychological factors that affect people in exercise environments.	

3.2 The Effects of Personality, Motivation and Aggression on Sports Performance

The key concept that underpins all studies in sport psychology is personality. It is clear that each person has the same brain structure and that their senses will all work in the same way to provide the brain with information. However, each person appears to be different in the decisions they make and how they behave in specific situations. Personality looks at these individual differences and how they affect performance.

There is a range of definitions of personality, each with its merits and drawbacks. It has been suggested that we all have traits and behaviour that we share with other people, but we also have some particular to ourselves. However, this idea does lack depth of information; as does Cattell's (1965) attempt to define personality: 'that which tells what a man will do when placed in a given situation'.

This suggests that if we know an individual's personality, we can predict their behaviour. However, human beings tend to be less than predictable and can act out of character, depending on the situation. Their behaviour may also be affected by their mood, fatigue or emotions.

Eysenck (1964) sought to address the limitations of previous definitions: 'The more or less stable and enduring organisation of an individual's character, temperament, intellect and physique which determines their unique adjustment to the environment.' Eysenck's statement that personality is more or less stable allows the human element to enter the equation and explain the unpredictable. He also makes the important point that personality is 'unique'. We may have behaviour in common with other people, but, ultimately, every person has a set of characteristics unique to themselves.

In summary, most personality theories state the following: personality is the set of individual characteristics that make a person unique and will determine their relatively consistent patterns of behaviour.

By giving labels to a person's character and behaviour, you have started to assess personality. By observing sportspeople, we are using a behavioural approach – assessing what they are like by assessing their responses to various situations. In reality, our observations may be unreliable because we see sportspeople in only one environment, and although we see them interviewed as well, we do not know what they are truly like. A cognitive psychologist believes we need to understand an individual's thoughts and emotions, as well as watching their behaviour. This we cannot do without the use of a questionnaire or an interview.

Personality Theories

Jarvis (2006) identifies four factors that will determine how an individual responds in a specific situation:

1 Our genetic make-up – the innate aspect of our personality that we inherit from our parents.

2 Our past experiences – these are important because if we have acted in a certain way in the past and it had a successful outcome, it is likely that we will act in the same way in the future; or if we have had a negative experience in the past, the same experience in the future will be seen as being threatening or stressful.

3 The nature of the situation in which we find ourselves – this will cause us to adapt our behaviour in a way that suits the situation.

4 Free will – a difficult concept in psychology, which suggests we have control over our thinking and thus our behaviour; it can be difficult to separate whether a person has chosen to behave in that way or is programmed by their genetics or past experiences.

Martens' Schematic View of Personality

Martens views personality as having three different depths or layers:

● Level 1 – the psychological core is the deepest component of personality and is at its centre. It includes an individual's beliefs, attitudes, values and feelings of self-worth. It is 'the real you' and, as a result, it is relatively permanent and seen by few people.

● Level 2 – typical responses are how we usually respond to situations and adapt to our environment. It is seen as the relatively consistent way we behave. Our typical responses are good indicators of our psychological core, but they can be affected by the social environment. A person who is very outgoing and sociable with his rugby-playing friends may become more reserved at a party with people he does not know.

● Level 3 – role-related behaviour is the shallowest level of our personality, and this level shows how we change our behaviour to adapt to the situation we are in. For example, throughout the day, we may play the roles of sportsperson, student, employee,

53

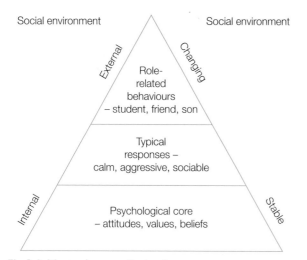

Social environment   Social environment

External   Changing

Role-
related
behaviours
– student, friend, son

Typical
responses –
calm, aggressive, sociable

Internal   Stable

Psychological core
– attitudes, values, beliefs

Fig 3.1 Martens' personality levels

friend, son/daughter, coach, and so on. In order to survive, we need to adapt our personalities, as it would not be appropriate to behave on the sports field in the same manner as when studying in class. We need to modify our personalities to suit the situation.

Trait Theory

The trait approach to personality relates to the first factor of personality. Jarvis (2006) identifies that personality is based in genetics. This is called the nature approach and says that we inherit personality at birth. This has some validity. For example, we can observe how different babies have different personalities from a young age. A trait is defined as 'a relatively stable way of behaving', suggesting that if a person shows a trait of shyness in one situation, they will be shy across a range of situations. Across a population, the traits people have are the same, but they show them to a greater or lesser extent, and this dictates their personality. This theory was very popular in the 1960s, but it is continually criticised for not considering that the situation may influence an individual's behaviour.

Situational Approach

The situational approach, or social learning theory, takes the view that personality is determined by the environment and the experiences a person has as they grow up. Other theories (e.g. trait theory) take the nature or biological approach to personality in that they see it as being largely genetic or inherited. The social learning theory sees personality as the result of nurture or past experiences.

Cox (2007) outlines the two mechanisms of learning: modelling and social reinforcement:

● Modelling: as we grow up, we observe and imitate the behaviour of significant others in our lives. At first, this is our parents and siblings, then our friends, teachers, sports stars and anyone we regard as a role model.
● Social reinforcement: this means that when behaviour is rewarded positively, it is more likely that it will be repeated. Conversely, behaviour negatively rewarded is less likely to be repeated. At an early age, our parents teach us right and wrong by positively or negatively rewarding behaviour.

In sport, there is a system of negative reinforcement to discourage negative behaviour on the sports field. Thus, rugby players are sent to the sin bin, cricketers are fined part of their match fee, and footballers are shown yellow and red cards. In particular, this theory shows why people behave differently in different situations. For example, an athlete may be confident and outgoing in a sporting setting, but shy and quiet in an educational setting. The athlete may have chosen positive role models in the sporting environment and had their successful performances rewarded. In the educational setting, they may have modelled less appropriate behaviour and had their behaviour rewarded negatively.

Interactional Approach

The trait theory of personality is criticised for not taking into account the situation that determines behaviour. The situational approach is criticised because research shows that while situation influences some people's behaviour, other people will not be influenced in the same way. The interactional approach considers the person's psychological traits and the situation they are in as equal predictors of behaviour.

$$behaviour = f \text{ (personality, environment)}$$

Thus, we can understand an individual's behaviour by assessing their personality traits and the specific situation they find themselves in. Bowers (1973) says the interaction between a person and their situation could give twice as much information as traits or the situational approach alone.

An interactional psychologist would use a trait–state approach to assess an individual's personality traits and then assess how these traits affect their behaviour in a situation (state). For example, an athlete who exhibits high anxiety levels as a personality trait would have an exaggerated response to a specific situation.

Neither personality traits nor situations alone are enough to predict an individual's behaviour. We must consider both to get a real picture.

Type A behaviour:

- Highly competitive and strong desire to succeed
- Achievement orientated
- Eat fast, walk fast, talk fast and have a strong sense of urgency
- Aggressive, restless and impatient
- Find it difficult to delegate and need to be in control
- Experience high levels of stress.

Type B behaviour:

- Less competitive
- More relaxed
- Delegate work easily
- Take time to complete their tasks
- Calm, laid-back and patient
- Experience low levels of stress.

Name of researcher/s	Questionnaire used and groups studied	Research findings
Schurr, Ashley and Joy (1977)	16PF: 1500 American students – athletes versus non-athletes	Athletes were more: • Independent • Objective • Relaxed. Athletes who played team sports were: • More outgoing and warm-hearted (A) • Less intelligent (B) • More group-dependent (Q2) • Less emotionally stable (C). Athletes who played individual sports were: More group-dependent (Q2) Less anxious (Q4) Less intelligent (B).
Francis et al. (1998)	EPQ: 133 female hockey players versus non-athlete students	Hockey players were: • More extroverted • Higher in psychoticism.
Ogilvie (1968)	16PF: athletes versus non-athletes	Athletic performance is related to: • Emotional stability • Tough-mindedness • Conscientiousness • Self-discipline • Self-assurance • Trust • Extroversion • Low tension.
Breivik (1996)	16PF: 38 elite Norwegian climbers	Research showed: • High levels of stability • Extroversion • Adventure seeking.
Williams (1980)	Female athletes versus female non-athletes	Athletes were: • More independent • More aggressive and dominant • More emotionally stable.

Table 3.1 Trait theory research (from Weinberg and Gould, 2007)

Type A and Type B Personalities

Friedman (1996) developed a questionnaire to diagnose people who were prone to stress and stress-related illnesses. However, it has some application to sport and exercise.

Type Bs will exhibit the opposite types of behaviour to type As. In sport, we see both personality types being equally successful. However, with people exercising recreationally, we see higher levels of retention on their exercise programmes. Type As would benefit from exercise, as it promotes type B-related behaviour. Type A behaviour is seen as causing a rise in a person's blood pressure and increasing the risk of coronary heart disease (CHD).

Personality and Sports Performance

The majority of research using trait theory was carried out in the 1970s and 1980s. Table 3.1 summarises this research.

Motivation

If a sports psychologist were asked why athletes of similar talents achieve different levels of performance, they would consider several factors, such as personality and ability to cope with stress. However, if one subject could be said to influence everything in sports psychology, it would be motivation – the reasons why we do what we do and behave and respond in the manner particular to us.

Psychologists would say that there is a reason for everything we do in life, and that some of these motives are conscious and some are unconscious. As a result, it can be difficult to assess our own motivating factors, let alone anyone else's.

Motivation is important to coaches and managers as they seek to get the best performances out of their athletes. Arsene Wenger and Alex Ferguson are two football managers who are seen as being great motivators of people.

Motivation can be a difficult subject to pin down and deal with because it is not steady and constant and depends on many factors. Most people will experience fluctuations in motivation. Some days they are fully prepared for the competition mentally, and on other days they just cannot seem to get themselves in the right frame of mind. This applies to everything we may do in a day, as sometimes it takes all our powers of motivation just to get out of bed!

Key term

Motivation:
- 'Motive – a desire to fulfil a need' (Cox, 2007)
- 'The internal mechanisms which arouse and direct behaviour' (Sage, 1974)
- 'The direction and intensity of one's effort' (Sage, 1977).

When examining motivation, five terms come up again and again:

- Fulfilling a need – all motivation arises as we seek to fulfil our needs. These may be basic biological needs, such as finding food and shelter, or more sophisticated needs, such as self-esteem or the need to belong and be loved.
- Internal state – a state is 'how we feel at any point in time', and this will be subject to change. As we see and feel things, they will trigger an internal state that will need actions to fulfil any needs.
- Direction – the direction of effort refers to the actions we take to move towards what we feel motivated by and feel we need.
- Intensity – the intensity of effort refers to how much effort the person puts into achieving their goal or into a certain situation.
- Energise behaviour – this shows how the power of the brain and the thoughts we have can give us the energy we need to produce the behaviour that is required to be successful in a certain situation.

Intrinsic and Extrinsic Motivation

To expand on Sage's definition, we can see motivation as coming from internal mechanisms or sources inside the body. We can call these intrinsic factors, or rewards coming from the activity itself. These include motives such as fun, pleasure, enjoyment, feelings of self-worth, excitement and self-mastery. They are the reasons why we do a sport and keep doing it.

Those who are intrinsically motivated engage in an activity for the pleasure and satisfaction they experience while learning, exploring or trying to understand something new.
(Weinberg and Gould, 2007)

The external stimuli, also called extrinsic rewards, come from sources outside the activity. This would include the recognition and praise we get from other people, such as our coach, friends and family. It could also be the approval we get from the crowd who support us. Extrinsic motivating factors would also include trophies, medals, prizes, records and any money derived from success.

Those who are extrinsically motivated engage in the activity because of the valued outcome rather than the interest in the activity solely for itself. (Weinberg and Gould, 2007)

Views of Motivation

Achievement motivation

Just as there are many views of personality, the same is true when examining motivation. In particular, we can examine the effect of the individual (trait) and the situation on motivation, and then how the two factors interact.

The personality view

This is called the trait-centred view and shows that motivation is the result of an individual's personality and how they think. For example, some sports people appear to be highly driven to succeed and will do anything they can to achieve their aim. Other people will be happy to let things pass them by and are unconcerned with their success or failure. These personal factors will also include the individual needs and goals a person may have, as these will drive their behaviour. However, it is clear that the individual will still be affected by the support they receive, and they will retain their motivation only if they have positive experiences. This can be related to the environments a person finds themselves in. For example, at school, our interest in a subject is generally either stimulated or dampened by the quality of the teaching we received.

The situation view

Clearly, the situation we find ourselves in has a major influence on our motivation level. This can explain why a person may be highly motivated on the football field, but less so in the classroom. Motivation can be influenced by the attractiveness of the environment and whether it is a comfortable place to be, or the style of the teacher or coach, or the motives of the other people in the environment. It is possible, however, that the environment has no effect on a person if their own motives are very strong. You may have found a situation where you did not get on with the coach or did not like the environment, but because the outcome mattered so much to you, you were successful in spite of this.

The interactional view

As in examining personality, we need to take a broader viewpoint when studying motivation, to consider both the personality of an individual and the situation they are operating within. The interactional viewpoint considers both these factors and says that if you want to get the most out of yourself and other people, you have to put the right people in the right situations. This is important in both sport and exercise settings, in getting the right fit between performers and activities. For a performer to be successful, they need the right internal motivating factors, the right environment and the right support and direction.

The Motivational Climate

Creating a motivational climate means influencing the factors that affect motivation in a positive way, to help increase the motivation levels of the participants in that environment. Three of the most influential factors are:

1 The behaviour of the leader
2 The environment itself
3 The influence of other people in the environment.

Behaviour of the leader

The leader's behaviour can seriously affect the behaviour of other people because the leader will set an example. If the people who are being led think that the leader does not care, then they may not care either; however, if the leader behaves in an upbeat and energetic way, this behaviour may be modelled.

The environment

Think about going to a gym that has grey walls and no decoration; it is cold and there are no staff. Compare this to walking into a gym that is painted brightly and has pictures of athletes achieving great feats, the staff are welcoming and there is upbeat music playing. The second environment is much more appealing to us, and we will be motivated to train there and also to return regularly.

The influence of other people

The motivation of an individual can be affected by social influences, in that other people will either offer approval or disapproval of their behaviour. The support and encouragement an individual receives from their family, friends, teachers and coaches can be vital in maintaining their motivation.

Aggression

Aggression in sport is a constant topic of discussion among performers and in newspapers. In most sports there is physical contact, and the line between what is acceptable and what is not acceptable is very fine. However, there is scope for verbal and emotional aggression as well as physical aggression. Most famously, we saw Zinedine Zidane commit an act of physical aggression on Marco Matterazzi in the 2006 World Cup final. We could say the physical aggression used was the result of verbal aggression on the Italian's part.

In reality, sport and the societies it is played within have become less aggressive because the threshold of what we see as being acceptable behaviour has risen. Violent acts have decreased in football as the number of cautionable offences has increased. In rugby union, players can face punishment after a match if a violent act is cited by the opposition. In 2009, Schalk Burger of the South African rugby team was banned from rugby for eight weeks, for gouging at the eye of British Lion, Luke Fitzgerald, during the second test. Julien Dupuy of Stade Français was banned for six months for the same offence on Stephen Ferris.

Fig 3.2 Aggression in sport

Fig 3.3 Referee cautioning a player

In general life, we refer to a range of behaviour where a person is being over-physical as being aggressive. Often these actions are mislabelled. Baron and Richardson (1994) defined aggression as 'any form of behaviour directed towards the goal of harming or injuring another living being who is motivated to avoid such treatment.'

In sport psychology, aggression has a specific meaning: aiming to harm or injure an opponent to gain an advantage, rather than playing in a hard manner. Gill (2000) gives us four criteria, which must all be met to allow us to label an action as aggressive:

1   There must be a physical or verbal behaviour.
2   It must involve causing harm or injury, whether it is physical or psychological.
3   It must be directed towards another living thing.
4   There must be the intention to cause harm or injury.

To summarise, aggression must actually involve a behaviour that is either physical or verbal in nature. Rather than just thinking or feeling that you want to do something, there must be an action.

The result of the aggressive action can be experienced either physically or psychologically (emotionally), and it must result in harm or damage to another person. While an act of physical aggression, such as throwing a punch, has a clear outcome of harm, so can saying something hurtful or offensive to another person.

It is important that the actions are carried out on another living thing because only they have feelings. So to throw your bat down in cricket when you are out is not an aggressive act, although it might be seen as unacceptable behaviour.

Finally, the most difficult aspect is that the act to cause harm must be intentional. If harm is caused by accident then it is not aggressive, but if there is intent to cause harm, it clearly is aggressive. The reason this is difficult is because only the individual knows what their intentions are and the officials have to make a judgement on this.

Key term

An aggressive act: when an individual intentionally causes physical or psychological harm to another living being.

You should be starting to realise that aggression has grey areas. We cannot tell whether an act is aggressive unless we know the motives of the person who produces the act. Plenty of sportspeople are injured, but not necessarily through acts of aggression. In order to be more specific about this area, we need to split aggressive acts into three distinct categories:

- **Assertive acts:** when a person plays with high energy and emotion, but within the rules of the game. For example, a footballer puts in hard, uncompromising tackles, or a tennis player is playing in a very tough and upbeat manner, but always within the rules. This is assertive play, because it is not intended to do any harm or cause any injury to the opponent, and uses force that is legitimate and within the rules.
- **Instrumental aggression:** when acts of aggression are used to achieve a non-aggressive goal, such as improving a team's chances of victory, they are not usually accompanied by feelings of anger. For example, if you target the opposition's star player for rough treatment by one of your team, but you are willing to accept the punishment, then you are committing instrumental aggression. This also explains the sport of boxing, where the aim is to hurt your opponent to win the fight, rather than

because you do not like your opponent. Also, in a rugby scrum, ruck or maul, players use a legitimate amount of force, but this may actually harm or injure an opponent.
- **Hostile aggression:** an act where the primary goal is to inflict harm or injury on an opponent purely for the sake of it, usually accompanied by feelings of anger. It often occurs when an individual is continually blocked from achieving a goal and their frustration and anger build up. For example, if a player is continually fouled or verbally abused, they may eventually respond aggressively as a result.

Theories of Aggression

Instinct theory

This theory says that all people have an instinctive, inborn need or tendency to be aggressive. This theory is based on the work of Sigmund Freud in the early twentieth century. He defined an instinct as 'an innate tendency to behave in a certain way'. An innate response is one that we have been born with, rather than one that has been learnt through experience. He said that man has two opposing instincts: the life instinct and the death instinct. He saw aggression as an innate instinct to ensure the survival of human beings and part of the death instinct.

Aggressive behaviour is not always inevitable. It can be directed towards another person or it can be displaced. This release of aggression is called catharsis. Some people say that they play rugby or football at the weekend to get rid of the tension and aggression that build up during the week. Other people will go swimming or running to achieve the same release of aggressive tendencies in a socially acceptable manner. This theory has also been used to explain why people fight at football matches as an outlet for their aggression, albeit in a less socially acceptable manner.

There is little research to support this theory, and it cannot explain why some people are more aggressive than others. Indeed, you may know some people who never show aggressive behaviour. It also differs across cultures, and this suggests there must be external influences that make the chances of aggression more likely.

Social learning theory

This theory offers an opposing view to the instinct theory, and says that aggression is learnt through modelling and imitative behaviour, rather than being an inborn instinct. Albert Bandura (1973) conducted research involving groups of children watching groups of adults playing with a doll. The children who watched the adults punching and beating up the

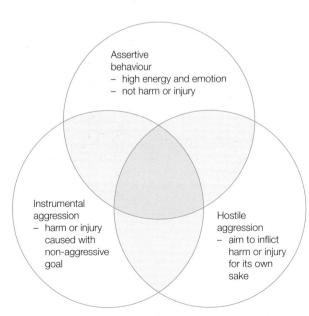

Assertive
behaviour
– high energy and emotion
– not harm or injury

Instrumental
aggression
– harm or injury
caused with
non-aggressive
goal

Hostile
aggression
– aim to inflict
harm or injury
for its own
sake

Fig 3.4 Referee cautioning a player

doll produced this reaction more than the group who watched the adults playing passively with the doll. This aggressive behaviour was increased when the children were positively rewarded for their actions.

Ice hockey has attracted a lot of research due to the regularity of fighting and fouling in the sport. Smith (1988) found that the violence in the game is the result of young amateur players modelling the professionals' behaviour.

It is easy to see how a young footballer may learn to be aggressive. At a football match, he sees a player making hard tackles, some of which are illegal and dangerous, and being cheered on by the crowd and his coach. The harder the player tackles, the more praise he gets, and he develops a following among fans who like this type of player. The young footballer learns that this is a positive way to behave and mimics the play in his own matches. Research has shown that aggressive acts are more likely to be imitated if produced by a person of the same sex and if they are witnessed live rather than on television or in cartoon form.

Social learning theory is a very convincing theory, and we can see how the levels of aggression in sport are accompanied by rises in the level of violence in society, particularly on television and in films. However, it fails to explain how people can witness the same events and the majority of them will not produce an aggressive response, while a minority will mimic the behaviour. For example, a boxing match will have a cathartic effect on some supporters and will cause an aggressive response in others. It comes back to personality type and brings in the instinct theory.

Frustration–aggression theory

This theory states that aggression is the direct result of frustration that has built up due to goal blockage or failure. This theory was first proposed by Dollard *et al.* (1939), who claimed that frustration would always produce aggression. However, in 1989, Berkowitz refined this theory by saying that frustration will lead to anger rather than aggression, particularly if we feel we have been unfairly treated, but we will not always produce an aggressive action. He went on to say that an aggressive action is more likely if aggressive cues are present (things related to aggression), but a person may be able to control their anger. Table 3.2 summarises the research and findings in this area.

Key learning points I

- Personality theories focus on whether personality is based in genetics (trait theory) or learnt from our environment (social learning theory).
- Motivation is defined as the direction and intensity of one's effort (Sage, 1974).
- Motivation can be **intrinsic** (coming from sources within the individual) or **extrinsic** (coming from sources outside the individual).
- Aggression is behaviour that is motivated by the desire to cause harm to another living being.
- Assertive behaviour is playing in an upbeat way, but within the rules and spirit of a sport.
- Aggression can be **instrumental** (aimed at winning) or **hostile** (aimed at causing harm for its own sake).

Name of psychologist/s	Nature of study	Outcomes of study
Widmeyer (1984)	A range of sports	Aggression facilitates performance in sport
Gill (2000)	A range of sports	Found no correlation between aggression and success
Lefebre and Passer (1974)	Belgian football	Found losing teams received more yellow cards for fouls than winning teams
Underwood and Whitwood (1980)	English First Division	No difference in the number of fouls committed by winning and losing teams

Table 3.2 Aggression–performance relationship

Student activity 3.1   2 hours   P1   P2   P3   M1   M2   D1

Task 1

Choose three performers in three different sports and then fill in the following table to show how their personality affects their performance.

Sports performers	Describe personality and how it affects sports performance	Explain personality and how it affects sports performance	Analyse personality and how it affects sports performance
1			
2			
3			

Task 2

Describe personality and the factors that affect it, taking into account factors such as the individual's personality, the situation the individual finds themselves in and the interaction of the two.

Task 3

Fill out the following two tables to show your understanding of aggression.

Types of aggressive behaviour	Describe each type, using an example	Explain each type, using an example
Assertion		
Hostile aggression		
Instrumental aggression		

Theory of cause of aggressive behaviour	Describe the cause of aggressive behaviour	Explain the cause of aggressive behaviour
Instinct		
Social learning		
Frustration–aggression		

Q Quick quiz 1

1. Decide whether each of the following statements is an example of intrinsic (I) or extrinsic (E) motivation:

    (a) I want to win medals.

    (b) I want to earn an England cap.

    (c) I want to reach my full potential.

    (d) I want to make money.

    (e) I want to play in a good team.

    (f) I want to play in front of large crowds.

    (g) I want to give the public enjoyment.

(h) I want to feel good about my performance.

(i) I want to be recognised by the public for my ability.

(j) I want to feel mastery in my own ability.

(k) I want to feel the joy of winning.

2. Decide whether each of the following examples is of hostile aggression, instrumental aggression or assertion:

(a) A footballer who has been hurt in a tackle kicks their opponent.

(b) A runner elbows a competitor during an 800 m race in order to get in front of them.

(c) A boxer lands a punch that knocks their opponent to the ground.

(d) A rugby player tackles an opponent and lands on top of them, causing their ribs to be bruised.

(e) A hockey player smashes their stick into an opponent's nose by mistake.

(f) A bowler hits the batsman on the helmet with a bouncing delivery.

(g) A rugby player tramples on an opponent's head in a ruck.

(h) In going for a cross, two players collide, causing a blood wound to each other's heads.

(i) An ice hockey player swears at an opponent who makes an illegal challenge.

(j) A tennis player kicks a ball away in a moment of rage.

3.3 The Impact of Arousal, Stress and Anxiety

P4 **P5** **M3** **D2**

Arousal and Anxiety

Arousal and anxiety are terms related to stress. Arousal is a response to stress and shows how motivated we are by a situation. The more aroused we become, the more interested and excited we are by a situation. We can see this when we watch a football match involving a team we support. We are so aroused that we are engrossed in the action to the point that we don't hear noises around us and time seems to go by very quickly. During a match that does not arouse us to the same extent, we find that our attention drifts in and out as we are distracted by things happening around us.

We can look at levels of arousal on a continuum that highlights the varying degrees of arousal:

Deep sleep → Mild interest → Attentive → Absorbed → Engrossed → Frenzied

Arousal and Attention Span

As arousal levels increase, they can affect a performer's attention span. If a performer has a broad attention span, they are able to pick up information from a wide field of vision. The narrower the attention span becomes, the less information the performer will pick up and the more they will miss. The attention span can be too broad, as the performer may try to pick up too much information.

Narrow attention span – high arousal

Broad attention span – low arousal

Optimal attention span – optimal arousal

Fig 3.5 Three attention spans

Anxiety

Anxiety can be seen as a negative aspect of stress, and it may accompany high levels of arousal. It is not pleasant to be anxious. It is characterised by feelings of nervousness and worry. Again, the stress and anxiety responses are unique to each individual.

Trait and State Anxiety

Trait anxiety means that a person generally experiences high levels of anxiety as part of their personality. They tend to worry and feel nervous in a range of situations and find them threatening. State anxiety is anxiety felt in response to a specific situation. It is anxiety related to a specific mood state. Usually, a person who has high trait anxiety will also experience higher levels of state anxiety. This is important for athletes because their levels of trait anxiety will determine their state anxiety in competition and, as a result, their performance.

Arousal and Performance

Arousal levels will have an influence on performance, but it is not always clear-cut what this relationship is. The following theories help to explain the relationship.

Drive Theory

Drive theory, initially the work of Hull (1943), states that as arousal levels rise, so do performance levels. This happens in linear fashion and can be described as a straight line.

The actual performance also depends on the arousal level and the skill level of the performer. Arousal will exaggerate the individual's dominant response, meaning that if they have learned the skill well, their dominant response will be exaggerated positively. However, if they are a novice performer, their skill level will drop to produce a worse performance.

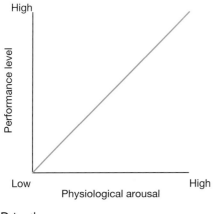

Fig 3.6 Drive theory

The Inverted U Hypothesis

This theory is based on the Yerkes and Dodson law (1908) and seeks to address some of the criticisms of the drive theory. This theory agrees that arousal does improve performance, but only up to a point, and once arousal goes beyond this point, performance starts to decline. Figure 3.7 shows the curve looking like an upside-down U.

This theory's main point is that there is an optimum level of arousal before performance starts to diminish. This is also called the ideal performing state (IPS) and is often referred to as the zone. At this point, the arousal level meets the demands of the task, and everything feels good and is going well.

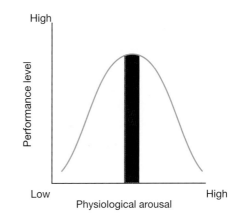

Fig 3.7 The inverted U hypothesis

Catastrophe Theory

This theory has been taken a step further by Fazey and Hardy (1988), who agree with the inverted U hypothesis, but say that once arousal level has passed, the IPS will drop off drastically rather than steadily. The point where performance drops is called the point of catastrophe. The Americans refer to this phenomenon, when performance drops, as choking. The history of sport is littered with examples of people or teams throwing away seemingly unassailable positions.

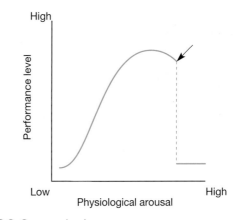

Fig 3.8 Catastrophe theory

Stress is usually talked about in negative terms. People complain that they have too much stress or are stressed out. Some sports people claim that the stress of competition is too much for them. However, we should not see stress as an entirely negative thing, because it provides us with the mental and physical energy to motivate us into doing things and doing them well.

Stressors are anything that causes us to have a stress response, and these are invariably different for different people. If we did not have any stress in our lives, we might not bother to do anything all day. We need stressors to give us the energy and direction to

63

get things done. This type of positive stress is called **eustress** (good stress). If we have too much stress it can become damaging, and we call this **distress** (bad stress).

- **Eustress** (*good stress*):
  - Gives us energy and direction
  - Helps us to be fulfilled and happy.
- **Distress** (*bad stress*):
  - Causes discomfort
  - Can lead to illness
  - Can cause depression.

Too much stress in our lives over a long period of time can seriously damage our health, causing coronary heart disease, high blood pressure, ulcers, impotence, substance addiction, mental health problems and suicidal tendencies.

Sport is a source of stress for some sports people. This is related to the experience of the performer, the importance of the competition, the quality of the opposition, the size of the crowd or previous events. The stress response will be specific to the individual. The feelings you have are the symptoms of stress, and they can be separated into physical (the effects on your body), mental (the effect on your brain) and behavioural (how your behaviour changed).

Key term

Stress: any factor that changes the natural state of the body.

The classic definition of stress sees the body as having a natural equilibrium or balance, when the heart rate and breathing rate are at resting levels and blood pressure is at normal level. Anything that changes these natural levels is a stressor. Theoretically, we could say we become stressed as soon as we get out of bed, as our heart rate, breathing rate and blood pressure all rise at this point. Indeed, to some people, the alarm going off is a real source of stress!

The Stress Process

McGrath (1970) sees the stress response as a process and defines stress as 'a substantial imbalance between demand (physical and psychological) and response capability, under conditions where failure to meet the demand has important consequences'.

Stress will occur when the person does not feel they have the resources to deal with the situation and that this will have bad consequences.

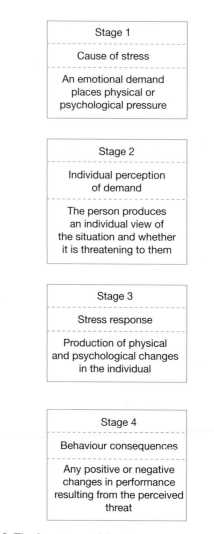

Fig 3.9 The four stages of the stress process

Causes of Stress

The causes of stress are many and varied, but, crucially, they are specific to an individual. For example, you can have two people in the same event, each with a different stress response.

The sources of stress can generally be divided into four categories:

- **Internal:** things we think about, such as past memories and experiences, current injuries, past injuries, our own feelings of self-worth, and so on
- **External:** things in our surroundings and our environment, such as competition, our opponents, the crowd, the weather, spiders and snakes, transport problems
- **Personal factors:** people we share our lives with, such as friends, family, partners; and life factors such as money and health
- **Occupational factors:** the job we do, the people we work with and our working conditions – in

64

sport, this could include our relationships with team-mates and coaches/managers.

Stress levels also depend on personality. Those people who have a predominantly type A personality will find more situations stressful, as will people who have a high N score using Eysenck's personality inventory.

The Physiology of Stress

When we perceive ourselves to be in a situation that is dangerous, our stress response is activated. This has been developed as a means of ensuring our survival, by making us respond to danger. For example, if we are walking home at night through dark woods and we hear noises behind us, the body will instigate physiological changes, called the 'fight-or-flight' response, as the body is preparing to turn and fight the danger or run away as fast as it can.

The response varies depending on how serious we perceive the threat to be. The changes take place in our involuntary nervous system, which consists of two major branches:

● Sympathetic nervous system
● Parasympathetic nervous system.

The sympathetic nervous system produces the stress response, and its aim is to provide the body with as much energy as it can to confront the threat or run away from it. The sympathetic nervous system works by releasing stress hormones, adrenaline and cortisol, into the bloodstream. The sympathetic nervous system produces the effects listed in Figure 3.10.

The parasympathetic nervous system produces the relaxation response, its aim being to conserve energy. It is activated once the stressor has passed.

Involuntary nervous system

Sympathetic nervous system	Parasympathetic nervous system
increased adrenaline production	decreased adrenaline production
increase in heart rate	slowed heart rate
increase in breathing rate	slower breathing rate
increased metabolism	slower metabolism
increased heat production	lower body temperature
muscle tension	muscle relaxation
dry mouth	dry skin
dilated pupils	smaller pupils
hairs on the skin stand on end (to make us look bigger)	
digestive system slows down	digestion speeds up
diversion of blood away from internal organs to the working muscles	

Fig 3.10 The involuntary nervous system

Sympathetic nervous system	Parasympathetic nervous system
Increased adrenaline production	Decreased adrenaline production
Increase in heart rate	Slowed heart rate
Increase in breathing rate	Slower breathing rate
Increased metabolism	Slower metabolism
Increased heat production	Lower body temperature
Muscle tension	Muscle relaxation
Dry mouth	Dry skin
Dilated pupils	Smaller pupils
Hairs on the skin stand on end (to make us look bigger)	
Digestive system slows down	Digestion speeded up
Diversion of blood away from internal organs to the working muscles	

Table 3.3 The involuntary nervous system

It is not healthy for the body to be in a constant state of stress because of the activation of the sympathetic nervous system. The excess production of adrenaline is dangerous because the body requires more cholesterol to synthesise adrenaline. This excess cholesterol production raises blood cholesterol levels and is a risk factor for coronary heart disease (CHD).

Symptoms of Stress

Stress has a threefold effect on the body, causing cognitive (mental), somatic (physical) and behavioural responses, as outlined in Table 3.4.

Cognitive response	Somatic response	Behavioural response
Reduced concentration	Racing heart rates	Talking, eating and walking quickly
Less interested	Faster breathing	Interrupting conversations
Unable to make decisions	Headaches	Increased smoking, drinking and eating
Sleep disturbances	Butterflies in the stomach	Fidgeting
Making mistakes	Chest tightness and pains	Lethargy
Unable to relax	Dry cotton mouth	Moodiness and grudge bearing
Quick losses of temper	Constant colds and illness	Accidents and clumsiness
Loss of sense of humour	Muscular aches and pains	Poor personal presentation
Loss of self-esteem	Increased sweating	Nervous habits
Loss of enthusiasm	Skin irritations	

Table 3.4 Symptoms of stress

Key learning points 2

- Arousal is a response to stress that describes how interested and motivated an individual becomes in a situation.
- Anxiety is a negative response to a stressful situation, characterised by nervousness and apprehension.
- Stress is any factor that changes the natural balance of the body.
- The theories of arousal show that changing levels of arousal will influence performance.
- The drive theory of arousal says that increases in arousal level will cause an increase in performance level, while the inverted U hypothesis suggests that increases in arousal level will cause an improvement in performance, but only up to a certain point; after this point, increases in arousal level will cause decrements in performance level.
- Symptoms of stress can be cognitive, somatic or behavioural.

Student activity 3.2 · 90 minutes · P4 · P5 · D2

Read the case study and answer the questions below.

1 Describe how Oliver experiences arousal and, using the theories of arousal, what effect changes in arousal have on his performance.

2 Explain how Oliver experiences arousal and, using the theories of arousal, what effect changes in arousal have on his performance.

3 Analyse how Oliver experiences arousal and, using the theories of arousal, what effect changes in arousal have on his performance.

4 Using Oliver as an example, describe how stress and anxiety affect him and what their causes are.

Oliver is a 16-year-old tennis player whose play is characterised by moments of brilliance mixed with temper tantrums. When Oliver trains in the gym, he loves to lift weights to increase his strength, and he finds that the more up for it he is, the heavier weights he can lift, so he spends time psyching himself up before lifting weights. Oliver loves the excitement of playing a match and feels that it gives him energy and helps to focus his attention. When Oliver plays tennis, he always starts off quite relaxed, but sometimes he is too relaxed to play well and will start to lose points. However, when he is in a losing situation, he starts to become worried and gets butterflies in his stomach, and this spurs him on to play better and get back into the match. Sometimes he wants to win so much that he starts to miss the service box or the base line, often by quite large margins. This can make him really angry, and when he loses his temper he quickly loses the match.

Q Quick quiz 2

1 Match each of the terms in the table below to the appropriate description.

Term	Description
Stress	An individual tends to get worried in most situations
Arousal	Feelings of worry associated with uncomfortable thoughts
Trait anxiety	Any force that changes the natural balance of the body
State anxiety	Racing heart rate and butterflies accompany feelings of worry
Cognitive anxiety	An individual experiences feelings of apprehension in certain situations
Somatic anxiety	Feelings of motivation and excitement produced in a situation

2 Fill in the blanks in the following paragraph.

According to drive theory, increased _____ levels will result in an increase in _____ levels; however, this works best for _____ performers, as arousal will exaggerate the dominant response, while for a novice it can produce a _____ in performance level. The inverted U hypothesis disagrees with drive theory, as it says that increased arousal levels will improve performance, but once arousal gets to a certain point, _____ will start to decline. The point at the top of the curve is called the _____ _____ _____.

3.4 The Psychology of Group Dynamics in Sports Environments

P6 M4

Throughout our sporting and social lives, we are involved in working in groups, such as our families, school groups, friendship groups and the sports teams in which we play. Sports teams have different characteristics – an athletics team will have different teamwork demands to a rugby or cricket team. However, all groups rely on the fundamental characteristic of teamwork.

Defining a group is not easy, but the minimum number of people required is two. A group can be seen as two or more like-minded people interacting to produce an outcome they could not achieve on their own. Groups involve interaction or working with other people in order to influence the behaviour of other people and, in turn, be influenced by them.

Key term

Group: a group should have:
- a collective identity
- a sense of shared purpose or objectives
- structured modes of communication
- personal and/or task interdependence
- interpersonal attraction.

(Weinberg and Gould, 2007)

A Group or a Team?

Generally speaking, an instructor will call people who are involved in an exercise class or dance class a 'group', and people playing cricket or rugby a 'team'. People involved in the group have a similar sense of purpose and may share common objectives. However, a team's members will actually be dependent on one another to achieve their shared goals and will need to support each other.

So why is the outcome of the group not always equal to the sum of its parts? For example, we can see in football that the teams with the best players do not always get the results they should. In 2006, the very talented Brazil and Argentina teams were knocked out at the quarter-final stage of the World Cup, and in 2004 the European Championships were won by Greece rather than the individually talented Portugal team. In cricket, the England one-day side is continually changing its players, as it seeks to find a team

rather than a group of individuals. We can even see the importance of a team when individual players come together in an event such as the Ryder Cup in golf. In 2004 and 2006, the British and European team beat the Americans emphatically, in large part because of the positive team feeling that had developed.

Stages of Group Development

A group of people coming together does not form a team. Becoming a team demands a process of development. Tuckman and Jensen (1977) proposed a five-stage model of group development:

1 Forming.
2 Storming.
3 Norming.
4 Performing.
5 Adjourning.

Each group will go through the five stages. The length of time they spend in each stage is variable.

Forming

The group comes together, with individuals meeting and familiarising themselves with the other members of the group. The structure and relationships within the group are formed and tested. If it is a team, the coach may develop strategies or games to break the ice between the group members. At this point, the individuals are seeing whether they fit in with this group.

Storming

A period of conflict will follow the forming stage, as individuals seek their roles and status within the group. This may involve conflict between individual members, rebellion against the leader or resistance to the way the team is being developed or managed, or the tactics it is adopting. This is also a period of intense inter-group competition, as group members compete for their positions within the team.

Norming

Once the hostility and fighting have been overcome, either by athletes leaving the group or accepting the common goals and values of the group, a period of norming occurs. Here, the group starts to cooperate and work together to reach common goals. The group pulls together and the roles are established and become stable.

Performing

In the final stage, the group members work together to achieve their mutual goals. The relationships within the group have become well established, as have issues of leadership and strategies for play.

It is unrealistic to see the group as being stable and performing in a steady way. The relationships within the group will change and develop with time, sometimes for the good of the group and sometimes to its detriment. As new members join the group, there will be a new period of storming and norming, as each person is either accepted or rejected. This re-evaluation of the group is often beneficial and stops the group becoming stale. Successful teams seem to be settled and assimilate two or three new players a year to keep them fresh. Bringing in too many new players can disrupt the group and change the nature of the group completely.

Adjourning

Once the group has achieved its goals or come to the end of its useful purpose, the team may break up. This may also be caused by a considerable change in the personnel involved or the management and leadership of the group.

Group Effectiveness

The aim of a group is to be effective by using the strengths of each person to better the effectiveness of the group. However, the outcome is often not equal to the sum of its parts. Steiner (1972) proposed the following model of group effectiveness:

Actual productivity = Potential productivity − Process losses

- Actual productivity = the actual performance achieved
- Potential productivity = the best possible performance achievable by that group, based on its resources (ability, knowledge, skills)
- Process losses = losses due to working as part of a group (coordination losses, communication problems, losses in motivation).

For example, in a tug-of-war team, each member can pull 100 kg individually, and as a team of four they pull 360 kg in total. Why do you think this would happen?

Social Loafing

One of the problems of working in groups is that it tends to affect motivation. People do not seem to work as hard in groups compared with working on their own. Research shows that rowers in larger teams put in less effort than those in smaller teams:

1 person = 100 per cent effort
2 people = 90 per cent effort
4 people = 80 per cent effort
8 people = 65 per cent effort.

This phenomenon is called the Ringelman effect, or social loafing, and is defined as the tendency of individuals to lessen their effort when part of a group.

Cohesion

Cohesion is concerned with the extent to which a team is willing to stick together and work together. The forces tend to cover two areas:

- the attractiveness of the group to individual members
- the extent to which members are willing to work together to achieve group goals.

To be successful in its goals, a group has to be cohesive. The extent to which cohesion is important depends on the sport and the level of interaction needed.

Key term

Cohesion: 'The total field of forces which act on members to remain in the group' (Festinger *et al.*, 1950).

Types of Cohesion

There seem to be two definite types of cohesion within a group:

- Task cohesion – the willingness of a team to work together to achieve its goals
- Social cohesion – the willingness of the team to socialise together.

It would appear that task cohesion comes first, as this is why the team has formed in the first place. If the group is lucky, they will find that they develop social cohesion as well, and this usually has a beneficial effect on performance. This is because if you feel good about your teammates, you are more likely to want success for each other as well as yourself.

Research says that cohesion is important in successful teams, but that task cohesion is more important than social cohesion. It does depend on the sport being played, as groups that need high levels of interaction need higher levels of cohesion. Research also suggests that success will produce increased cohesion, rather than cohesion coming before performance. Being successful helps to develop feelings of group attraction, and this will help to develop more success, and so on. This can be seen with the cycle of success, in that once a team has been successful it tends to continue being successful – success breeds success.

Leadership in Sport

The choice of a manager, coach or captain is often the most important decision a club's members have to make. They see it as crucial in influencing the club's chances of success. Great leaders in sport are held in the highest regard, irrespective of their talent on the pitch.

> ## Key term
>
> **Leadership:** 'The behavioural process of influencing individuals and groups towards goals' (Barrow, 1977).

Leadership behaviour covers a variety of activities, which is why it is described as multi-dimensional. It includes:

- decision-making processes
- motivational techniques
- giving feedback
- establishing interpersonal relationships
- confidently directing the group.

Leaders are different from managers. Managers plan, organise, budget, schedule and recruit, while leaders determine how a task is completed.

People become leaders in different ways; not all are appointed. Prescribed leaders are appointed by a person in authority – a chairman appoints a manager, a manager appoints a coach, a principal appoints a teacher. Emergent leaders emerge from a group and take over responsibility. Emergent leaders can be more effective, as they have the respect of their group members.

Theories of Leadership

Sport psychologists have sought to explain leadership effectiveness for many years, and they have used the following theories to help understand effective leadership behaviour.

Trait Approach

In the 1920s, researchers tried to show that characteristics or personality traits were stable and common to all leaders. Thus, to be a good leader, you needed to have intelligence, assertiveness, independence and self-confidence. Therefore, a person who is a good leader in one situation will be a good leader in all situations.

Behavioural Approach

The trait approach says that leaders are 'born', but the behavioural approach says that anyone can become a good leader by learning the behaviour of effective leaders. Thus, the behavioural approach supports the view that leadership skills can be developed through experience and training.

Interactional Approach

Trait and personal approaches look at personality traits. The interactional approach looks at the interaction between the person and the situation. It stresses the following points:

- Effective leaders cannot be predicted solely on personality.
- Effective leadership fits specific situations, as some leaders function better in certain circumstances than others.
- Leadership style needs to change to match the demands of the situation. For example, relationship-orientated leaders develop interpersonal relationships, provide good communication and ensure everyone is feeling good within the group. However, task-orientated leaders are concerned with getting the work done and meeting objectives.

Social Facilitation

Social facilitation is the change in performance that occurs due to the presence of others – whether the presence is an audience or fellow competitors. There is no doubt that our performances change as the result of the presence of other people. Think about how you feel when your parents or friends come to watch you, or when you start to perform in front of an audience.

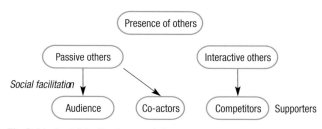

Fig 3.11 Social facilitation model

Zajonc (1965) defined the different types of people present, separating them into those people who are competing against you and those people who are merely present and not competing.

> ## Key term
>
> **Social facilitation:** 'The consequences upon behaviour which derive from the sheer presence of other individuals' (Zajonc, 1965).

Co-actors are people involved in the same activity, but not competing directly. Triplett (1898) did some of the earliest experiments in sport psychology. He examined co-action in the following three conditions, using cyclists:

1 Unpaced.
2 Paced (co-actor on another bike).
3 Paced competitive (co-actors pacing and competing).

Triplett's findings were that cyclists in condition 2 were 34 seconds per mile faster than cyclists in condition 1, while cyclists in condition 3 were 39 seconds per mile faster than cyclists in condition 1.

The reasons for social facilitation are not always clear. Triplett concluded that in his experiment it was due to the physical effects, such as suctioning and sheltering resulting from travelling behind another rider; and psychological effects, such as encouragement, anxiety, pressure and competitiveness, which are felt as the result of cycling with someone else. Triplett concluded that it did not matter if the cyclists were competing. What was important was that 'The bodily presence of another rider is stimulus to a rider in arousing the competitive instinct.'

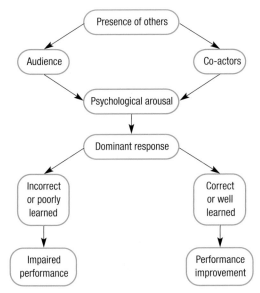

Fig 3.12 Zajonc's expanded model (1965)

Zajonc's expanded model (Figure 3.12) showed that whether the audience or co-actors have a positive or negative effect on performance depends on how well the skill has been learnt. A poorly learnt skill will become worse, while a well-learnt skill will be improved. This links in well with the effect of stress on performance, and it can be seen that the presence of others would cause more stress.

Zajonc also looked at the relationship between the audience effect and the standard of the performer. His results are shown in Figure 3.13.

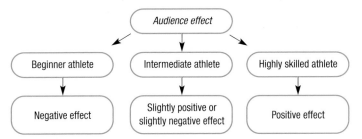

Fig 3.13 Audience effect and the standard of performer

The effect also depends on the nature of the task – whether it is strength- or skill-related. Strength tasks will usually be enhanced by the presence of others. However, skilled tasks (especially poorly learnt skills) may suffer. Social facilitation effects tend to disappear as the individual gets used to them.

Cottrell (1968) said that it is not the mere presence of an audience that creates arousal, but that the type of audience is also very important. For example, a blindfolded audience had no facilitation effect. The following factors will affect social facilitation:

● Audience expertise: an expert audience will increase arousal level
● Type of audience: a pro-winning audience will have more of a facilitation effect than a pro-enjoyment audience
● Performer's evaluation of the audience: the performer decides what they think the audience wants and is aroused accordingly
● Size: a larger audience will have more of a facilitation effect.

Home Advantage

Home advantage is the view that the team playing at home has a disproportionately higher chance of winning in relation to the team playing away from home. This phenomenon was apparent in cricket, as home teams are more often successful in test matches. For example, England beat Australia to win the Ashes in 2005 and 2009, yet they were beaten 5-0 in Australia in 2006 when they tried to retain the Ashes. In the football World Cup of 2006, which was held in Germany, all four semi-finalists were European countries.

There are many reasons why home teams are more successful. Some of these are physical and some are psychological:

● Familiarity with the surroundings and the surfaces
● A supportive home crowd who give positive approval
● Less intimidation from opposing supporters

71

- The territory is theirs and claimed by display of their playing colours
- There is less travel involved in getting to the match
- Travel can cause boredom and staleness
- Players do not have to stay in unfamiliar surroundings and eat unfamiliar food
- Home teams are more likely to play offensively
- Away teams may not be treated well by their opponents

- Referees and officials may unconsciously favour the home team to seek the crowd's approval.

Home advantage may be seen as being a disadvantage to the away team rather than an advantage to the home team. It is the job of the coach and psychologist to find ways of minimising this away disadvantage.

Key learning points 3

- A group is defined as two people who have to work together to achieve an outcome they could not achieve individually.
- Members of a team will have greater dependence on each other to achieve their outcome than members of a group.
- The model of group effectiveness states that the actual productivity of a group will equal the potential productivity (best possible outcome of the group) minus process losses (losses due to the problems of working as a group).
- Process losses include problems with coordination, communication and motivation of individuals in the group.
- Social loafing describes the tendency of individuals to exert less effort when working as a part of a group than they would individually.
- Cohesion is described as the total sum of forces that cause individuals to remain in a group.
- The leader in the group can influence its effectiveness, especially if they are able to adapt their personality to the demands of the situation they find themselves in.
- Social facilitation suggests that the presence of other people will have a benefical effect on the performance of the individual.

Q Quick quiz 3

Match each of the terms in the table below to the appropriate description.

Term	Description
Social loafing	The degree of attraction an individual feels towards a group
Task cohesion	Loss of performance caused by working as part of a group
Leadership	The presence of other people can have a beneficial effect on performance
Social cohesion	The tendency for an individual to give less effort when part of a group
Process losses	The process of influencing individuals or groups towards achieving their goals
Social facilitation	The extent to which team members want to work together

Student activity 3.3

 1 hour   P5   M3   D2

Read the case study, in which Patrick, a former professional player, talks about two teams he played for in his career, then answer the questions below.

1 From Patrick's explanation, identify four factors that contributed is the dynamics of his two groups.

2 From Patrick's explanation, identify four factors that contributed to the dynamics of his two groups.

I played for several teams in my career, but when I was a young player I was lucky to have a brilliant manager. At the beginning of the season, he would tell each player what their role was in the team, and then he would bring the team together and tell us how he wanted us to play together. We each knew our individual role, and as long as we performed it we were kept in the team. I remember the manager taking players off early in matches because they were not doing their job. He was a hard manager to please, but his methods worked well and we were very successful. My second team was managed by an ex-player who I knew from the first club, and he put together a team of players that he had played with and trusted. We were never the most talented group of individuals, but once we were on the pitch, we all worked for each other and achieved more than the individual sum of our talents should have achieved. The manager always took us out on Monday nights, when we would go for a meal, go bowling or play darts, which helped to build a solid bond between us, and we cared for each other on and off the pitch. This manager was so successful that he moved to a bigger club; he was replaced by a new manager who was not successful because he didn't understand how the club worked and he could never explain how he wanted us to play.

3.5 Psychological Factors that Affect People in Exercise Environments

P7   M5

Many people in Britain have been persuaded to start exercising, as they are aware of the benefits of exercise. People are also persuaded by impressive facilities and the atmosphere of fitness centres. Research shows that despite the best of intentions, most people will fail to stick to their training programmes.

According to Weinberg and Gould (2007), the most rapid dropout occurs in the first three months, when 33 per cent of people will have stopped their exercise programme, while after six months, 52 per cent of people will have dropped out. Figure 3.14

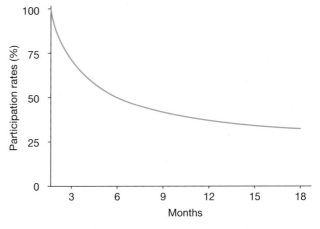

Fig 3.14 Change in participation in exercise over time

shows the important point that if a person can keep exercising for nine months, they are highly likely to keep going. Why is the nine-month point so important?

Behaviour change is difficult for people because what we did yesterday is pretty much what we will do today. Everything we do, we tend to do in the same way, because we develop 'rituals' that work for us. For example, if you look at how you get yourself up in the morning and get ready for the day, you will probably do it the same way every day. Therefore, adding in exercise causes us to change our rituals, and at first it feels uncomfortable because it requires a lot of conscious effort. However, the more often we repeat the ritual, the easier it becomes, as it gets integrated into an unconscious behaviour. To make the change into an automatic behaviour takes around six to nine months, by which time most people will have given up as the effort is too great.

This means that for a person to be successful, the exercise has to fit into their life, and it is best to set down regular times and develop a consistent routine. Also, a person has to understand the 'value' of the ritual. For example, most people clean their teeth twice a day because it has a clear health and hygiene value. Most people think they should exercise, but are not always clear as to the value of exercise to them.

There are strategies to prevent dropout and promote adherence to exercise programmes, as the following sections show.

Setting Goals and Targets

In order to direct an individual's efforts and give them something to work for, we can set goals. This has to be done with great care, so as not to negatively affect motivation. To help us do this, we can use the acronym SMART:

- **Specific** goals – related to a particular aspect of fitness (such as strength or endurance)
- **Measurable** – the goal must be quantifiable (expressed in figures)
- **Achievable** – the goal must not be set too high
- **Realistic** – the goal must be realistically achievable
- **Time-constrained** – there must be a time-frame (set a date).

Goals can be set in the long term and the short term. A long-term goal may be achieved over the course of a year, and can be broken down into shorter-term goals, such as one-month, three-month or six-month goals. We can use outcome goals, which are related to the final result, and process goals, which are goals we can meet to help us achieve the outcome goal. For example, if a person's outcome goal is to lose 3 per cent body fat over a three-month period, their process goal may be to exercise three times a week for the first month.

The best way to set goals is to answer three questions:

1 What do I want to achieve? (Desired state)
2 Where am I now? (Present state)
3 What do I need to do to move from my present state to my desired state?

Then present this on a scale:

Present state				Desired state
1	2	3	4	5

1 Write in your goal at point 5 and your present position at point 1.
2 Decide what would be halfway between points 1 and 5; this is your goal for point 3.
3 Then decide what would be halfway between your present state and point 3; this is your short-term goal for point 2.
4 Then decide what would be halfway between point 3 and the desired state; this is your goal for point 4.
5 All these goals are outcome goals and must be set using the SMART principle.
6 Work out what needs to be done to move from point 1 to point 2. These are your process goals and, again, must use the SMART principle.

It is best to use a goal-setting diary to keep all goal-setting information in the same place, and to review the goals on a weekly basis.

Decision Balance Sheet

Taking the decision to exercise can be set out on a decision balance sheet. Imagine that a person who is contemplating exercise is going through a period of behaviour change and they have two choices: taking action or not taking action. Each course of action will bring them some pleasure and some pain, and this exercise helps them understand this. Hopefully the pleasure that change brings in the long term will outweigh any pain it causes in the short term. Unfortunately, some short-term pleasure has to be foregone. However, this continued behaviour would result in long-term pain (illness, dysfunction).

An example of a decision balance sheet is shown in Table 3.5.

People should become aware that their change will be done for two reasons: first, to gain the benefits of change; second, to avoid the consequences of not taking action. The following can then help them take action:

- **Prompts:** a man puts up posters or reminders around the house to keep reminding himself to

Decision: Training three times a week in the gym			
Pain of taking action	**Pleasure of taking action**	**Pain of not taking action**	**Pleasure of not taking action**
Loss of time	Look slimmer	Stay fat	Get to watch more television
Physically uncomfortable	Feel fitter	Feel tired and lethargic	Allowed to eat chips
Getting home later	Have more energy	Develop diabetes and heart disease	Able to go to the pub
Less available money	Can binge on chocolate		

Table 3.5 Example of a decision balance sheet

exercise. This could also be done with coloured dots on mirrors or other places that catch the eye regularly.

- **Rewards for attendance/completing goals:** the same man is provided with an extrinsic reward for completing the goal or attending the gym regularly. This may be something to pamper him, such as a free massage, and should not be something that conflicts with the goal – such as a slap-up meal!
- **Social support approaches:** you can help people exercise regularly by developing a social support group of like-minded people with similar fitness goals, so they can arrange to meet at the gym at certain times. This makes it more difficult for people to miss their exercise session. Also, people should try to gain the backing of the people they live with to support them, rather than tease or criticise them.

Barriers to Exercise

We have to be realistic that people will have aspects of their lives that may decrease their chances of success. A barrier is not a good word to use because it suggests such aspects cannot be overcome; it is better to look at factors to consider and take into account.

- **Lack of time:** 69 per cent of inactive people state lack of time as a barrier to exercise. In reality, it may be poor time management or making exercise a low priority, as they seem to find time to go to the pub or watch television. A good way of looking at this is by saying that if you don't find time now to be more healthy, you will have to find time later in life to be ill!
- **Lack of energy:** due to the amount of time people work, they can start to experience stress and mental fatigue; 59 per cent of non-exercisers said this was a barrier for them. The way around this is

to explain that exercise can help to relieve stress and energise the individual. Providing breaks in the day can make an individual more productive.

- **Lack of motivation:** motivation is a most unstable aspect of personality and can change in line with a change of priorities, such as when work gets busy or family demands increase. The individual has to remember the benefits of their exercise and the value behind these benefits.

Other factors that may cause barriers include cost, lack of facilities, lack of support or feeling insecure. These factors need to be taken seriously and then actions put in place to overcome them.

Models of Behaviour Change

Transtheoretical Model of Change

When a person goes through a period of behaviour change, they will experience a series of distinct stages. The best known model was developed by Prochaska and DiClemente (1983) and is called the

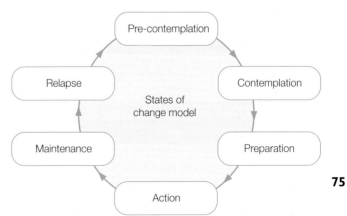

Fig 3.15 Prochaska and di Clemente's transtheoretical model of behaviour change

75

transtheoretical model of change. We will apply it to a person changing from a state of inactivity to a state of activity; it can be applied to any period of behaviour change, such as stopping smoking or dieting.

1 **Pre-contemplation:** this stage occurs when a person is inactive, happy to stay inactive and has no intention of changing their behaviour.

2 **Contemplation:** this stage occurs when a person has the intention to start exercising in the near future.

3 **Preparation:** they may be preparing physically and psychologically, but they have not yet made the behaviour change.

4 **Action:** the period of behaviour change has begun and they have started out on their exercise programme. This period lasts for as long as the change remains a conscious effort. The period is usually around six to nine months.

5 **Maintenance:** once the behaviour change has been integrated into the person's life and they are maintaining the change, they will be in this stage.

6 **Relapse:** the individual has returned to their original state and has dropped the newly acquired behaviour.

The health belief model

This states that the likelihood of an individual engaging in behaviour to preserve good health depends on the value they place on preventing disease and illness. An individual will also consider the costs and benefits of exercise or any other measures they take. This fits in with the decision balance sheet, which most people use unconsciously; when they consider they are potentially at risk, they will be pushed into preventative action.

The theory of planned behaviour

The theory of planned behaviour (Ajzen, 1985) states that intentions are the best predictors of actual behaviour. Intentions are produced by the individual's attitude to a particular behaviour. For example, if a person has a positive attitude to exercise (thinks it is important and looks forward to exercise), it is likely that they will intend to exercise regularly. However, intentions do not always result in actual behaviour, because the individual's perception of their ability to perform the behaviour will also affect their success or failure. This is called perceived behavioural control, and if a person intends to go to a gym but is concerned that they will not know what to do when they get there, they are less likely to go or keep going.

Key learning points 4

● Changing behaviour to become more physically active is a difficult process, and if an individual can maintain an exercise programme for over nine months, it is likely that they will have changed their behaviour permanently.

● Strategies such as goal setting and using a decision balance sheet can help to support the period of behaviour change.

● Models of behaviour change can help us to understand the process individuals go through as they change their behaviour.

Student activity 3.4   30 mins   P7   M5

Fill in the following table to show your understanding of the psychological factors that affect people in exercise environments.

Identify three factors that affect people in exercise environments	Explain each of the factors you have identified that affect people in exercise environments
1	
2	
3	

References

Barrow, J. (1977) The variables of leadership: a review and conceptual framework. *Academy of Management Review*, 2, 231–51.

Bowers, K.S. (1973) Situationism in psychology: an analysis and a critique. *Psychological Review*, 80, 307–36.

Cattell, R.B. (1965) *The Scientific Analysis of Personality*, Penguin.

Cottrell, N.B. (1968) Performance in the presence of other human beings: mere presence, audience and affiliation effects, in E. Simmell, R. Hoppe and G. Milton (eds), *Social Facilitation and Imitative Behaviour*, Allyn & Bacon.

Cox, R. (2007) *Sports Psychology: Concepts and Applications*, Wm C. Brown Communications.

Eysenck, H. (1964) *Manual of Eysenck Personality Inventory*, University of London Press.

Fazey, J. and Hardy, L. (1988) *The Inverted U Hypothesis: A Catastrophe for Sport Psychology?* British Association of Sports Sciences Monograph, no. 1, NCF.

Festinger, L.A., Schachter, S. and Back, K. (1950) *Social Pressures in Informal Groups: A Study of Human Factors in Housing*, Harper.

Friedman, M. (1996) *Type A Behaviour: Its Diagnosis and Treatment*, Plenum Press.

Gill, D. (2000) *Psychological Dynamics of Sport and Exercise*, Human Kinetics.

Grout, J. and Perrin, S. (2004) *Mind Games*, Capstone.

Hull, C.L. (1943) *Principles of Behaviour*, Appleton-Century-Crofts.

Jarvis, M. (2006) *A Student's Handbook*, Routledge.

McClelland, D.C., Atkinson, J.W., Clark, R.W. and Lowell, E.J. (1953) *The Achievement Motive*, Appleton-Century-Crofts.

McGrath, J.E. (1970) Major methodological issues, in J.E. McGrath (ed.), *Social and Psychological Factors in Stress*, Holt, Rinehart & Winston.

Nicklaus, J. (1976) *Play Better Golf*, King Features.

Sage, G. (1974) *Sport and American Society*, Addison-Wesley.

Sage, G. (1977) *Introduction to Motor Behaviour: A Neuropsychological Approach*, Addison-Wesley.

Schurr, K., Ashley, M. and Joy, K. (1977) A multivariate analysis of male athlete characteristics: sport type and success. *Multivariate Experimental Clinical Research*, 3, 53–68.

Steiner, I.D. (1972) *Group Processes and Productivity*, Academic Press.

Triplett, N. (1898) The dynamogenic factors in pacemaking and competition. *American Journal of Psychology*, 9, 507–33.

Tuckman, L. and Jensen, M. (1977) *Stages of Small Group Development Revisited*, Group and Organisational Studies.

Weinberg, R.S. and Gould, D. (2007) *Foundations of Sport and Exercise Psychology*, Human Kinetics.

Williams, J.M. (1980) Personality characteristics of the successful female athlete, in W.M. Straub, *Sport Psychology: An Analysis of Athlete Behavior*, Movement.

Yerkes, R.M. and Dodson, J.D. (1908) The relationship of strength and stimulus to rapid habit formation. *Journal of Comparative Neurology and Psychology*, 18, 459–82.

Further reading

Cox, R. (2007) *Sports Psychology: Concepts and Applications*, Wm C. Brown Communications.

Thatcher, J., Thatcher, R., Day, M., Portas, M. and Hood, S. (2009) *Sport and Exercise Science*, Learning Matters.

Weinberg, R.S. and Gould, D. (2007) *Foundations of Sport and Exercise Psychology*, Human Kinetics.

Useful websites

www.istadia.com/sport-psychology.php

A vast amount of information, including articles and blogs; registration necessary to access all materials

www.bbc.co.uk/wales/raiseyourgame

Contains visual, audio and written resources for sports psychology and other areas of sport science

www.5min.com/Video/How-to-Develop-Motivation-for-Sport-34094922

A series of five-minute videos on motivation and a range of other topics in sport psychology

4: Research Methods for Sport & Exercise Sciences

4.1 Introduction

This unit explains methods used in research by sport and exercise scientists. It will enable you to understand research in all disciplines of sport and exercise science. It should allow you to develop research skills, including collecting information, handling information, and mathematical and statistical skills, so that you can carry out your own research. Numbers and mathematical concepts put off a lot of students, but the purpose of research methods (and this unit in particular) is to help you understand and interpret the meaning of information and to look at alternative methods of collecting data.

The difference between quantitative research and qualitative research will be examined. Quantitative research is based on numerical evidence (e.g. heart rate), while qualitative research places more emphasis on what people do or say (e.g. answers given in an interview).

By the end of this unit you should know:

● key issues in research methods for sport and exercise sciences
● data collection techniques for sport and exercise sciences
● qualitative data analysis techniques for sport and exercise sciences
● quantitative data analysis techniques for sport and exercise sciences.

Assessment and grading criteria

To achieve a PASS grade the evidence must show that the learner is able to:	To achieve a MERIT grade the evidence must show that, in addition to the pass criteria, the learner is able to:	To achieve a DISTINCTION grade the evidence must show that, in addition to the pass and merit criteria, the learner is able to:
P1 describe qualitative and quantitative research		
P2 identify key issues that affect research in sport and exercise sciences	**M1** explain key issues that affect research in sport and exercise sciences	**D1** analyse key issues that affect research in sport and exercise sciences
P3 outline the types, techniques and classifications of data that are common in research in the sport and exercise sciences		
P4 describe two ethical and legal issues associated with research in sport and exercise sciences	**M2** explain the implications of not working both ethically and legally when conducting research in the sport and exercise sciences	**D2** analyse the implications of not working both ethically and legally when conducting research in the sport and exercise sciences.
P5 describe the three main stages of qualitative data analysis in the sport and exercise sciences	**M3** justify, for a selected research-based example, the most appropriate research design and techniques for qualitative data collection and data analysis	
P6 describe two contrasting quantitative data analysis techniques used in the sport and exercise sciences.	**M4** justify, for a selected research-based example, the most appropriate research design and techniques for quantitative data collection and data analysis.	

4.2 Key Issues in Research Methods for Sport and Exercise Sciences

Broadly speaking, information gathering or research in sport and exercise science can be divided into two types: quantitative and qualitative.

Quantitative research tends to involve numerical data (numbers) and is usually designed to establish differences, relationships or causality.

- Differences – for example, to test the theory that netball players have greater aerobic fitness than hockey players.
- Relationships – for example, to test the theory that a sportsperson's anxiety levels are related to their performance.
- Causality – for example, to test the theory that an increase in potassium ions are responsible for the ventilation threshold.

Quantitative research involves measuring things and seeing how they change or what they are related to. For example, you could measure the percentage body fat of a group of people before and after a training programme. You could then investigate how their body fat percentage changed. If percentage body fat went up, you would deduce that the training had brought about this change, or at least had helped towards it.

Qualitative research places more emphasis on people's ideas, opinions and behaviour, and is designed to explain differences, relationships or causality. As a coach, it may be that one of your athletes keeps getting injured while training. You could carry out an in-depth study into this one person (case study). Included in this study could be interviews and logs of the athlete's training; you could even observe their behaviour in training. From

Fig 4.1 A person carrying out quantitative research

this information, you would hope to determine any reasons for their consistent injuries.

Key term

Case study: an in-depth examination of a single event.

Both quantitative and qualitative methods are useful, and often it is best to use a combination of the two methods to obtain the best results.

Student activity 4.1   30 minutes   P1

Write a report that:
- describes qualitative research, giving examples of when and how it can be used
- describes quantitative research, giving examples of when and how it can be used.

Reliability

One of the key issues in research is reliability. This is concerned with how repeatable something is. That is, if you measured the same thing on separate occasions, would you record the same value? Let us say that you are going to take your resting heart rate every morning before you get up. You would expect the value not to change much over a number of weeks. If you recorded the same or similar values each morning, this would display reliability. You would then know that the way you were measuring your heart rate was reliable.

> ## Key term
> **Reliability:** the ability of something to perform consistently (i.e. if you were to repeat the test, you would you get the same results).

The two major obstacles to good reliability in sport and exercise research are:

- errors – mistakes caused by people measuring the wrong thing or not knowing how to measure something correctly
- day-to-day differences within subjects.

Good training with the equipment to be used, attention to detail and checking that the equipment is working correctly can overcome errors. Differences within subjects are a lot harder to account for. Even when measuring physiological variables, using accurate equipment, it is difficult to record exactly the same value. On different days, people eat different amounts, sleep for different lengths of time, undertake different levels of physical activity, have differing mental states, and so on. The resting heart rate will vary from day to day due to these factors.

Researchers try to minimise these effects by standardising the test situation. In the above example, you could record heart rate at the same time each morning – before breakfast and before the person has had the opportunity to be affected by what happens that day, both physiologically and psychologically. It is also good practice for researchers to make repeated observations and then report the average value; this averages out any errors or variations.

Validity

Another key issue is validity. This refers to the meaning of the information. Did you measure what you set out to measure? You may have decided, as a cricket coach, to measure the aerobic fitness of your players by getting them to perform the bleep test. Your results may be very reliable, but are they valid? Do the results of the bleep test relate to levels of fitness in your players? This is a difficult question to answer. It is often difficult, especially in a field setting, to measure exactly the variable you are looking at. A cricket coach could not practically measure the aerobic capacity (VO_2max) of his players, but he could quite easily measure their performance on the bleep test and relate it back to VO_2max values.

> ## Key term
> **Validity:** whether the selected test actually measures the correct variable.

Choosing a valid test can be a problem in sport and exercise science research. Frequently, people measure certain things and then try to make general statements about what they have found. For example, the sit-and-reach test is often used to measure flexibility; however, it incorporates only leg and back flexibility. Even then, there is debate about its usefulness in measuring this. So, to make statements about an athlete's overall flexibility based on this one test would be incorrect; it would not be valid. When drawing conclusions based on what you have measured, it is important to be specific about those conclusions, unless you have taken a range of measurements.

Objectivity

Another key issue is objectivity. If two different people obtain a similar value for a measurement, it is said to be objective. As a measure of the number of times your heart beats, heart rate recorded at the radial artery is an objective measure. Two different people would obtain similar values when measuring somebody's pulse. It is a simple matter of counting the number of beats in a given time, then converting this to beats per minute. Measuring blood pressure (at the brachial artery with a manual sphygmomanometer) would be less objective. The person measuring blood pressure has to decide the value of systolic pressure, based on when they can hear a constant tapping sound (the Kortikoff sound). Similarly, diastolic pressure is recorded on the absence of a rhythmic tapping sound. Both these points will be slightly subjective – that is, different people could record them differently.

> ## Key term
> **Objectivity:** to be unbiased in our point of view or decision-making process.

Measuring systems should be designed to be objective; however, this is not always possible. Physiological measures (heart rate, respiratory rate) tend to exhibit the most objectivity. Difficult areas in which to achieve objectivity are when an opinion is required or when people are expected to judge performance. For example, scoring in gymnastics can be subjective. This is why detailed scoring systems, involving a number of judges, have been developed to try to overcome this problem.

Accuracy and Precision

When you are testing and assessing athletes, you need to take special care when interpreting the results of tests. It is possible to measure things only to a certain degree of accuracy. The accuracy of a recording will depend on the precision of the equipment used. If you weigh somebody on a set of bathroom weighing scales (the ones with a marker on a dial to indicate weight), their weight might record 84 kg. If you used a set of digital scales, these might show a recording of 84.88 kg. When weighing somebody, is 84 kg accurate enough? Is the extra precision important?

Precision alone is not enough. In the above example, the scales might not be working correctly, so if they reported a value of 81.24 kg, they would be precise, but wrong.

Accuracy is a measure of how close you are to recording the actual value of something that you intend to measure. If you were measuring heart rate

with a heart rate monitor and it displayed a value of 144 beats per minute (b.p.m.), yet the real heart rate was 150 b.p.m., the monitor would be inaccurate.

Key terms

Precision: the degree of agreement of a measurement.

Accuracy: how close something is to its actual value.

Key learning points

- Quantitative research is usually designed to establish differences, relationships or causality.
- Qualitative research is usually designed to explain differences, relationships or causality.
- Key issues in research include:
  - Validity: does the test measure what it is meant to measure?
  - Reliability: if you performed the test again, would it give the same results?
  - Accuracy: how close is the reading to its actual value?
  - Precision: what is the degree of agreement of a measurement?

Student activity 4.2 · 60–90 mins · P2 M1 D1

Task 1

Draw a spider diagram to identify the key issues that affect research in sport and exercise sciences.

Task 2

Write a report that explains and analyses the key issues that affect research in sport and exercise sciences.

Quick quiz

1 Give three examples of research questions you could try to answer using *quantitative* research methods.
2 Give three examples of research questions you could try to answer using *qualitative* research methods.
3 Which tests would be valid to measure a person's:
   (a) aerobic fitness?
   (b) flexibility?
   (c) muscular endurance?
   (d) speed?
4 How would you check to find out if a test was reliable?
5 Describe the differences between accuracy and precision.

4.3 Data Collection Techniques for Sport and Exercise Sciences

P3

Types of Data – Primary and Secondary

Why do we need to take measurements in sport and exercise science? Measurement allows us to quantify things (e.g. it is possible to give a value for the number of times a heart beats in a minute). With sufficient measurement, data can be produced, so heart rate over a given time could be displayed. The production of data is important in science, as it allows for analysis. Hence, it would be possible to examine what happens to heart rate during a set time period or in a given situation (e.g. during exercise). Does heart rate increase, decrease or stay the same during exercise? This analysis, in turn, allows interpretation to infer meaning. The reason for an increased heart rate could be examined. Why did the heart rate go up? What caused it?

Data that you measure yourself is called **primary** data. Somebody else's data that you use is called **secondary** data. If you were examining the number of yellow and red cards for the teams competing in the last three football World Cups, you would need to collect the data from these competitions. This might involve looking up information on the internet, for example. This would be secondary data, which was originally recorded by somebody other than you.

Data Collection Techniques

Data collection is the process of obtaining information. The method used will depend on whether you are interested in collecting quantitative or qualitative information.

Qualitative Techniques

Interviews

This is where the researcher will ask a person a series of questions. Interviews tend to be used mainly with qualitative research. A good interview will rely on trust and rapport to obtain information. Interviews are good at assessing somebody's attitude towards something. They allow for probing or follow-up questions, such as: What do you mean by...? This can lead to a deeper level of understanding. On the negative side, interviews are time-consuming, they can be open to biases on the part of the interviewer and can result in the interviewee giving answers that are socially acceptable.

During interviews, information is usually recorded via a voice recorder or camcorder. A voice recorder is less obtrusive, as some people feel nervous when faced with a camera. However, the use of a camcorder can give some non-verbal information that may prove beneficial. If neither is available, you will have to record responses by hand. To become a good interviewer requires both ability and practice. If the answers obtained are to be valid, it is essential that the respondent is relaxed and at ease. It is vital that the answers given are genuine and, for this reason, it is important that you do not influence the response by the nature of your questioning or even by your presence. As with questionnaires, your research is relying on what the subject says, which may or may not be the truth. Techniques can be used to test the validity of a person's answer (i.e. repeated or similar questions can be asked to see if the answers are the same).

Focus groups

A focus group involves a group of people (five to ten) who focus on certain given topics. The researcher will guide the session, so that the issues discussed are relevant to the research. Focus groups are very good for exploring people's ideas. As with interviews, issues can be probed in more detail. Due to the group situation, people may feel less self-conscious than when being interviewed one to one. This may result in the answers being more honest. As with the interview, information can be recorded and analysed after the event.

Focus groups do have some limitations. Leading the group and facilitating discussion is a difficult skill to master. Often, one or two people dominate the group. A lot of time can be spent discussing unnecessary information.

Observations

A further means of gaining information or data for research is to observe the subject in a given situation. Observations are common in psychology-based research – seeing what a person will do in a certain situation. This method is used because it is less obtrusive than administering a questionnaire or asking questions in an interview. Also, people do not always do what they say they will do! Coaching is another area that relies on observations for obtaining information. In some sports, elaborate systems have been developed to code categories of actions or behaviour. These systems can be used by researchers to analyse coach or player behaviour, as well as being used by the coach themselves to help players improve their performance. A good example of this is in football, where notational analysis systems, designed to examine the amount of activity (walking, running, jumping) undertaken by players of different positions, can be used to devise individualised training programmes.

There are many methods of observation:

- The observer may be external to the group, such as a coach observing their own players' performances
- The observer may be part of the group – imagine that you wanted to look at football hooliganism; the best way to do this would be by becoming part of the crowd and experiencing what happens.

Observations are useful because you can see what actually happens and you are not just relying on what people say they will do. Observations are especially useful with individuals who have weak verbal skills or with people who are unwilling to talk about what they do. As with the previous methods of data collection, investigator effects may have an impact – people may react differently when they know they are being observed. It could be that the behaviour you wish to observe occurs when you are not there. All methods of data collection will have limitations.

Quantitative Techniques

Quantitative techniques are mainly based on gathering numerical information. They can also give rise to qualitative information. Questionnaires would be such an example. Imagine you have designed a questionnaire to measure the amount of exercise people do. Quantitative information could be in the form of the number of times a week somebody exercises, while qualitative information might be the reasons why they exercise or how they feel when they are exercising.

Questionnaires

A very common method of collecting data in qualitative and quantitative research is to use a questionnaire. A questionnaire is a method of surveying people's opinions or habits by asking subjects to respond to questions.

The major limitation with a questionnaire is that the results consist of what people say they do or believe, and this is not always reliable. Careful planning is essential if you hope to get valid results. You can use techniques to try to identify whether people are telling the truth. One way to do it in a questionnaire is by repeating questions or asking very similar questions. If a person is telling the truth or answering each question properly (and not just skimming through the questions), you would expect the same answer to these repeated or similar questions.

You need to think about what you wish to get out of the questionnaire (i.e. what information you hope to collect). Careful consideration also needs to be given to the actual questions asked. There are two common types of question that could be asked in a questionnaire. These are closed questions and open questions:

- A **closed question** is one where you give a certain number of choices and the person has to pick one. An example would be: How do you rate your fitness? The possible answers would be: Not at all fit, Slightly fit, Moderately fit, Very fit or Extremely fit. You know the answer will be from this list.
- **Open questions** have no list. The question is open-ended, such as: How could you improve your level of fitness? In this case, the range of possible answers is almost endless.

A further concern is the order in which you put the questions. Often, questionnaires collect general information first – age, gender, job, sport played, and so on. This gets people into the habit of answering the questions. They are then more likely to complete the questionnaire. If the questions become more difficult or detailed, it may be necessary to provide examples.

A major problem with research involving questionnaires is people either not completing the questionnaire sufficiently or not completing it at all. To obtain the best results from a questionnaire, it should be relatively short, as you are more likely to get a response.

You also need to think about how you are going to present your results. A lot of open questions may give you lots of information, but this will be hard to summarise in a table or graph. Too many open questions are difficult to analyse and therefore time-consuming. Numerical data are easier to analyse, so you should try to code the possible answers (Yes = 2, No = 1). There are different ways that questions can be coded. Scaled questions can be in the form of the Likert scale, for example, which indicates a person's level of agreement with a statement or question.

Using the previous example on fitness, the following is a scaled question: How do you rate your fitness?

Not at all fit	Slightly fit	Moderately fit	Very fit	Extremely fit
1	2	3	4	5

With a scaled answer, the person must pick the answer that they feel is most suitable from those available. If you want more than one answer, then a ranked question would be better. An example might be: Which sport do you enjoy participating in most?, where 1 is the most preferred and 5 is the least, and where the options are basketball, rugby, cricket, running and cycling. The respondent would then rate each sport from 1 to 5, based on their level of enjoyment of that sport.

Sometimes you may be looking for one answer, a simple yes or no, as in the question: Have you ever been skiing? In this example, only two choices are needed – you have either been skiing or you have not. If necessary, further categories can be used, such as a 'Do not know' option.

When designing a questionnaire, you are trying to make it as easy as possible to fill in, but also easy for you to report the results accurately and clearly.

You should try to avoid leading questions – that is, ones where you are suggesting the answer in the question. For example, asking: Do you think football players receive too much money? could be considered a leading question, as it almost implies that footballers are paid too much money.

You should also avoid unclear terms. If a question begins with 'usually' or 'mostly', how often is that – once a day, once a week or something different? In addition, try not to use jargon or technical terms. If you ask a member of the public: How many times per week do you take part in aerobic exercise?, they may not understand the term 'aerobic'. They may not answer the question or may answer it incorrectly.

Not only do the questions need to be made very clear, but so too does how you want them to be answered. Will there be tick boxes or do respondents circle a number, for example?

Once you have designed your questionnaire, try it out on a small group of people first (not the ones you plan to use it on later). Is it liable to cause offence? Check the wording that you have used. If you ask: Which sports do you enjoy? and then proceed to give a list, what if somebody wants to specify a sport you have not listed? You could include 'Other' in the list or ask: Which of the following sports do you enjoy? Is the method of response easy? People tend to fill in questionnaires as quickly as they can. They do not want to spend time having to complete the answers. Are there any overlapping categories? Asking how old somebody is and then having answers of 16–20, 20–24, for example, is annoying to a 20-year-old. Which category are they in?

Questionnaires offer an inexpensive way of gathering large amounts of information in a relatively short time. As previously stated, the information provided can be analysed using qualitative and quantitative techniques. Normally, questionnaires guarantee anonymity. This would make it difficult to have follow-up questions or to clarify if there are issues or misunderstandings. Reply rates are low with questionnaires, as you get answers only from the people who are motivated enough to fill them in. This will impact on any results you obtain.

Key terms

Anonymity: keeping identity a secret.

Closed environment: a situation that is tightly controlled, where things do not change.

Laboratory and Field-based Data Collection

Tests are generally divided into laboratory-based tests and field-based tests. Laboratory tests are performed in a closed environment.

In a closed environment, things are closely controlled and maintained. The advantage of this is that there are fewer factors that will affect the results. Let's say you wanted to perform a fitness test on one of your athletes. In a laboratory-based test, the room temperature would be constant, the amount of exercise can be measured exactly and there will be no effects from spectators or fellow players. These conditions make the results reliable. That means you could reproduce the test conditions easily and be able to compare results from one test to another.

It would seem, therefore, that laboratory tests are very useful, and they are. But sport is not played in a lab! This is the reason for field-based tests, or tests that are performed in a real-life setting. If you were a football coach and you wished to measure your players' fitness, you could do this out on the football pitch, on grass, where players play their games. You could organise the bleep test on the pitch. The results will be affected by the weather, the state of the pitch, the player's footwear, and so on, but at least the results can be related to football (i.e. running on grass).

Classifications of data

A group or set of numbers is referred to as data. The resting heart rates of a group of people would be a set of data. Data can include more than one type of measurement – for example, the height and weight of a number of people. With any type of measurement, the thing measured is called a variable. This is because the measurement can vary. In sport and exercise, a variable is something that we measure (blood pressure, anxiety levels, flexibility). If the variable can be recorded using a, it is described as a numeric variable.

However, not all variables or sets of data have to use numbers. If you were recording the gender of a group of people, instead of numbers you could use labels (male and female). Variables with letters or words in place of numbers are called string variables.

Data can be classified according to the type of measurement. The simplest type of measurement uses what is called a nominal scale, in which categories are given nominal values. Let's say gender was to be recorded in a table – males could be denoted by a 2 and females by a 1. These values would be nominal; they have no meaning, they just identify which category each person belongs to. As the values have no numerical meaning, 2 is not twice as good as 1. They are just labels to separate each category. Nominal data is sometimes referred to as discrete data, because you can only have discrete values (male/female, yes/no).

The next type of measurement is ordinal. Ordinal values also use numbers to signify categories, but these numbers also give a ranking value (Liverpool = 1st, Arsenal = 2nd, Manchester United = 3rd). In the example given, each number indicates a football league position – Liverpool is first, Arsenal is second, and so on. This sort of data gives us a lot more detail than nominal data (we can now say who is the tallest, quickest or heaviest), although it does not provide as much detail as we might like. In the league position example, the team in first place may be one point ahead of the team in second place, while the team in second place could be three points in front of the team in third place. This type of data only gives a rank order (first, second, third) and not an exact value.

A more detailed type of numerical measurement is interval or ratio-level data. These are two different types of data, but are often referred to as one, as they are very similar.

An interval scale has equal distances between each value, hence its name. It is normally given by units of measurement. An example is the Fahrenheit scale. Ratio scales are all units of measurement with set distances between values, but they also have a zero point, determined by nature (time, distance, weight) or what is called an absolute zero. Therefore, a distance of 20 km is twice that of 10 km. The same cannot be said for Fahrenheit – that is, 20 °F is not twice as hot as 10 °F.

Interval or ratio data are continuous. Continuous data can have any numeric value, with any number of decimal places. The time taken to run the 100 m would be a continuous measure (a value of 11.43 seconds). Interval or ratio data can be converted into ordinal or nominal scales, but this is not true the other way round. If you were to measure the exact height of some people, you could then categorise the subjects into the following groups based on their height: tall = 1, medium height = 2, short = 3. This would be converting ratio data into ordinal data.

Research Design

There are a number of steps involved in designing a research project:

1 You need a question that you are going to ask (e.g. How does exercise affect heart rate?).
2 You need to ask yourself what you think will happen, based on any previous research (e.g. Does heart rate increase with exercise?).
3 You need to collect the data (e.g. measure heart rate during exercise).
4 You have to examine the results in line with your expectations (e.g. Does heart rate go up, and by how much?).

The most common type of research design is to have two groups: one that undertakes some form of training or treatment and one that does not. You would then test both groups at the start of the research and both groups at the end of the research and see if there is a difference. This is termed a pre-test/post-test research design. For example, if you wanted to determine if relaxation reduces anxiety before a game, you could have two groups: the first group would receive training in relaxation techniques, while the other would not. For this experiment you could make a hypothesis.

Key term

Hypothesis: a theory you plan to test.

Instead of just saying that relaxation has an affect on anxiety, it is normal to give three hypotheses:

● The null hypothesis
● The alternative hypothesis
● The directional hypothesis.

In the above example, the hypotheses would be as follows:

● Null hypothesis: there will be no difference in pre-game anxiety between groups one and two.
● Alternative hypothesis: there will be a difference in pre-game anxiety between the two groups.
● Directional hypothesis: group one (which undergoes training in relaxation techniques) will rate their pre-game anxiety lower than group two (the group that has no relaxation technique training).

Not all research uses the pre-test/post-test design. It may be that you are not looking at the effects of anything you do. You might wish to examine how much sport and physical education children do in schools and the effect it has on the sport they take part in outside school. In this case, what you are measuring is how much sport is played outside school. The thing you change would be the amount of sport and physical education done in school. But you cannot change this, as the school, local education authority and the government determine it. What you can do is compare one school with another, one area with another, or even one country with another (e.g. France and England). This is termed a comparative study.

Another method of research is to compare evidence or information over time, instead of comparing one region with another. You may wish to see how the amount of physical education in schools has changed over the years. This method works if you have the data or can obtain them. If there was little or no data, you would have to set up a study to review things in the future. Let us imagine that you wish to see the effect of school sport and physical education on the health of children in your area. However, you have no information on the current state of health of the children. What you would have to do is monitor the sport and physical education participated in by the children, and their level of health. You would have

to do this over a period of time to see if their health improved, declined or stayed the same. This type of study is called a longitudinal study. It is often used in the study of health and disease. It requires time, with some longitudinal research lasting for many years. Therefore, this method would not be suitable for a small research project.

Key learning points 2

- Data can be primary or secondary.
- Qualitative techniques include: interviews, focus groups and observations.
- Quantitative techniques include: questionnaires, laboratory-based data collection, field-based data collection.
- Classifications of data include: discrete, ordinal, interval and radio.
- Types of research design include: crosssectional, experimental, case study, longitudinal and comparative.

Student activity 4.3   30–60 mins   P3

Task 1
Draw a spider diagram to illustrate the different types, techniques and classifications used in sport and exercise sciences research.

Task 2
Write a report that outlines the different types, techniques and classifications used in sport and exercise sciences research.

4.4 Ethical and Legal Issues in Sport and Exercise Sciences Research

P4   M2   D2

A lot of testing, measuring and research in sport and exercise science involves working with other people (e.g. athletes, clients of a health club). The British Association of Sport and Exercise Sciences (BASES) has a code of conduct for its members when working with athletes.

The general principles should be followed by anybody conducting research in any area of sport and exercise science. It is important to respect the rights of other people and ensure they are not

negatively affected by your tests or work. This is especially true when working with children. Your subjects should be made aware of their right to withdraw from a test or programme of exercise at any time during the study. The decision to undertake a test or exercise programme rests with the individual; if they decide they do not want to continue, you must stop the test. You should explain the full procedures and programmes that any individual will be following, give them details of the group they will be in, if any, and tell them who will be testing them. This is an important part of testing, as it allows you to be sure that the subject is clear about what they are doing. You do not want the results to be affected by a lack of understanding on the subject's part.

As always, confidentiality is important. You should make this clear to all involved and ensure that the identity of all your subjects and their information is used only for research purposes and that any information produced will not display their names. It may be necessary to prove that the above considerations have been adhered to. For example, you may be conducting some research at a local health club, and one of the clients is injured while undergoing a fitness test. The manager of the club will want to know if it was your testing that caused the injury. In such a case, it is not only important that you have stuck to certain guidelines while testing and that you were suitably qualified, but also that you can show this to be the case. You could find that the injured person decides to sue you or the club for negligence.

Informed Consent

An informed consent form is a document that has been signed to show that your subjects have been informed of the test (told what is going to happen) and have given their consent (agreed to undertake the test). An informed consent form should explain what risks may be involved in the study. It can also include a list of possible benefits. The form must make it clear that cooperation in the research is voluntary and that the subject can withdraw their consent at any time. The form may also contain some detail on the testing procedure. With children, or if the test is very complicated, the procedures can be made easier to understand. The subjects should be encouraged to ask questions if they have concerns.

It is a vital part of the form that the subject signs to say they have read it, understood what is in it and are happy to be part of the study.

Data Protection Act

Any information on a subject, athlete or client should be kept confidential. This is in line with the Data Protection Act 1984. Records (hard copy or computerised) should be kept where only authorised personnel can access them. When reporting information to other people, personal details should be left out. For example, if you were reporting back to a group of athletics coaches regarding some research you had carried out on strength training, you would not include in your report or presentation the names of the subjects you had used. It would be sufficient for you to give general background information, such as age, gender, ability level, years of training, and so on.

Key learning points 3

- BASES has produced a code of conduct that takes into account ethical and legal issues involved in sport and exercise sciences research.
- Ethical and legal issues must be taken into account in research where people are being used for the investigation.

Student activity 4.4   ⏱ 60–90 mins   P4 M2 D2

Time: 60–90 minutes

As the majority of research in sport and exercise sciences requires human subjects, it is very important that the research is carried out in line with ethical and legal guidelines, to ensure the health and welfare of the subjects and to maintain the reputation of sport and exercise sciences.

1 Select two ethical and two legal issues associated with sport and exercise sciences.

2 Explain and analyse the implications of not working ethically and legally when carrying out research in sport and exercise sciences.

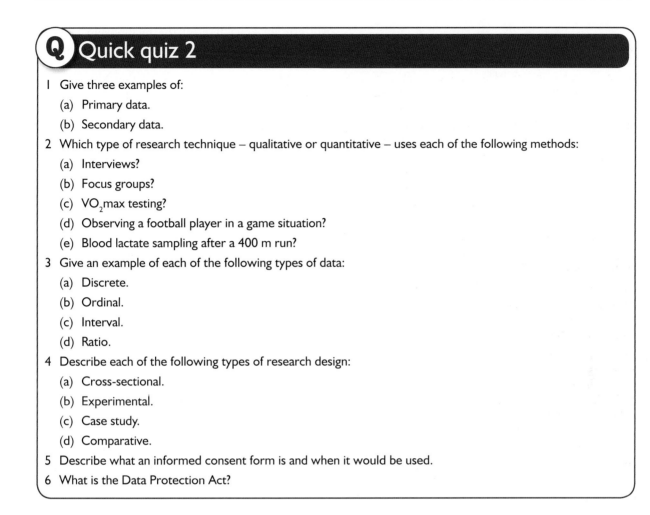

Q Quick quiz 2

1 Give three examples of:
   (a) Primary data.
   (b) Secondary data.

2 Which type of research technique – qualitative or quantitative – uses each of the following methods:
   (a) Interviews?
   (b) Focus groups?
   (c) VO_2max testing?
   (d) Observing a football player in a game situation?
   (e) Blood lactate sampling after a 400 m run?

3 Give an example of each of the following types of data:
   (a) Discrete.
   (b) Ordinal.
   (c) Interval.
   (d) Ratio.

4 Describe each of the following types of research design:
   (a) Cross-sectional.
   (b) Experimental.
   (c) Case study.
   (d) Comparative.

5 Describe what an informed consent form is and when it would be used.

6 What is the Data Protection Act?

4.5 Qualitative Data Analysis Techniques for Sport and Exercise Sciences

Stages of Data Analysis

With qualitative data, there tends to be lots of information (e.g. long lists of answers to questions or descriptions of behaviour). This information needs to be reduced into a manageable amount. This process of data reduction is called coding – that is, grouping the data into meaningful segments.

In qualitative analysis, there are no right and wrong answers. You interpret the data as you see fit. Coding can be time-consuming, especially if the amount of data is large. To this end, computer software has been written to analyse the data. Currently, the most popular qualitative data analysis packages are NUD-IST, ATLAS and Ethnograph.

Displaying Data

Frequently in qualitative research, diagrams are drawn to show how something works or to clarify the relationship between various things. People do exercise for health and fitness benefits, which will overlap with each other. In addition, people exercise for social or psychological benefits, which, again, are interlinked. In diagrammatic form, this may look like Figure 4.2.

Verifying Data

It is important in any form of research to verify that the data you have is accurate and that the conclusions you reach are valid. In qualitative research, this is done via triangulation. This is a method of cross-checking information using different sources or different methods of data collection. It is a common technique used by detectives and journalists. If two people say the same thing independently of each other, it is more likely to be true.

89

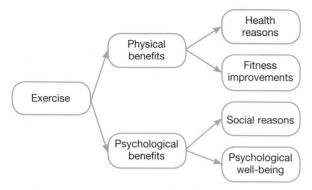

Fig 4.2 Example of a diagram that presents conclusions

Key learning points 4

● The two types of data that can be used for research are primary and secondary.
● Qualitative techniques include interviews, focus groups and observation.
● Classifications of data include discrete, ordinal, continuous, interval and ratio.
● Types of research design include experimental, cross-sectional, case study, longitudinal and comparative.

4.6 Quantitative Data Analysis Techniques for Sport and Exercise Sciences

Data Analysis

Numerical analysis of data is called statistics. Descriptive statistics are about describing data (i.e. the average value or the range of numbers). Inferential statistics are more detailed. They examine things like relationships or differences in data. They can be used to determine the answer to your research question or your hypothesis. Relationships look at how one thing affects another and can be analysed using correlations. Differences decide if one group is different from another.

Correlations

To measure if two things are related, a correlation can be performed. Correlation means association or relationship. For example, the question: Is heart rate related to environmental temperature? can be answered with a test of correlation. The correlation

will give an exact level of the relationship between the two things. This value or number is called the correlation coefficient and is normally given by the letter 'r'. If two things are in an exact relation with one another – as one goes up, so does the other – they have a positive correlation.

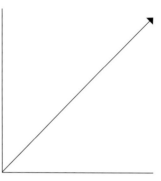

Fig 4.3 A perfect positive correlation

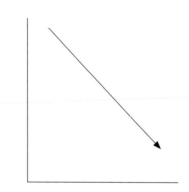

Fig 4.4 A perfect negative correlation

The correlation coefficient (r) to represent this is $+1$. If there is no relationship, r is 0. However, if the relationship is the other way round – one goes up as the other goes down – this is a negative correlation. In this case, r would be -1. Therefore, you can see that r can be between $+1$ and -1. A high correlation, association or relationship is just that; it does not necessarily mean that one thing causes the other.

Once you have measured r, what does it mean? When a correlation is calculated, a probability or significance value is also given, in addition to the r value. This significance value is a number (e.g. 0.10). The value gives the likelihood of what you are testing being true. For example, if you were testing a relationship and you had a significance value of 0.10, this would mean that 10 times in 100 you would be wrong if you said there was a relationship. The good side of this is that 90 times in 100 you would be correct. In social science (sports science, psychology), the customary significance value is 0.05 (being wrong 5 times in 100). If the significance value is higher than 0.05, then there is no relationship (or at least, it is not significant). Statistically, the specific significance value of 0.05 is written as p < .05.

A Pearson product–moment correlation is one type of test that can be performed. In order to do this, a number of criteria must be met. The main assumptions are as follows:

● Data must be from related pairs – they should be collected from the same subject (e.g. height and mass from the same person).
● Data should be interval or ratio (explained previously).
● Each variable should be normally distributed (normality).

If the assumptions for a Pearson product–moment correlation are not met, a Spearman rank–order correlation is performed.

If the relationship were significant, the statistics would be reported as (r = .931, p < .05). The significance value is less than 0.05. This means the relationship is meaningful.

Difference Tests

Difference tests can be divided into two types: parametric and non-parametric. Parametric statistics should be used when the data are normally distributed and interval or ratio level. Non-parametric statistics are used when the data are not normally distributed.

Difference tests are used for studying the effect of something on a group of individuals – for example, how training affects fitness levels. The outcome of difference tests is reported in the same way as a correlation, but, rather than a relationship, a significant difference is referred to. For example, there is a significant difference (t = 1.352, p < .05) in heart rate between a group that does exercise and a group that does not.

With parametric statistics, the most frequent difference tests are t-tests. An independent t-test is used when investigating differences among groups. A dependent t-test is used when you are investigating a difference inside the group. If the data are not parametric, t-tests cannot be performed, and alternative tests are used. The Mann-Whitney U test is a non-parametric difference test that can be used with different groups. The Wilcoxon matched-pairs test is a non-parametric test that can be used within the same group. Another non-parametric test is the chi-square test. It looks at the frequency of occurrence of something.

Sampling

When we are conducting research, we want to use the results to explain what could or would happen to anybody. However, measuring everybody is not possible, so we often look at a small group of the population. This is called a sample. A value (e.g. the average height) that is taken from a sample is called a statistic.

The best way of selecting a sample is by random sampling. Random sampling is a system where a group of subjects is selected at random from a bigger group. Anybody in the group has an equal chance of being selected for the group. With the use of random sampling, the chance of bias is reduced.

Key term

Bias: the error that occurs when estimating a value from a sample of a population.

Organising and Displaying Data

For numbers, one method of organising the values is to chart them as a frequency distribution. One type of frequency distribution is a scatter plot. This type of plot records a point for each time a certain value occurs. Instead of showing a series of points, vertical bars can be used. This is called a histogram, as shown in Figure 4.5, created using Statistical Package for Social Scientists (SPSS).

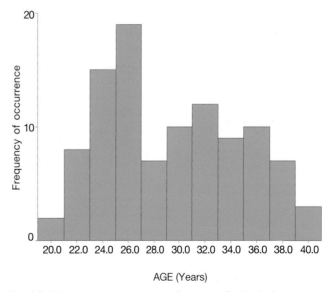

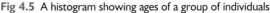

Fig 4.5 A histogram showing ages of a group of individuals

SPSS is similar to Microsoft Excel®, in that it allows you to record and display data. It is often used due to its versatility when using statistics. The most

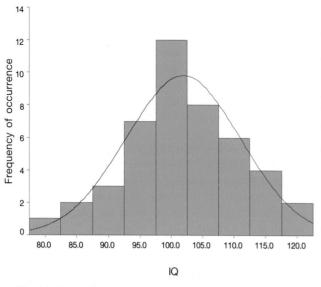

Fig 4.6 Data displaying normal distribution

important consideration when displaying data is the presentation. The data should be displayed in the most effective format (there is no need to include raw data). Tables of data should contain units and must have a suitable title. Graphs should also incorporate units and labels and contain a title. Any picture, photograph or diagram, including graphs and histograms, but not tables, is referred to as a figure.

Normally distributed data peaks in the middle. In the example in Figure 4.6, if we measured IQ for a sample of the population, we could say that the majority of people have an average IQ, while a small number have high and low values.

Normally distributed data is described as bell-shaped when plotted on a graph. In an exact normal distribution, the mean, median and mode are all the same. If the distribution is asymmetrical, the data are not normally distributed, which can be due to skewness (the peak is more to the left or right) or kurtosis (the curve is excessively peaked or flat).

Measures of Central Tendency and Variability

With a group of numbers, it is possible to use one number to represent them all. This number is the average, or, as it is correctly termed, the central tendency. The three most commonly used measures of central tendency are as follows:

- The **mean** is the sum of all the numbers divided by the amount of numbers. This is the most common type of average. When people refer to the average, they are normally talking about the mean. The mean of 8, 12, 16 and 24 would be 15.
- The **median** is a value that divides a group of numbers exactly in half. Half the numbers are higher and half are lower. If there is an odd number of values, the median is the middle one. With an even number of values, the median is the average of the two middle values. The median of 23, 47, 50, 67 and 88 is 50.
- The **mode** is the most frequently occurring value in the list of numbers. For individuals of the following ages, 17, 18, 19, 20, 20, 20, 23 and 27, the mode is 20.

Statistics can also be used to give an idea of the variation of the data. Variation in a set of numbers could be the difference in the scores (e.g. weight) across the group. The set of numbers could represent the weight of a subject measured a number of times. The terms between-subject variation and within-subject variation are used to describe these two issues.

The easiest measure of variation to calculate is the range or the difference between the biggest and smallest (e.g. if your oldest subject is 24 and the youngest is 18, the range is 6 years). The problem with measuring the range is that, to a large degree, it relates to group size: the more people you measure, the bigger the range will be.

A different, but more complicated measure of variation in scores is the standard deviation. The simplest explanation of this is the spread of the scores around the mean. The mean and standard deviation are sometimes shown together (e.g. average height was 1.67 m $+/-0.22$ m).

Interquartile range is similar to range, but it takes out the top and bottom 25 per cent of the numbers.

The type of dispersion data that you report will depend on the measure of central tendency that you use. With mean, the standard deviation is used; the median uses interquartile range; and with the mode it is range.

Outliers

Outliers are unusual data measurements. They can be the result of error or they may be correct readings caused by a strange event (a subject has an abrupt change in heart rate). The trouble with outliers is that some information (like the average) can be greatly affected. If this is the case, the median could be used instead of the mean, as the outlier would not affect it. Many people try to ignore outliers. But you need to think long and hard about doing this. Was the data point a mistake or is it a genuine reading? If you have any uncertainty, you can include results both with and without outliers, to see how much they differ.

Key learning points 5

- Quantitative techniques include laboratory-based data collection and field-based data collection.
- Parametric tests: statistical tests that can be performed on normal data.
- Non-parametric tests: tests for data that are not normally distributed.
- Distribution: the grouping of the data.
- Displaying data: showing the results of numerical analysis, commonly in tables and graphs.
- Central tendency: the average value.

Student activity 4.5 — 90–120 mins — P5 P6 M3 M4

For these tasks, you will need to select two research-based examples in sport and exercise sciences; one example should be appropriate for qualitative research and the other should be appropriate for quantitative research.

Task 1

- Write a report that describes the three main stages of qualitative data analysis.
- Describe a selected qualitative research design, then justify the research design and techniques for qualitative data collection and data analysis.

Task 2

- Write a report that describes two contrasting quantitative data analysis techniques that could be used in sport and exercise sciences research.
- Describe a selected quantitative research design, then justify the research design and techniques for quantitative data collection and data analysis.

Q Quick quiz 3

1 Describe data reduction coding.

2 List three different ways of displaying qualitative data.

3 When would you use a correlation coefficient test?

4 When would you use a t-test?

5 For the following data of heart rates from two different circuit training classes:

(a) Work out the mean, median and mode heart rates for each class.

(b) Carry out a t-test to determine the differences between the heart rates for each class.

(c) Display the data in the most appropriate way.

(d) Were there any outliers in the two sets of data? If so, identify and explain each one.

(e) Do the data follow a normal distribution? Explain your answer.

Class 1	123	132	117	143	129	136	118	134	111	127	124	115
Class 2	136	128	136	131	115	117	151	147	126	135	128	138

Further reading

Clegg, F. (1993) *Simple Statistics: A Course Book for the Social Sciences*, Cambridge University Press.

Silverman, D. (2005) *Doing Qualitative Research: A Practical Guide*, 2nd edn, Sage Publications.

Thomas, J.R. and Nelson, J.K. (2005) *Research Methods in Physical Activity*, 5th edn, Human Kinetics.

Useful websites

www.coachesinfo.com/index.php

Free access to a number of regularly updated articles on a wide range of sports, describing methodology of research; registration necessary for full access.

www.visionlearning.com/library/module_viewer.php?mid=109

A short introduction, with quiz, to demonstrate how to use graphs to represent scientific data effectively.

math.youngzones.org/stat_graph.html

Concise summary of the pros and cons of which type of graph to use to represent data

5: Research Project in Sport & Exercise Sciences

5.1 Introduction

Research is about finding solutions to problems, obtaining facts and determining what is the truth. A research project allows you to bring different areas of study together. You can use your knowledge of sport and exercise science to investigate a particular topic or question you have an interest in. It could be related to a certain sport (e.g. fitness in football referees), general issues in sport and exercise (e.g. the amount of physical activity undertaken by schoolchildren), or it may arise from one of the disciplines within sport and exercise (e.g. sports injuries). Whatever topic you choose, you will have to spend a large amount of time working independently. This will include reading literature, collecting and analysing data, and writing up the whole project. The aim of this unit is to help you achieve such a project.

By the end of this unit you should be able to:

● plan a sport science- or exercise science-based research project
● conduct a sport science- or exercise science-based research project
● produce a sport science- or exercise science-based research project
● review a sport science- or exercise science-based research project.

Assessment and grading criteria

To achieve a PASS grade the evidence must show that the learner is able to:	To achieve a MERIT grade the evidence must show that, in addition to the pass criteria, the learner is able to:	To achieve a DISTINCTION grade the evidence must show that, in addition to the pass and merit criteria, the learner is able to:
P1 plan a sport science- or exercise science-based research project	**M1** explain how the selected research design and research methods will ensure that data collection and analysis is valid and reliable	
P3 collect and record data from the research project conducted	**M2** correctly analyse collected data, describing techniques used	**D1** correctly analyse data, explaining techniques used
P4 produce a full research report, using a standard scientific structure		
P5 carry out a review of the research project conducted, describing strengths, areas for improvement and future recommendations.	**M3** carry out a review of the research project, explaining strengths, areas for improvement and future recommendations.	**D2** carry out a review of the research project, justifying future recommendations for further research.

5.2 Planning a Sport Science- or Exercise Science-based Research Project

Often the hardest part of the plan is getting started. Thinking of a good idea takes time. It is useful to have a number of topics you hope to look at, and then if one idea proves impractical or too hard to test, you have an alternative. A good research question is something that you can answer, such as: Are netball players fitter than football players? Is body weight related to upper body strength? It also needs to be practical, so that you can test it. You need to think about the time available, what resources and equipment you have and the subjects you can use. It needs to be of importance, so that your conclusions have an implication for somebody or something. How will your research help an athlete, coach, official, teacher, administrator or manager? Finally, your research should be interesting so that others will read it and you will stay focused enough to complete it. It could take more than six months for you to finish the whole project.

What is to be the focus of your study? If you do not already have an idea in mind, you need to come up with one. Many people find this the hardest part of the research project. A good way to start is to think about a sport or type of exercise that you know a lot about or that takes your interest. If, for example, you are a keen cyclist, you may wish to do a project on some aspect of cycling. Another way to narrow the area is to do it by a discipline within sport and exercise science. For example, you may decide to do a project involving biomechanics. You could even combine the two areas to arrive at a project that incorporates the biomechanics of cycling.

Writing an Introduction

Your plan will need to have an introduction, which should be the background to the research. This will include why you picked this idea, what you may already know about this topic or what you might have recently found out. Try to predict the usefulness of your research. Remember that the research needs to be of some practical use. There is little point in asking a group of relatively unfit people to follow a 12-week training plan consisting of cycling, running and swimming, and having as your objective to see if aerobic fitness levels increase after the training programme. You would be able to predict the results in advance with some certainty. It would be better to look at different training methods, intensities or durations and see how they compared.

Now that your ideas are becoming more specific, you can start to decide on a title. Do not worry about this too much, as the title may change slightly as you find out more about your research area.

Aims and Objectives

The aim or objective of the research must be clear. Along with finding a good title, this is an area that people find hard to get right at first. You may have a general idea for a project (e.g. fitness in football players), but not a specific aim. Using fitness in football players as an example, what would you test, and who would you test? The topic is too general. It needs to be focused on one particular aspect of fitness in football players.

Contrast this with the following topic: the anaerobic fitness levels of college male first-team and second-team football players. This project is far clearer. What is to be measured is specific – anaerobic fitness. But you would still need to decide how to measure it and justify your chosen method. The people you are going to investigate are clearly stated. The objective is very clear. Therefore you have something that you can test. You might suggest that first-team players will have a higher level of anaerobic fitness than second-team players. This would be easy to test, by measuring it in both sets of players and then comparing the values.

Having a good question to test helps make the research clear. It helps you to think about how you intend to collect the data. The aim will define the scope of your project. If you are looking at fitness in young male footballers, this is what your conclusions should be about. You might like to generalise to older footballers, or females or rugby players, but you would be speculating. So remember, keep the research focused on one area. For example:

Title: Do isotonic sports drinks increase cycling endurance performance?

Aim: To assess whether isotonic sports drinks increase the time that a person can perform endurance cycling.

Objectives:
- Find out how sports drinks affect endurance performance.
- Use primary data taken from laboratory testing to see how endurance performance is affected by drinking sports drinks.
- Be able to provide cyclists recommendations for how sports drinks can affect their endurance performance.

97

Hypothesis

Your project should also have some sort of hypothesis. A hypothesis is basically a theory that you plan to prove or disprove through your research. A hypothesis will include two variables and a prediction of what you think will happen – for example, drinking sports drinks while cycling will improve endurance performance.

A null hypothesis is where it is expected that there will be no relationship between the two variables – for example, there will be no difference in cycling endurance performance if a cyclist drinks a sports drink.

Hypotheses are usually used when you are carrying out quantitative research. However, when you are using qualitative research, it is not always necessary or appropriate to include a hypothesis in your project; instead, you would state what you think you will find out from the research.

Collection of Evidence

Next in your plan you should include how you aim to collect your data. This will include:

- Scope
- Research design
- Equipment
- Reliability
- Validity
- Methods of data collection
- Sample
- Ethical considerations
- Legal considerations

Scope

The scope of your project is basically who the results of project would be applicable to. For example, if you were to carry out your research on eight people, the results would probably only be applicable to that population. So if you selected eight male club cyclists to test if sports drinks affect their endurance, the results would really only be applicable to males who are at the same club level.

Research Design

The research design will depend on what you are hoping to examine. If you aim to examine the effect of a training programme on a particular measure, such as flexibility, you would need to record the value of this measurement before and after the training programme. This would allow you to see if what you were measuring had changed and to infer that your training plan had caused the change. This is referred to as a pre-test/post-test research design.

Another research design method is the double-blind design, which is where one group of subjects is given something that, for example, may increase/affect their performance, while another group is given a placebo.

Key term

Placebo: dummy medication/treatment.

The term 'double blind' is where neither the tester nor the subject knows if they have the 'real' performance enhancer or the placebo. This way, neither the tester nor the subject can influence the results.

Equipment

The equipment you are going to use will depend on what you are going to measure. The main considerations you have are these:

- Can you get access to the equipment you need and do you have the skills to use it?
- Do you need to book a room or a video camera?
- Do you know how to do this?

Check with your tutor that you have access to all the equipment that you need during the planning stages of your research project.

Methods of Data Collection

Besides determining how to measure things, careful thought needs to be given to how you record the data. It could be that you have to devise a score sheet or record sheet on which to write data. You may be intending to use a computer-based system to store the results directly. Is there enough space on the system? Do you need portable storage? What about backing up the data?

Sample

Your sample is the people that you plan to test in your research project. For most people, after actually deciding on a topic, this is one of the most difficult areas. The first thing to remember is that you cannot test everybody, as it would take too long. Therefore, you need to pick a group. This is called a sample. You will need to think about the types of people that you have access to and if they would be willing to take part in your project. If you are a member of a sports club or gym, you may find that the members are happy to volunteer. If you would like to research elite sports players, you will probably have to ensure that you can access secondary data, as you would be very unlikely to have access to them to carry out your own testing! You will also need to consider the group that you plan to test. On the whole, the individuals need to be very similar in order to attain more meaningful data; therefore, it is a good idea to select either males or females and ensure that they are of a similar age and, where appropriate, build, ability, and so on.

Reliability

The reliability of the tests you are planning to form should also be taken into account.

> ## Key term
>
> **Reliability:** if a test is repeated, it will give the same results.

If you recorded the same thing on two separate occasions, would you expect the value to be the same? Imagine you were coaching a cyclist, and to monitor his training and recovery you recorded his resting heart rate each morning. Assuming your cyclist was not overtraining or suffering from an illness, you would expect the resting heart rate to remain fairly constant over a number of weeks. If you measured similar values each morning, this would display good reliability. You would then be assured that your measuring technique was reliable. If the values did change, you could then be sure it was due to something other than your measuring – your athlete might be suffering from a cold, which may have elevated their resting heart rate.

Validity

The validity of the tests used also needs to be considered.

> ## Key term
>
> **Validity:** whether the test actually measures what it is supposed to measure.

Many fitness tests are available to measure different aspects of fitness. Therefore, you need to be sure that the test you are using does actually measure the component of fitness that you are interested in. For example, if you want to measure the flexibility of a person and choose the sit-and-reach test, you are actually only measuring the flexibility of their back and hamstrings. This may not be a true representation of their overall flexibility, as they may have very flexible shoulders and hips.

Ethical and Legal Issues

You will also need to take into account ethical and legal considerations. For example, you might be interested in how anabolic steroids can affect performance, but it would unethical to administer anabolic steroids to people as they are harmful to health. You will also need to consider if someone with specific qualification is needed to run any part of the test, such as a VO_2max test. Will the test be safe? What happens if there is an accident? Have you told the subjects what they have to do? Have they completed an informed consent form?

> ## Key term
>
> **Informed consent:** a form that clearly explains what a person needs to do, which they sign to agree that they have understood what is expected from them.

Fig 5.1 A person completing an informed consent form

Action Plan

A good research project requires a good action plan. The plan is crucial to set out clearly what is to be done and why it is necessary. By writing the plan, a lot of the problems that you may otherwise have encountered can be avoided. You should also devise a timetable for the implementation of the project. Include deadlines for:

- Researching information
- Carrying out testing
- Analysing results
- Writing up individual sections of the research.

99

Key learning point 1

● A research plan should include clear aims and objectives, scope, research design, reliability and validity of selected tests, sample, data collection methods, data analysis methods, ethical and legal considerations.

Student activity 5.1   5–8 hours   P2

Consider what subject area of sport and exercise sciences interests you – for example, exercise physiology, biomechanics, sport psychology – then start to think of a research project that you could carry out that is in line with your interests.

Produce a plan for a sport science- or exercise science-based research project. Your plan should include:

- Title

- Aims
- Objectives
- Scope of the project
- Research design
- Sample you plan to use
- Data collection methods
- Data analysis methods
- Appropriate ethical and legal considerations.

Q Quick quiz 1

1 Identify the null hypothesis for the following hypotheses:
   (a) Netball players have higher aerobic fitness compared to hockey players.
   (b) Football players are more flexible than rugby players.
   (c) Swimmers with larger feet can swim faster than swimmers with smaller feet.
   (d) Long-distance runners show more introverted traits than long-distance cyclists.
2 Describe what reliability means.
3 Describe what validity means.
4 Why do you think samples usually consist of either males or females?
5 What is a double-blind research design?
6 What is a placebo and why is it used?
7 Carry out research to find out what the placebo effect is.

5.3 Conducting a Research Project

Resources

Once the topic of research has been decided, the next consideration is obtaining information about the topic. The first part of any research project will consist of reporting what is already known about the subject area. This will form the literature review. The evidence gathered will be from either a primary or a secondary source. Primary data or information is that which is reported directly by the author who measured or observed it. Secondary data is reported from the original primary source by another author. If you include information from a secondary source, you are trusting that the information has been recorded and analysed correctly.

Libraries

A lot of information for your project will be obtained using some form of library information system. All libraries have a method of cataloguing their information, and contain a large and varied amount of different resources, including books, e-books, journals, e-journals, newspapers, videos and CD-ROMs. All this information needs to be made available to anybody who requires it, hence the use of library catalogue or searching systems.

The system will be a database of all records of information (books, journals, newspapers), using a standard format of recording the information. The most common method of cataloguing information is by the authors who wrote it. If you know the name of an author, you can enter their name into the system and it will report all the books by that author. Most systems will have more than one way of searching. As well as being listed by author, books will be listed by title. Keyword searches are another method of looking for information (e.g. injuries). To widen the search still further, the system may have a subject search, which will include all works in a subject area (e.g. sports therapy).

Textbooks are a reliable source of information, which means that you can be certain that the information they contain is accurate. Textbooks have usually been written by subject specialists and are then reviewed by experts, to ensure the work is accurate. If the textbook is endorsed by the examining board, it means that the content of the book is in line with the specifications of the course.

There is a range of textbooks available for the specific course that you are on, and they may well be in your library for you to look through. There are also more specific textbooks available that concentrate purely on that particular topic – for example, if you are studying an anatomy unit, you may wish to use textbooks that are written purely about anatomy.

More and more people are using electronic sources of information. Many libraries subscribe to e-books and e-journals, so the material can be read on the computer screen. There are also searchable databases that have been developed in certain subject areas. SPORTSDiscus is one example; it is a database of information from across the globe in the area of sport and exercise science. It can be accessed via the internet and a subscription is required.

The Internet

Undoubtedly, you will also want to use the internet to obtain information. The internet will have two uses. First, it can be used as a way to access information contained within libraries. It can also be used to access general information contained on the millions of web pages on the internet.

Information presented on the internet should be treated with some caution. Books, for example, are checked to make sure the information in them is correct, but this is not the case with the internet. Information can be posted on a website by anybody. It does not have to be reviewed or checked in any way. Having said that, the internet does contain some very useful websites. A good use of the internet, and one that saves a lot of time, is obtaining information that would normally have to be sent by post. You might want to obtain some information from the American College of Sport Medicine, which you can find on its website. You might be after the medal table from the Beijing Olympics, or maybe the results from football league games.

Journals

Journals are written by subject specialists, reviewed by subject experts and come out at regular intervals throughout the year. As they are published so frequently, the information they contain is up to date and will cover detail of current facts and trends relating to the subject area. Most libraries will stock a range of relevant journals and you can also access some journals via the internet (however, some charge a subscription cost in order for you to access the journal – check to see if your centre has a subscription to the journal you are interested in). If you are hoping to achieve distinction grades, journals are a very good source of information to help you attain this level of understanding.

Taking Notes

In order to help ensure that you remember all the information you are researching, it is a good idea to take notes. For some people, the very act of writing something down will help them to remember that information. Note-taking also means that you do not have to reread the whole unit or section of the journal if you have forgotten it; all you will need to do is read your notes.

Remember to keep to the topic in question; keep the task or question set close by, so that you can keep checking that you are sticking to the task at hand and not researching work that is irrelevant. For example, if the task asks you to explore the aerobic energy system, only research this topic; you will not get extra marks for writing about the anaerobic energy system because the question has not asked for this information.

1 Skim through the information to check that it is suitable for your work.
2 Make a note of the details of the book or article that you are using.
3 Actively read the work – have a pen in your hand and start to make notes.
4 Write down any relevant quotes that think you may use in your work.
5 Summarise information in your own words.

Using Quotes

Once you have read through a range of resources, you should try to put this information into your own words. However, in order to help justify what you say, it is a good idea to include quotes in your work.

A quote is a sentence or two taken from one of your research sources that is written word for word. In order to show that you are quoting the material, you must place the quote in speech marks and then state the name of the author(s) of the source, and the year in which it was published, in brackets after the quote. For example:

'Journals are written by subject specialists, reviewed by subject experts and come out at regular intervals throughout the year' (Stafford-Brown and Rea, 2010).

This is good practice and should be encouraged.

Quotes are used to help to substantiate work that you have written. For example:

People are taking much less exercise these days, more people drive to work or school and spend more time pursuing sedentary leisure activities. 'The average adult watches over 26 hours of television each week' (Stafford-Brown and Rea, 2010).

If you have written a summary of information that has come from more than one textbook, you can write the summary in your own words, with no speech marks, and quote the authors at the end of the paragraph. For example:

Aerobic fitness training has been shown to have many cardiovascular benefits. Resting heart rate decreases, stroke volume increases, hypertrophy of the left ventricle occurs, new capillaries form (capillarisation) and there is an increase in haemo-globin content of the blood due to an increase in the number of red blood cells (Stafford-Brown *et al.*, 2010; Wesson *et al.*, 2006).

When there are more than two authors, it is possible to write the name of the lead author (the first one printed on the book) and then write '*et al.*' which literally means 'and the rest'. However, when you come to write your bibliography or reference page, you must list the names of every author involved in writing the book you have used.

Your quote should not really be any longer than about two sentences. It is not good practice to quote large chunks of text, as this just shows that you are able to copy work, but does not demonstrate your understanding of that work.

Referencing your Work

Any sources that you have used quotes from or have used to help you to research your assessment activity should be included in a reference section or bibliography, located at the end of your work. The types of source you have used will determine the way in which each source is referenced.

Book

Author (year) *Book Title* (edition – if not the 1st). Publisher. Pages used.

For example, Stafford-Brown, J. and Rea, S. (2007) *BTEC National in Sport*, Hodder Arnold, pp. 116–20.

Journal

Author (year) Article title. *Journal*, volume, issue no., pages used.

For example, Swaine, I.L (1997) Cardiopulmonary response to exercise in swimmer using a swim bench and a leg-kicking ergometer. *International Journal of Sports Medicine*, 18, 359–62.

Website

Author (year (look for the © at the bottom of the page) *Web page title*. Full web page address (date you accessed the page).

For example, McKenzie, B. (2002) Cardiovascular tests. www.brianmac.demon.co.uk/cvtesting.htm (accessed 22 February 2010).

Newspaper

Author (year) Article title. *Newspaper,* pages used.

For example, Layer, G. (2004) Wide of mark on participation. *Times Higher Education Supplement,* p.76.

How to Avoid Plagiarism

Plagiarism is a term given to a situation where a person has copied work from another person or another source and passed it off as their own. This is a form of cheating, and any person found to have plagiarised work in their assignments will not pass that assignment and will usually face further questioning from their tutor or quality manager. Examples of plagiarism include copying work from another student, copying work from a textbook and copying text or diagrams from the internet. Any other information you would like to use should be put into your own words or put into a quote. If you would like to copy diagrams from the internet, you must acknowledge that the work is not your own and give details of the website you have used next to the diagram.

Equipment

While you are collecting research information from the library and the internet, you also need to be thinking about actually collecting some data or doing some testing. Do you need to book a room or a gym? Is it available at the time you wish to use it? Do you need to book a video camera and can you use it? When you pick it up, will the battery be charged? Will it have a spare? Why not have a dry run through everything first, just to check it all works. If you encounter any problems, write them down, then go away and think about what you need to change.

	Yes	No

1. Do you have a bone or joint problem which could be made worse by exercise?
2. Has your doctor ever said that you have a heart condition?
3. Do you experience chest pains on physical exertion?
4. Do you experience light-headedness or dizziness on exertion?
5. Do you experience shortness of breath on light exertion?
6. Has your doctor ever said that you have a raised cholesterol level?
7. Are you currently taking any prescription medication?
8. Is there a history of coronary heart disease in your family?
9. Do you smoke? If so, how many?
10. Do you drink more than 21 units for a male, 14 units for a female?
11. Do you have diabetes?
12. Do you take physical activity fewer than three times a week?
13. Are you pregnant?
14. Are you asthmatic?
15. Do you know of any other reason why you should not exercise?

If you have answered yes to any questions please give more details

_____

_____

If you have answered yes to one or more questions, you will have to consult with your doctor before taking part in a programme of physical exercise.

If you have answered no to all questions, you are ready to start a suitable exercise programme.

I have read, understood and answered all questions honestly, and confirm that I am willing to engage in a programme of exercise that has been prescribed to me.

Name   Signature

Trainer name   Trainer signature

Date

Figure 5.2 Example of a Physical Activity Readiness Questionnaire (PAR-Q)

Ethical and Legal Issues

It is essential that you keep confidential any results and information from your project. That means you should not mention people's names in your study. You could use letters or numbers to differentrate people if need be. This is in line with the Data Protection Act 1984. In sport and exercise research, special consideration is needed because the research involves humans as subjects.

Any experiments that you design need to be ethical. For example, asking people to undertake training or a diet that could have negative effects is unethical. A great deal of thought therefore needs to go into designing the project. Even when you are happy that the research is ethical, the health and safety of your subjects is vital. The American College of Sport Medicine suggested that researchers should adhere to the Declaration of Helsinki, which has a code of practice for measurements in humans.

If your research involves working in a school, you may need to have a CRB check done to ensure that you have not committed any crimes that would prevent you from working with children.

If the testing you are planning to perform requires the participants to take part in a physical test, you should make sure that they all complete a health-screening questionnaire to ensure that they are fit and able to take part in your tests. A PAR-Q (Physical Activity Readiness Questionnaire) is a commonly used questionnaire that will help you determine if the participants you have selected are suitable to participate. An example is shown in Figure 5.2.

There is a range of questionnaires available, but they all ask similar questions.

Informed Consent Form

Your participants should also complete an informed consent form prior to participation in any tests.

An informed consent form lets a subject know what to expect during the exercise test, and the associated risks involved. It also stresses that any participation in the tests is voluntary and that the subject has the choice to stop at any point. An example of an informed consent form is shown in Figure 5.3.

Data Collection Methods

Most projects will involve recruiting a group of people to test. The group you choose is called the sample. If you were examining the amount of exercise under-taken by college students, it would not be practical

---

1. Explanation of the test(s)
You will perform a test that will vary in its demands on your body. Your progress will be observed during the test and stopped if you show signs of undue fatigue. You may stop the test at any time if you feel unduly uncomfortable.

2. Risks of testing
During exercise certain changes can occur, such as the rising of blood pressure, fainting and raised heart rate, and in rare cases heart attacks or even death. Every effort is made through screening to minimise the risk of these occurring during testing. Emergency equipment and relevantly trained personnel are available to deal with any extreme situation which occurs.

3. Responsibility of the participant
You must disclose all information in your possession regarding the state of your health or previous experiences of exercise, as this will affect the safety of the tests. If you experience any discomfort or unusual sensations it is your responsibility to inform your trainer.

4. Freedom of consent
Your participation in this test is voluntary and you are free to deny consent or stop the test at any point.

I have read this form and understand what is expected of me and the tests I will perform. I give my consent to participate.

Subject signature

Print name

Date

Tester's signature

Print name

Date

Fig 5.3 Example of an informed consent form

Fig 5.4 A person undergoing a VO₂max test

to question all students, so you would just question a sample. The sample you use should not be biased in any way. They would not all be the same age, or all from one course, unless you specifically state '18-year-old college students'. Your sample will be made up of volunteers or those who are available at the time, such as your classmates. You should try to avoid any bias in your research, as this limits any conclusions that you make.

Key term

Bias: influence in an unfair way.

You may be a keen netball player and want to prove that netball players have higher VO₂max compared to hockey players.

Your choice of subjects could bias your results in favour of this being proved correct. For example, you might choose netball players who play at a higher level than the hockey players. Or you might choose netball players who play in positions that require high levels of aerobic fitness, such as the centre and the wings, and then choose hockey players who play in positions that require low levels of aerobic fitness, such as the goalkeeper. This would bias your sample and probably prove your theory to be correct.

You may wish to conduct your test in a realistic environment. This is called a field-based test. If you use specialist facilities, this is termed a laboratory test. The advantages of doing laboratory tests are that they are more controlled, as you do not have to worry about external factors like the weather. But remember, sport is not played in a lab, so field tests, although difficult, may give you a truer picture of what is actually happening.

Accuracy and Precision

If you are using specialist equipment, it is essential that you can use it correctly. Your major consideration will be how true are the data that you collect. Data should be accurate and precise, and for this to be the case, a certain level of knowledge and skill on the part of the tester will be required. The data can be only as precise as the measuring system. If a metre rule has only centimetre increments, you will be able to record only to the nearest centimetre (i.e. 1.75 m, not 1.755 m). The accuracy of the data relates to how close your measurement is to what you actually intend to measure. Checking that equipment is calibrated correctly will help ensure accuracy.

An example of calibrating a piece of equipment would be to pass a sample of a known percentage of oxygen through a gas analyser and check that it is giving the correct reading. If it is not, the piece of equipment should be adjusted until it is producing an accurate reading. Some pieces of equipment should be calibrated prior to every use, such as an online gas analyser, but other equipment, like weighing scales, rarely needs calibration.

Questionnaires

Not all research involves collecting and analysing numbers. Some research requires information on a person's behaviour or attitude towards something. This is common in qualitative research. Questionnaires, interviews and observations are used to gather evidence, and, although the data or information is in a different format to quantitative research, the question of truthfulness or exactness is just as important. Is the information you obtain valid? If you set out to measure anxiety levels and do so using a questionnaire, are the answers you receive accurate? Does your questionnaire actually measure anxiety? Do people tell the truth? All these issues need to be addressed.

What about reliability? If you repeated your questionnaire in similar situations, would you obtain similar results?

The design of the questionnaire, the type of questions and the way they are worded can all affect the validity and reliability of your results. This will also be the case if you decide to conduct individual interviews rather than administer questionnaires.

Recording Results

A clear data sheet can save both time and confusion when recording results. Imagine you have designed a questionnaire to investigate the amount of sport and exercise undertaken by college students. Once all the completed questionnaires have been returned, you need to record all the results in a clear and effective format. Putting them in one table will allow you to see all the results together and will be better for subsequent analysis.

There are many ways of recording data. For example, you could record the most common answer. This is called frequency analysis: looking at how often something occurs. You could even list things as the most frequent, the second most frequent, the third most frequent, and so on. This is called putting things in rank order. It is important to do this sort of analysis with your data so that you can start to make sense of it.

You may have used a questionnaire asking a series of questions and then coded the answers. For example, the possible answers may be: Strongly agree, Agree, Disagree, Strongly disagree. By giving these answers numbers from 1 to 4, you can more easily carry out data analysis (e.g. what is the average reply?).

You could convert your answers to percentages and work out what percentage agrees or what percentage answered 'yes' to a question. If you have a long list of answers or a lot of possible answers, you can examine the range of responses. If you were measuring heart rates of a group during a fitness test, you could use all these methods. Who has the highest heart rate (rank order), how many had heart rates between 131 and 140 beats per minute (b.p.m.) compared with 141 and 150 b.p.m., or what was the average, or what percentage were below a certain figure (frequency analysis)? Even what the difference was between the highest and the lowest (range). The list of options is almost endless.

Use of Media

Numbers are fairly easy to record, as are written responses. Verbal replies require a little bit more thought. You could just write down what you hear when somebody is speaking. This method is called transcribing. It is a lot more convenient and a lot more accurate to take an audio recording or a video recording. These two methods allow you to play the recording over and over again, so you can ensure that you get an accurate account of what was said. Video will even lend itself to observation of the individual, as well as hearing what they say. This may give you more detailed information than the audio recording alone.

Whichever method of data collection you use, at some point the information will be converted into an electronic format, such as a spreadsheet, a database, or an audio or video file. This needs to be kept safe and it is wise to keep a duplicate copy.

Preliminary Analysis

When collecting data, it is good to look over it to check that it looks as it should. Do you notice any discrepancies? Are the responses to your questionnaires as expected? If all the answers are 'No' or 'Disagree', perhaps you need to redesign your questionnaire. If you are measuring heart rate and the results are not what you might reasonably have expected, are you sure the heart rate monitors are recording correctly? A little bit of time spent looking at the results early on could save you time in the long run. You may even start to get a pattern of how the results are going, enabling you to draw some initial conclusions.

Storing Information

When conducting a research project you should always keep your original data. These are the raw data.

Key term

Raw data: the original data collected (e.g. questionnaires, tally charts).

Raw data can come in many forms – heart rate readings, heights, weights, video footage, questionnaires, data sheets and notes of an interview. If you keep these data, you can then go back at any time and refer to them to clear up any questions you may have. As with any data, it is worth copying the information in case the originals are lost or damaged. This is especially the case with any electronic data. Files can become wiped, corrupt or infected, computers can crash and data can be lost, so back-ups are essential. Remember to use different types of storage. Electronically, data can be saved on your hard drive, the school or college hard drive, your flash drive, CDs, DVDs and even on the internet.

Key learning points 2

● When carrying out a research project, it is important to ensure that you can use the required equipment safely and appropriately.
● If your subjects need to take part in any physical tests, you should ensure that they have completed an informed consent form and a PAR-Q.
● Ensure you have appropriate documentation to record the data collected.
● All data collected from your testing should be kept confidential and stored securely.

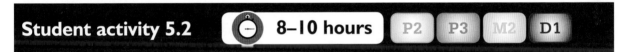

Student activity 5.2 ⏱ 8–10 hours P2 P3 M2 D1

Task 1

Collect and record data from the research project that you have conducted.

Task 2

Examine the data that you have collected from your

research project, then write a report that correctly analyses the data collected. In your report, make sure that you describe and explain the techniques used in your analysis process.

Q Quick quiz 2

Select the appropriate term from the list below to match each of the following definitions:

- Raw
- Journals
- Plagiarism
- Calibration
- Bias
- Frequency analysis
- Quote
- Informed consent form
- Primary
- Secondary.

1 To influence in an unfair way.

2 The process of checking and adjusting equipment to ensure it gives accurate readings.

3 A sentence or two taken from a research source that is written out word for word.

4 The original data collected during the research.

5   When a person copies someone else's work and passes it off as their own.

6   Written by subject specialists, reviewed by subject experts and published at regular intervals throughout the year.

7   When using a questionnaire, this process involves recording the most common answer.

8   Subjects should complete one of these before taking part in your research tests.

9   This type of data or information is reported directly by the author who measured or observed it.

10 This type of data is reported from the original source by another author.

5.4 Producing a Sport Science- or Exercise Science-based Research Project

Scientific Structure of the Research Report

The project will be reported in writing. The general structure of a written project is given below. Obviously on the front will be the title page, followed by:

● Preliminary pages
  – Abstract
  – General contents
  – Contents page for figures and tables
  – Contents page for appendices
  – Acknowledgements
● Introduction
● Literature review
● Method
● Results
● Discussion
● Conclusion
● References
● Appendix.

Title Page

This should have on it the title of the study, the person who wrote it and the year. You may wish to include the name of your college.

Abstract

This is a summary of all sections of the report. It is a review of the entire project. The abstract must be clearly separated from the main body of the report. Normally in the region of 250 words, it will contain information on the aim, research plan, outcomes and overall conclusions. This summary of the research appears as the first page of the report, but is usually written last, since you cannot summarise until the end.

Contents Page

This will list the units or the sections of the report, together with the number of the page on which each begins. There should be separate contents sections for figures and tables and appendices.

Acknowledgements

This is the part of the project where you can write something personal and thank those people who may have helped you during the project. It could include thanks to your supervisor for support, and there might be others who you would like to mention.

Introduction

The purpose of the **introduction** is to give an outline of the research area. It should address the question of why you are doing the project. The introduction sets the tone of the project. What is the project all about? How did you become interested in it? It should make the objective of the project clear. It should be interesting enough to make the person reading want to find out more. The end of the introduction should be the aim of the research.

Literature Review

This is an in-depth analysis of the research. It will be a detailed look at all areas within the project. Key terms need to be defined. You should explain why your research is needed and how athletes, coaches and physical educators will benefit. Try to evaluate what is already known about your research topic. You can use many sources of information for your literature review. Conclude the review with a statement of what it is you are going to test.

Method

This should be relatively simple to write, as it explains what you did. It can be divided into subsections. In the first part, you should explain about the subjects – how many, what groups, give details on the average age, what sports they play or their current fitness level. This will give a good indication of the subjects that you have in your project. Next you should include your research design – how you collected your information. After the research design, provide a list of the equipment you needed to use. The final part of the method is to report the protocol and procedures of the tests you undertook. Provide enough information so that anybody reading it could reproduce exactly what you did.

Results

This section contains the actual data collected by you. They should be presented in as clear a format as possible and make it easy to read what you found. You do not need to include lists of numbers or piles of questionnaires unless you are specifically asked for this. Results can be summarised using descriptive statistics. Patterns that you see in the data need to be described (e.g. heart rate increases with time). Tables and graphs are the best way of presenting lots of data, but you need to write about what is in the table or graph. What was the average heart rate? What did heart rate go up to? What time did heart rate start to decrease? These are the sorts of things you need to be looking for. Besides describing results, statistics are used to analyse results to allow conclusions to be made. These are called inferential statistics. They allow you to make accurate statements about your results. Consider an investigation to see if a given training programme lowered the resting heart rate of a group of individuals. Your results might show that the average resting heart rate of the training group is 58 b.p.m., while that of a control group (a group of subjects who did no training) is 61 b.p.m. There is a difference of 3 b.p.m., but is this meaningful or is the difference just due to chance? A statistical difference test (e.g. t-test) would be able to establish if the difference in the values is significant – large enough to mean something. Where calculations are performed in analysing data, a sample calculation is helpful to explain the analysis. This can be included in the main text or in an appendix.

Discussion

This is the most central part of your research, as it is your chance to explain what has happened and why. This section should include an analysis of the results. Do not merely repeat the results that you have just described. Try to give a summary of what you found. Always refer back to the aim of your project and to what you said in the literature review. Did your idea of what was going to happen come true, and if not, why not? Also explain what went wrong and why. What could you have done better, or were there things beyond your control? Explain how the project could be improved. After this, discuss the implications of your findings. Ask yourself of what

use is the information you have found. Finally, give suggestions for future research. This is an important part of research, to present ideas about what needs doing next.

Conclusion

This should be statements of fact. What are your main findings? These should relate back to the aim of your research. The conclusion does not need to be too long or detailed. Just list the findings and do not start new arguments or ideas here.

References

This section will list the references used in the report. In the text, you will have quotes or citations referring to other people's work, and then at the end of the report you will have a detailed list. The Harvard system of referencing is commonly used in academic work. You need to report the reference in the text itself by giving the author of the work and the year of publication. The full title of the work is given in the references section. If work is transferred into your own words – paraphrasing – quotation marks are not needed. If a quote is included in the text, you should use single quotation marks.

In your report, the reference would appear like this: 'Recovery for athletes is essential (Child, 2004)'. If you are referencing more than one book, you can name them all, in order of date of publication: 'The stresses imposed by training can be harmful (Child, 1999; Tyzack, 2002; Watt, 2003)'. If more than one author was involved in the work, you would reference them all: '(Ball, Brees, Chance and Stokes, 1989)'. You do not need to consistently list all authors. Once you have listed them once, you can from then on refer to the first author, followed by *et al.* This is only the case if there are more than two authors – for example, 'Ball *et al.* (1989) have shown that...' You may come across two authors with the same surname. If this is the case, use initials to distinguish between them: 'A report (Barton, R., 2006) has indicated...' If you need to reference more than one article by the same author in the same year, add letters to the different references: 'Thomas (2000a, 2000b) showed that...'

Sometimes it may be necessary to refer to letters, emails or conversations. These are called personal communications. They would be referenced as follows: 'In a telephone conversation on 10 August 2005, Mr J.A. Gilbert pointed out that...', or 'Mr D. Goodchild's letter dated 1 May 1998 claimed that...'

You may need to refer to work with no author's name: 'A recent report by the American College of Sports Medicine (2001) states...', or 'the *Teesside Times* (15 July 2007, p. 4) reported that...'

There are guidelines for entries in the list of

references, depending on what you are referring to. Books are referenced as follows:

Thomas, J.R. and Nelson, J.K. (2005) *Research Methods in Physical Activity*, 5th edn, Human Kinetics.

Journals and periodicals are referenced as follows:

Morris, T. (2000) Psychological characteristics and talent identification in soccer. *Journal of Sports Sciences*, 18, 715–26.

Online (electronic) material is a little different, as it has not been published in the traditional way. Sometimes the date it was posted on the internet is given. Whether this is the case or not, the date you accessed the material should be stated. Therefore, an online reference would appear as follows:

Sport England (2006) Equity and inclusion. www. sportengland.org/index/about_sport_england/ equality_standard_for_sport.htm (accessed 22 February 2010).

Appendix

After the reference section comes the **appendix**. Here you can include any information that does not readily fit into the rest of your report. This is where you would put your raw data (which would otherwise just fill up the results section) and data collection sheets. You can refer to any part of the appendix in the main body of the report. Multiple appendices should be labelled as Appendix A, B, C, and so on. If you refer to an appendix in your report, you could do it like this: 'Appendix A shows that…', or 'Crowd attendances are on the increase (see Appendix A)'.

Drawing Conclusions

The final part of a research project is to draw the whole process together. When discussing the results, you should attempt to cover three main areas. Initially, in conjunction with the statistical analysis, evaluate the results. What happens to the values you are measuring? Do they go up, down, stay the same or fluctuate? Are there any differences, similarities or relationships? Are your values in line with what you would expect based on previous evidence? After the analysis, be critical of your results. Are your results valid? Do they display reliability and objectivity? What errors did your investigation contain and how did this affect your results? What may limit any conclusions you aim to make? Finally, what are the implications of your results? What have you found out and what does it mean?

To recap, be analytical, be critical and draw clear conclusions.

Internal Coherence

A good report will follow the format laid out above. In addition to being in the right format, it should read well. The sections should link together well, so if you have talked about something in your review of literature, you should refer to it in your discussion. Always keep in mind the aim of your project and constantly refer back to it. Discuss what you find in relation to what you set out to do. Make sure there is a direct link from the aim to the conclusion. If you set out to investigate whether children from one school were fitter than those from another, were they? If they were not, say so. Remember you will not always be able to prove what you had hoped to prove.

Presentation of the Report

When writing up the project, it is important that it looks good and reads well. For it to look good, you need to be familiar with word-processing software and spreadsheets. Using IT to record, report and present the results will go a long way to making it look professional. For it to read well, you need to concentrate on sentence structure, grammar, the order in which you write things and, most importantly, you need to think about the reader.

Oral Presentation

Normally on completion of their research, people are asked to give a short presentation. Your presentation might include video footage, handouts or a computer slide show. It is not possible in a short presentation to cover the whole project, so pick out the main parts. Start by introducing your area of research and explain why you chose it. State the main literature relating to your project. After this, explain the method and list the main results. Graphs and tables are helpful at this point. The most important part of the presentation (and the bit that will show you understand the research) is where you discuss the findings. Why did certain things happen, or not happen? What went right and what went wrong? What are the implications of the study? Finish the presentation with your conclusions and remember to relate these back to your original aims.

When giving a presentation from a computer, try not to include too much information on any one slide. Use the slides to talk around the topic rather than just reading them out. Try to include some pictures or diagrams that people will find interesting. Maintain eye contact. Look confident – it is your research and you know what you did.

Key learning points 3

A research project should consist of the following sections:
- Preliminary pages
  - Abstract
  - General contents
  - Contents page for figures and tables
  - Contents page for appendices
  - Acknowledgements
- Introduction
- Literature review
- Method
- Results
- Discussion
- Conclusion
- References
- Appendix.

5.5 Reviewing a Sport Science- or Exercise Science-based Project

P5 **M3** **D2**

The evaluation of the project is useful to you as a learning experience and to anyone that might listen to, read or hear what you have done. You could evaluate your project by performing a SWOT analysis:

- **Strengths**: these will be things you have learned from the project. They could be personal things – how to collect data, how to present information – or, more generally, things like the results of your study.
- **Weaknesses**: these will be your limitations or the limitations of your research. You may have been limited in the people you could test or you may not have been able to measure what you first set out to measure. Being clear in your limitations shows you have a good understanding of your research, so do not think this a negative thing.
- **Opportunities**: if you were to do the study all over again, what would you do? What could somebody else do if they were to follow up your study? How could they improve on what you did?
- **Threats**: are there any things that question the validity of your information? Are you sure the conclusions you arrived at are true? Is the information all your own?

Be specific and give examples. If you think your data presentation was one of your strong points, where is the evidence? Include an example of one of your graphs.

Future Recommendations

This is the reflective part of the research. Use the information from the SWOT analysis. What would you change? What did not work as expected? If you could go back several months, what would you do differently? Even more importantly, what advice can you give to somebody who wants to do research in the same area? What things could they investigate that would add to what you have found? You can always improve on things, so do not be afraid to say what went wrong in your own study, as it shows you have an understanding of the research that you undertook.

Key learning points 4

- The key components in a research project include:
  - Title page
  - Abstract
  - General contents page
  - Contents page for tables and figures
  - Contents page for appendices
  - Acknowledgements
  - Introduction
  - Literature review
  - Method
  - Results
  - Discussion
  - Conclusion
  - References.
- Once the project is complete, it is a good idea to review the project and identify strengths, areas for improvement and provide recommendations for future research.

Student activity 5.3   🕐 12–15 hours   P4   P5   M3   D2

Task 1

Write up your research project using the following headings:

- Title page
- Abstract
- General contents page
- Contents page for tables and figures
- Contents page for appendices
- Acknowledgements
- Introduction
- Literature review
- Method
- Results
- Discussion
- Conclusion
- References.

Task 2

Write a review of your research project which describes and explains strengths and areas for improvement. Include in your review future recommendations for future research, giving justification for each one that you have included.

Ⓠ Quick quiz 3

Write a brief description of what should be included in each of the following sections in a research project:

1 Title page
2 Abstract
3 General contents page
4 Contents page for tables and figures
5 Contents page for appendices
6 Acknowledgements
7 Introduction
8 Literature review
9 Method
10 Results
11 Discussion
12 Conclusion.

Further reading

Thomas, J.R. and Nelson, J.K. (2005) *Research Methods in Physical Activity* (5th edn), Human Kinetics.

Useful websites

www.bases.org.uk

Membership website for sports professionals, providing details of job vacancies, careers advice, forums for coaching and sports science-related topics; limited access to non-members

www.pponline.co.uk/encyc/sports-performance-analysis-coaching-and-training-39

Online article detailing how sports analysis can help coaching and training

6: Sports Biomechanics in Action

6.1 Introduction

Biomechanics is concerned with internal and external forces acting on the human body, and on implements used during sport (bats, balls, etc.), and the effects produced by these forces. Biomechanics is used to analyse sports technique, which allows athletes or coaches to improve performance or avoid injury. The coaching process involves observing performance, evaluating it in comparison to what should be done and then instructing the performer as to how they can improve. The observation process is more than merely looking at a performer; this unit will focus on different methods of analysing performance.

By the end of this unit you should:

- be able to perform a notational analysis for sport
- know how to compare a numerical model to sporting performance
- know how to compare a technical model to sporting performance
- be able to provide feedback on performance to an athlete or team.

Assessment and grading criteria		
To achieve a PASS grade the evidence must show that the learner is able to:	**To achieve a MERIT grade the evidence must show that, in addition to the pass criteria, the learner is able to:**	**To achieve a DISTINCTION grade the evidence must show that, in addition to the pass and merit criteria, the learner is able to:**
P1 describe five relevant performance criteria for an individual or team-based sport		
P2 perform two notational analyses on a chosen sport, with some support	**M1** compare the two notational analyses, using statistics, data representation and literature to explain the strengths and areas for improvement	
P3 produce a numerical model, using three numerical components, and compare it to a sporting performance, with some support		
P4 produce a technical model, using four technical components, and compare it to a sports performance, with some support	**M2** explain and justify the methodology for either the numerical or technical models	**D1** evaluate findings for either the notational analyses, numerical or technical models, commenting on their influence on performance within the chosen sport
P5 provide feedback on performance, to an athlete, or team, using information gathered from one of the analyses performed, prescribing future action, with support.	**M3** provide detailed feedback and prescribe future action for the athlete or team from either the notational analyses, numerical or technical models.	**D2** justify the prescribed future actions for either the notational analyses, numerical or technical models.

6.2 Notational Analysis for Sport

P1   P2   M1

As the name 'notational analysis' suggests, you note

Key terms

Notational analysis: a simple method of recording what happens during a sporting contest.

Performance criteria: something that you measure to record performance.

down what happens while observing the performers. This single recognised process makes it easier to allow for comparison between observers, players, teams and games.

The things that you decide to measure are called performance criteria. These can be based on what an individual player does or on what the team does – or you can include both. For example, in volleyball you could record the number of times a player serves in court (equally you could record this for the whole team); or you could record the number of times a team returns the ball after service. If you require more detail, you could record the exact outcome of the serve – that is, does the ball hit the net (and not go over), does the ball land out of court, is the ball returned or does it land in the opponent's part of the court (an ace)? This is only one part of a volleyball match, so you could also record passes (volley), hits (smash) and blocks. You would then start to gather a lot of detail on a player's or a team's performance.

Data Representation

Different things can be measured in different sports. In football, you could measure passes, shots, fouls, interceptions, headers, tackles, dribbling and saves. You could even measure time spent walking, jogging, running and sprinting. In basketball, you might measure passes, shots (both 2-point and 3-point), free throws, fouls, assists, rebounds and dribbles. In tennis, you could record serves, second serves, and backhand and forehand shots. In cricket, you might consider (for a batsman) scoring shots, non-scoring shots and played and missed. The number of sports and the criteria you could measure are almost endless and will depend on the detail you wish to obtain.

As we saw in the football example, not only can you measure skill, but you can also measure effort. You can examine the amount of time a player is walking, running, sprinting, jumping, and so on. The best way to gather any of this information is in the form of a tally chart or checklist (see Table 6.1). This can then be stored easily on a database or in a spreadsheet. Remember, you need to think about what you are going to record.

Take football as an example. It is no good just counting the number of passes each player makes. It would be better to divide up these criteria further. You could have successful short passes (less than 5 m), unsuccessful short passes, successful long passes (over 5 m) and unsuccessful long passes. Similarly with headers, just recoding the number gives little information. Why not include defensive headers and attacking headers? Then, under the attacking headers, you could have on-target and off-target.

Fig 6.1 A football manager making notes

Team: Middlesbrough Mavericks Opponents: Stourport Swifts Date: 1 May 2006
Set No: 1
1112

Player	Serve		Reception		Volley or dig		Smash		Block		Time on court
	+	−	+	−	+	−	+	−	+	−	Minutes
1	IIII	I			IIIIIIIIIII	IIIII					22
2	I	II	I		III	I	III	I	I	IIII	22
3	III		I		IIIIIIII	III					22
4	II			II	IIII	II	IIII	II	II	III	14
5	I	I	IIIII	I	IIIII		IIII	III	I	II	22
6	II	I	IIII	I	IIIII	III	III	I	II	IIIII	22
7											
8	II	I			IIII	II	I		I	II	8
9											
10											

Table 6.1 Example of a data representation table

Data Analysis

Recording the information should be fairly straightforward. If you have completed an activity such as that outlined for football above, you will have realised that the two biggest problems you will encounter are the time it takes (a game of football could last for two hours, including breaks) and how much you have to concentrate. For this reason, you may wish to look at only part of the game. This is common when doing notational analysis. Having obtained the data, the difficult job for a coach is understanding what is going on and making the necessary changes. When you have a detailed list of what has happened during the game, you need to condense this into a more manageable format. The best way to do this is to look at totals, percentages and averages. Total numbers – for example, the number of shots, number of passes or number of serves – give you an indication of player involvement. You would expect your midfield player in football to have more passes (and more successful passes) than your forward. However, you may want your forwards to have had more shots on goal. Remember, the analysis you perform is only as good as the data you collect from the game.

Statistics

> **Key term**
>
> **Statistics:** the process of describing and analysing data.

The number of passes a player makes may tell you how involved they were, but if you have a number of successful and unsuccessful passes, you could work out pass completion percentages. Take the following example from a football match:

Player A makes 30 passes during a game and 15 are successful, while player B makes ten passes and eight are successful. What can you work out from this information?

Player A makes more passes, but only has a 50 per cent success rate. Player B makes fewer passes, but with 80 per cent success. Does this mean player A works harder but that player B is more skilful? You would need to check other statistics to confirm this. It should at least give you some ideas as to what you should be working on in training.

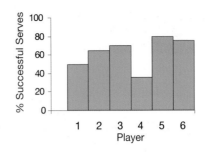

Fig 6.3 Sample bar chart

Fig 6.2 Football players passing the ball

Graphical Representation

The reason you are collecting all this information is to try to improve a player's or a team's performance. You will need to explain to the team or player what they are doing right or wrong. This can be more easily done using graphs than tables of numbers (a picture paints a thousand words).

Imagine, as a volleyball coach, that you have been working on the serve in training. From your next match you could record service information. You may have successful serves for each player, which could be put into a graph and displayed in training. You could do this using a simple bar chart.

Alternatively, you may have a football coach who is trying to get their team to pass the ball more. You could record the number of passes for the outfield players and display this information in a pie chart. The player who has the greatest slice of the pie is the one who has passed the most. You could look at this over a series of games. You could then look at the average number of passes by the team in one game compared to another. You will also need to think about which type of average you use (see Unit 4: Research Methods for Sport and Exercise Sciences). Let's say you want to look at the average number of passes per game and also the most common type of pass (e.g. less than 5 m back or square, less than 5 m forward, more than 5 m). For the average number, you would take the mean (total passes divided by number of players). However, for the most common, you would look at the mode (the one that occurs the most).

Key learning points 1

- Notational analysis – a method of recording the performance of individuals and teams.
- Performance criteria – the things that you measure (e.g. passes, catches).
- Data analysis – what you do with the data you have collected (e.g. calculate averages or percentages).

Student activity 6.1

🕐 **60 minutes**   P1   P2   M1

Task 1

Using the following table, describe five relevant performance criteria of a sport of your choice (team or individual).

Performance criteria	Description
1.	
2.	
3.	
4.	
5.	

Task 2

Use the following template to conduct two notational analyses on a sport of your choice.

Player	PC 1 (+ve)	PC1 (−ve)	PC 2 (+ve)	PC2 (−ve)	PC 3 (+ve)	PC3 (−ve)	PC 4 (+ve)	PC4 (−ve)	PC 5 (+ve)	PC5 (−ve)
1.										
2.										
3.										
4.										
5.										
6.										
6.										
8.										
9.										
10.										

Notes: PC = performance criteria
+ve = positive
−ve = negative

Task 3

To achieve a merit, you need to compare the data that you gained from each notational analysis using statistics, then present the results graphically and show the strengths and weaknesses you have found in the performers.

Q **Quick quiz 1**

Complete the following table by choosing the appropriate term from the list below to match each of the definitions.

- Notational analysis
- Performance criteria
- Data representation
- Statistics
- Data analysis

Term	Definition
	Presenting figures in an organised way
	Process of describing and analysing data
	Measures of performance
	A method of recording what happens during a sporting contest
	What you do with figures once they have been collected

6.3 Comparing a Numerical Model to Sporting Performance

P3

Teaching skills requires not only knowing what to teach (i.e. being aware of the correct technique), but also knowing how to eliminate errors and avoid actions that limit performance or cause injury. Developing a model of a skill allows a coach to observe, analyse and then correct the athlete's technique, by comparing their performance with a standard.

The first part of developing a model of performance is to determine the aim of the skill in question. In the volleyball serve, the objective is to strike the ball so that the opposition either cannot return the ball or will find it difficult to do so. It is also important that the serve is legal (no foot fault or time fault; ball travels within playing area). To achieve this objective, accuracy is important, as are timing and power. If the ball is mis-hit, or is hit too softly or inaccurately, it will be easier for the opposition to return the ball.

The next step is to devise a theoretical model of the skill. This could be done with the help of a video of an elite performer, or it may be that this has already been done and the information is available in a book or on the internet. The skill can be divided into phases and the biomechanical features of each phase identified. It is common to divide skills

into three phases. It is important to identify where one phase ends and the next begins. Most striking, kicking, hitting and catching skills are divided into the following:

1. Preparation phase.
2. Force-production phase.
3. Recovery phase.

Examining the volleyball serve (see Figure 6.4), it has a preparation phase that consists of holding the ball in the non-striking hand and drawing the hitting hand back. The force-production phase involves bringing the hitting hand into contact with the ball. The recovery phase is to stop the movement of the body and be ready for the next action.

Even repetitive skills, like running, swimming or cycling, can be divided into three similar phases. Take running as an example. The preparation phase could be the foot landing on the floor (the heel strike in normal running). Driving off from the front of the foot is the force-production phase. Recovery will be bringing the foot through, ready for another heel strike. If the skill is more complex, such as the triple jump, the skill can be broken into major phases that are then subdivided into further sections.

With the skill divided into parts, it is then possible to analyse each phase. For the volleyball serve, what position is the hitting hand in? What position are the hitting arm and shoulder in? What about the trunk and the legs? How is power generated? Where is the

a) Preparation phase   b) Force production phase   c) Recovery phase

Fig 6.4 Skill phases

ball struck? How is topspin created or does the ball float? Look at stability and timing.

There are many ways to analyse movements. We are going to concentrate on two:

- Numerical models – those involving things that can be measured in numbers (e.g. speed, distance, force)
- Technical models – those involving technique aspects of a skill (e.g. foot position, hand position, centre of gravity movement).

Numerical Model Production

As with all methods of movement analysis, the objective is to look at what a particular athlete does in comparison to the correct model. The correct model could be based on what is in a coaching manual or determined by observing an elite performer. The important thing is to have an accurate starting point from which to make comparisons.

There are many numerical components that can be examined in sporting performance, including linear motion, angular motion and projectiles.

Linear Motion

The action of objects (e.g. balls, people) can be described by measures such as distance, displacement, speed, velocity and acceleration. These quantities, which are used to describe the motion of objects, can be divided into two categories: vector and scalar. These two categories can be separated from each other by their definitions.

Distance and displacement are quantities that have similar meanings, yet the definitions are different. Distance is a scalar value that measures the length of the path a body follows during motion. Displacement

is a vector quantity that refers to how far from an initial position an object has moved, or, to put it more simply, its change in position. If an athlete ran 2 km north, then 2 km south, they would have run a distance of 4 km, but a displacement of 0 km. Displacement being a vector quantity, the 2 km north is cancelled by the 2 km south.

Key terms

Scalar: a simple measurement with no direction.

Vector: a measurement in a certain direction.

Speed and velocity are related to distance and displacement. Speed is a scalar – it is a measure of how fast something is moving. If something is not moving, speed is zero. Speed is determined by the equation:

$$\text{Speed} = \text{distance} \div \text{time}$$

The units usually used for speed are metres per second (m/s), but miles per hour or kilometres per hour/second are also used.

Velocity is a vector – it measures an object's rate of change of position. Envisage a person jumping up and down, yet always returning to the same position. If measured over time, although they were moving up and down, their change in position is zero, since they would return to the floor. Similarly, an athlete completing a lap of a 400 m track would cover a distance of 400 m, but a displacement of 0, as their finishing position is the same as their starting position.

The equation to work out velocity is:

$$\text{Velocity} = \text{displacement} \div \text{time}$$

As with speed, the units for velocity are metres per second squared (m/s^2), but direction also needs to be included (e.g. south at 30°).

Acceleration is a vector quantity that is measured by the rate at which velocity changes. Therefore, an object is accelerating if it is changing its velocity. Decelerating is the opposite of accelerating, so it is slowing down. People often refer to a person accelerating if they are moving fast, but an athlete can be running very fast and still not be accelerating. Accelerating is velocity increasing; constant velocity, even if very fast, is zero acceleration.

The equation to measure acceleration is:

$$\text{Acceleration} = \text{change in velocity} \div \text{time taken}$$

It can be worked out by finding:

- V_f = final velocity
- V_i = initial velocity
- t = time interval.

The units for acceleration are metres per second per second (ms^{2s}).

Angular Motion

In sport, movement or motion is quite often not in a straight line, such as a golf swing or the action of the leg in running. However, the same concepts and principles used to describe linear motion can be used to explain motion in a circle. The major difference in measuring angular motion is the unit that it is measured in. With linear motion, metres (m) are used to determine distance and displacement, and all following units are taken from that (e.g. $m.s^{-1}$, $m.s^{-2}$). With angular motion, changes in position are measured by angles, the units of which are degrees (°).

The position of a particular object, such as a golf club, at any moment in time, is its angular position. This is measured with reference to something else – for example, the ground, a vertical line or another object. If angular position changes, as would be the case in a golf swing, the difference between the starting position and the final position is called the angular displacement. It is symbolised by the Greek letter theta (θ). The rate of change of angular displacement is termed angular velocity. It is calculated in the same way as linear velocity, but instead of displacement divided by time, it is angular displacement divided by time.

The average angular velocity (ω) of something rotating is the angular displacement divided by the time taken to move through this displacement or angle. Hence:

$$\text{Angular velocity} = \text{angular displacement} \div \text{time}$$

- ω = average angular velocity
- θ = angular displacement
- t = time taken.

The symbol for angular velocity is the Greek letter omega (ω) and is measured in degrees per second (°s^{-1}).

Angular acceleration can be calculated from angular velocity and is defined as the rate of change of angular velocity:

$$\text{Angular acceleration} = \text{angular velocity} \div \text{time}$$

- a = average angular acceleration
- ω_f = final angular velocity
- ω_i = initial angular velocity
- t = time taken.

When examining linear motion, an object's resistance to move is called inertia and is determined by its mass. With angular motion, this resistance to movement is not only caused by the object's mass, it is also due to where this mass is located. For example, a golf club has a large proportion of its mass at the club head, while a tennis racket has its mass distributed more evenly. The golf club would have greater angular inertia. Angular inertia is more commonly called moment of inertia and is calculated as:

Moment of inertia = mass of any particle within the object × (distance from particle to axis of rotation)^2

The units for moment of inertia are kgm^2. From the equation, you can see that the distance the majority of the mass is from the axis of rotation has more effect on angular inertia than the object's mass. If you increase an object's mass, you increase its moment of inertia by the same level (so a heavy cricket bat is harder to swing than a light cricket bat). However, if you increase the distance between the majority of the mass and the axis of rotation (i.e. you make the object longer), the effect on inertia is the increase in distance squared (double the distance results in quadrupling the effect on inertia). Thus, swinging a driver (a long club) in golf is a lot harder than swinging an iron (a shorter club). Golf club designers are addressing this issue by designing drivers that are relatively light, using materials such as carbon fibre and titanium.

Since inertia exists (i.e. objects are reluctant to move), a force is needed to produce any movement. This will also be the case with angular motion. Imagine a tennis player putting topspin on a ball – to spin the ball they must produce a force towards the top of the ball. This force allows the ball to spin in an angular motion. In the case of the player who has just hit the topspin, if you are sitting near the umpire's chair and the tennis player hitting the topspin is on the right-hand side of the court, the direction of the force will be anticlockwise. If the same player put a clockwise force on the ball, this would be backspin.

Projectiles

Projectile motion is the study of an object in flight. Factors affecting the flight path of an object include:

● Amount of force applied to the object
● Point of force application (where the object is hit)
● Direction of force.

Take the volleyball serve as an example. The harder the ball is hit (i.e. the more force applied), the further and faster the ball will go. Where you hit the ball (i.e. point of application of force) will affect the direction it goes in. Hit it below the centre line and it will go up in the air, which is what is needed for a volleyball serve. The final thing that is important to consider is how the ball is struck (i.e. direction of application of force). If the ball is hit near the centre with a forward motion, this will impart topspin. If the ball is hit lower down with a downward motion, this will produce backspin. A spinning ball will behave more directly in the air than one that is not spinning.

Fig 6.5 A downhill skier

Key term

Gravity: the force caused by the pull of the earth's mass.

Many sports involve projectiles – for example, balls, javelins, shuttlecocks and even humans in the long jump and high jump. A projectile is any object that has no external forces acting on it other than gravity. The flight-path shape of a projectile would be symmetrical if we discount air resistance and lift. In reality, air resistance (which causes drag force) and aerodynamic factors (that cause lift) will act to affect the flight path of a projectile.

Any object moving through air, and especially water, will experience a drag force. This resists the motion of the object. The greater the speed of the moving object, the greater the drag force. For example, a cyclist experiences far greater drag forces than a runner. That is why slipstreaming plays such a vital part in cycling. A cyclist can save as much as 30 per cent of his or her energy by cycling close behind a competitor or teammate.

The drag force also depends on the size and shape of the object. A downhill skier in a tuck position, wearing a racing suit, will generate less drag force than a recreational skier standing more upright, wearing salopettes and a ski jacket.

The final factor that affects drag is the density of the medium of transport. Water creates more drag than air.

The flow of air around a projectile depends on the shape of the projectile. A smooth, symmetrical shape will have a symmetrical flow around it. However, in sport, many objects are not symmetrical. An aerofoil is not symmetrical. Air travels faster over the top of an aerofoil than underneath it. This means that the air pressure is lower above the aerofoil than below it. The difference in pressure creates an upward force that causes the aerofoil to lift.

Various sporting objects experience lift, such as the javelin or discus. In some cases, an aerofoil is turned upside down and used to create a downward force. Spoilers on the back of racing cars force them towards the ground, making them less likely to skid off track.

Spin plays a part in the flight path of an object or projectile. A spinning or rotating object (e.g. a football kicked on one side), has more interference with the air than if it were not spinning. This causes the air to slow down on the side that is moving into the air and speed up on the side that is moving with the air. This difference in air speed causes an unequal pressure, and just as an aerofoil creates lift, so the spinning ball will dip, lift or swerve, depending on the direction of spin. In the case of a golf ball, which is usually hit with backspin, the ball will lift. However, it could be used for swerve (bending a football round a wall) or topspin (causing a volleyball to dip).

The surface of the object (or the balls) will have an effect on its trajectory. Examples of this are the golf ball and the cricket ball. A golf ball is covered in dimples, which means the interaction between the surface of the ball and the surrounding air is increased. If a golf ball is hit with backspin, the dimples amplify the amount of lift force. This means the ball will travel further, which gets it closer to the hole, potentially reducing the number of shots.

There is a problem, though, with the dimples – not only do they increase the amount of lift on a golf ball, but they also bring out any sideways movement. This is why golf balls can be hooked or sliced quite dramatically.

Key term

Trajectory: the flight path of an object such as a ball.

In the case of a cricket ball, the seam has a key effect on its flight. The movement of air over the ball, as with any ball, interacts with the surface of the ball. But because the ball has a seam, when the air hits this, it disrupts the flow of air around the ball. As with the golf ball, this causes uneven air pressure around the ball, which generates sideways movement or swing. The plan of the swing bowler in cricket is to bowl so as to cause this movement. This requires the seam to be in a certain position when the ball is released. Cricket players also polish the ball on one side to make it smooth, so that when the air passes over the smooth side, the change in air pressure is even greater than normal, and hence the ball moves more.

A long jumper could be thought off as a projectile once they have taken off.

The shape of the flight path of a projectile can be measured, including angle of release or take-off. These factors will have a big impact on how far the object will travel. If the angle of release is too high, the object will go up in the air, but will not go far. If the angle of release is too low, the object will return to the ground before it has had much chance to go very far. Obviously the higher from the ground the object is released, the longer it is in the air and so the further it can go.

Measurement of Movement

A more simplistic method of numerical modelling (rather than measuring velocity, etc.) is to just measure position, such as joint angles. As with the other methods of analysis, the skill is broken down into smaller phases and the position of each can be recorded. Various joint angles could be measured (e.g. ankle, hip, knee), and even the position of the centre of gravity.

Detailing the movement of the centre of gravity is sometimes useful because it allows you to concentrate on just one point, rather than the whole body. Also, if you know the position of the centre of gravity in relation to the body, it will give an indication of the weight distribution or balance of the individual.

Joint angles can be measured from taking a video of the skill. This is far easier than measuring joint angles during performance. If you need to measure joint angles during performance, you would need to use a goniometer (this is like a big protractor).

Key term

Centre of gravity: a point through which the whole body can be said to act – the centre point.

Methodology for Recording Performance

Having decided on what the ideal skill is, we can now measure where our current athlete is. So far as using the numerical model is concerned, the best method of obtaining information is with the use of a video. This can easily be stored in a digital format and allows the performance to be played back at a later date to calculate numerical information.

The major limitation of using video is that you will have only two-dimensional information of a three-dimensional skill. Some skills will not be affected by this, such as running in a straight line. It is possible to record using more than one camera and combine this information.

When using a camcorder to obtain performance information, there are a few things you need to remember. The image on the screen is smaller than occurs in real life. When measuring angles this has no impact. If you are examining the golf swing, the angle between the golf club and the golfer's body is the same in real life as on the screen. However, when looking at distance this is not the case. Using the same example, if you measured the distance between the golfer's feet and the golf ball, it would not be the same in real life compared with on the television screen. This is referred to as perspective error.

Key term

Perspective error: objects appearing smaller than in real life when replayed on a screen.

It is therefore important that when you take a recording of a skill you have a reference object, such as a metre rule. When you play back the recording on a television, you can be sure you know what distance equates to one metre. A similar thing can be done to ensure you know exactly what angle is vertical. If the metre rule is held vertically, you can use this to determine exact distance and exact angles in relation to vertical.

Your second important consideration is time. If you want to measure speed (e.g. club speed for a golfer or take-off speed for a long jumper), you need to be able to measure time. The easiest way to measure time is to determine how many frames per second the recording was made at. If you record performance with a camcorder using video, the recording will be played back at 25 frames per second on a television. This means that each frame lasts for 1/25 of a second. If you now want to measure club speed for a golfer driving a golf ball, and you can measure on screen that the club has moved 200 degrees in five frames, you have a simple calculation. Angular velocity (change in angle with time) is equal to angular displacement divided by the time it takes to move that displacement. In the above example we would have 200 degrees divided by the time it takes for five frames (remember, one frame is 1/25 of a second). That would give 200 degrees divided by 5/25 second, which is equal to 1000 degrees per second.

Fig 6.6 A golfer taking a swing

Student activity 6.2 — ⏱ 45 minutes — P1

Produce a numerical model, using three numerical components, and compare it to a sporting performance. The following table shows how it could be done for a javelin throw:

Numerical component	Example 1	Example 2
1. Angle of release		
2. Angle of attack		
3. Height of release		

6.4 Comparing a Technical Model to Sporting Performance

P4   M2   D1

As with the numerical model of analysing sports performance, for the technical model you also need first to describe the ideal: what the skill looks like performed by an elite-level performer.

The technical model uses more of a qualitative method of description. Rather than looking at the run-up speed, an athletic coach would examine run-up technique (looking at knee lift, balance, arm movement). A cricket coach would look at position of hands on the bat (grip), the position of feet in relation to the body and how balanced the individual is (stance).

There is a long list of skills in different sports that can be analysed (e.g. serving, hitting, kicking, catching, throwing, jumping, running, passing). The majority of information on correct technical models will be found in coaching manuals. Good coaches remember most of the technical points related to their sport.

As with any method of modelling performance, the idea is to compare your performance (or your athlete's) with the correct (or ideal) model. The key to successful coaching is to be able to see where the two performances are different. You must then be able to bring about improvement. You need to highlight the areas that need improving or that contain errors.

If you are teaching the volleyball serve, one of your players may consistently serve to the left-hand side of the court. You have worked out that this is caused by them bringing their arm across their body in the recovery phase. You now need to decide how to correct the error. You might wish to break the movement down into its phases and concentrate on one phase, or you could run through the action in slow motion. A video of the correct technique could be shown. Whatever you decide, it is important that, after a period of coaching, you repeat the observation to see if your player has improved.

In group coaching sessions with beginners, coaches are performing this sort of analysis all the time. They are looking at what actions the individuals are doing and then suggesting corrections based on what they see. As the performance becomes more specialist, the knowledge of the coach needs to increase accordingly. Recording the performance (via video) is useful, as this allows the coach more time to observe the performance accurately.

Key learning points 3

- Technical model of performance – describing performance based on technique (e.g. stance, balance, grip, body position).
- Technical components – more qualitative than mechanical components; what things look like.

Q Quick quiz 3

When analysing a tennis player, list eight technical components you could assess.

Student activity 6.3 — 90 minutes — P4 M2 D1

1. Using a skill of your choice (e.g. a tennis serve, a javelin throw or a footballer taking a free kick), find or make a recording of an elite performer.

2. Use a camcorder or video recorder to make your own recording of a non-elite performer performing the same skill.

3. Compare the performance of the elite performer to the performance of the non-elite performer by listing where they are similar and where they are different. Be specific and use technical language of the sporting activity.

4. Explain and justify the methodology you used for either the numerical model in Student Activity 6.2 or the technical model used in this Student Activity.

5. Evaluate the findings for either the notational analyses performed in Student Activity 6.1, the numerical model used in Student Activity 6.2 or the technical model used in this Student Activity.

6.5 Providing Feedback on Performance

Using biomechanical analysis to improve technique is based on four steps:

● Describing the ideal model
● Recording what your athlete is doing
● Comparing the two to see what needs improving
● Instructing the athlete on how to improve.

No one method of gaining information is best, as there are many ways to analyse performance. We have concentrated on two: numerical models and technical models. We could easily have looked at anatomical models of performance, ones based on examining what happens at joints (flexion, extension, etc.) and muscles (eccentric, contraction, etc.). All methods are useful and can be combined to provide a wealth of information on performance. Whichever method is used to analyse the performance, one of the main roles of the coach is instructing the athlete how to improve.

The information the coach has may seem clear to them, but remember that this may not be the case for the athlete. When giving feedback on performance (telling the athlete how they performed) and giving guidance on how to improve (telling the athlete what they need to do next), the coach should follow the guidelines given below.

Coaching Feedback

Clarity of Information/Appropriate Language

Keep it simple and make it understandable. Do not use terms that the athlete would not understand.

For example, telling a golfer, 'The club head needs to come through faster', is easier to understand than saying, 'Increase the angular velocity of the club'.

Type of Feedback

Use different forms of feedback. You could tell the athlete what you want them to do, but you could also show them via a demonstration. People tend to remember only about 10 per cent of what they are told, but can remember far more of what they see. You could list the main coaching points, so your athlete can use them when practising alone. Written feedback can vary from a simple list of what is required, to details of things like heart-rate training zones.

Positive and Negative Feedback

Discuss strengths and weaknesses. Tell the athlete what they are good at, as people like to hear this (this is positive feedback) and it motivates them. However, do not neglect the areas for improvement – what will make a performer better. Negative feedback can also be used in the following way: every time the ball goes out, the team does five push-ups. When coaching, talk about good and bad aspects. Remember that if everything were good, there would be no need for the coach, and if everything were bad, people would stop performing (many people play sport because of the enjoyment they get from it).

Evidence-based Feedback

Base things on fact. What information did you acquire from your notational analysis or your analysis of technical performance? Do not just coach things for the sake of coaching them. Concentrate on what you need to. If you are a volleyball coach and you have determined that serving is a problem, practise serving, give feedback on serving and aim to improve this area. You should also take into account other things that may be affecting performance. Are your athletes fit enough, motivated enough, skilful enough to perform what you are asking of them?

Confidentiality

Athletes are people. Some athletes may prefer it if you discuss their weak points confidentially. Your athletes may be lacking in self-confidence, and the way you provide feedback can have an impact on this. You may wish to start and finish on something positive and have the negative part in the middle. Remember that performance may fluctuate from day to day (e.g. due to the weather, how the person is feeling, what they have had to eat). It is worth keeping in mind that we all have bad days – even the coach!

The level and amount of feedback is related to the ability level of the athlete. As performance progresses, feedback should change from general to precise. With beginners, mistakes are normally quite general and related to the whole movement, so general feedback is good. Beginners may require more motivational-type feedback. As the athlete becomes more skilful, the nature of the feedback needs to change. The feedback should be more specific, concentrating on details. Often, good performers can start to analyse their own performance, so feedback should encourage this.

Timing of feedback is another important issue. Feedback should be given soon after the performer has done the skill. If not, there is a risk that they will not be able to relate what you are doing to the actions they performed.

Goal Setting

Once you have explained to the group or individual how they are performing, it is important to outline a way forward. You should give your team or athlete a clear action plan as to what they should do next. Action plans should contain targets or goals. Goals are things that your athletes can work towards and measure how well they are doing. Goals can be divided up into short-term (for next week), medium-term (for next month) and long-term (for next season). All the goals you set need to be SMART:

● **S**pecific
● **M**easurable
● **A**chievable
● **R**ealistic
● **T**ime-constrained.

Specific

The goal must be specific to what you want to achieve. This may be an aspect of performance or fitness. It is not enough to say, 'I want to get fitter.'

You need to say, 'I want to improve strength, speed or stamina, etc.'

Measurable

Goals must be stated in a way that is measurable, so they need to state figures. For example, 'I want to improve my first serve percentage' is not measurable. However, if you say, 'I want to improve my first serve success by 20 per cent', it is measurable.

Achievable

It must be possible to actually achieve the goal.

Realistic

We need to be realistic in our setting of goals and look at what factors may stop us achieving them.

Time-constrained

There needs to be some sort of time frame – by the end of the season, by the end of next month.

Imagine you are a volleyball coach and your analysis of a player's serve has shown you that the particular player has a success rate of 50 per cent (from your notational analysis) and lacks a follow-through of the hitting arm (from your technical analysis). How could you set SMART goals?

Improving service technique may be a good long-term goal, but in the short term you need something more specific. A good short-term goal would be to increase accuracy of service. This can be measured easily. You could measure serves in court and serves out of court (you could even be more specific and see if these change during different sets). You might set a target of 60 per cent for the next match. To know if this is achievable, look at the time frame you have given. Is the player going to get enough practice between now and the next match? Is 60 per cent a realistic target to expect? What service success do your other players have? Remember to include time constraints; so you might expect 60 per cent next match, but 70 per cent by the end of the season.

Future training should be based on the observations you make of your athletes. You can set goals related to both individuals and teams. The goals can be based on skills, fitness or even psychological techniques. Whichever you use, it is good to relate training back to previous performance, so athletes will see the reasons for and the benefits of doing the training.

Key learning points 4

- Feedback – the way feedback is given is important, as is the type of feedback.
- Strengths and weaknesses – both play a part in improving performance.
- Goal setting – goals are an important focus for training and they should be SMART.

Student activity 6.4   ⏱ 40 minutes   P5 M3 D2

Based on one of the analyses you performed in Student Activities 6.1, 6.2 or 6.3, provide feedback to an athlete or a team. You may include statistics or data representation and use goal setting to link to future performance.

To achieve M3, this feedback needs to be detailed, and to achieve D2 you need to justify the future actions you have prescribed.

Further reading

Hall, S.J. (2002). *Basic Biomechanics*, Maidenhead: McGraw-Hill.

Thatcher, J., Thatcher, R., Day, M., Portas, M. and Hood, S. (2009). *Sport and Exercise Science*, Learning Matters.

Walder, P. (1994). *Mechanics and Sport Performance*, Feltham Press.

Useful websites

www.getbodysmart.com

Free tutorials and quizzes from an American site that looks at human anatomy and physiology, helping you to see the structure of the different body systems.

www.innerbody.com

Free and informative diagrams of the different body systems, including respiratory, cardiovascular, skeletal and muscular

www.instantanatomy.net

Free useful anatomy pictures and information, mainly from a medical viewpoint.

7: Exercise, Health and Lifestyle

7.1 Introduction

A person's lifestyle can have a huge impact on their long-term health. Lifestyle plays a key role in the prevention of a large number of diseases, including coronary heart disease, cancer and obesity. This unit will give you the knowledge and skills to assess the lifestyle of an individual, provide advice on lifestyle improvement and plan a health-related physical activity programme.

By the end of this unit you should:

● know the importance of lifestyle factors in the maintenance of health and well-being
● be able to assess the lifestyle of a selected individual
● be able to provide advice on lifestyle improvement
● be able to plan a health-related physical activity programme for a selected individual.

Assessment and grading criteria

To achieve a PASS grade the evidence must show that the learner is able to:	To achieve a MERIT grade the evidence must show that, in addition to the pass criteria, the learner is able to:	To achieve a DISTINCTION grade the evidence must show that, in addition to the pass and merit criteria, the learner is able to:
P1 describe lifestyle factors that have an effect on health	**M1** explain the effects of identified lifestyle factors on health	
P2 design and use a lifestyle questionnaire to describe the strengths and areas for improvement in the lifestyle of a selected individual	**M2** explain the strengths and areas for improvement in the lifestyle of a selected individual	**D1** evaluate the lifestyle of a selected individual and prioritise areas for change
P3 provide lifestyle improvement strategies for a selected individual	**M3** explain recommendations made regarding lifestyle improvement strategies.	**D2** analyse a range of lifestyle improvement strategies.
P4 plan a six-week health-related physical activity programme for a selected individual.		

7.2 Lifestyle Factors

P1 **M1**

Physical Activity

Our lifestyle has become much more sedentary over the years. We now have methods of transport that require little physical exertion. Cars and buses have replaced walking and cycling. Recent studies have shown that 30 per cent of children go to school by car, and fewer than 50 per cent walk. This country has less time dedicated to PE lessons than any other country in the European Union. There are now relatively few manual occupations, and the majority of people's careers are spent in an office-based environment. Everyday tasks such as laundry, cleaning and cooking require little effort, as they are all aided by labour-saving devices. It is now even possible to go shopping by sitting in front of a computer and logging on to the internet.

For entertainment, the average person spends less time participating in active leisure pursuits and prefers to sit in front of the TV. The average adult watches over 26 hours of television each week, which is a virtually totally sedentary activity. Children also spend much less time pursuing activity-based play and choose computer games, videos or the TV to occupy their free time. All these factors have led to many people taking part in very low levels of physical activity.

Physical activity can increase a person's basal metabolic rate by around 10 per cent. This elevated basal metabolic rate can last for up to 48 hours after the completion of the activity. By taking part in physical activity kilocalories will be expended. The number of kilocalories used depends on the type and intensity of the activity. The more muscles that are used in the activity and the harder you work, the more kilocalories will be used up to perform the activity. For example, swimming the front crawl uses both the arms and the legs and will therefore use more calories to perform than walking, which mainly uses the leg muscles.

The body weight of the person will also have an impact on the number of kilocalories burnt while taking part in a physical activity. The heavier the person, the more kilocalories are required to move the heavier weight. So a heavier person will burn more calories than a lighter person when performing the same activity at the same intensity.

Key term

Physical activity: the state of being active.

National Recommended Guidelines

In order to gain the health benefits of physical activity, adults should aim to participate in physical activity for 30 minutes at least five times a week. Our national recommended guidelines for children state that they should participate in moderate-intensity exercise for 60 minutes per day, but the European Health Study 2006 found that they should be exercising for 90 minutes per day to gain the health benefits of physical activity.

Health Benefits of Physical Activity

Taking part in regular exercise has consistently been shown to have many benefits to a person's physical and mental health. Many types of disease can be alleviated or prevented by taking part in regular exercise.

Coronary heart disease and physical activity

Coronary heart disease (CHD) is the leading cause of death in the Western world. One-third of all deaths associated with CHD are due to not taking part in physical activity. Coronary heart disease is a narrowing of the coronary arteries, which are the blood vessels that pass over the surface of the heart and supply it with blood. CHD is usually a result of a build-up of fatty material and plaques within the coronary blood vessels. This is known as atherosclerosis.

Key terms

Coronary blood vessels: blood vessels that supply blood to the heart.

Atherosclerosis: build-up of fatty material in the coronary blood vessels, which makes their diameter smaller.

When a person with CHD takes part in a physically demanding task, the coronary arteries may not be able to supply the heart muscle with enough blood to keep up with the demand for oxygen. This will be felt as a pain in the chest (angina). If a coronary artery becomes completely blocked, the area of the heart muscle served by the artery will die, resulting in a heart attack.

Taking part in regular exercise appears to reduce the risk of heart disease directly and indirectly. Research has shown that exercise:

131

- Increases levels of HDL cholesterol
- Decreases the amount of triglycerides in the bloodstream.

Key terms

HDL cholesterol: the 'good' cholesterol that acts to clean the artery walls, which in turn reduces atherosclerosis.

Triglycerides: another type of fat; high levels in the bloodstream have been linked with increased risk of heart disease.

Hypertension: high blood pressure.

Fig 7.1 A normal lung (left) beside the lung of a smoker (right)

Hypertension and physical activity

A person is deemed to have hypertension if their blood pressure consistently reads at 140/90 or higher. Hypertension is a very common complaint, and around 15 to 25 per cent of adults in most Western countries have high blood pressure. If a person with hypertension does not reduce their blood pressure they are more at risk of suffering a stroke or a heart attack.

Psychological Benefits of Physical Activity

A number of studies have attempted to explore the effects of exercise on depression and found that exercise increases self-esteem, improves mood, reduces anxiety levels, increases the ability to handle stress and generally makes people happier than those who do not exercise. It is thought that one cause of depression may be a decreased production of certain chemicals in the brain, specifically adrenaline, dopamine and serotonin. Exercise has been shown to increase the levels of these substances, which may have the effect of improving a person's mood after taking part in exercise. For the last decade or so, exercise has been prescribed as a method of combating depression.

Smoking

You are probably aware that smoking is bad for you. It actually kills around 14,000 people in the UK each year, and 300 people die in the UK every day as a result of smoking. These deaths occur through a range of diseases caused by smoking and include a variety of cancers, cardiovascular disease and an array of chronic lung diseases.

The products in a cigarette that appear to do the most damage include tar, nicotine and carbon monoxide.

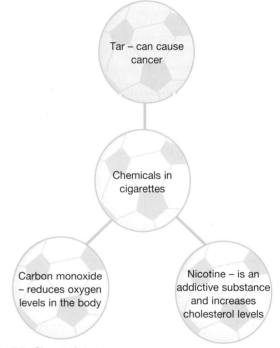

Fig 7.2 Chemicals in cigarettes

Smokers are making themselves much more likely to suffer from a range of cancers; 90 per cent of people suffering from lung cancer have the disease because they smoke or have smoked. You are also four times more likely to contract mouth cancer if you are a smoker. Other forms of cancer that have been linked to smoking include cancers of the bladder, oesophagus, kidneys and pancreas, and cervical cancer.

Cardiovascular Disease

Cardiovascular disease is the main cause of death in smokers. The excess cholesterol produced from smoking narrows the blood vessels.

When the blood vessels become narrower, blood clots are more likely to form, which can then block the coronary blood vessels. A blockage in these vessels can lead to a heart attack. It is estimated that 30 per cent of these heart attacks are due to smoking.

Alternatively, the blood clot may travel to the brain, which can lead to a stroke; or it could travel to the kidneys, which could result in kidney failure; or the block may occur in the legs, which can lead to gangrene, for which the main treatment is amputation.

Chronic Lung Disease

The following diseases are more prevalent in smokers:

- Emphysema – a disease that causes breathlessness due to damaged alveoli
- Bronchitis – makes the person cough excessively because of increased mucus production in the lungs.

Key term

Alveoli: air sacs in the lungs in which gaseous exchange takes place.

Smoking is responsible for 80 per cent of these conditions, which basically block air flow to and from the lungs, making breathing more difficult. These diseases tend to start between the ages of 35 and 45.

Other Smoking-Related Health Risks

Smoking can also damage health in a variety of other ways. A person who smokes may suffer from some of the following:

- High blood pressure
- Impotence
- Fertility problems
- Eye problems
- Discoloured teeth and gums
- Mouth ulcers
- Skin more prone to wrinkles.

Alcohol

Alcohol is a legal drug that may be consumed by people aged 18 or over – although by the age of 16, over 80 per cent of young people in the UK have tried alcohol. In fact, in the UK, people aged between 16 and 24 are the heaviest drinking group of the population. Studies reveal that one in two men and one in four women drink more than the recommended daily benchmarks, and over a quarter of males and females drink more than double the recommended daily amount.

The recommended daily benchmarks for alcohol consumption are based on adult drinking; there are no recommendations for children and young people as they should be refraining from alcohol consumption by law.

Recommended Daily Intake

The Health Education Authority recommends that women should drink no more than two units of alcohol per day and males should drink no more than three units per day. Both males and females should have at least two alcohol-free days per week.

It takes around an hour for the adult body to get rid of one unit of alcohol, and this may well be slower in young people.

Effects of Alcohol on the Body

Alcohol affects the brain so that it compromises our judgement and suppresses our inhibitions. It decreases our physical coordination and sense of balance, and makes our vision blurred and speech slurred. Excessive drinking can lead to alcohol poisoning, which can cause unconsciousness, coma and even death. Excessive alcohol consumption can often make a person vomit, and vomiting while unconscious can lead to death by suffocation, as the vomit can block the air flow to and from the lungs. The effects of alcohol have also been implicated in a large proportion of fatal road accidents, assaults and incidents of domestic violence.

Diseases Associated with Excess Alcohol Consumption

Alcohol consumption in excess of the recommended daily guidelines will often cause physical damage to the body and increase the likelihood of getting diseases such as cancer, cirrhosis, high blood pressure, strokes and depression.

Cirrhosis

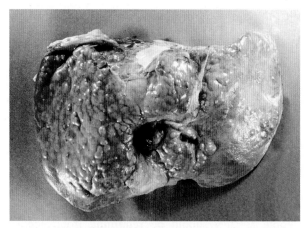

Fig 7.3 A liver affected by cirrhosis

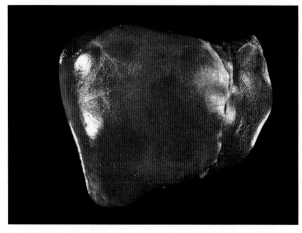

Fig 7.4 A healthy liver

Excessive alcohol consumption can result in cirrhosis of the liver. The liver is the largest organ in the body. It is responsible for getting rid of poisons from the blood, helps our immune system in fighting infection, makes proteins that help our blood to clot and produces bile, which helps with the breakdown of fats. The disease damages the liver and produces scar tissue. The scar tissue replaces the normal tissue and prevents it from working as it should. Cirrhosis is the twelfth leading cause of death by disease and causes 26,000 deaths per year.

Cancer

Around 6 per cent of deaths from cancer in the UK are caused by alcohol (*Oxford Textbook of Medicine*, 2003). A range of cancers have been linked with excess alcohol consumption; these include:

- Cancer of the mouth
- Cancer of the larynx
- Cancer of the oesophagus
- Liver cancer

- Breast cancer
- Bowel cancer.

Depression

Alcohol consumption has been linked with anxiety and depression. One in three young people who have committed suicide drank alcohol before they died, and more than two out of three people who attempt suicide have drunk excessively.

Stress

When we perceive ourselves to be in a situation that is dangerous, our stress response is activated. This has been developed as a means of ensuring our survival by making us respond to danger. For example, if you are walking home at night along a dark street and you hear noises behind you, your body will instigate physiological changes, called the 'fight-or-flight' response, as your body is preparing to turn and fight the danger or run away as fast as it can.

Adrenaline and cortisol are the main hormones released when we are stressed, which have the effect of:

- Increasing the heart rate
- Increasing the breathing rate
- Decreasing the rate of digestion.

It is not healthy for the body to be in a constant state of stress because of the excess production of adrenaline and cortisol. This results in excess cholesterol production that raises blood cholesterol levels and is a risk factor for CHD.

Stress and Cardiovascular Disease

If the excess hormones and chemicals released during stressful periods are not 'used up' through physical exertion, the increased heart rate and high blood pressure place excess strain on our blood vessels. This can lead to vascular damage. Damaged blood vessels are thicker than healthy blood vessels and have a reduced ability to stretch. This can have the effect of reducing the supply of blood and oxygen to the heart.

Stress and the Immune System

Stress can decrease our body's ability to fight infection, which makes us more susceptible to suffering from illnesses. This explains why we catch more colds when we are stressed.

Stress and Depression

Stress is also associated with mental health problems, and in particular with anxiety and depression. Here the relationship is fairly clear. The negative thinking that is associated with stress also contributes to these.

Diet

Our diets have changed significantly over the years. Today we have the largest range of foods available to us, but we are choosing to eat foods that are high in saturated fats and simple carbohydrates. Fast-food restaurants are flourishing because they are used so regularly by our society. Today, the nation's diet tends to be lacking in a number of important nutrients, including fibre, calcium, vitamins and iron. This is because a high proportion of the population relies on snacks and fast foods as their main source of nutritional intake. As a result, the Western diet is generally high in fat and sugars, resulting in a huge increase in obesity.

Estimates in 1990 suggested that 1 in 20 children aged 9 to 11 could be classified as clinically obese. If a person is obese they are much more likely to suffer from coronary heart disease, which is currently the biggest killer in Britain. As we are continuing to rely on foods that do not give us the right balance of vital nutrients, a number of people are suffering from poor nutrition. This not only impairs physical and mental functioning, but can also increase the risk of suffering from a range of diseases, including anaemia, diabetes and osteoporosis. A number of nutrition experts have also linked poor nutrition to emotional and behavioural problems that are seen to occur much more frequently among children today; these include hyperactivity and attention deficit disorders.

A healthy diet contains lots of fruit and vegetables. It is based on starchy foods, such as wholegrain bread, pasta and rice, and is low in fat (especially saturated fat), salt and sugar. Current recommendations for a healthy diet are shown in Table 7.1.

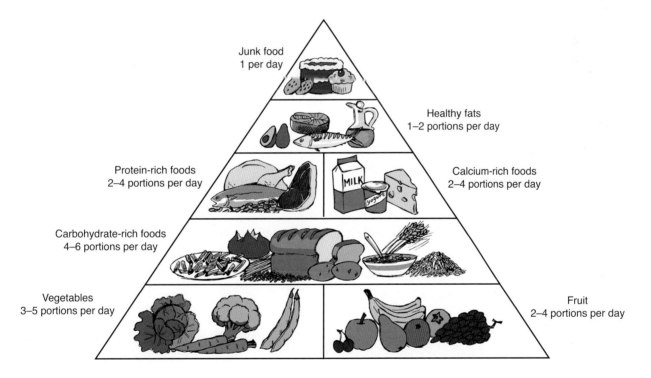

Junk food
1 per day

Healthy fats
1–2 portions per day

Protein-rich foods
2–4 portions per day

Calcium-rich foods
2–4 portions per day

Carbohydrate-rich foods
4–6 portions per day

Vegetables
3–5 portions per day

Fruit
2–4 portions per day

Fig 7.5 The nutrition pyramid

Food	Amount we should eat	Function	Example of food sources
Carbohydrates	50–60%	Provide energy for sports performance	
Sugars		Provide short bursts of energy	Jam, sweets, fruit, fizzy drinks, sports drinks
Starch		Provide energy for longer periods	Pasta, rice, bread, potatoes, breakfast cereals
Fat	25–30%	Provides energy for low-intensity exercise, e.g. walking	
Saturated fats		Insulate the body against the cold	Mainly animal sources: cream, lard, cheese, meat
Unsaturated fats		Help to protect internal organs	Mainly plant sources: nuts, soya, tofu
Protein	10–15%	For growth and repair	Meat, eggs, nuts, fish, poultry

Table 7.1 Recommendations for a healthy diet

Vitamin	Food sources	Function
A	Carrots, liver, dark green vegetables, mackerel	Maintains good vision, skin and hair
B group	Cereals, liver, yeast, eggs, beef, beans	Helps to break down food to produce energy
C	Most fresh fruits and vegetables, especially citrus fruits	Fights infection; maintains healthy skin and gums; helps with wound healing
D	Oily fish, eggs	Helps to build bones and teeth
E	Nuts, whole grains, dark green leafy vegetables	Antioxidant that prevents damage to cells
K	Leafy green vegetables, peas, milk, egg yolks	Helps to form blood clots

Table 7.2 Sources and functions of vitamins

Mineral	Food sources	Function
Iron	Liver, lean meats, eggs, dried fruits	Blood production
Calcium	Milk, fish bones, green leafy vegetables	Helps to build strong bones and teeth; helps to form blood clots
Sodium	Salt, seafood, processed foods, celery	Maintains fluid balance in cells; helps in muscle contraction
Potassium	Bananas	Works with sodium to maintain fluid balance, aids muscle contraction, maintains blood pressure
Zinc	Meats, fish	Tissue growth and repair

Table 7.3 Sources and functions of minerals

Key learning points 1

- People are much more sedentary today and many are not meeting national recommended guidelines.
- Children should be physically active for at least 60 to 90 minutes per day.
- Adults should be physically active for at least 30 minutes five times per week.
- People who take part in physical activity are less likely to suffer from CHD, hypertension, diabetes, obesity and depression.
- Smoking has been shown to cause cancer, chronic lung disease and cardiovascular disease in some people.
- Adult males should have no more than three units of alcohol per day and adult females should have no more than two. Males and females should both have at least two alcohol-free days per week.
- Excess alcohol consumption has been shown to cause cirrhosis, cancer and depression in some people.
- Stress can cause cardiovascular disease, decrease the immune system's response to infection and cause depression in some people.
- Today, many people are eating fast food and not taking in the right quantities of macronutrients, vitamins and minerals.
- A healthy diet contains lots of fruit and vegetables, is based on starchy foods such as wholegrain bread, pasta and rice, and is low in fat (especially saturated fat), salt and sugar.

Q Quick quiz 1

Match each description in the table below to the condition it describes, choosing from the following:

- Excess alcohol consumption
- CHD
- Hypertension
- Emphysema
- Cirrhosis.

Description	Condition
A disease that causes breathlessness due to damaged alveoli	
Damage and scarring to the liver	
A blood pressure reading of 140/90 or higher	
The build-up of fats in the coronary blood vessels	
This can lead to poisoning, unconsciousness and coma	

7.3 Assessing the Lifestyle of an Individual

When assessing the lifestyle of an individual, you will need to gather as much information on them as possible. This can be done effectively through a comprehensive questionnaire. It will be part of an initial consultation and must cover the following as a minimum requirement:

- Medical history
- Activity history
- Lifestyle factors
- Nutritional status
- Any other factors that will affect the person's health.

137

Lifestyle Questionnaire

Section 1: Personal Details

Name_____

Address _____

_____

_____

_____

Home telephone _____

Mobile telephone _____

Email _____

Occupation_____

Date of birth _____

Section 2: Physical Activity Levels

1 Does your occupation require you to take part in physical activity? If so, what?

_____

_____

2 What are your medium-term goals over the next three months?

_____

_____

_____

_____

3 What are your short-term goals over the next four weeks?

_____

_____

_____

_____

Section 3: Current Training Status

1 What are your main training requirements?

  (a) Muscular strength.

  (b) Muscular endurance.

  (c) Speed.

  (d) Flexibility.

  (e) Aerobic fitness.

  (f) Power.

  (g) Weight loss or gain.

  (h) Skill-related fitness.

  (i) Other (please state)

_____

2 How would you describe your current fitness status?

_____

_____

3 How many times a week will you train?

_____

4 How long do you have for each training session?

_____

Section 4: Your Nutritional Status

1 On a scale of 1 to 10 (1 being very low quality and 10 being very high quality), how would you rate the quality of your diet?

_____

2 Do you follow any particular diet?
   (a) Vegetarian.
   (b) Vegan.
   (c) Vegetarian plus fish.
   (d) Gluten-free.
   (e) Dairy-free.
3 How often do you eat? Note down a typical day's intake.

_____
_____
_____
_____
_____

4 Do you take any supplements? If so, which ones?

_____
_____

Section 5: Your Lifestyle

1 How many units of alcohol do you drink in a typical week?_____
2 Do you smoke?_____ If yes, how many a day?_____
3 Do you experience stress on a daily basis?_____
4 If yes, what causes you stress (if you know)?

_____

5 What techniques do you use to deal with your stress?

_____

Section 6: Your Physical Health

1 Do you experience any of the following?
   (a) Back pain or injury.
   (b) Knee pain or injury.
   (c) Ankle pain or injury.
   (d) Swollen joints.
   (e) Shoulder pain or injury.
   (f) Hip or pelvic pain or injury.
   (g) Nerve damage.
   (h) Head injuries.

2 If yes, please give details.

_____

_____

_____

3 Are any of these injuries made worse by exercise?

_____

4 If yes, what movements in particular cause pain?

_____

5 Are you currently receiving any treatment for any injuries? If so, what?

_____

Section 7: Medical History

1 Do you have, or have you had, any of the following medical conditions?

(a) Asthma.

(b) Bronchitis.

(c) Heart problems.

(d) Chest pains.

(e) Diabetes.

(f) High blood pressure.

(g) Epilepsy.

(h) Other

_____

2 Are you taking any medication? (If yes, state what, how much and why.)

_____

Name

Signature   Date

One-to-one Consultation

It is always a good idea to follow up a lifestyle questionnaire with a consultation with the individual. The person running the consultation must know when to ask questions and prompt the client, and when to listen and take notes. The main rule of thumb is that the client should be doing most of the talking in a consultation; the consultant's role is to ensure that questions are answered accurately and fully. The client should be made aware that their lifestyle questionnaire and the follow-up consultation are confidential, and the questionnaire should be stored in a secure place.

Communication Skills

When conducting a consultation, you will need to use skills such as questioning and listening. One of the aims of the consultation is to develop rapport with your client, which means that they will start to trust you and accept the advice that you give to them.

Questioning

The consultation is a chance to gain information from your client so that you can use that information to help them improve their lifestyle; however, the quality of the information you gain will depend on the quality of the questions that you ask. There are different types of questions, such as:

- Closed questions
- Open questions
- Indirect questions.

Closed questions can be answered with a simple yes

or no, or by a short phrase. They are used to obtain facts or to clarify a certain point, for example:

- Where do you live?
- What is your occupation?
- Have you tried changing your diet?

Open questions will require a longer and more thoughtful response, as they are used to invite the client into a discussion or to explore an issue, for example:

- What activities do you enjoy doing?
- How are you getting on with your training?

Indirect questions are a softer introduction to a question and they may feel less intrusive, so are good for gaining sensitive information, for example:

- Do you mind me asking what you are trying to achieve?
- I was wondering whether you had thought about giving up smoking?

When you are choosing questions, you need to think about the information you are aiming to gather, as this will influence whether you ask a closed, open or indirect question. You should also think about the wording you use in your question and make sure that the client will understand it, rather than using wording that you think makes you look intelligent!

Listening

Listening is the second part of good communication and is vital in establishing rapport. If you are a good listener, people will like talking to you and you will gather all the information that you need. The following are guidelines on how to listen to people:

- Clear your mind of thoughts, as it is not easy to listen to listen and think at the same time.
- Avoid jumping to conclusions or prejudging a person by how the person looks or talks.
- Establish eye contact, but keep your eyes soft so the client does not feel you are staring at them.
- Once the client has answered your questions, summarise the main points of what they have said and even take notes.
- Give the client your full attention and avoid fidgeting.

As you are consulting, you also need to consider non-verbal communication, which is body language and facial expressions. It is best to keep your body language open, which means that you should not cross your arms or legs, as they look like a barrier, and you should sit in a posture that makes it look like you are interested – for example, leaning forward slightly, but not in a threatening way. You should keep your expression relaxed and maintain eye contact when you are listening. Taken together, working on your questioning and listening skills and your non-verbal communication will help improve your consultation skills.

Key learning points 2

- A lifestyle questionnaire should address levels of activity, alcohol consumption, smoking, stress levels and diet. A one-to-one consultation should follow up a lifestyle questionnaire.

Q Quick quiz 2

Which of the following statements are true and which are false?

1 There should be an equal amount of talking between the trainer and the client during a consultation.
2 Once rapport has been created, the client will accept the advice that you offer.
3 Indirect questions can be used to put a client at ease.
4 'How do you feel your training is going?' is a closed question.
5 When you are listening, it is important to summarise what the client is telling you.

7.4 Lifestyle Improvement

P3 M3 P2

Physical Activity

When designing a physical activity programme, it is important to make the programme as personal as possible. It must meet the needs of the individual it is written for or it will result in the person being unhappy or unsuccessful. The key to this is gathering as much information as possible on the individual, by asking questions such as:

- What activities do you like to take part in?
- What have you done in the past that you enjoyed?
- Do you like to exercise alone or with other people?

You should take into account the facilities in the person's area. Do they live near a gym or leisure centre? One of the biggest factors to put people off going to a gym is if it is quite some distance away and takes them a while to get there. If the gym is close to where they live or work, this makes it a much more viable option. They could go to the gym in their lunch break or on the way to or from work.

Increasing Daily Activity

It is actually unnecessary to join a gym or go to a swimming pool to increase physical activity levels. There are lots of ways to attain the benefits of physical activity by just adapting everyday life. If a person takes the bus or train to work, they could get off one or two stops earlier and walk the remaining distance. If a person drives to work, they could park further away from their workplace and walk the remaining distance. If cycling to work is a viable option, it is not only good for you but is also cheaper and better for the environment. Many new cycle paths are being constructed to encourage people to cycle. Choosing options such as walking up a flight of stairs instead of taking a lift or escalator also help to increase a person's activity levels.

Fig 7.6 Gardening can increase heart rate and help tone muscles

Housework and gardening are productive ways of increasing daily activity levels. Vacuum cleaning and dusting the home, or digging the garden or mowing the lawn will increase heart rate and help tone muscles.

Reducing Alcohol Consumption

If a person is dependent on alcohol they must seek help to prevent the damage it does to their body and mind and to those around them.

In order to determine if a person is drinking more than the government recommended amounts of alcohol, it is a good idea to keep a 'drinking diary'. This involves noting what, how much and when that person drinks alcohol. If the person is just over the limit, simple changes could help them cut down. If they usually drink strong lager, they could opt for one that contains less alcohol. Or if they usually drink wine, they could have a spritzer instead, as this will make their drink last longer and help them to drink less. If they regularly meet up with friends in pubs, they could try to find alternative venues, such as a juice bar or coffee shop.

A GP can provide confidential advice and support. In order to help prevent the withdrawal symptoms of drinking, they may be prescribed antidepressants (e.g. Valium). Two drug treatments are also available to help a person stop drinking. A drug called Disulfiram makes the person feel very ill if they drink even a small amount of alcohol. Another drug called Acamprosate helps to reduce a person's craving for alcohol, but it does have many unpleasant side-effects. A person may attend organisations such as Alcohol Concern and Alcoholics Anonymous to help them stop drinking alcohol.

Stopping Smoking

Smokers have both a physical and a psychological addiction to smoking. The combination of these two factors makes cigarettes one of the most addictive drugs used today. Determining whether you are more physiologically than psychologically addicted to smoking will help to decide the best course of action in trying to stop smoking.

First of all, a person needs to think about why they smoke and identify the things they do that always make them want to light up. Once these triggers have been identified, the person can attempt to remove themselves from them. The next step is to decrease the person's dependence on nicotine. Either they can slowly decrease the amount of cigarettes they smoke over a set period or they could use a nicotine replacement therapy, such as a nicotine patch and/or nicotine gum. This process helps the person break the cigarette habit and also slowly reduces the amount of nicotine being taken into the body.

The NHS has set up a smoking helpline and runs clinics to help advise people on how to give up smoking. Each year there is a national no-smoking day, which has also been effective in making people think about giving up smoking and giving them a clear target day to attempt to stop.

Reducing Stress through Stress Management Techniques

The main methods of stress management are:

- Progressive muscular relaxation
- Mind-to-muscle relaxation
- Meditation/centring.

Progressive Muscular Relaxation

Progressive muscular relaxation (PMR) involves a person tensing and relaxing the muscle groups individually and sequentially to relax their whole body and mind. It is also called 'muscle-to-mind' relaxation, as muscles are tensed and relaxed to induce complete relaxation. Each muscle is tensed and relaxed to teach the person the difference between a tense muscle and a relaxed muscle. After a muscle is tensed, the relaxation effect is deepened, which also has an effect on the involuntary muscles.

The technique is practised using a series of taped instructions, or with the psychologist giving the instructions. It usually starts at the hands by making a tight fist and then relaxing. The tensing and relaxing carries on up the arms into the shoulders, face and neck, then down to the stomach and through the hips and legs.

These sessions last between 20 and 30 minutes, and need to be practised about five times a day to gain the maximum effect. Each time they are practised they have an increased effect and a person can relax more quickly and more deeply. The aim is that when the person needs to use the relaxation technique quickly, they can induce relaxation using a trigger, such as tensing the hand or the shoulders.

Mind-to-muscle Relaxation

Mind-to-muscle relaxation is also called imagery and involves the use of a mental room or a mental place. This is a place where a person can quickly picture themselves to produce feelings of relaxation when they need to relax.

Again, it involves the person using a taped script, or a psychologist giving instructions. Usually the psychologist asks a person to build a mental picture of a room. This is a room where they can feel relaxed and where there is somewhere to sit or lie down. It should be decorated in a pleasing manner. Alternatively, the person may imagine a relaxing place, such as somewhere they went on their holidays, or a beach or quiet place where they feel calm and relaxed. They are taught to imagine this place in detail and to feel the sensations associated with being there. They do this about five times, so that eventually they can go there when they need to and are able to relax more quickly and more deeply. As the person relaxes their mind, they feel the sensations transferring to their muscle groups and they can achieve overall body relaxation. It tends to work best for individuals who have good imagery skills. Other people may feel that PMR is more effective for them.

Meditation/Centring

Meditation/centring techniques involve the person focusing on one thing, such as their breathing (centring) or a mantra (meditation). By focusing their attention they become more and more relaxed. Again, these feelings of relaxation can eventually be produced when needed.

Diet

Food Preparation

The way food is prepared has a huge impact on its nutritional value. We should eat a fair amount of potatoes, but if you fry the potatoes to make chips, the food then belongs in the fats and oils food group, as it now has such a high concentration of fat.

You can prepare foods in certain ways to make them much healthier.

Breads and grains
- Use lots of wholemeal pasta and a small portion of sauce to prepare pasta dishes.
- Make sandwiches out of thick slices of wholemeal bread.
- Mash sweet potatoes and regular potatoes in larger than usual quantities for a shepherd's pie topping.

Fruits and vegetables
- Eat dried fruit, fresh fruit or vegetable sticks (e.g. carrot sticks) as snacks.
- A selection of vegetables or salads can accompany each main meal.
- Make fruit-based puddings, such as poached pears or apple and blackberry crumble.
- Add dried or fresh fruit to breakfast cereals.
- Include more vegetables in casserole dishes.

Meat, fish and vegetarian alternatives
- Use lean meat and remove skin and fat where possible.
- Grill meats wherever possible.
- Include pulses in meat dishes to reduce the fat

content and increase the fibre content, such as kidney beans in a chilli.

- Try to eat two portions of oily fish per week.

Milk and dairy foods

- Choose semi-skimmed or skimmed milk and low-fat or reduced-fat cheeses.
- Replace cream with fromage frais or yoghurt.
- Use strong-tasting cheese in cooking so that you require smaller amounts.

Foods containing fat and foods containing sugar

- Do not fry foods containing fat as it will just add more fat to them. Instead, grill or dry-bake them (without oil) in the oven.
- Use small amounts of plant-based cooking oils (e.g. olive oil or rapeseed) when frying foods.
- Make salad dressings with a balsamic vinegar base instead of oil.
- Sweeten puddings with dried or fresh fruits instead of sugar.
- Drink fresh water instead of fizzy drinks.

Timing of Food Intake

There is a saying that you should 'Eat breakfast like a king, lunch like a prince and dinner like a pauper.' This basically means that you should have your main meal at breakfast time, have a good-sized lunch and then eat your smallest meal at dinner time. The reasoning behind this saying is to have enough energy for the day and then to digest the food properly before going to bed. Heavy meals eaten before bedtime, such as a curry, take a long time to digest, which may disturb sleep. Any excess calories eaten during this meal will most probably be turned into body fat, as very few people actually take any form of exercise after a late heavy meal.

Key learning points 3

- Physical activity levels can be increased by adapting an individual's daily activities.
- A drinking diary can make a person aware of how much alcohol they are consuming.
- Nicotine replacement therapy and NHS support can help people stop smoking.
- Relaxation techniques, such as PMR and mind-to-muscle relaxation, can help reduce stress.
- The way foods are prepared and the timing of their intake can have an impact on an individual's health.

Q Quick quiz 3

Fill in the blank spaces to complete the following sentences.

In order to help a person improve their lifestyle it is important to increase their _____ _____ . It would be beneficial to _____ or _____ to work rather than take the car. When at home, gardening and housework can be used to raise the _____ _____ . It would improve health if alcohol consumption was reduced by keeping a _____ _____ , or, if a person smokes, by using _____ _____ _____ . Stress can cause people to smoke or drink more alcohol, but it can be reduced by using _____ techniques or using _____ to take them to a mental place or room. Also, diet can be improved by eating less _____ and more _____ and _____ .

7.5 Planning a Health-related Physical Activity Programme

Collecting Information

When a trainer sits down to design a physical activity programme, they need to consider a range of factors to ensure that the programme is appropriate and that it will benefit the person rather than harm them. They will need to consider the following factors:

- PAR-Q responses – have any contraindications to exercise been identified?
- Medical history – does the client have any conditions which may affect the training programme and choice of exercises?
- Current and previous exercise history – this will give an idea about the current fitness level of the client.
- Barriers to exercise – does the client have constraints such as time, cost, family responsibilities or work commitments?
- Motives and goals – what is the client aiming to achieve and what is their time-scale?

- Occupation – what hours does the client work, and is their work manual or office-based?
- Activity levels – what amount of movement does the client do on a daily basis?
- Leisure-time activities – are these active or inactive?
- Diet – what, how much and when does the client eat?
- Stress levels – how does the client deal with stress, either through work or in their home life?
- Alcohol intake – how much does the client consume and how often?
- Smoking – is the client a smoker or ex-smoker, and how much do they smoke?
- Time available – the client needs to fit the training into their schedule and the trainer needs to be realistic when planning the programme.

Goal Setting

Short-term goals are set over a brief period of time, usually from one day to one month. A short-term goal may relate to what you want to achieve in one training session or where you want to be by the end of the month.

Long-term goals run from three months to a period of several years. You may even set some lifetime goals, which run until you retire from your sport. In sport, we set long-term goals to cover a season or a sporting year. The period between one and three months would be called medium-term goals.

Usually, short-term goals are set to help achieve the long-term goals. It is important to set both short- and long-term goals, but particularly short-term goals, because they will give a person more motivation to act immediately.

When goals are set, you need to use the SMART principle to make them workable. SMART stands for:

- **S**pecific
- **M**easurable
- **A**chievable
- **R**ealistic
- **T**ime-constrained.

Specific
The goal must be specific to what you want to achieve. It is not enough to say, 'I want to get fitter'. You need to say, 'I want to improve strength/speed/stamina.'

Measurable
Goals must be stated in a way that is measurable, so a goal needs to state figures, for example, 'I want to cut down my alcohol intake to five units per week.'

Achievable
It must be possible to actually achieve the goal.

Realistic
We need to be realistic in our setting of goals and look at what factors may stop us achieving them.

Time-constrained
There must be a time-scale or deadline for the goal. This allows you to review your success. It is best to set a date by which you wish to achieve the goal.

Strategies to Achieve Goals
Some commonly used and effective strategies are as follows:

- **Using a decision balance sheet**: an individual writes down all the gains they will make by exercising and all the things they may lose through taking up exercise. Hopefully, the gains will outweigh the losses and this list will help to motivate them at difficult times.
- **Prompts**: an individual puts up posters or reminders around the house that will keep giving them reminders to exercise. This could also be done with little coloured dots on mirrors or other places where they look regularly.
- **Rewards for attendance/completing goals**: the individual is provided with an extrinsic reward for completing the goal or attending the gym regularly. This may be something to pamper themselves, such as a massage, and should not be something that conflicts with the goal – such as a slap-up meal!
- **Social support approaches**: you can help people to exercise regularly by developing a social support group of like-minded people with similar fitness goals, so that they can arrange to meet at the gym at certain times. This makes it more difficult for people to miss their exercise session. Also, try to gain the backing of the people they live with, to support them rather than teasing or criticising them.

Principles of Training

In order to develop a safe and effective training programme, you will need to consider the principles of training. These principles are a set of guidelines to help you understand the requirements of programme design. They are:

- Frequency
- Intensity
- Time
- Type
- Overload
- Reversibility
- Specificity.

145

- **Frequency:** this is how often the person will train per week.
- **Intensity:** this is how hard the person will work. It is usually expressed as a percentage of maximum intensity.
- **Time:** this indicates how long the person will train for in each session.
- **Type:** this shows the type of training the person will perform and needs to be individual to each person.
- **Overload:** this shows that to make an improvement, a muscle or system must work slightly harder than it is used to. This may be as simple as getting a sedentary person to walk for ten minutes or getting an athlete to squat more weight than have done previously.
- **Reversibility:** this principle states that if a fitness gain is not used regularly, the body will reverse it and go back to its previous fitness level. It is commonly known as 'use it or lose it'.
- **Specificity:** this principle states that any fitness gain will be specific to the muscles or system to which the overload is applied. Put simply, this says that different types of training will produce different results. To make a programme specific, you need to look at the needs of the person and then train them accordingly. For example, a person who was overweight would need to take part in lots of low-intensity cardiovascular training in order to burn fat.

Appropriate Activities

When you are devising your training programme you need to be sure that you are including activities that are appropriate to your client. If your client is obese, a training programme that includes jogging would probably not be appropriate. This kind of exercise is a high-impact exercise which places a lot of stress on the joints. If a person is obese, they will be stressing their joints to a greater degree, which means they would be much more likely to injure or damage their joints. Therefore, walking or swimming would be much more appropriate, as these activities place much less stress on the joints.

You should also try to include activities that you know your client enjoys. That way, they will be much more likely to continue their exercise programme.

Exercise Intensity

The intensity of exercise can be monitored by expressing it as a percentage of maximum heart rate. Your maximum heart rate is the maximum number of times your heart could beat. To find this out, you would have to work to your maximum intensity, which

for most people would clearly be unsafe. Therefore, we estimate the maximum heart rate by using the following formula:

$$\text{Maximum heart rate} = 220 - \text{age}$$

So, for a 17-year-old, their maximum heart rate would be $220 - 17 = 203$ beats per minute (b.p.m.).

To work out the heart rate training zone, we take percentages of heart rate maximum. If we work between 60 and 90 per cent, we would be working in the aerobic training zone, where the exercise we are performing is effective in improving aerobic fitness without being dangerous. However, it is still a wide range for a heart rate to be within, so we change the zone depending on the fitness level of the participant.

Rate of perceived exertion (RPE) is another measure used to monitor exercise. RPE is scale that can be used by the participant to rate how hard they feel they are working between two extremes. Rather than monitoring heart rate, the participant is introduced to the scale and then asked during the aerobic session where they feel they are. Below is Borg's modified RPE scale.

1 Extremely light.
2 Very light.
3 Moderate.
4
5 Somewhat hard.
6
7 Hard.
8 Very hard.
9 Extremely hard.
10 Maximal exertion.

To achieve aerobic fitness gains, the participant needs to be working at around 6 to 7 on the modified scale.

Key learning points 4

- Ensure you collect all relevant information from your client to assess their lifestyle and determine any contraindications.
- Ensure you set short-term and long-term goals.
- Apply the principles of training to your training programme.
- Ensure your training programme incorporates appropriate activities.
- Ensure your client exercises at the appropriate intensity.
- Effective zones for different groups as a percentage of maximum heart rate (MHR) are: beginners – 60 to 70 per cent of MHR; intermediate – 70 to 80 per cent of MHR; advanced – 80 to 90 per cent of MHR.

Student activity 7.1  3 hours

Read through the following case study and then complete the tasks that follow.

> Eddie is a full-time student who is studying a demanding course at university; he attends lectures from 9 a.m. to 5 p.m. every day. He also loves playing sport and plays football and cricket for the university; he also enjoys golf. Although he enjoys playing sport, he does not enjoy the training and feels that it gets in the way of his social life. He enjoys socialising and spends most evenings in the pub, even sometimes the night before a match. He worked out his alcohol consumption as 35 units per week, but he thinks it could be higher, and he has been smoking on what he sees as being a 'social basis', consisting of three to four cigarettes a day.
>
> Eddie does not really have a weight issue and he is able to get good food from the canteen. He knows he needs to eat fruit and vegetables, so he makes sure that he eats as much fresh food as he can and only occasionally eats takeaways. However, he hardly ever eats breakfast as he prefers to spend the time in bed.
>
> In terms of his current activity, Eddie plays football at the weekend and he does have a bike, but he chooses to get the university bus each day and occasionally goes training with the football team, which is mainly circuit training.

Task 1

Choose three lifestyle factors from the case study and describe the effect each one has on Eddie's health and well-being. To achieve a merit you need to explain the effects that each of the three lifestyle factors may have on Eddie's health and well-being.

Task 2

P2 M2 **D1**

1 Design a lifestyle questionnaire that could be used describe the strengths and weaknesses of Eddie's lifestyle.
2 Use a role-playing exercise with a fellow student; you should play the role of the consultant and your fellow student should play the role of Eddie. In this role play, use the questionnaire to gain as much information about Eddie as you can.

To achieve **P2** you need to describe the strengths and areas for improvement of Eddie's lifestyle. To achieve **M2** you need to explain these strengths and areas for improvement. To achieve **D1** you need to evaluate Eddie's lifestyle and make a list of priorities for changing and improving it.

Task 3

P3 M3 D2

Now that you have analysed the areas that Eddie has to improve, you need to decide the strategies you are going to use to help him to do this (**P3**). To achieve **M3** you need to explain why you have made these recommendations to improve Eddie's lifestyle. To achieve **D2** you need to analyse the effectiveness of these chosen methods.

Task 4

Now that you have looked at Eddie's lifestyle you need to focus on his physical activity and produce a six-week physical activity plan to help improve his health. Be sure to incorporate his current activity into the plan. You can use the following template to help him.

	Week 1	Week 2	Week 3	Week 4	Week 5	Week 6
Monday						
Tuesday						
Wednesday						
Thursday						
Friday						
Saturday						
Sunday						

Further reading

Baechle, T. and Earle, R. (2008) *Essentials of Strength Training and Conditioning*, Human Kinetics.

Dalgleish, J. and Dollery, S. (2001) *The Health and Fitness Handbook*, Longman.

Sharkey, B.J. and Gaskill, S.E. (2006). *Fitness and Health*, Human Kinetics.

Useful websites

www.bbc.co.uk/science/humanbody/

Interactive tests and puzzles about how the human body works

www.bhf.org.uk/keeping-your-heart-healthy/default.aspx

Tips from the British Heart Foundation on how to keep your heart healthy

www.getbodysmart.com

Free tutorials and quizzes from an American site that looks at human anatomy and physiology, helping you to see the structure of the different body systems.

www.innerbody.com

Free and informative diagrams of the different body systems, including respiratory, cardiovascular, skeletal and muscular

www.netfit.co.uk/nutrition/nutrition/index.htm

Free useful food facts with the focus on health and fitness.

8: Fitness testing for sport & exercise

8.1 Introduction

The ability to conduct fitness testing is a vital skill for the sport scientist to possess. All athletes and people starting exercise need to know where they are at any point in time so they can work out how close they are to where they want to be.

This unit will start by looking at a battery of fitness tests that can be used with athletes and people taking exercise, and will consider any advantages or disadvantages with these methods. Then we will look at screening techniques and health-monitoring tests that are used to identify whether a person is healthy enough to perform these fitness tests, which can push an individual to the limits of their fitness. Once we have knowledge of the tests, we will look at how these tests can be administered safely and how the data you gain from the tests can be interpreted.

By the end of this unit you should:

- know a range of laboratory-based and field-based fitness tests
- be able to use health-screening techniques
- be able to administer appropriate fitness tests
- be able to interpret the results of fitness tests and provide feedback.

Assessment and grading criteria		
To achieve a PASS grade the evidence must show that the learner is able to:	**To achieve a MERIT grade the evidence must show that, in addition to the pass criteria, the learner is able to:**	**To achieve a DISTINCTION grade the evidence must show that, in addition to the pass and merit criteria, the learner is able to:**
P1 describe one test for each component of physical fitness, including advantages and disadvantages	**M1** explain the advantages and disadvantages of one fitness test for each component of physical fitness	
P2 prepare an appropriate health-screening questionnaire		
P3 devise and use appropriate health-screening procedures for two contrasting individuals		
P4 safely administer and interpret the results of four different health-monitoring tests for two contrasting individuals	**M2** describe the strengths and areas for improvement for two contrasting individuals using information from health-screening questionnaires and health-monitoring tests	**D1** evaluate the health screening-questionnaires and health-monitoring test results and provide recommendations for lifestyle improvement
P5 select and safely administer six different fitness tests for a selected individual, recording the findings	**M3** justify the selection of fitness tests, commenting on suitability, reliability, validity and practicality	
P6 give feedback to a selected individual, following fitness testing, describing the test results and interpreting their levels of fitness against normative data.	**M4** compare the fitness test results to normative data and identify strengths and areas for improvement.	**D2** analyse the fitness test results and provide recommendations for appropriate future activities or training.

8.2 Laboratory-based and field-based fitness tests

Tests are conducted to assess each different component of fitness. It is important to choose the components of fitness relative to the person you are working with. This will depend on their own goals and the activities they are involved in, be it sport or exercise.

Performance-related fitness

Performance in sport and exercise is dependent on a range of components of fitness. These are shown in Figure 8.1.

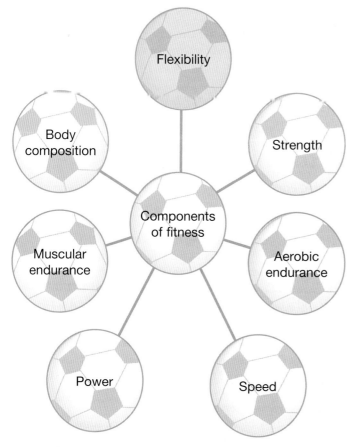

Fig 8.1 Components of fitness

Test protocols

The following is a list of test protocols:

● sit and reach
● one repetition maximum
● grip strength dynamometer
● multi-stage fitness test

● step test
● 40-metre sprint
● vertical jump
● Wingate test
● one-minute press-up test
● one-minute sit-up test
● skinfold assessment
● bioelectrical impedance
● hydro-densitometry.

We will now look at each of these in turn.

Flexibility

The **sit and reach test** measures the flexibility of the muscles in the lower back and hamstrings. This test is safe to perform unless the athlete has a lower back injury, particularly a slipped disc. The test is performed in the following way:

1 Warm the athlete up with five minutes' jogging or cycling.
2 Ask the athlete to take off their shoes and any clothing that will limit movement.
3 The athlete sits with their legs straight and their feet against the board. Their legs and back should be straight.
4 The client reaches as far forward as they possibly can and pushes the marker forward.
5 Record the furthest point the marker reaches.

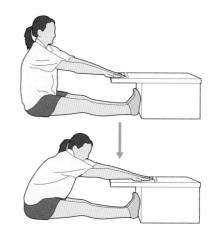

Fig 8.2 Sit and reach test

This test is quick and easy to administer and perform; however, it is a fairly non-specific test as it tells us something about the range of movement in the back, hamstrings and calves, but we may not be able to identify where there are restrictions or tight muscles. Also it tells us nothing about the range of movement in other important muscle groups, such as the chest, quadriceps or hip flexors.

Category	Males (cm)	Females (cm)
Elite	>27	>30
Excellent	17 to 27	21 to 30
Good	6 to 16	11 to 20
Average	0 to 5	1 to 10
Fair	–8 to –1	–7 to 0
Poor	–9 to –19	–8 to –14
Very poor	<–20	<–15

Table 8.1 Categories for sit and reach scores (adapted from Franklin, 2000)

Strength

The **one repetition maximum** (1 RM) is a measure of absolute strength and is the maximum weight that can be moved once with perfect technique.

This is clearly a dangerous test to perform unless the client is of an advanced skill level and is very well conditioned. The test will also require a thorough warm-up prior to its performance.

The test is performed in the following way:

1 Choose an exercise requiring the use of large muscle groups, such as a bench press or a leg press.
2 Warm up with a light weight for ten repetitions.
3 Give one minute rest.
4 Estimate a resistance that can be used for three to five repetitions.
5 Give two minutes' rest.
6 Estimate a load that can be used for two to three repetitions.
7 Give two to three minutes' rest.
8 Decide on a load that can be used for one repetition.
9 If successful, then give two to four minutes' rest.
10 Add a little more weight and complete one repetition.
11 Weight is gradually added until the client fails.
12 1 RM is the last weight that can be completed successfully.

There are no normative tables for 1 RM tests as they are used to monitor progress and strength gains. They can also be used to decide on training loads for the individual.

The **grip strength dynamometer** is a static test to assess muscular strength in the arm muscles. Unfortunately, it will give no indication as to the strength of other muscle groups. The test involves squeezing a hand-grip dynamometer as hard as possible. The test is conducted in the following way:

1 Adjust the handle to fit the size of your hand.
2 Hold the dynamometer in your strongest hand and keep the arm hanging by your side with the dynamometer by your thigh.
3 Squeeze the dynamometer as hard as you can for around five seconds.
4 Record the results and repeat after about a minute.
5 Take your best recording.

Aerobic endurance

The **multi-stage fitness test** was developed at the University of Loughborough and is known as the 'bleep' test because athletes have to run between timed bleeps. The test will give you an estimation of your VO_2max, which is the measure of your aerobic fitness level. You will need the pre-recorded CD or tape and a flat area of 20 metres, with a cone at either end. This test can be used with large groups, as all the athletes will run together. The procedure is as follows:

1 Mark out a length of 20 metres with cones.
2 Start the tape and the athletes run when the first bleep sounds. They will run the 20 metres before the second bleep sounds.
3 When this bleep sounds, they turn around and run back.
4 They continue to do this and the time between the bleeps gets shorter and shorter, so they have to run faster and faster.
5 If an athlete fails to get to the other end before the bleep on three consecutive occasions, they are out.
6 Record at what point the athlete dropped out.
7 Using Table 8.2, you can find out the athlete's predicted VO_2max.

This is an excellent field-based test which can be used to assess and monitor the fitness levels of individuals and groups of people. The results are dependent on the motivation level of the participants and how willing they are to drive themselves to their limits.

The **Canadian step test** is a simple and straight-forward test to perform, and measures how heart rate increases with steady-state exercise.

You need a step 30 cm high, a heart-rate monitor and a stopwatch. This test is carried out in the following way:

1 The client steps up and down for three minutes while you monitor their heart rate.
2 You keep the client at a steady state by saying 'up, up, down, down' at a normal speech rate. The client should complete 24 steps per minute.
3 At the end of the third minute, record their heart rate.
4 Compare the result to the normative data for males and females shown in Tables 8.3 and 8.4.

Category	Males (mm/O2/kg/min'''1)	Females (mm/O2/kg/min'''1)
Extremely high	>70	>60
Very high	63–69	54–59
High	57–62	49–53
Above average	52–56	44–48
Average	44–51	35–43

Table 8.2 Categories for predicted VO_2max scores (adapted from Baechle and Earle, 2008)

Age	Excellent	Good	Above average	Average	Below average	Poor	Very poor
18–25	<79	79–89	90–99	100–105	106–116	117–128	>128
26–35	<81	81–89	90–99	100–107	108–117	118–128	>128
36–45	<83	83–96	97–103	104–112	113–119	120–130	>130
46–55	<87	87–97	97–105	106–116	117–122	123–132	>132
56–65	<86	86–97	98–103	104–112	113–120	121–129	>129
65+	<88	88–96	97–103	104–113	114–120	121–130	>130

Table 8.3 The classification for males measured in b.p.m. (adapted from Franklin, 2000)

Age	Excellent	Good	Above average	Average	Below average	Poor	Very poor
18–25	<85	85–98	99–108	109–117	118–126	127–140	>140
26–35	<88	88–99	100–111	112–119	120–126	127–138	>138
36–45	<90	90–102	103–110	111–118	119–128	129–140	>140
46–55	<94	94–104	105–115	116–120	121–129	130–135	>135
56–65	<95	95–104	105–112	113–118	119–128	129–139	>139
65+	<90	90–102	103–115	116–122	123–128	129–134	>134

Table 8.4 The classification for females measured in b.p.m. (adapted from Franklin, 2000)

Fig 8.3 Canadian step test

This is a safe test to use with clients and provides a useful means to monitor progress. It will not provide any information regarding their maximal aerobic capacity.

Speed

The **40-metre sprint** is a test for pure speed. You will need a flat running surface and a tape measure to ensure the distance is correct. You also require a stopwatch and a person who can time the run. The test is conducted in the following way:

1 The athlete warms up for several minutes.
2 They then do the 40-metre run at a speed less than their maximum.
3 The athlete starts the test behind the line, with one or two hands on the ground.
4 The starter will shout 'go' and the athlete sprints the 40 metres as quickly as possible.

5 This run should be repeated after two or three minutes and the average of the two runs taken.

This test is a good, accurate test of pure speed; it is dependent on the competence of the testers to accurately record the times of the performers.

Power

The **vertical jump** is a test of power, with the aim being to see how high the athlete can jump. It is important that you find a smooth wall, with a ceiling higher than the athlete can jump. A sports hall or squash court is ideal. The test is conducted in the following way:

1 The athlete rubs chalk on their fingers.
2 They stand about 15 cm away from the wall.
3 With their feet flat on the floor, they reach as high as they can and make a mark on the wall.
4 The athlete then rubs more chalk on their fingers.
5 They then bend their knees to 90 degrees and jump as high as they can up into the air.
6 At the top of their jump they make a second chalk mark with their fingertips.
7 The trainer measures the difference between their two marks – this is their standing jump score.
8 This test is best done three times, so the athlete can take the best of their three jumps.

Category	Males (seconds)	Females (seconds)
Elite	<4.6	<5.5
Excellent	4.6–4.7	5.5–5.7
Good	4.8–5.0	5.8–8.3
Average	5.1–5.5	8.4–8.7
Below average	>5.6	>8.7

Table 8.5 Categories for the 40-metre sprint test (adapted from Franklin, 2000)

Rating	Males (cm)	Females (cm)
Excellent	>70	>60
Very good	61–70	51–60
Above average	51–60	41–50
Average	41–50	31–40
Below average	31–40	21–30
Poor	21–30	11–20
Very poor	<21	<10

Table 8.6 Ratings for males and females in the vertical jump test (adapted from Franklin, 2000)

Fig 8.4 Vertical jump test

Fig 8.5 Wingate test

Anaerobic Capacity

The **Wingate test** is a maximal test of anaerobic capacity and is thus suitable only for highly conditioned clients. It is used to measure peak anaerobic power and anaerobic capacity. It is carried out in the following way:

1 The client warms up for around two to three minutes at increasing intensities until their heart rate is 180 b.p.m.
2 Once they are ready, the client cycles as fast as they can for 30 seconds at a calculated load. The load is calculated for use on the Monark cycle ergometer. For a person aged under 15 years, the load is their body weight in kilograms × 0.35 g. For an adult, it is their body weight in kilograms × 0.75 g. A 70 kg adult's workload would be worked out in the following way: 70 × 0.75 = 52.5 kg.
3 The client is instructed to start and then given two seconds to achieve their maximum speed, at which point the workload is added.

4 The client pedals for 30 seconds as fast as they can, and the tester needs to count the number of revolutions of the flywheel every five seconds.
5 There needs to be a second tester who records the scores as they are called out for each five seconds.
6 At the end of the 30 seconds, the client cools down at a light workload.

To work out the power for each five-second interval, you need to use the following equation:

Power = load (kg) × revolutions of flywheel in five seconds × radius of flywheel × 12.33

This score is then divided by their body weight in kilograms to calculate the power per kilogram of body mass.

To analyse the results you need to do the following:

● Plot a graph with power in watts (y-axis) against time in seconds (x-axis).
● The peak anaerobic power is the highest power score in a five-second period.

155

- The minimum anaerobic power is the lowest score in a five-second period.
- The power decline can be calculated in the following way:

$$\text{Power decline} = \frac{\text{Peak power} - \text{Minimum power}}{\text{Peak power} \times 100}$$

You will need to use Table 8.7 to record the results and then work out the power achieved.

This is a test of maximal aerobic capacity and should be used only with advanced, well-conditioned performers. Again, its accuracy is dependent on the motivation of the individual to push themselves to their maximum capacity.

Muscular endurance

The **one-minute press-up test** is a test of muscular endurance in the chest and arms. You will need a mat and a stopwatch.

It is carried out in the following way:

1 This test involves the male starting in the press-up position, with their hands facing forwards and below the shoulders, back straight and pivoting on their toes. Females will perform the test from their knees, with their knees, hips and shoulders all in line and their lower legs resting on the ground.
2 The subject will go down until their chest is 2 cm off the floor and push up to a straight elbow. They must maintain a straight back.
3 The number of press-ups performed in one minute without rest is recorded.
4 If a client is unable to maintain good technique or shows undue fatigue, the test must be stopped.

Time (s)	Number of revolutions of flywheel	Power (watts)	Power per kg of body mass
0–2			
2–7			
7–12			
12–17			
17–22			
22–27			
27–32			

Table 8.7 Recording the information from the Wingate test

Age	Excellent	Very good	Good	Fair	Needs improvement
20–29	36	29–35	22–28	17–21	<17
30–39	30	22–29	17–21	15–20	<15
40–49	25	17–24	13–16	8–12	<8
50–59	21	13–20	10–12	7–9	<7
60–69	18	11–17	8–10	5–7	<5

Table 8.8 Categories for males measured in the number of completed press-ups (adapted from Franklin, 2000)

Age	Excellent	Very good	Good	Fair	Needs improvement
20–29	30	21–29	15–20	10–14	<10
30–39	27	20–26	13–19	8–12	<8
40–49	24	15–23	11–14	5–10	<4
50–59	21	11–20	7–10	2–6	1
60–69	17	12–16	5–11	2–4	1

Table 8.9 Categories for females measured in the number of completed press-ups (adapted from Franklin, 2000)

Age	High	Above average	Average	Below average	Low
17–19	>49	44–48	37–43	24–36	<24
20–29	>44	39–43	32–38	20–31	<20
30–39	>39	34–38	27–33	16–26	<16

Table 8.10 The classification for males measured in the number of completed sit-ups (adapted from Franklin, 2000)

Age	High	Above average	Average	Below average	Low
17–19	>42	32–41	25–31	19–24	<19
20–29	>36	27–35	21–26	15–20	<15
30–39	>30	22–29	17–21	11–16	<11

Table 8.11 The classification for females measured in the number of completed sit-ups (adapted from Franklin, 2000)

The **one-minute sit-up test** is a test of muscular endurance in the abdominals. You will need a mat and a stopwatch.

The test procedure is as follows:

1 The athlete lies on the floor with their fingers on their temples and their knees bent.
2 On the command of 'go', the athlete sits up until their elbows touch their knees.
3 They then return to the start position, with the back of their head touching the floor. That will be one repetition.
4 The athlete does as many repetitions as they can in one minute.

Body composition

In very simple terms, a person's body weight or mass can be split into two categories: fat mass and lean body weight (all that is not fat).

● Fat mass is made up of fat (adipose tissue).
● Lean body weight consists of:
  – muscle
  – water
  – bone
  – organs
  – connective tissue.

This shows that you can lose weight by reducing any of the components of the body. However, lean body weight could be seen as healthy weight, as it contributes to the performance of the body. Fat weight in excess would be unhealthy weight, as it would cause a loss in performance as it requires oxygen without giving anything back to the body.

It is necessary to take a body fat measurement to show that the weight loss is fat and not muscle.

It is impossible to turn muscle into fat or fat into muscle. This is because they are completely different types of tissue in the body. A good training programme will produce a loss of fat or excess fat and a gain in muscle tissue. So while it may look like one is turning into the other, this is not the case. This happens particularly when an athlete does weight training.

157

1. **Triceps brachii**
With the client's arm hanging loosely, a vertical fold is raised at the back of the arm, midway along a line connecting the acromion (shoulder) and olecranon (elbow) processes.

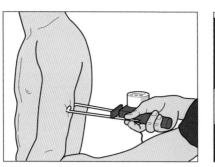

2. **Biceps brachii**
A vertical fold is raised at the front of the arm, opposite to the triceps site. This should be directly above the centre of the cubital fossa (fold of the elbow).

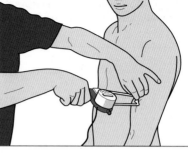

3. **Subscapular**
A fold is raised just beneath the inferior angle of the scapula (bottom of the shoulder-blade). This fold should be at an angle of 45 degrees downwards and outwards.

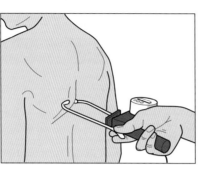

4. **Anterior suprailiac**
A fold is raised 5–7 cm above the spinale (pelvis), at a point in line with the anterior axillary border (armpit). The fold should be in line with the natural folds downwards and inwards at up to 45 degrees.

Fig 8.6 Body fat measurement

Area	Description of site
Triceps	This is taken halfway between the shoulder and elbow on the back of the arm. It is a vertical pinch.
Biceps	This is taken 1 cm above the site for the triceps on the front of the arm. It is a vertical pinch.
Subscapular	This is taken 2 cm below the lowest point of the shoulder blade. It is taken at a 45-degree angle.
Suprailiac	This is taken just above the iliac crest (hip bone), directly below the front of the shoulder.

Table 8.12 Description of four sites for measuring body composition

The **skinfold assessment** test is carried out using skinfold calipers. It is conducted using the Durnin and Wormsley sites, and is carried out as follows:

1 Take the measurements on the left-hand side of the body.
2 Mark up the client accurately.
3 Pinch the skin 1 cm above the marked site.
4 Pull the fat away from the muscle.
5 Place the calipers halfway between the top and bottom of the skinfold.
6 Allow the calipers to settle for one or two seconds.
7 Take the reading and wait 15 seconds before repeating for accuracy.
8 Add up the total of the four measurements.
9 Calculate body fat percentage using Table 8.13.

This test has proved to be an accurate method of assessing and monitoring body composition; however, it is very dependent on the tester's competence to correctly identify the skinfold sites and then to take the measurement accurately. This does involve a fair amount of skill and practice.

The **bioelectrical impedance** technique involves placing electrodes on one hand and one foot and then passing a very small electrical current through the body. The theory is that muscle will conduct the electricity, while fat will resist the path of the electricity. Therefore, the more electricity that comes out of the body, the more muscle a person has, and the less electricity that comes out, the more fat a person has.

This technique has benefits over skinfold measurement because it is easier to do and does not mean that the client has to remove or adjust any clothing. However, it has been shown to be not such an accurate measure of body fat percentage, as it is dependent on how well hydrated the individual is at any point.

Hydro-densitometry, or underwater weighing, is a technique based on the Archimedes principle.

Males		Females	
Sum of skinfolds	Body fat %	Sum of skinfolds	Body fat %
		14	9.4
		16	11.2
		18	12.7
20	7.1	20	14.1
22	9.2	22	15.4
24	10.2	24	18.5
26	11.2	26	17.6
28	12.1	28	17.6
30	12.9	30	19.5
35	14.7	35	21.6
40	18.3	40	23.4
45	17.7	45	25.0
50	19.0	50	28.5
55	20.2	55	27.8
60	21.2	60	29.1
65	22.2	65	30.2
70	23.2	70	31.2
75	24.0	75	32.2
80	24.8	80	33.1
85	25.6	85	34.0
90	28.3	90	34.8
95	27.0	95	35.6
100	27.6	100	38.3
110	27.8	110	37.7
120	29.9	120	39.0
130	31.0	130	40.2
140	31.9	140	41.3
150	32.8	150	42.3
160	33.6	160	43.2
170	34.4	170	44.6
180	35.2	180	45.0

Table 8.13 Body fat measurements for males and females (adapted from Franklin, 2000)

It involves a person being weighed on land and then when fully submerged in water. Muscle and bone are denser than water, while fat is less dense. A person with more bone and muscle will weigh more in water, have a higher body density and therefore less fat. Once the weight on land and weight in water are taken, a formula is used to work out percentage body fat.

This technique involves the use of a large pool of water and significant amounts of equipment. It is impractical for use outside a sport science laboratory.

Fig 8.7 Underwater weighing

Key learning points 1

- Blood pressure, resting heart rate, lung function, body mass index and hip-to-waist ratio are all static tests which are performed to see if the client is healthy enough to perform the dynamic fitness tests.
- Performance-related fitness is made up of the following components: flexibility, strength, aerobic endurance, speed, power, muscular endurance and body composition.
- Flexibility is measured by a sit and reach test.
- Strength is measured by one repetition maximum and grip strength dynamometer.
- Aerobic endurance is measured by the multi-stage fitness test and the step test.
- Anaerobic capacity is measured by the Wingate test.
- Speed is measured by the 40-metre sprint test.
- Power is measured by the vertical jump test.
- Muscular endurance is measured by the one-minute press-up test and the one-minute sit-up test.
- Body composition is measured by skinfold assessment, bioelectrical impedance and hydro-densitometry tests.

Classification	Males (% body fat)	Females (% body fat)
Under-fat	<6	<14
Athletes	6–13	14–20
Fitness	14–17	21–24
Acceptable	18–25	25–30
Overweight	26–30	31–40
Obese	>30	>40

Table 8.14 Calculating your body fat percentage (adapted from Franklin, 2000)

Student activity 8.1   ⏱ **45 minutes**   P1   M1

Fill in the following table to demonstrate your knowledge of the tests for the different components of fitness and their advantages and disadvantages.

Component of fitness	Description of a test for component of fitness	Description of test's strengths and weaknesses	Explanation of test's strengths and weaknesses
Flexibility	Sit and reach test – where the person sits with their feet against a board and slowly bends forwards to see how far they can reach.	It is an easy-to-use test for flexibility, but it does not give us very specific scores.	The test is easy to explain and easy for the participant to perform. It is safe and we can get the results quickly. However, it gives us a score that measures flexibility in the back, hamstrings and calves, but cannot be used to identify range of movement specifically in one of the areas or any other joint/muscle in the body. It gives us a general measure of flexibility but lacks specificity.
Strength			
Aerobic endurance			
Speed			
Anaerobic endurance			
Muscular endurance			
Body composition			

Ⓠ Quick quiz 1

Match each fitness test in the table below to the component of fitness that it tests, choosing from the following:

- flexibility
- strength
- aerobic endurance
- speed
- anaerobic capacity
- muscular endurance
- body composition.

Name of test	Component of fitness tested
Wingate test	
Bioelectrical impedance	
I RM	
One-minute press-up test	
40-metre sprint	
Sit and reach test	
Multi-stage fitness test	

8.3 Using health-screening techniques

Before you start to conduct fitness tests with an athlete or a person who wants to start exercising, you will need to conduct a detailed fitness consultation. This will consist of the following:

● health-screening questionnaire

● informed consent form
● identification of coronary heart disease risk factors
● identification of any causes for medical referral.

Health-screening questionnaire

You will need to have prepared a detailed questionnaire to cover areas such as medical conditions, illnesses and injuries, as well as history of exercise and lifestyle factors. A sample questionnaire is shown here.

Section 1: Personal Details

Name_____

Address _____

_____

_____

_____

Home telephone _____

Mobile telephone _____

Email _____

Occupation_____

Date of birth _____

Section 2: Sporting Goals

1 What are your long-term sporting goals over the next year or season?

_____

_____

2 What are your medium-term goals over the next three months?

_____

_____

_____

3 What are your short-term goals over the next four weeks?

_____

_____

_____

_____

Section 3: Current Training Status

1 What are your main training requirements?
   (a) Muscular strength.
   (b) Muscular endurance.
   (c) Speed.
   (d) Flexibility.
   (e) Aerobic fitness.
   (f) Power.
   (g) Weight loss or gain.
   (h) Skill-related fitness.
   (i) Other (please state).

_____

2 How would you describe your current fitness status?

_____

_____

3 How many times a week will you train?

_____

4 How much time do you have available for each training session?

_____

Section 4: Your Nutritional Status

1 On a scale of 1 to 10 (1 being very low quality and 10 being very high quality), how would you rate the quality of your diet?

_____

2 Do you follow any particular diet?
   (a) Vegetarian.
   (b) Vegan.
   (c) Vegetarian and fish.
   (d) Gluten-free.
   (e) Dairy-free.

_____

3 How often do you eat? Note down a typical day's intake.

_____

_____

_____

_____

4 Do you take any supplements? If so, which ones?

_____

_____

Section 5: Your Lifestyle

1 How many units of alcohol do you drink in a typical week? _____

2 Do you smoke? _____ If yes, how many a day? _____

3 Do you experience stress on a daily basis? _____

4 If yes, what causes you stress (if you know)?

_____

_____

_____

5 What techniques do you use to deal with your stress?

_____

Section 6: Your Physical Health

1 Do you experience any of the following?

   (a) Back pain or injury.

   (b) Knee pain or injury.

   (c) Ankle pain or injury.

   (d) Swollen joints.

   (e) Shoulder pain or injury.

   (f) Hip or pelvic pain or injury.

   (g) Nerve damage.

   (h) Head injuries.

2 If yes, please give details.

_____

_____

_____

3 Are any of these injuries made worse by exercise?

_____

4 If yes, what movements in particular cause pain?

_____

5 Are you currently receiving any treatment for any injuries? If so, what?

_____

Section 7: Medical History

1 Do you have or have you had any of the following medical conditions?

   (a) Asthma.

   (b) Bronchitis.

   (c) Heart problems.

   (d) Chest pains.

   (e) Diabetes.

   (f) High blood pressure.

   (g) Epilepsy.

   (h) Other.

2 Are you taking any medication? If yes, state what, how much and why.

Section 8: Informed Consent

Name

Signature

Trainer's name

Trainer's signature

Date

Notes

1 **Explanation of the tests.**
You will perform a series of tests which will vary in their demands on your body. Your progress will be observed during the tests and stopped if you show signs of undue fatigue. You may stop the tests at any time if you feel unduly uncomfortable.

2 **Risks of exercise testing.**
During exercise certain changes can occur, such as raised blood pressure, fainting, raised heart rate and, in a very small number of cases, heart attacks or even death. Every effort is made through screening to minimise the risk of these occurring during testing. Emergency equipment and relevantly trained personnel are available to deal with any extreme situation that occurs.

3 **Responsibility of the participant.**
You must disclose all information in your possession regarding the state of your health or previous experiences of exercise, as this will affect the safety of the tests. If you experience any discomfort or unusual sensations, it is your responsibility to inform your trainer.

4 **Benefits to expect.**
The results gained during testing will be used to identify any illnesses and the types of activities that are relevant for you.

5 **Freedom of consent.**
Your participation in these tests is voluntary and you are free to deny consent or stop a test at any point.
I have read this form and understand what is expected of me and the tests I will perform. I give my consent to participate.

Client's signature

Print name

Date

Trainer's signature

Print name

Date

Informed consent

An informed consent form lets a client know what to expect during the exercise test, and the associated risks involved in exercise or training. It also stresses that any participation in the tests is voluntary and that they have the choice to stop at any point.

An example of an informed consent form is shown at the end of the health-screening questionnaire above.

Risk of coronary heart disease

Coronary heart disease (CHD) is a leading cause of death in all industrialised countries. It is caused by a narrowing of the coronary arteries, which limits the amount of blood flowing through the arteries.

Key term

Coronary arteries: blood vessels that bring oxygenated blood to nourish the muscle cells of the heart muscle.

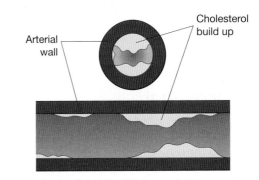

Fig 8.8 Build-up of cholesterol in an artery

165

Arteries losing their elasticity is part of the ageing process. However, there are many lifestyle factors that cause damage or narrowing of the arteries. Obstructions are created as cholesterol and fatty plaques are laid down in the artery, causing a narrowing of the artery space.

The coronary arteries are found only in the heart and they supply the heart with oxygen to enable it to pump. When these arteries narrow or become blocked, the blood supply to the heart is reduced. As a result, carbon dioxide builds up in the heart muscle and this causes pain, which is called angina. Angina feels like a crushing pain on the chest. If this pain becomes a shooting pain into the left arm and the neck, the person is having a heart attack.

The following lifestyle factors will increase an individual's chance of having CHD:

- diet high in fat (particularly deep-fat fried foods)
- diet high in table salt (sodium chloride)
- obesity (particularly abdominal fat)
- smoking
- excess alcohol consumption
- older age
- male gender
- high blood pressure
- type 2 diabetes.

Fig 8.9 Smoking will increase an individual's chance of having CHD

If you consider that a person has a high risk of CHD, it is best to refer them for GP clearance before you start to train them.

Medical referral

To ensure that you offer a proper 'duty of care' to your client, you will need to refer them to a GP if you have any doubt regarding how safe it is for them to exercise. If your client has any of the following, they must be referred to their GP:

- high blood pressure (over 160/100)
- poor lung function
- excess body fat (40 per cent or more for a female, 30 per cent or more for a male)
- high resting heart rate (100+ b.p.m.)
- medication for a heart condition (e.g. beta blockers).

Likewise, if they experience any of the following, they must also be referred to their GP:

- Muscle injuries
- Chest pain or tightness
- Light-headedness or dizziness
- Irregular or rapid pulse
- Joint pain
- Headaches
- Shortness of breath.

Health-monitoring tests

Tests can be split into two clear categories: those that measure health and those that measure fitness. Health tests are carried out to see if the individual is healthy enough to do the fitness tests or whether they need to receive GP clearance. Health tests will be static in nature while fitness tests will be dynamic and involve bodily movement and exertion.

The health tests conducted are:

- heart rate
- blood pressure
- lung function
- waist-to-hip ratio
- body mass index (BMI).

Resting heart rate

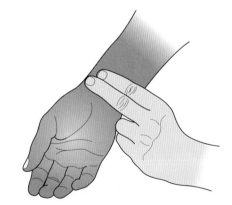

Fig 8.10 Taking a pulse rate

To measure the resting heart rate, you can use a heart rate monitor or do it manually. The best time to take a person's resting heart rate is before the person gets out of bed and experiences the stresses of the day. To perform it manually, complete the following steps:

1 Let your client sit down and rest for about five minutes.
2 Find their radial pulse (wrist) or brachial pulse (front of elbow).
3 Place your middle and index fingers over the pulse. The thumb has a pulse of its own and will produce an inaccurate reading.
4 Count the pulse for 60 seconds and record the result before repeating for another 60 seconds.
5 If there is a large variation in readings you should take a third reading.

Here is a reference for resting heart rates for men and women:

Category	Males (b.p.m.)	Females (b.p.m.)
Normal	60–80	60–80
Average	70	76
Proceed with caution	90–99	90–99
GP referral	100+	100+

Table 8.15 Heart rate reference tables for males and females (adapted from Franklin, 2000)

Blood Pressure

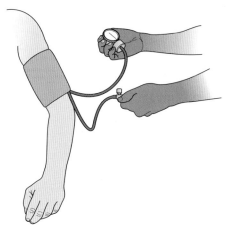

Fig 8.11 Taking a blood pressure reading

Blood pressure is the pressure blood exerts on the artery walls and is a clear indication of general health. It is vital to measure blood pressure before a client exercises, because it will tell you whether they are at risk of having a heart attack.

We need to split this up into the short-term and long-term. Short-term means the blood pressure rises for a period and then falls again, while long-term means that the blood pressure remains high all the time.

Blood pressure is taken by a blood pressure meter and stethoscope, or it can be done using an electronic blood pressure meter.

1 Allow the client to be relaxed for about five minutes.
2 Ask the client to sit down, with their left arm resting on a chair arm. Their elbow should be at 45 degrees, with the palm of the hand facing up.
3 Find the brachial pulse – it should be on the inner side of the arm, just under the biceps muscle.
4 Place the cuff just clear of the elbow (about 2–3 cm above the elbow). The bladder of the cuff (the part which inflates) should be directly over the pulse.
5 Place the earpieces of the stethoscope in your ears and place the microphone over the brachial pulse.
6 Inflate the cuff up to 200 mmHg.
7 Slowly open the valve by turning it anticlockwise and release the pressure.
8 Listen out for the first time you hear the thud of the heart beat and make a mental note of it. This is the systolic blood pressure reading.
9 Keep deflating the cuff, and when the heart beat becomes muffled or disappears, this is your diastolic reading.
10 Keep deflating the cuff and, if necessary, repeat after around 30 seconds.

Lung function

We need to assess lung function to see whether the airways between the mouth and the alveoli are clear and conducive to good air flow. Poor lung function will limit the amount of oxygen that can be delivered to the bloodstream and the tissues.

Lung function can be measured using a micro-spirometer or a hand-held peak flow meter.

To use a peak flow meter, work through the following steps:

1 Ask the client to hold the peak flow meter directly in front of their mouth.
2 Ask them to turn their head to the side and take three deep breaths.
3 On the third breath, ask them to put their mouth around the end of the tube and, ensuring a good lip seal, blow as hard as they can into the tube.
4 Say that it should be a short, sharp blow, as if they were using a pea shooter.
5 Repeat twice more and take the highest reading. This is called their peak expiratory flow rate (PEFR).

167

Age	1.55 m	1.60 m	1.65 m	1.70 m	1.75 m	1.80 m	1.85 m	1.90m
25	515	534	552	570	589	607	625	644
30	502	520	539	557	576	594	612	632
35	489	508	526	544	563	582	600	619
40	476	495	513	531	550	568	586	606
45	463	482	501	519	537	556	574	593
50	450	469	487	505	524	543	561	580
55	438	456	475	493	511	530	548	567
60	424	443	462	480	498	517	535	545
65	412	430	449	460	486	504	522	541
70	399	417	436	454	472	491	509	528

Table 8.16 PEFR for males (adapted from Franklin, 2000)

Age	1.45 m	1.50 m	1.55 m	1.60 m	1.65 m	1.70 m	1.75 m	1.80m
25	365	383	400	416	433	449	466	482
30	357	374	390	407	423	440	456	473
35	348	365	381	398	414	431	447	464
40	339	356	372	389	405	422	438	455
45	330	347	363	380	397	413	429	446
50	321	338	354	371	388	404	420	437
55	312	329	345	362	379	395	411	428
60	303	320	336	353	370	386	402	419
65	294	311	327	344	361	377	393	410
70	285	302	318	335	352	368	384	401

Table 8.17 PEFR for females (adapted from Franklin, 2000)

The PEFR is a measurement of the power of the lungs. It is a hypothetical figure which tells us how much air would pass through our lungs if we breathed in and out at our maximum power for one minute. It is hypothetical because it cannot really be measured, as we would faint after about 15 seconds of breathing at maximum power.

You will need to know the gender, age and height of the client to work out their acceptable score.

The PEFR for males and for females are shown in Tables 8.16 and 8.17.

If your client's score is 100 below the acceptable figure, this is classified as poor lung function and they should be referred to their GP before they exercise.

Body mass index

Body mass index is used to give us an idea of whether a client is obese. It then gives the extent of their obesity.

This is worked out by using the following formula:

Body mass index (BMI) = weight in kilograms divided by height in metres squared.

For a male who weighs 75 kg and is 1.80 m tall: $75 \div 1.80^2 = 23.1$. Thus his body mass index will be 23.1 kg/m^2.

What does this mean? Table 8.18 shows the classification for overweight and obesity.

The body mass index has serious limitations because it does not actually measure body composition. It can be used as a quick measure to see if a person is over-fat, but it is inaccurate because it does not make a distinction between muscle and fat. Thus, someone with a lot of muscle may come out as fat!

Hip-to-waist ratio

Hip-to-waist ratio is taken as an indicator of the health risks associated with obesity, and in particular the risk of coronary heart disease. Fat stored in the abdominal area is a greater risk factor for CHD because it is closer to the heart and can more easily be mobilised and taken to the heart.

Hip-to-waist ratio is calculated in the following way, using a tape measure.

● Waist measurement is taken at the level of the navel, with the stomach muscles relaxed and after a normal expiration. The tape measure is put around the waist and a horizontal reading is taken.
● Hip measurement is taken with the client standing up and is the widest measurement around the hips. It is usually taken at the level of the greater trochanter, which is at the top of the femur.

The ratio is worked out by dividing the waist measurement by the hip measurement. For a male with a 26" waist and 30" hips, this would be: $26 \div 30 = 0.87$.

What do these scores mean? Table 8.19 shows the classification for hip-to-waist ratio.

A male with a score above 0.90 and a female with a score above 0.80 will have an increased risk of developing CHD.

	Obesity class	BMI (kg/m2)
Underweight		< 17.5
Normal		17.5–24.9
Overweight		25–29.9
Obesity	I	30–34.9
Obesity	II	35–39.9
Extreme obesity	III	>40

Table 8.18 BMI classification of overweight and obesity

	Hip-to-waist ratio	Classification
Males	> 1.0	High risk
	0.90–0.99	Moderate risk
	< 0.90	Low risk
Females	> 0.85	High risk
	0.80–0.85	Moderate risk
	< 0.80	Low risk

Table 8.19 CHD risk classification from hip-to-waist ratio scores

Key learning points 2

● Before a fitness test is conducted, a health-screening form and an informed consent form must be completed.
● A client must be screened for risk of CHD. Risk factors include poor diet, obesity, smoking, excess alcohol intake, male gender and type 2 diabetes.

Student activity 8.2 ⏱ 90 minutes P2 P3 P4 M2 D1

- Using the health-screening questionnaire provided as a template (see page 162), design your own questionnaire that covers personal details, goals, current activity levels, lifestyle factors and medical history.
- Use the health-screening questionnaire for two individuals who have different goals and a different health status (e.g. conditioned and unconditioned).
- Use the following table to record and analyse the results of four health-related tests for the two individuals:

Name of test	Result of test	Interpretation of test: fit and healthy/proceed with caution/ GP referral
Resting heart rate		
Blood pressure		
Lung function		
Body mass index		
Strengths:		
Areas for improvement:		

Evaluate the information gained from the health-screening questionnaire and the fitness tests and make recommendations on how each individual could improve their lifestyle.

Q Quick quiz 2

1 Describe why coronary heart disease develops.
2 State three occasions when you would refer someone to the GP before letting them start exercising.
3 What is the difference between a static test and a dynamic test?
4 A high hip-to-waist ratio may indicate a raised risk of which medical condition?

8.4. Administering appropriate fitness tests

In order to administer fitness tests safely and effectively, you need to follow certain procedures. The test protocols have been described earlier in this unit, but you also need to ensure that the tests are valid and reliable, and that the individual being tested is appropriately prepared. You also need to be aware of any signs that would suggest that you ought to terminate the test.

Validity and reliability

These two terms must be considered before a test is conducted. The two questions you must ask yourself are:

1 Does this test actually test what I say it tests?
2 If this test were to be repeated, would I get the same results?

The first question tests validity. For example, a speed test using a shuttle run may actually test a person's ability to turn, which is more about agility than speed.

The second question tests its reliability. The conditions of the test must always be identical, making it most likely that the same results will be produced. However, there are many factors that may change, such as the temperature of the environment, the physical state of the athlete and the technique of the tester. All these may alter the results produced.

The purposes of fitness testing

The purposes of fitness testing are to:

- ensure that the person is safe to exercise
- find out their current position in terms of the components of fitness
- identify the strengths and weaknesses of each of their components of fitness
- gain information to allow a specific training programme to be written
- be able to monitor any changes in fitness
- provide an opportunity to educate individuals about health and fitness.

Pre-test procedures

When testing people, it is important that the tests are safe for the client, and also that the conditions the tests are performed in are consistent and stable.

The following should be taken into consideration in relation to the client:

- They should have medical clearance for any health conditions.
- They should be free of injuries.
- They should be wearing appropriate clothing.
- They should not have had a heavy meal within three hours of the test.
- They should have had a good night's sleep.
- They should not have trained on the day and should be fully recovered from previous training.
- They should have avoided stimulants such as tea, coffee or nicotine for two hours before the test.

The following should be taken into consideration regarding the environment:

- Heating in the area should be at room temperature (around 18 °C).
- The room should be well ventilated.
- The room should be clean and dust-free.

Test sequence

The order in which tests are conducted must be considered because it may change the accuracy of the results you produce. You may even have to do different tests on different days to produce the best results.

Your knowledge of sport science can help you to decide which tests should be done first and for how long the athlete will have to rest between tests. For example, a test that requires effort over a long period of time or works to failure will require one to two hours of recovery. A test requiring a high level of skill or coordination needs to be done first because skill level decreases when a person is tired. The correct order to follow would be:

- sedentary tests – height, weight, body composition, flexibility
- agility tests
- maximum power and strength tests
- sprint tests
- muscular endurance tests
- aerobic endurance tests.

Reasons to terminate a fitness test

There will be occasions when it becomes unsafe to continue with a test due to physiological changes within the client. The following is a list of specific situations when a test should be stopped:

- chest pains or angina-like symptoms
- excessive increase in blood pressure (250/115)
- shortness of breath and wheezing
- leg cramps or pain
- light-headedness, nausea or pale, clammy skin

171

- heart rate does not rise with exercise intensity
- irregular heart beat
- client requests to stop
- signs and symptoms of severe exhaustion
- equipment fails.

Key learning points 3

- Tests can be split into two types: those which test health and are static in nature and those which test fitness and are dynamic in nature.
- Before conducting a test, you must consider whether both the client and the environment are in an appropriate state for the test to take place.
- A valid test is one that tests what it says it will test.
- A reliable test is one that would yield the same results if it were to be repeated.

Q Quick quiz 3

Fill in the blank spaces to complete the following sentences, choosing from the list of words below.

- Safe
- Reliable
- Sedentary
- Strengths
- Valid
- Coordination
- Maximal
- Weaknesses.

When administering a fitness test, you must make sure it is _____ by considering whether it tests what it says it is testing, and also how to make it _____, which means that if you did the test again you would get the same results. Fitness testing is done to make sure the person is _____ to exercise and to identify their _____ and _____. It is important to do the _____ tests first and then tests requiring _____, and finally tests requiring _____ effort.

8.5. Interpreting the results of fitness tests and providing feedback

Once you have completed a fitness test, it is important to give detailed feedback to the individual. Before you conduct a test, you need to say what you are testing and explain how the test will be conducted. Feedback is given once you have conducted the test, written down the result and then worked out how the result compares with the normative tables.

Feedback should be given in the following format:

- Repeat the component of fitness that has been tested.
- Tell the individual what the result of the test was.
- Explain what you have tested and what the score represents.
- Tell the individual where they fit within the population norms.
- Tell the individual what the implications of the result are in terms of their health and fitness.
- Discuss what recommendations you would make for the future.

If you have carried out a blood pressure test, for example, you would give feedback in this specific way:

- 'I have just taken your blood pressure.'
- 'Your blood pressure was 120/80 mmHg.'
- 'Blood pressure is the pressure of blood in the arterial system. 120 mmHg is the pressure during the contraction phase of the heart beat, and 80 mmHg is the pressure during the relaxation phase of the heart beat.'
- 'This score is within the normal healthy range.'
- 'It means you are healthy enough to take part in sport and exercise.'

The scores of all fitness tests must be recorded in writing to ensure you have the information available in the future when you come to retest.

Recommendations

Once you have completed all the tests, you will be able to write an action plan or a report on the individual. This should cover the following information:

- current situation, highlighting strengths and weaknesses
- client's aims and objectives
- changes to be made, with options
- actions – a step-by-step guide to achieving aims.

Key learning points 4

● When giving feedback, you must let the individual know what you were testing, what score they achieved, what their score means and any implications this score may have.

● Once fitness tests have been completed, you can write an action plan for the individual, with recommendations for them to improve their health and fitness.

Student activity 8.3   3 hours   P5   P6   M3   M4   D2

Task 1

● Choose six fitness tests specifically identified for the individual that you have selected to test.

● Justify why you chose these six tests for this individual (think about choosing tests specific to the goals and fitness needs of that individual).

● Develop a table and record the scores for each of the six tests.

Task 2

● Once your selected individual has done the fitness tests and you have recorded their results, you should prepare and then present feedback to the individual in the form of a consultation. You should have worked out how their score fits into the normative data for each test, and what the implications of the results are.

● As part of the consultation, summarise by identifying the individual's strengths and weaknesses and then provide recommendations for their future training activities.

References

Baechle, T. and Earle, R. (2008) *Essentials of Strength Training and Conditioning,* Human Kinetics.

Davis, R., Bull, C., Roscoe, J. and Roscoe, D. (2005) *Physical Education and the Study of Sport,* Elsevier Mosby.

Franklin, B. (2005) *American College of Sports Medicine's (ACSM) Guidelines for Exercise Testing and Prescription,* 6th edn, Lippincott, Williams and Wilkins.

Wesson, K., Wiggins-James, N., Thompson, G. and Hartigan, S. (2005) *Sport and PE: A Complete Guide to Advanced Level Study,* Hodder Arnold.

Further reading

Baechle, T. and Earle, R. (2008) *Essentials of Strength Training and Conditioning,* Human Kinetics.

Coulson, M. (2007) *The Fitness Instructor's Handbook.* A & C Black.

Sharkey, B.J. and Gaskill, S.E. (2006) *Fitness and Health,* Human Kinetics.

Useful websites

www.topendsports.com/testing/tests.htm
Over 100 fitness tests to try, all divided into different fitness categories

www.bases.org.uk
Membership website for sports professionals, providing details of job vacancies, careers advice, forums for coaching and sports science-related topics; limited access to non-members

www.1st4sport.com
Provides qualifications for sports professionals covering a wide range of sports-related activities

9: Fitness Training & Programming

9.1 Introduction

Developing the correct training programme is vital to the success of the individual athlete and the team. Top-class athletes build their life around the requirements of their fitness training and have a dedicated coach for this purpose. Fitness will be important to any individual who is involved in physical activity to give them the best chances to succeed.

By the end of this unit you should:

- know different methods of fitness training
- be able to plan a fitness training session
- be able to review a fitness training programme.

Assessment and grading criteria		
To achieve a PASS grade the evidence must show that the learner is able to:	To achieve a MERIT grade the evidence must show that, in addition to the pass criteria, the learner is able to:	To achieve a DISTINCTION grade the evidence must show that, in addition to the pass and merit criteria, the learner is able to:
P1 describe one method of fitness training for six different components of physical fitness	**M1** explain one method of fitness training for six different components of physical fitness	
P2 produce training session plans covering cardiovascular training, resistance training, flexibility training and speed training	**M2** produce detailed session plans covering cardiovascular training, resistance training, flexibility training and speed training	**D1** justify the training session plans covering cardiovascular training, resistance training, flexibility training and speed training
P3 produce a six-week fitness training programme for a selected individual that incorporates the principles of training and periodisation		
P4 monitor performance against goals during the six-week training programme		
P5 give feedback to an individual following completion of a six-week fitness training programme, describing strengths and areas for improvement.	**M3** give feedback to an individual following completion of a six-week fitness training programme, explaining strengths and areas for improvement.	**D2** give feedback to an individual following completion of a six-week fitness training programme, evaluating progress and providing recommendations for future activities.

9.2 Different Methods of Fitness Training

Components of Fitness

Fitness can mean different things to different people and has been defined in different ways. When we examine fitness we need to ask 'What does this person have to be fit for?' or 'What functions does this person have to perform?' From this starting point we can build up a picture of their fitness requirements and then look at what can be done to develop their fitness.

Fitness is defined by the American College of Sports Medicine (ACSM) (1990) as:

> 'a set of attributes that people have or achieve that relate to their ability to perform physical activity.'

Fitness is clearly related to performance and developing the attributes to achieve this performance.

Physical Fitness

Physical fitness can be seen to be made up of the following factors.

Aerobic endurance is also called cardiovascular fitness or stamina. It is the individual's ability to take on, transport and utilise oxygen. It is a measure of how well the lungs can take in oxygen, how well the heart and blood can transport oxygen, and then how well the muscles can use oxygen. When working aerobically we tend to perform repetitive activities using large muscle groups in a rhythmical manner for long periods of time.

Muscular endurance is how well the muscles can produce repeated contractions at less than maximal (submaximal) intensities. When training for muscular endurance we usually do sets of 15 to 20 repetitions. Most movements we produce in sport and everyday activities will be at submaximal intensities and all people will benefit from muscular endurance training.

Flexibility is the range of motion that a joint or group of joints can move through. Flexibility is often not given the amount of attention it should have in a training programme because people do not always see its importance. However, improving flexibility can improve performance because a greater range of motion will result in greater power development and will help to prevent injury and pain caused through restrictions in movement.

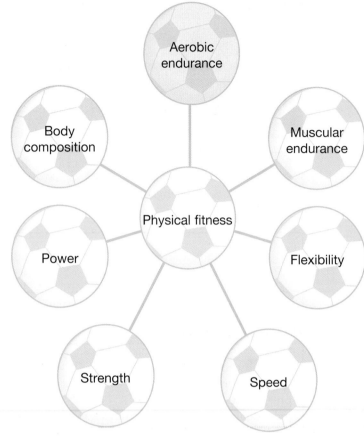

Fig 9.1 Physical fitness

Speed is the rate at which the body or individual limbs can move.

Strength is the maximum force a muscle or group of muscles can produce in a single contraction. Heavy weight lifting or moving a heavy object will require strength. For example, if you have to push-start a car the success or failure of this effort will be an expression of your muscular strength. To train for strength we usually do sets of 1 to 5 repetitions.

Power is the production of strength at speed and can be seen when we throw an object or perform a sprint start. To move a heavy load quickly we need to use our power. Activities such as jumping to head a ball or a long jump will require us to express our power.

9.3 Methods of Physical Fitness Training

P1 **M1**

Flexibility Training

Flexibility is the 'range of motion available at a joint' and is needed in sports to:

- enable the athlete to have the range of motion to perform the movements needed
- prevent the athlete from becoming injured
- maintain and improve posture
- develop maximum strength and power.

What Happens to Muscles When we Stretch?

The stretching of muscles is under the control of the sensory nerves. There are two types of sensory nerves which are involved in allowing muscles to stretch and relax. They are muscle spindles and Golgi tendon organs (GTOs). The sensory nerves work to protect the body from becoming injured and will contract if they think a muscle is at risk of becoming damaged. This is one of our basic survival instincts because when we were hunter-gatherers injury would render us incapable of finding food and our families would starve.

The muscle spindles are sensory receptors which become activated as the muscle lengthens (due to its potential danger). When the muscle has reached a certain length they tell the nervous system to contract the muscle and prevent it being stretched any further. This protects the muscle against damage. If you perform the patella knee tap test this activates the muscle spindles. When this test is conducted, the knee extends due to the contraction of the quadriceps muscle activated by the muscle spindle. This is also called 'the myotatic stretch reflex'.

When we stretch a muscle we try to avoid this by stretching in a slow and controlled manner. The muscle spindles contract the muscle, which makes it feel uncomfortable or slightly painful. This is called the 'point of bind' where the muscle has contracted to avoid any damage.

When the point of bind is reached the stretch should be held for around ten seconds. This is because after ten seconds the muscle will relax and the pain will disappear. This relaxation is brought on by the action of the GTOs. GTOs are found in tendons and they sense how much tension there is in the muscle. Once the GTOs sense that the muscle is not in danger of damage they will override the muscle spindles and cause the muscle to relax. This is the

effect that you want a stretch to have; it is called 'the inverse stretch reflex'. Once the muscle has relaxed you can either stop the stretch there or stretch the muscle a bit more until the point of bind is reached again and the process starts again.

There are various methods of stretching muscles.

Static Stretching

This is when a muscle is stretched in a steady, controlled manner and then held in a static or still position. It is taken to the point where the muscle contracts and a slight pain is felt. This is called 'the point of bind'. At this point the stretch is held until the muscle relaxes and the discomfort disappears.

A static stretch can be a maintenance stretch or a developmental stretch. A maintenance stretch is held until the discomfort disappears and then the stretch is stopped. A developmental stretch is different because when the muscle relaxes and the discomfort disappears the stretch is applied further to a second point. It is taken to a point when the discomfort is felt again, it is held until the muscle relaxes and then applied again. It lasts for around 30 seconds while a maintenance stretch will last for around 10 seconds.

Proprioceptive Neuromuscular Facilitation

This type of stretching, known as PNF, is an advanced type of stretching in order to develop the length of the muscle. It needs two people to be involved: one person to do the stretching and one to be stretched.

It is carried out in the following way.

- The muscle is stretched to the point of bind by the trainer.
- At this point the trainer asks the athlete to contract the muscle and push against them at about 40 to 50 per cent effort.
- This contraction is held for 10 seconds.
- When the muscle is relaxed the trainer stretches the muscle further.
- Again a contraction is applied and then the muscle is re-stretched.
- This is done three times.

This is a more effective way of developing the length of the muscle as the contraction will actually cause the muscle to relax more quickly and more deeply.

Ballistic Stretching

This means a 'bouncing' stretch as the muscle is forced beyond its point of stretch by a bouncing movement. Ballistic stretches are performed in a rapid, repetitive bouncing movement. It is a high-risk method of stretching due to the risk of muscular damage but it may be used in specific sports such as

177

gymnastics. It must never be used on people training for health and fitness reasons rather than sports.

Resistance Training

Resistance training means using any form of resistance to place an increased load on a muscle or muscle group. Resistance training can be done to develop muscular endurance, strength or power depending upon the number of repetitions chosen, resistance chosen and speed the movements are performed at. Muscular endurance training involves a high number of repetitions (12–20) performed with relatively low weights, while strength training involves low repetitions (1–5) with relatively heavy weights and power training is performed by moving weights at speed so involve low repetitions (1–5) with relatively heavy weights.

Resistance can be applied through any of the following methods:

- free weights
- resistance machines
- cable machines
- gravity
- medicine balls
- air
- water
- resistance bands
- manually.

The following are popular methods of resistance training:

- resistance machines
- free weights
- cables
- plyometrics
- circuit training.

A range of resistance machines have been developed to train muscle groups in isolation. They were

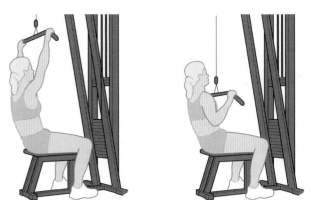

Fig 9.2 Resistance training with a machine

originally developed for body builders but their ease of use and safety factors make them a feature of every gym in the country. These machines target individual muscles and replicate the joint actions these muscles produce.

Free weights involve barbells and dumbbells and are seen to have advantages over resistance machines. Mainly, they allow a person to work in their own range of movement rather than the way a machine wants them to work. Also, when a person does free weights they have to use many more muscles to stabilise the body before the force is applied. This is particularly so if the person performs the exercise standing up. They also have more 'functional crossover' in that they can replicate movements that will be used in sports and daily life. This is seen as a huge advantage.

Cable machines are becoming increasingly popular because, again, they involve the use of many more muscles than resistance machines, and therefore burn up more calories. Once again, they can produce

Objective	Muscular strength	Muscle hypertrophy	Muscular endurance	Power
Repetitions or duration	1–5	6–12	12–20	1–2 for single-effort events 3–5 for multiple-effort events
Recovery period	3–5 mins	1–2 mins	30–60 secs	2–5 mins
Sets per exercise	2–6	3–6	2–3	3–5
Frequency per week	1–2 on each muscle group	1–2 on each muscle group	2–3 on each muscle group	1–2 sessions

Table 9.1 Shows the repetition ranges for targeting components of fitness.
(Adapted from Baechle and Earle, 2000)

Fig 9.3 Depth jumping is one example of plyometric activity

movements that are not possible on resistance machines. For example, a golfer will need to perform rotation-type movements and can do these on cable machines.

Plyometrics

Plyometric training develops power, which is producing strength at speed. It usually involves moving your body weight very quickly through jumping or bounding. Any sport that involves jumping in the air or moving the body forwards at pace will need power training.

Examples of plyometric training include:

- jumping on to boxes and over hurdles
- depth jumping
- vertical jumps and standing long jump
- medicine ball throws
- hopping
- bounding
- squat and jump
- press-up and clap.

It is a very strenuous type of training and an athlete must have well-developed strength before performing plyometrics. Before you take a plyometric session you must make sure the athlete is well warmed up and that you have checked the equipment and the surfaces thoroughly. Ideally, you should use a sprung floor or a soft surface.

Circuit Training

A circuit is a series of exercises arranged in a specific order and performed one after the other. There are normally eight to twelve stations set out and organised so that each muscle group is worked in rotation. Each exercise is performed for a certain number of repetitions or a set time period. Circuits are used predominantly to develop muscular endurance or aerobic fitness – this depends upon the resistances used, the speed of the movements and the length of time on each station. For muscular endurance the participant works flat out on each station for about 30 seconds, while to develop aerobic endurance the time period on each station is increased to 45 seconds with a slower speed of movement. They can be made specific to various sports by including exercises for the muscles used in that sport and some of the skills specific to that sport.

When planning a circuit you need to ask several questions:

- What is the objective of the session?
- How many participants will I have?
- What is their level of fitness?
- How much space have I got?
- What equipment is available?

A basic circuit session should contain exercise to improve aerobic fitness or raise the pulse rate, exercises to work the upper body, lower body and the core. When designing the circuit layout be careful not to place all the exercises for the same muscle group beside each other as this will cause undue fatigue. The circuit should follow the normal structure of a routine:

- warm-up
- main session
- cool-down
- flexibility.

The warm-up will include a pulse raiser, mobility and dynamic stretches. For example:

- walk
- walk with bicep curls and shoulder presses
- slow jog with shoulder circles
- jog
- dynamic stretches such as squat and press, step back and chest stretch
- jog with knee raises and heel flicks
- run
- jumps and hops
- sprint.

The main session should include eight to twelve exercises from Table 9.2.

179

Aerobic fitness or pulse raisers	Shuttle runs Skipping Box step-ups Box jumps Jumping jacks Star jumps Spotty dogs Grapevines
Upper body	Press-ups Bench press with dumbbells Cable seated rows Bent-over row Shoulder press Bicep curls Tricep curls Lateral raises Dumbbell pullovers Medicine ball chest passes Medicine ball chest pass & press-up Medicine ball overhead throws
Lower body	Squats Lunges Split squats Side lunges Squat thrusts Hurdle jumps Ladder work Step-ups with dumbbells
Core exercises	Swiss ball curls Swiss ball back extension Plank Bridge Superman Rotations with medicine ball Medicine ball rotate and throw

Table 9.2

The cool-down should progressively lower the pulse, but it can be combined with some stretching as well. It could follow this example:

● run (1 minute)
● jog (1 minute)
● brisk walk (1 minute)
● stretch trapezius, pectoralis major, latissimus dorsi, triceps, deltoids
● standing stretches of adductors, calves and quads
● kneeling stretches of hip flexors and lower back
● lying stretches of hamstrings and gluteus medius and minimus.

Aerobic Endurance Training

Continuous training is also called 'steady-state' training and involves an individual maintaining a steady pace for a long period of time. To be effective it needs to be done for a period of over 20 minutes. It is useful for developing a strong base of aerobic fitness, but it will not develop speed or strength.

While continuous training has a role to play it can be limited in its benefits, particularly if the athlete does the same session each time they train. While initially it will have given them fitness gains there will be limited benefits after about four weeks once the body has adapted to the work. It may also produce boredom and a loss of motivation to train.

Interval training is described as having the following features: 'a structured period of work followed by a structured period of rest'. In other words, an athlete runs quickly for a period of time and then rests at a much lower intensity before speeding up again. This type of training has the benefit of improving speed as well as aerobic fitness. Interval training also allows the athlete to train at higher intensities than they are used to, and thus steadily increase their fitness level and the intensity they can work at. The theory is that you will be able to run faster in competition only if you train faster – and interval training allows this to occur. Intervals can be used to improve performance for athletes and fitness levels for people involved in exercise.

Interval training can be stressful to the systems of the body and it is important to ensure that an individual has a good aerobic base before raising the intensity of the training.

Once an athlete has reached the limit of their aerobic system they will start to gain extra energy from their anaerobic system (lactic acid system); this is demonstrated by an increased accumulation of lactic acid in the blood. The point where blood lactic acid levels start to rise is called the lactate threshold. Interval training can be designed to push an athlete beyond their lactate threshold and then reduce the exercise intensity below the lactate threshold. This has the effect of enabling the athlete to become better at tolerating the effects of lactic acid and also increasing the intensity they work at before lactic acid is produced. Well-designed interval training sessions can produce this desirable effect.

The intensity of interval training is higher than continuous work and thus there will be more energy production to sustain this high-intensity work. More energy production equals more calories burnt during training, which could lead to a faster loss of body fat (if the nutritional strategy is appropriate). As the intensity is higher more waste products are built up, resulting in a greater oxygen debt and a longer period of recovery. This longer period of recovery results in more oxygen being used post-exercise and more energy used to recover. Therefore, more energy is used during exercise and also after exercise, multiplying the potential effects of fat loss.

The main benefits of interval training are:

● improved speed
● improved strength
● improved aerobic endurance
● improved ability to tolerate the effects of lactic acid
● increased fat burning potential
● increased calorie output
● improved performance.

Interval training can be used to develop aerobic fitness as well as anaerobic fitness. When designing interval training sessions you need to consider how long the periods of work are in relation to the periods of rest. The following are recommended guidelines for training with each of the three energy systems.

● Aerobic interval: 1 or half a unit of rest for every unit of work.
● Lactic acid intervals: 2 to 3 units of rest for 1 unit of work.
● ATP/CP intervals: 6 units of rest for 1 unit of work.

As the intensity increases, more rest is required to guarantee the quality of each interval. If you were training for aerobic fitness you may do four minutes' work then have two minutes' rest (1:1/2). If you were training for lactic acid intervals you would have one minute's work and two or three minutes' rest.

Sample Aerobic Interval Session

First estimate the maximum heart rate as 220 minus age and then you can work out the percentage of maximum heart rate.

For a 20 year old:
Maximum heart rate = 220 − 20 = 200 bpm
70% of max HR = 200 × 0.7 = 140 bpm
80% of max HR = 200 × 0.8 = 160 bpm
90% of max HR = 200 × 0.9 = 180 bpm

You will need to find out what workload (speed) produces each heart rate when you are running.

Basic interval
Work = 4 minutes   Rest = 2 minutes
4 sets of 4 minutes at 70% effort with 2 minutes' rest in between

Pyramid interval
Work = 3 minutes   Rest = 1.5 minutes

Warm-up
3 mins @ 80% of max HR

Rest
3 mins @ 85% of max HR

Rest
3 mins @ 90% of max HR

Rest
3 mins @ 85% of max HR

Rest
3 mins @ 80% of max HR

Cool-down

Treadmill hills pyramid
Find the speed that produces 70% of max HR and stay at this speed throughout the interval programme; then vary the gradient on the treadmill.

Work = 2 mins   Rest = 1 min

Warm-up
2 mins @ 2% gradient

Rest
2 mins @ 4% gradient

Rest
2 mins @ 6% gradient

Rest
2 mins @ 4% gradient

Rest
2 mins @ 2% gradient

Cool-down

Alternately the gradients could be set at 3%, 6%, 9%, 6% and 3%.

Sample Anaerobic Session

Lactic Acid System
6 sets of 45 seconds (or 300 m) at 90–95% effort with 90 seconds' rest
4 sets of 75 seconds (or 500 m) at 80–85% effort with 150 seconds' rest

ATP/PC System
10 sets of 50 metres at 100% effort with 1 minute rest

Fartlek is a Swedish term; it literally means 'speed play' and it involves an athlete going out and running at a range of different speeds for a period of 20 to 30 minutes. This type of training is excellent for replicating the demands of a sport such as football, rugby or hockey where different types of running are required at different times. It can be used to develop aerobic or anaerobic fitness depending on the intensity of the running. It can also be used in cycling or rowing training. Fartlek running involves finding a base speed at around 60 to 70 per cent of maximum intensity and then fast bursts of work at 75, 80, 85 and 90 per cent mixed up into longer or shorter time periods. It can be used to challenge the different energy systems and demands of sports as well as reducing the boredom of training for long periods of time.

Core Stability

If we were to take our arms and legs off our body we would be left with the body's core, which can be said to be the working foundation of the body and is responsible for providing the base to develop power. If we have a strong core we will be able to generate more force and power through the arms and legs; this is important when we kick a football or hit a tennis ball.

The body is made up of layers of muscles and the abdominal area is no different as it has deep, middle and outer layers which work together to provide stability.

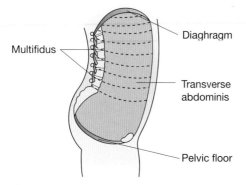

Fig 9.4 Outer layer of core muscles

The outer layer of muscles are the best known abdominal muscles with the rectus abdominis at the front, the erector spinae at the back and the internal and external obliques at the sides.

The middle layer is deeper muscle, which forms a cylinder or unit around the vertebrae. At the top we have the diaphragm and at the bottom the pelvic floor muscles, while across the back we have the multifidus, and around the front and sides we have the transverse abdominis (TVA). The TVA is the key muscle here and is described as being 'the natural weight belt' because a weight belt replicates its shape and function.

The role of the inner muscles is to stabilise the vertebrae, ribs and pelvis to provide the stable working base or foundation. These muscles contract a fraction of a second before the arms or legs are

moved when the body is functioning correctly. If this does not happen the chances of damaging the spine are increased.

The deep layer is tiny muscles which sense the position of the vertebrae and control their movement to keep them in the strongest position and prevent injury.

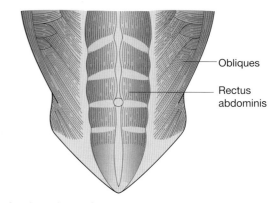

Fig 9.5 Inner layer of core muscles

Activating the core muscles can be done in two ways. First, by hollowing or pulling in the abdominals or by bracing, which means contracting the muscles without them moving out or in. Different trainers will recommend different techniques depending upon their own experiences and training.

Abdominal Training

The concepts of abdominal training are changing rapidly. The traditional method has been to do hundreds of sit-ups in pursuit of a perfect six-pack and then, in the late 1990s, abdominal cradles were introduced into gyms to aid people further. The 2000s have seen the introduction of Swiss balls and functional abdominal exercises into training programmes. There is still some confusion over what is the best way to train the abdominals. We need to look at a couple of misconceptions first before looking at what is the best way to train.

'Sit-ups will help me lose fat in the abdominal area'

No, you cannot spot-reduce fat because the muscle below the abdominal fat is separate from the fat itself and you can never be sure from where the losses in fat due to exercise will come. The way to lose abdominal fat is to increase activity level and have a correct nutritional strategy.

'Sit-ups will give me the six-pack I want'

Not necessarily, because overdoing abdominal work can cause a shortening of the abdominal muscles and pull your posture forwards, making the abdominal area shorter, squeezing the fat together and making you look fatter. In fact, if you perform back extensions it will make your posture more upright and help to keep the abdominals contracted and make them look more toned.

'Sit-ups are the best abdominal exercise'

This is debatable because sit-ups produce concentric and eccentric muscular contractions. The abdominals will contract isometrically when we train and move around in daily life. Therefore, surely we should replicate this isometric contraction when we train as it will have the best 'functional crossover' to daily life.

When we train the core muscles we need to target the deeper muscles; this is done by producing isometric or static contractions.

Any exercise where you are standing up or supporting your body weight will be a core exercise. For example, a press-up is an excellent core exercise because the core muscles work to keep the back straight and the back will start to sag when these muscles become fatigued. All standing free weight and cable exercises require the core to stabilise the vertebrae while they are being performed. However, there are some specific core exercises that can be performed (see Figure 4.6).

Fig 9.6b Side plank

Fig 9.6c Bridge

The use of a Swiss ball to perform exercises requires an extra load on the core muscles and works them harder, as will using cables to exercise.

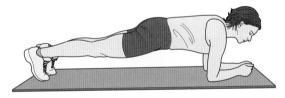

Fig 9.6a Plank

Fig 9.7 Swiss ball abdominal crunches

Q Quick quiz 1

Match the following: (a) the definition to the component of fitness and (b) the training method to the correct component of fitness that it works on.

Component of fitness	Definitions	Training methods
Aerobic endurance		
Muscular endurance		
Flexibility		
Speed		
Strength		
Power		

(a) Choices of definition
  • The range of motion a joint or group of joints can move through
  • The ability to take on, transport and utilise oxygen
  • The rate that individual limbs can move
  • The production of strength at speed
  • The maximum force a muscle or group of muscles can produce in a single contraction
  • The ability of muscles to produce repeated contractions

(b) Training methods
  • plyometrics
  • PNF stretching
  • Resistance training (high weights, low repetitions)
  • Resistance training (Low weights, high repetitions)
  • Steady state running
  • Interval training.

Student activity 9.1   ⏱ 40 minutes   P2   M1

Methods of fitness training

Complete Table 9.3 to describe and explain different methods of fitness training for six different components of fitness.

Component of fitness	Describe one method of fitness training for this component	Explain one method of fitness training for this component
Aerobic endurance		
Muscular endurance	E.g. Resistance training, which would be 8–10 exercises with a low weight but high repetitions.	E.g. Resistance training on free weights, resistance machines or cables using a low weight (about 60–70 of maximum) and high repetitions (12–20). Working all muscle groups and doing 2–3 sets per exercise.
Flexibility		
Speed		
Strength		
Power		

Table 9.3

9.4 Planning a Fitness Training Session

Principles of Training

To develop a safe and effective training programme you will need to consider the principles of training. These principles are a set of guidelines to help you understand the requirements of programme design. The principles of training are:

- Frequency
- Intensity
- Time
- Type
- Overload
- Reversibility
- Specificity.

Frequency means how often the athlete will train per week, month or year. It is recommended that a beginner trains three times a week while a competitive athlete may train ten or twelve times a week.

Intensity is how hard the athlete works for each repetition. It is usually expressed as a percentage of maximum intensity. Intensity can be increased by adding more weight to be lifted, or increasing speed or gradient on the treadmill.

Time indicates how long they train for in each session. The recommended length of a training session is around 45 minutes before fatiguing waste products build up and affect training technique.

Type shows the type of training they will perform and needs to be individual to each person. A training effect can be achieved by varying the exercises an individual does – moving them from a treadmill to a rower, or a seated chest press to a free weight bench press.

Overload shows that to make an improvement a muscle or system must work slightly harder than it is used to. The weight that produces overload depends upon what the individual is currently used to at that moment. This may be as simple as getting a sedentary person walking for ten minutes or getting an athlete to squat more weight than they have previously. Overload can be achieved by changing the intensity, duration, time or type of an exercise. Reversibility says that if a fitness gain is not used regularly the body will reverse it and go back to its previous fitness level. Any adaptation which occurs is not permanent. The rule is commonly known as 'use it or lose it'.

Specificity states that any fitness gain will be specific to the muscles or system to which the overload is applied. Put simply, this says that different types of training will produce different results. To make a programme specific you need to look at the needs of the athletes in that sport and then train them accordingly. For example, a footballer would need to run at different speeds and have lots of changes of direction. A golfer would need to do rotational work but sprinting speed would not be so important. A runner would need to do running predominantly, and they may get some aerobic gain from swimming or cycling but it would not achieve the best result.

There are other principles too.

Progressive Overload

To ensure an athlete continues to gain fitness they need to keep overloading their muscles and systems. This continued increase in intensity (how hard they work) is called progressive overload. If you keep training at the same intensity and duration the body will reach a plateau where no further fitness gains are made. Therefore, it is important to keep manipulating all the training variables to keep gaining adaptations.

Who Will You Train?

You need to be prepared to train a range of individuals including elite performers, trained or well conditioned individuals and untrained or de-conditioned individuals. You may also train individuals who are training for a specific sport or have special requirements or medical conditions. You will have been able to identify the strengths and weaknesses of each individual by carrying out the health screening questionnaire, performing the static health tests and the dynamic fitness on the individual and then analysing their strengths and areas that need improvement.

Planning the Programme

Once you have identified the training needs of the individual through the screening process then you can design their training programme. Each programme will have a different content dependent upon the goals of the individual; however, the structure of the training programmes will be fairly similar. It should look like Table 9.4.

Type of training	Description of amount	Guidance
CV training – warm up	3–5 minutes	This involves a gradual increase of intensity to raise the heart rate steadily
Flexibility	2–3 dynamic stretches	These stretches involve moving the joints and muscles through the full range of movement in a controlled manner to replicate movements coming up in the main session
Resistance 1	4–5 exercises to cover the main muscle groups (pecs, lats, glutes, quads and hamstrings)	Sets and repetitions are dependent upon the training goals of the individual. Exercises could include free weights, resistance machines or cable exercises
CV training	Between 5 and 20 minutes, dependent upon the goals of the individual	Could involve steady state work or intervals. It may be done for speed or aerobic endurance and involve running, rowing or cycling
Resistance 2	4–5 exercises to cover a selection of the minor muscle groups (biceps, triceps, deltoids, claves)	Sets and repetitions are dependent upon the training goals of the individual. Exercises could include free weights, resistance machines or cable exercises
CV training	Between 5 and 20 minutes dependent upon the goals of the individual	Could involve steady state work or intervals. It may be done for speed or aerobic endurance and involve running, rowing or cycling
Core training	2–3 exercises to cover the abdominals, back muscles (erector spinae) and obliques	This could include dynamic exercises, such as sit ups, crunches or back extensions or static exercises, such as the plank or a bridge
CV training – cool down	3–5 minutes	This involves a gradual decrease of intensity to lower the heart rate steadily
Flexibility	8–10 stretches on all the muscles worked in the session	This would include developmental stretches on those muscles which are tight (e.g. pecs, hamstrings) and static stretches on all the other muscles worked

Table 9.4 The structure of a typical training programme

A typical training session for an untrained beginner may look like Table 9.5.

Type of training	Name of exercise	Amount
CV training – warm up	Treadmill	5 minutes
Flexibility	Dynamic stretches: chest, back, legs	×10 on each exercise
Resistance 1	Squats Bench press Seated row Leg extension Leg flexion	2 × 15 on each exercise with 20–30 seconds rest between sets and exercises
CV training	Rower	5–10 minutes
Resistance 2	Shoulder press Bicep curls Tricep press Calf raises	2 × 15 on each exercise with 20–30 seconds rest between sets and exercises
CV training	Static bike	3–5 minutes
Core training	Sit ups on stability ball Back extensions on stability ball	2 × 10 repetitions on each exercise
CV training – cool down	Treadmill	3–5 minutes
Flexibility	Quads Hamstrings (developmental) Pecs (developmental) Lats Glutes Biceps Triceps Deltoids Calves	All stretches to be held for 10 seconds, except the developmental stretches, which will be held for 30 seconds.

Table 9.5 A typical training session for an untrained beginner

Q Quick quiz 2

Match the components of fitness to their correct definition:

Component of fitness	Definition
Frequency	
Intensity	
Time	
Type	
Overload	
Reversibility	
Specificity	

Choice of definitions:

- if a fitness gain is not used it will be lost
- how often the athlete will train per week, month or year
- the individual's choice of training
- any training gain will only be of benefit to the muscles/energy system to which it is applied
- how hard the individual works
- working a muscle or system slightly harder than it is used to
- how long each session will last

9.5 Planning a Fitness Training Programme

Collecting Information

As an effective fitness coach it is important to be able to write an appropriate fitness training programme. There is a process that you need to go through to write an effective training session for a client.

Stage 1 – Gathering information: the first step is to gain relevant information about the person so that you can plan a personal training programme. The key is to build up a picture of the individual and what their life is like. Then you can look at what exercises you will plan for them. This is done through a questionnaire, which the client will fill out on your first meeting. (See Unit 8 Fitness Testing for Sport & Exercise, for a sample questionnaire.)

What a person does or does not do in their life will have an effect on their health and fitness levels as well as their chances of being able to keep the training programme going. The following factors need to be taken into consideration.

- Occupation – hours worked and whether work is manual or office-based.
- Activity levels – amount of movement they do on a daily basis.
- Leisure time activities – whether these are active or inactive.
- Diet – what, how much and when they eat.
- Stress levels – either through work or their home life and how they deal with it.
- Alcohol intake – how much they consume and how often.
- Smoking – whether they are a smoker or ex-smoker and the amount they smoke.
- Time available – the client needs to fit the training into their schedule and the fitness trainer needs to be realistic when planning the programme.
- Current and previous training history – this will give an idea of the current fitness level of the client and also their skill level.

Stage 2 – Establishing objectives: to ensure the success of the fitness programme it needs to be specific to the outcome a person wants. Once we have found this out we can establish goals. Their objective could be any of the following:

- cardiovascular fitness

- flexibility
- muscular strength
- muscular size
- muscle tone
- power.

Once the objectives have been established it is time to set goals to achieve these objectives.

Stage 3 – Goal setting: when setting goals it is important to ensure they follow the SMART principle – that they are specific, measurable, achievable, realistic and time-constrained. These goals should be set for the year or season, then for three months, one month and down to one week or one day. (For a full guide on how to set goals effectively see Unit 21: Applied Sport & Exercise Psychology.)

This goal-setting information should be kept in the training diary along with records of each training session.

Periodisation

Periodisation means a progressive change in the type of training that is being performed to gain maximum fitness benefits. It needs to be carefully planned and would show progression from one type of training to another. For example, a sprinter will focus on developing their strength base and muscular endurance in the autumn before working on improving power and speed as they get closer to the competitive season. All training for sports performance needs to be periodised. For people training in the gym, they can periodise their training by changing the volume and intensity of their training so that they train different energy systems and for different components of fitness.

For example, consider a competitive sports performer who has six weeks to prepare for the new season. They may realise that they need to train for aerobic endurance, anaerobic endurance and speed,

as well as muscular endurance and power. They will periodise their cardiovascular training and their resistance training by manipulating the volume and intensity of their training. An example is provided in Table 9.6.

Macrocycle, mesocycle and microcycle are terminology specific to periodisation. The macrocycle is the largest unit of the training cycle and would cover the overall objective of the training. It will last for the length of a season or a training year. It is broken down into smaller units or mesocycles. A mesocycle is an individual phase of training and would cover a period of around a month depending upon the objective of the phase of training. A microcycle would represent each individual training session and its content. The plan would be periodised by looking at the big picture, or the macrocycle, then broken down into mesocycles, each contributing to the big picture and then the small detail of each session would be to consider how to achieve the aim of each mesocycle.

A Training Diary

A training diary is used to record all the training sessions completed, to enable the individual to monitor their progress. It should include the following details:

- date of each session
- detail of what was done in each session
- a record of the performances in training
- notes on how the athlete felt
- reasons as to why the athlete felt that way
- competition results
- fitness testing results
- performance reviews with their coach.

This can then be used to demonstrate progress, keep the athlete motivated and then to understand any improvements which have been made (or not).

Number of sets × number of repetitions	Week 1	Week 2	Week 3	Week 4	Week 5	Week 6
2 × 20	2 × 20					
2–3 × 15		2–3 × 15				
3 × 12			3 × 12			
3 × 10				3 × 10		
4 × 8					4 × 8	
5 × 5						5 × 5

Table 9.6 Example of a periodised six-week training plan for resistance training

189

Student activity 9.2

⏱ **90 minutes** | P2 | P3 | P4 | M2 | D1

Developing a six-week training programme

Read the following case study and then answer the questions that follow:

CASE STUDY

Harry is a 21-year-old who wants to start playing tennis again after having stopped playing when he left school 3 years ago. Since then he has been working in a sedentary job, which involves him sitting in front of a computer every day, and his favourite leisure activities are playing computer games and going to the cinema to watch horror films. He knows his diet is poor as he eats a lot of fried chicken and he is starting to put on a bit of weight around the middle. At his consultation he says he wants to get fit enough to start playing tennis again, and he is particularly worried that he gets breathless very easily.

At the consultation Harry and his trainer decide upon the following goals:

- Improve his aerobic fitness to help him keep going during his matches.
- Improve his speed so he can move around court quickly.
- Improve his muscular strength and endurance to his improve his hitting.
- Develop his flexibility so he can stretch for the ball.
- Develop his core strength so he can produce the strength and power he needs.

(a) Using the layout presented in Table 9.6, produce a training session for Harry covering cardiovascular training, resistance training, flexibility and speed training.

To gain a merit the programme needs to be produced with detail, and to gain a distinction you need to justify your training programme by explaining why you have chosen the exercises that you did for Harry.

(b) Harry has got 6 weeks until he has his first tennis match. Using the following template, show how his training will develop over this six-week period. You need to consider the principles of training and how frequency, intensity, time and type will change over the six weeks to ensure progressive overload on the muscles and energy systems.

(c) How will you monitor Harry's performance over the six weeks of the training programme?

This is an example for you to use as a practice before you prepare a six-week training programme for a selected individual, and then monitor their progress over the six weeks.

Component of fitness	Week 1	Week 2	Week 3	Week 4	Week 5	Week 6	Comments
Cardiovascular training							
Resistance training – Muscular endurance							
Resistance training – Strength							
Speed							
Flexibility							

Table 9.7 Template for six-week training period (tennis player)

9.6 Reviewing a Fitness Training Programme

P4 **P5** **M3** **D2**

The programme is planned out in detail and implemented with great energy and enthusiasm; likewise it must be evaluated in an organised manner. The athlete must keep a training diary for every session, whether it covered physical training, technical development or mental skills. Only then can it be accurately and systematically evaluated.

The athlete can evaluate the success and effectiveness of their training in the following ways:

- repeating their fitness tests
- evaluating performances
- reviewing their training diary
- measuring whether their goals have been achieved.

Based on all this information, the next stage of the training programme can be developed.

The diary can also be used to evaluate the reasons why the athlete did or did not achieve their goals, and any modifications or interventions can then be planned.

References

Baechle, T. and Earle, R. (2008) *Essentials of Strength Training and Conditioning*, Human Kinetics.

Elphinston, J. and Pook, P. (2009) *The Core Workout: a Definitive Guide to Swiss Ball Training for Athletes, Coaches and Fitness Professionals*, Core Workout.

Further reading

Ansell, M., (2008) *Personal Training*, Exeter: Learning Matters.

Baechle, T. and Earle, R., (2008) *Essentials of Strength Training and Conditioning*, Human Kinetics.

Coulson, M., (2007) *The Fitness Instructor's Handbook*, London: A&C Black.

Dalgleish, J. and Dollery, S. (2001) *The Health and Fitness Handbook*, Harlow: Longman.

Useful websites

www.topendsports.com/testing/tests.htm
Over 100 fitness tests to try, all divided into different fitness categories.

www.netfit.co.uk/previous.htm
Extensive range of exercise and training techniques, some sports specific, others more general

---

Student activity 9.3 ⏱ **45 minutes** **P5** **M3** **D2**

Reviewing the training programme

Once the selected individual has completed the six-week training programme, you need to review their progress and then prepare to give them feedback. You can use the following information to base your review on:

- Information in the training diary on their progress over the six weeks.
- Progress towards their goal.
- Feedback from other people involved in the training.

To achieve a pass you need to give feedback and then describe their areas of strength and those that they need to improve on; to move to a merit you need to explain their areas of strength and those requiring improvement and to achieve a distinction you need to evaluate their progress by looking at the factors that have contributed to their progress or worked against it and then offer recommendations for future training activities.

10: Sport & Exercise Massage

10.1 Introduction

Massage can be used to remedy problems and enhance an athlete's performance. It helps athletes to relax after training and competitions, and helps to restore the body to a pre-exercise state.

This unit will explore the benefits of sport and exercise massage, and explain the basic skills and techniques required to assess an athlete's specific needs and complete an appropriate massage.

By the end of this unit you should:

- know the effects and benefits of sport and exercise massage
- know the roles of sport and exercise massage professionals
- be able to identify the sport and exercise massage requirements of athletes
- be able to perform and review sport and exercise massage techniques.

To achieve a PASS grade the evidence must show that the learner is able to:	To achieve a MERIT grade the evidence must show that, in addition to the pass criteria, the learner is able to:	To achieve a DISTINCTION grade the evidence must show that, in addition to the pass and merit criteria, the learner is able to:
P1 describe the effects and benefits of sport and exercise massage	**M1** explain the beneficial effects of sport and exercise massage	
P2 describe the roles of sport and exercise massage professionals		
P3 carry out pre-treatment consultations on two different athletes	**M2** explain the sport and exercise massage requirements of two different athletes	**D1** compare and contrast the sport and exercise massage requirements of two athletes
P4 describe six contraindications to massage treatment		
P5 produce a treatment plan for two athletes (IE4, IE5, IE6, TW1, TW2, TW3)		
P6 demonstrate appropriate sport and exercise massage techniques on two athletes		
P7 review the treatment plan for two athletes, describing future treatment opportunities.	**M3** explain the appropriate sport and exercise massage treatment for two athletes.	**D2** evaluate the appropriate sport and exercise massage treatment for two athletes.

10.2 The Effects and Benefits of Sports Massage

As participation in sport and exercise becomes increasingly popular and the rewards for success increase, greater demands are placed on today's athletes. When they attempt to improve their performances, athletes push themselves to their physical and psychological limits. If inevitable injuries are ignored and become chronic, they not only hinder rehabilitation but also affect performance, which makes the athlete susceptible to further injury.

Key term

Sports massage: the systematic manipulation of the soft tissues of the body for therapeutic purposes to aid individuals participating in physical activity.

Sports massage is therefore an expanding industry which aims to aid an athlete's recovery and enhance performance. It is carried out at most major sporting events around the world.

The aims of sports massage are to restore normal functional activity to the musculo-skeletal system. Massage should therefore be an integral part of every athlete's pre- and post-training and competition routines, and should be viewed with similar importance to warming up and cooling down.

The general benefits of massage fall into three specific categories:

- mechanical
- physiological
- psychological.

Mechanical benefits to the athlete are:

- stimulation of soft tissues
- stretching of soft tissue to improve flexibility
- breaking down scar tissue
- correction of posture and limb alignment to improve body awareness
- reducing tension and associated pain
- reducing soreness and pain after an activity.

Physiological benefits to the athlete are:

- improved circulation via stimulation of the sympathetic nervous system to increase the supply of oxygen and nutrients to the injured tissue, thereby promoting healing
- improved circulation to remove waste products from the soft tissues via the lymphatic system
- improved circulation to reduce swelling post-injury
- sedative effect on the parasympathetic nervous system to reduce tension, induce relaxation and relieve pain
- stimulation of the nervous system to prepare the muscles for activity.

Psychological benefits to the athlete are:

- promoting relaxation
- creating a sense of well-being
- increasing confidence prior to competition

In summary, the above effects will allow athletes to train more often, at a higher intensity and with fewer physical problems. It is therefore an essential part of an overall training programme.

Key term

Soft tissues: ligaments, tendons, muscles, connective tissue and skin.

Student activity 10.1   50 minutes   P1   M1

The effects and benefits of sport and exercise massage

Task

Produce a leaflet which a sports and exercise massage professional could hand out to clients that describes and explains the benefits of sports massage.

Include in your leaflet the mechanical, physiological and psychological effects and benefits of sports massage.

10.3 The Role of the Sports Massage Professional

P2

A sports massage professional has a varied job: preparing athletes for competition, helping them warm down after competition, and then dealing with any injuries or symptoms. They can also treat other people who are active but not athletes.

Knowledge

In order to practise, the therapist ideally requires a sports therapy diploma, accredited by the Vocational Training Charitable Trust (VTCT), which can be studied at most further education colleges. It is also possible to study at degree level at a limited number of universities, and private training organisations offer an excellent range of courses and career opportunities. Details of these courses can be found on the internet.

To be an effective sports therapist, you need a thorough basic knowledge and a range of physical and personal skills, including being professional, honest and reliable, as well as having good listening and communication skills.

The therapist also needs to know their limits and when to seek advice or refer a client to a medical colleague. The diagnosis of certain conditions may require more extensive training and expertise. Treatment could be provided once the all-clear was given from a specialist. For this reason many therapists work alongside other specialists such as physiotherapists, and this relationship is often mutually beneficial.

Treatments Applied

Sports massage professionals may be required to perform a range of treatments in addition to the basic sports massage techniques. They may need to deal with injured and recovering athletes and therefore need to know about strapping, stretching, resistance training, first aid and modalities such as heat, ice and electrotherapy.

Types of Business Setting

The sports massage professional usually has to deal with administration and may choose to set up their own business. This business could be located anywhere, but usually they are at sports clubs, leisure centres, gyms and medical centres. Some will travel to clients' homes and others will diversify, offering additional personal training services. To this end, it is useful to have a sound knowledge of sport-specific techniques and the rigours of competition.

Fig 10.1 An athlete receiving sports therapy

In summary, a sport and exercise massage therapist has a huge role to play in the treatment of sports injuries, the conditioning of athletes and the treatment of the general public.

Key learning points 1

The aim of a sport and exercise massage is to restore normal function to an athlete's body. Massage can provide a variety of benefits to an athlete including:
- mechanical
- physiological
- psychological.

A sport and exercise massage professional requires suitable qualifications to carry out sports massage therapy. A range of physical and personal skills are required for a career in sport and exercise massage. A sports massage therapist needs to know and be able to perform a range of different treatments.

Key learning points 2

- Qualifications are necessary to become a sports therapist, as is a thorough knowledge base.
- Certain personal and physical attributes are required if you are considering a career as a sports therapist.
- The career can be varied and rewarding, with high levels of satisfaction.

Q Quick quiz I

1 What are the main aims of sport and exercise massage?
2 List and describe five mechanical benefits of massage.
3 List and describe five physiological benefits of massage.
4 List and describe five psychological benefits of massage.
5 Describe three different roles of a sports massage therapist.
6 Describe three treatments which a sports massage therapist may need to use.

Student activity 10.2   45 minutes   P2

Roles of a sport and exercise massage professional

A sport and exercise massage professional has many roles and responsibilities, and it is important for anyone interested in embarking on such a career to realise what these roles and responsibilities are.

Task 1

Design a spider diagram that lists the different roles and responsibilities of a sport and exercise massage professional.

Task 2

Write a sentence or two that describes each role and responsibility that you have included in your spider diagram.

10.4 Identifiying Sport and Exercise Massage Requirements of Athletes

The Indications for Sports Massage

The following problems would indicate a need for sports massage based on the benefits which it can offer:

- pain post-injury or following training and competition
- swelling
- reduced flexibility
- reduced strength
- muscle tension
- pre-event nerves
- post-event fatigue or soreness
- routine part of training schedule to minimise the chance of the above situations arising
- injury prevention.

Once you are clear about the effects of massage, you can proceed to client assessment. This initial consultation is as important as the treatment itself, and an accurate record must be kept along with details of the subsequent physical examination.

The consultation begins with questioning the client; this is called the *subjective* assessment. It enables the therapist to build up a picture of the current issues, the client's history and what they aim to achieve from treatment.

Prior to any questioning, you should make your client aware of any health and safety issues that are specific to your facility, and the location of fire exits, fire procedures, etc.

The initial questions will establish the cause, nature and irritability of their symptoms:

- What is your presenting problem?
- If there has been an injury, how and when did it occur?
- If there has been no injury, how long have you had the problem?
- Did the problem occur immediately or gradually?

- How would you describe the symptoms, eg dull ache, sharp pain?
- Has there been any swelling, redness or increased temperature?
- Is the problem improving, remaining the same or becoming worse?
- How is this currently affecting your function and performance?

Once you have this detailed information about the client's current status, you need to build up a picture of their history:

- How is your general health?
- Have you any history of medical problems?
- Are you taking any medication?
- What physical activities are you involved in?
- At what level are you competing?
- What is your training schedule?
- What injuries, if any, have you previously suffered?
- What treatments have you previously had?

The information that you are given needs to be recorded on a record form similar to that shown within Fig 10.2.

At this point you may have identified a contraindication (see details on next pages), or may have concerns beyond your level of expertise. If so, you may choose to refer your client to their doctor before progressing with treatment.

You should at this stage have a good idea of their problem, but you will need to verify this by examining the client. This is called the *objective* assessment. If appropriate, it may be necessary for the client to remove clothing, often down to their underwear, with their dignity being maintained at all times. A basic

Key terms

Haematoma: bruising.
Abrasion: grazed skin.

understanding of anatomy is essential for these next stages.

- You need to observe the client for limping, swelling, muscle wasting, bruising, haematomas, abrasions, redness or other abnormal signs.
- You then need to test the range of movement in the areas adjacent to their problem. First, ask the client to move and assess their willingness (active movement), then move the area yourself within a comfortable range (passive movement). This will assess the flexibility of the tissues in question.
- You then need to assess any muscle weakness by resisting certain movements or asking them to perform certain functional tasks.
- Finally, you need to palpate (touch) the problem area to check for muscle spasm, increased temperature, tenderness or pain.

This will complete your client assessment and provide you with all the necessary information to move on to the treatment stage. The information you are given needs to be recorded on a form which also includes the client's details. This form is an accurate record of your assessment and subsequent treatment, and needs to be signed and dated on every entry. The information disclosed by the client is strictly confidential and should not be discussed without their authority.

Student activity 10.3 45 mins P3 M2 D1

Case study: Pre-treatment consultation

The following two athletes have come to you as a sport and exercise massage professional to treat their specific conditions.

Athlete 1 is a 38-year-old male. He is a swimmer, and trains every other day. He chooses mainly to swim the front crawl stroke. His main area for concern is his right shoulder which is painful. On closer examination, he is unable to lift his right arm above shoulder height without experiencing some pain.

Athlete 2 is a 25-year-old female who has knee pain. She takes part in club football, playing once a week and training three times a week. She sustained this

injury two weeks ago in her last football game from another player; the player tried to tackle her but missed the ball and kicked her knee. Most of the bruising has now gone but she is still in some pain and walks with a limp.

Both clients have no contraindications to massage and are both otherwise fit and healthy.

Task 1

Write a report to show how you would carry out a pre-treatment consultation on both athletes. (This will help to prepare you for the demonstration of a pre-treatment consultation of two athletes required for you to attain P3, M2 and D1.)

Task 2

Write a report that explains, compares and contrasts the two athletes' sport and exercise massage requirements.

Name: _____ Occupation: _____

Age: _____ D.O.B.: _____

Address: _____

Tel: Day: _____ Eve: _____ Mob: _____

Sex: _____ Height: _____ Weight: _____

Sport played: _____ Frequency/intensity: _____

GP name/address: _____

Medical history: _____

Present complaint: _____

History of injury: _____

I confirm that the information I have given is accurate to the best of my knowledge and I have not withheld any details. I accept that I will receive sports massage therapy at my own risk.

Signed: _____ Date _____

Print name: _____ Therapist signature: _____

Notes – physical assessment _____

Fig 10.2 Pre-massage questionnaire

The Contraindications for Sports Massage

Under certain circumstances, conditions may be present that sports massage may make worse, and hence it should not be carried out. These conditions are collectively known as contraindications. The massage therapist needs to know what they are and how to deal with them.

- A body temperature over 37.7° Celsius (100° Fahrenheit), or feeling unwell: these symptoms suggest a period of illness, and as massage improves circulation, it may also spread toxins and could make the condition worse.
- Skin diseases and disorders: the skin may become inflamed due to allergies or medical conditions such as eczema and psoriasis. Infections can be recognised by swelling, redness, pain and heat. Massage can cause further irritation and may spread the infection through the client to the therapist, and even to a subsequent client.
- Vascular diseases: phlebitis is the inflammation

of veins, and can often accompany a blood clot called a thrombosis. The clot may be disturbed by massage, causing a blockage elsewhere in the blood vessels of the heart, lungs or brains, all with serious consequences. Caution should be taken if there is swelling, increased temperature and pain in the calf muscles. If a clot is suspected, urgent medical attention should be sought. Attempts to massage an area where varicose veins are present could also cause further damage and pain.

Key term

Vascular: relating to the blood vessels.

- Recently injured areas: the site of an injury may be acutely inflamed with swelling, heat, redness, pain and probable dysfunction. Massage may act to disturb the healing process, thus making the condition worse by increasing circulation and therefore causing further swelling.

The above conditions may need a medical opinion and the client should be advised to see a doctor.

- Pregnancy: care should be taken if the client is

experiencing nausea and vomiting. Massage of the back and abdomen must be avoided during the first 16 weeks of pregnancy as friction could promote miscarriage. In the later stages of pregnancy, massage of the lower limbs may reduce swelling and aid relaxation in areas such as the upper back and shoulders.

● Other medical conditions: clients presenting with a medical history of cancer, diabetes, tuberculosis, multiple sclerosis or other serious medical conditions should be advised to gain medical clearance from their doctor prior to treatment.

Student activity 10.4 ⏱ 40 minutes P4

Massage treatment is not appropriate for people who have certain contraindications to massage. It is vital that both the sports and exercise massage therapist and the client are aware of these contraindications.

Task

Prepare a leaflet to be handed out to patients that describes six contraindications to massage treatment

Key learning points 3

● The aim of sports massage is to restore normal function. Its benefits can be divided into mechanical, physiological and psychological.
● The indications for sports massage are wide-ranging and need to be known by both the therapist and client.
● Be aware of the contraindications to avoid making the client feel worse; seek medical advice if you are not certain whether to proceed.

Treatment Plan

The results of the assessment should be discussed with the client, along with how you intend to treat their problem and what this aims to achieve. Your plan will involve informing the client of the treatments which you propose to use and the number of treatments that may be required to achieve satisfactory results. This may include the client having to

perform a home exercise programme such as guidance for stretches, on strengthening and posture, or how to use heat and ice.

The client is then in a position to give you their informed consent for you to proceed. Any charges should be made clear prior to the assessment, and any payments received should be accurately recorded.

Key learning points 4

● The assessment results and subsequent treatment plan should be shared with the client so that they can offer their informed consent to treatment.
● A considerable amount of organisation is needed to prepare the environment, equipment, the therapist and the client, in order to portray a professional image and strike up an appropriate rapport.
● Awareness of health and safety legislation and customer rights is essential, and hygiene and hand-washing are particularly important.
● It is important to understand which massage medium to use – oils, powders or creams.

Student activity 10.5   45 mins   P5

Treating two clients with sport and exercise massage

Having carried out a pre-treatment consultation on two clients, you now need to decide how you will treat them through sport and exercise massage.

Task

Produce a treatment plan for each of your two athletes; make sure that you complete a full assessment of each athlete and produce a record card which details the treatments that you intend to give.

10.5 Performing and Reviewing Sport and Exercise Massage Techniques

Environment, Appearance and Equipment

You will often have to be flexible as to where you work. The environment will often be beyond your control, especially if working at a sporting event. Care is essential to create an environment as near to the ideal as possible. This would involve the following:

● privacy for the client
● a clean, tidy and well-ventilated room
● warmth to promote relaxation, especially if the client has to undress.

The therapist should have:

● a professional appearance, unhurried and confident
● clean hands – wash basin, soap, towels and waste disposal available
● short nails with no polish and no jewellery
● short sleeves and no wristwatch.

The following equipment should be available:

● massage couch with adjustable height and pillows
● privacy screens (for a private changing area)
● massage oils, creams or powders
● massage cologne to remove oils
● towels to cover areas not being massaged and to provide a comfortable temperature.

Client comfort is paramount, so the couch should ideally be adjustable with a face hole and a ready supply of pillows to support the head or limbs. It is also important for the therapist to be comfortable as they will adopt positions for sustained periods, day in

day out, so the height of the plinth and your position requires careful attention to convey relaxation and confidence to the client.

Safe practice needs to be implemented, and an understanding of health, safety and hygiene regulations is important. Massage is often a personal experience for both therapist and client, and although you may have a professional manner and do not indulge in inappropriate behaviour, complaints may still arise. An awareness of consumer rights is therefore beneficial.

Client Preparation

Success depends not only on diagnosis, treatment and physical skills, but also on personal skills. It is essential that a professional rapport is developed with the client. This can be achieved by:

● relaxing the client and putting them at ease
● showing a caring attitude when listening to their concerns
● being professional at all times
● maintaining client confidentiality
● explaining the treatment course and the desired effect
● using tact and respecting their privacy and dignity.

Once the treatment has commenced, the client must be able to relax. Experience will allow you to work out whether the client wishes to talk or not.

Massage oils are used to allow smooth movement over the client's body and prevent friction. Vegetable oils such as olive and sunflower oils are commonly used as they have little fragrance and are easily absorbed by the skin. Aromatherapists use essential oils which have specific effects and should therefore only be used following appropriate training. If using oils, sports cologne should be applied post-treatment to remove any excess. The traditional lubricant for Swedish massage is talcum powder but this can cause extra friction and subsequent discomfort on dry skin. The finer powder may also be inhaled over time by the therapist, endangering their health. But as certain clients still prefer it, you should still consider using it with caution. Less frequently used are certain creams and lotions.

Massage Techniques

The three main techniques used are:

- effleurage
- petrissage
- frictions.

Other techniques are also used, including tapotement, vibrations and trigger points.

Effleurage

This involves a variety of stroking movements and is used at the beginning and end of a massage. It can be applied with varying degrees of pressure and is broken into light and deep stroking. Light stroking is performed with the whole hand, keeping the fingers together and with the hand relaxed. The speed and pressure will vary as the massage proceeds. The initial light stroking enables the therapist to spread the oil and identify tension in the muscle, even starting to relax the muscle. Gradually more pressure is applied, with the aim of assisting fluid flow through the tissue spaces, vessels and veins. The movement should occur up the limb towards the superficial lymph glands which can be found in the groin, back of the knee and the armpit.

Pressure should be consistent throughout a stroke, but can be increased by placing one hand on top of another or using the heel of the hand, finger pads or thumbs. The aim is to relax and sedate initially, then to stretch tissues, increase flow and drainage, reduce swelling, reduce pain by nerve stimulation, and remove waste products.

Petrissage

This is also known as kneading, as the basic movement involves compressing then releasing the tissues. Direct pressure is performed in a circular motion using the palm of the hand to compress muscle tissue onto underlying structures. More localised pressure can be applied using the fingertips, thumbs and even the elbows.

The next stage is similar to kneading but is known as 'picking up' as it involves lifting the tissues up perpendicular to the underlying tissues then squeezing with the forefinger and thumb prior to release. Once the tissue is released, blood returns to it, bringing with it the essential oxygen and nutrients for healing. This technique also aims to mobilise tissues and reduce tension, promote lymph drainage and encourage relaxation.

Student activity 10.6   30 mins   P6

Effleurage massage

Working in pairs, practise effleurage on each other's calf muscles, with strokes starting at the foot and ending at the back of the knee. Relax your partner with gentle stroking movements, warming the muscles and spreading the oils. Promote circulation, increase pressure and stimulate lymph drainage to the major superficial glands. Gradually end the massage using further gentle stroking techniques. Reflect on each other's performance and remember that practice makes perfect.

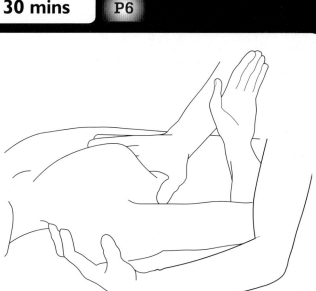

Fig 10.3 Effleurage

Student activity 10.7   10 mins   P6

Petrissage massage

Practise this technique in a similar way to effleurage. This time decide for yourself which muscles would benefit most from this technique.

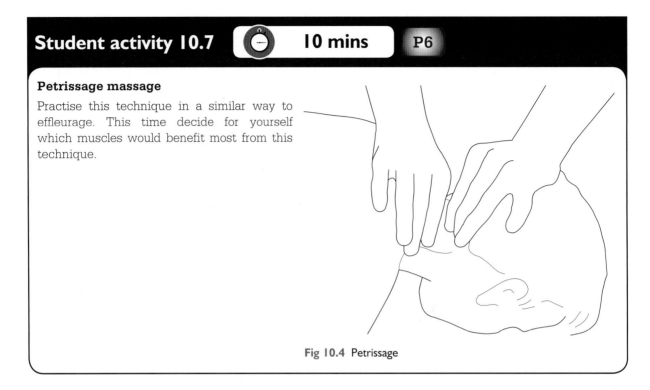

Fig 10.4 Petrissage

Frictions

These are small movements over a localised area using the pads of the fingers or thumbs. Unlike other techniques they are often used where there is little soft tissue, such as the elbows, knees and ankles. Considerably more pressure is applied than during petrissage.

The action is initiated by bracing with the heels of the hands, then holding the thumbs steady and moving the fingers in a circular motion. The fingers do not move across the skin but they do move the skin across the deeper tissue. By increasing the pressure you can stimulate the deep muscle tissue and the breakdown of recently formed scar tissue by separating adhesions between repaired muscle

Student activity 10.8   10 mins   P6

Frictions massage

Practise this technique in the same way as the other two. Decide what injuries and which parts of your body would benefit most.

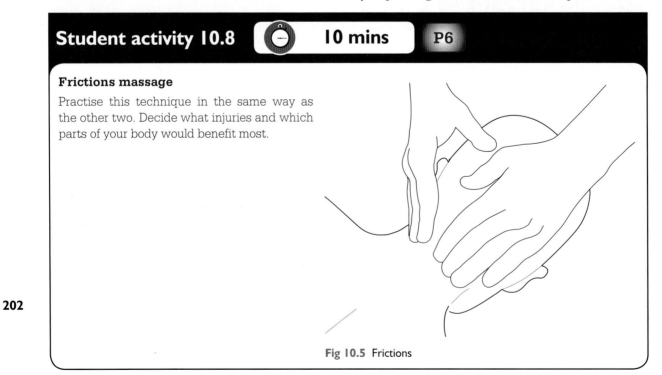

Fig 10.5 Frictions

fibres. There can be a degree of discomfort but only for a short time. This aims to stimulate blood flow, separate adhesions, minimise the effects of scar tissue, promote flexibility and promote healing.

Tapotement

This is also known as percussion and can be divided into cupping and hacking.

Cupping involves the therapist making a cup shape with their hands and, with the palms down, they strike the muscle making a dull thud, which should sound different from the slap of a flat palm. Moving the hands rapidly up and down the muscle has the effect of improving superficial circulation and stimulating the muscle.

Hacking has a similar effect and involves using the outside of the hands with the palms facing each other to strike the muscle, usually targeting the larger muscle bulks such as the quadriceps.

Fig 10.6 Tapotement (hacking)

Vibration

This is often used to finish off a massage. It involves the therapist supporting a muscle with one hand and vibrating the other hand from side to side as they move up and down the muscle. This aims to stimulate the muscle, and to promote blood flow and increase flexibility.

Trigger Point

This massage involves the therapist applying sustained pressure in one specific place, using a finger, thumb or even an elbow. The trigger point is an area of high tension in the muscle where the fibres have failed to relax. It can cause local or referred pain where symptoms are felt at a distance away from the trigger point. Pressure is applied and the pain it creates will tend to subside after ten seconds, after which greater pressure can be applied and sustained for up to a minute. The aim is to gain relaxation and allow blood to return to the muscle.

Order of Routine

Usually the techniques described above are performed in the order given, with the massage finishing with effleurage. The time you spend on each technique may vary depending on the needs of your client.

Evaluation

It is important to evaluate the effect of treatment by:

- asking for immediate feedback
- stretching and loading affected muscles
- performing specific tests
- receiving client feedback once they return to sporting action.

Based on the feedback, you may prescribe more treatments or a change of technique. If symptoms persist, referral to another medical professional such as a doctor, physiotherapist, chiropractor or osteopath may be advised.

Key learning points 5

- There are three main massage techniques that are the basis of treatments; these need to be practised diligently in order to gain maximum benefit and to instil confidence in the client.
- Additional techniques are also available and it is important to learn when to use all the techniques and for which body parts certain techniques are most suitable.
- An evaluation after the treatment is an essential part of the overall management.

Q Quick quiz 2

Trigger point	Effleurage	Vibration	Frictions
Tapotement	Feedback	Petrissage	Medical professional

Select a word or words from the boxes above to answer the following questions:

1 This massage technique involves a variety of stroking movements.

2 This massage technique involves lots of small movements applying pressure.

3 This massage technique involves kneading movements.

4 This massage technique involves cupping and tapping.

5 This massage technique requires sustained pressure in one specific place.

6 This massage technique is usually used at the end of the massage.

7 A client should provide you with this after their treatment.

8 If the client continues to suffer from the same problem after a series of massage treatments, to whom should they be referred?

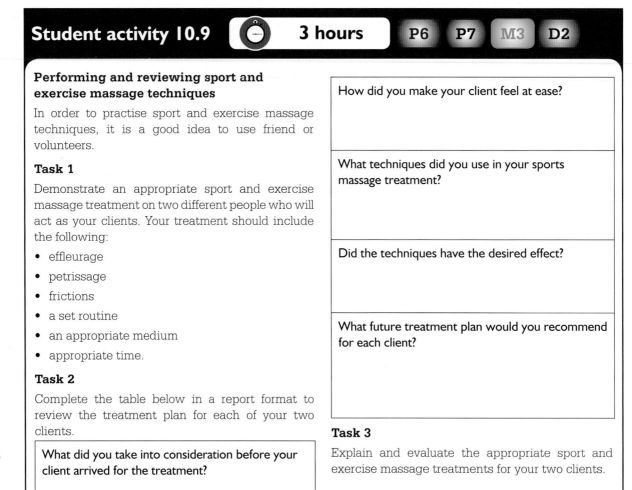

Student activity 10.9   3 hours   P6   P7   M3   D2

Performing and reviewing sport and exercise massage techniques

In order to practise sport and exercise massage techniques, it is a good idea to use friend or volunteers.

Task 1

Demonstrate an appropriate sport and exercise massage treatment on two different people who will act as your clients. Your treatment should include the following:

- effleurage
- petrissage
- frictions
- a set routine
- an appropriate medium
- appropriate time.

Task 2

Complete the table below in a report format to review the treatment plan for each of your two clients.

> What did you take into consideration before your client arrived for the treatment?

> How did you make your client feel at ease?

> What techniques did you use in your sports massage treatment?

> Did the techniques have the desired effect?

> What future treatment plan would you recommend for each client?

Task 3

Explain and evaluate the appropriate sport and exercise massage treatments for your two clients.

References

Cash, M. (1998) *Sports and Remedial Massage*, Mosby.

Dawson, L., Dawson, K. A. and Tiidius, P. M. (2004) 'Evaluating the influence of massage on leg strength, swelling and pain following a half marathon', *Journal of Sports Science Medicine*, 3, 37–43.

Lewis, M. and Johnson, M. I. (2006) 'The clinical effectiveness of therapeutic massage for musculoskeletal pain: a systematic review', *Physiotherapy*, 92 (3), 146–58.

Paine, T. (2000) *The Complete Guide to Sports Massage*, A & C Black.

Preyde, M. (2000) 'Effectiveness of massage therapy for sub acute low back pain: a randomised controlled trial', *Canadian Medical Association Journal*, 162, 1815–20.

Tiidius, P. M. and Shoemaker, J. K. (1995) 'Effleurage massage, muscle blood flow and long-term post-exercise strength recovery', *International Journal of Sports Medicine*, 15, 478–83.

Van der Dolder, P. A. and Roberts, D. L. (2003) 'A trial in to the effectiveness of soft tissue massage in the treatment of shoulder pain', *Australian Journal of Physiotherapy*, 49, 183–8.

Watt, J. (1999) *Massage for Sport*, The Crowood Press.

Useful websites

www.eorthopod.com

Provides patient guides, video & news on latest scientific literature for sports injuries and traumas

www.brianmac.co.uk/massage.htm

Provides information about the three main sports massage techniques and when to use these

http://www.wonderhowto.com/how-to-sports-massage-5258/

Free videos demonstrating the correct way to apply sports massage

12: Sports nutrition

12.1 Introduction

As we seek to gain an extra edge in our sporting performances and to maximise the effects of our training, so the spotlight has fallen on areas other than training. Nutrition has been shown to be an area of increasing interest. We know that training brings benefits and we know that eating properly brings benefits. So if we combine the correct training with the correct nutritional strategy, the gains are multiplied. Nutrition is as important for people who are seeking to improve their sporting performance as it is for those seeking fitness gains or weight-management objectives.

By the end of this unit you should:

- know the concepts of nutrition and digestion
- know energy intake and expenditure in sports performance
- know the relationship between hydration and sports performance
- be able to plan a diet appropriate for a selected sports activity.

Assessment and grading criteria

To achieve a PASS grade the evidence must show that the learner is able to:	To achieve a MERIT grade the evidence must show that, in addition to the pass criteria, the learner is able to:	To achieve a DISTINCTION grade the evidence must show that, in addition to the pass and merit criteria, the learner is able to:
P1 describe nutrition, including nutritional requirements, using recommended guidelines from public health sources associated with nutrition		
P2 describe the structure and function of the digestive system		
P3 describe energy intake and expenditure in sports performance	**M1** explain energy intake and expenditure in sports performance	
P4 describe energy balance and its importance in relation to sports performance	**M2** explain the importance of energy balance in relation to sports performance	**D1** analyse the effects of energy balance on sports performance
P5 describe hydration and its effects on sports performance		
P6 describe the components of a balanced diet	**M3** explain the components of a balanced diet	
P7 plan an appropriate two-week diet plan for a selected sports performer for a selected sports activity.	**M4** explain the two-week diet plan for a selected sports performer for a selected sports activity.	**D2** justify the two-week diet plan for a selected sports performer for a selected sports activity.

12.2 Nutrients

P1

Key term

Nutrients: chemical substances obtained from food and used in the body to provide energy, as well as structural materials and regulating agents to support growth, maintenance and repair of the body's tissues.

Nutrients can be divided into two main groups: macronutrients and micronutrients. The three macronutrients are:

- carbohydrate
- protein
- fat.

Macronutrients are needed in large amounts in the diet and all provide energy for the body. They are also used to build the structures of the body and produce functions needed to sustain life.

The two micronutrients are:

- vitamins
- minerals.

They are needed in smaller amounts in the diet and contain no energy themselves. They work in conjunction with the macronutrients to produce life-sustaining functions and are needed to unlock the energy present in the macronutrients.

There are other food groups such as water and fibre. Water is not usually regarded as a nutrient because it has no nutrient value despite being highly important in sustaining life. Fibre is a type of carbohydrate so it would be part of that food group.

Carbohydrate

Almost every culture relies on carbohydrate as the major source of nutrients and calories – rice in Asia, wheat in Europe, the Middle East and North Africa, corn and potato in the Americas.

Carbohydrate should provide between 50 and 60 per cent of calorie intake and its main role is to supply energy to allow the body to function. The energy content of carbohydrate is that 1 g provides 4 kcals.

There are many sources of carbohydrate, such as bread, rice, pasta, potatoes, fruit, vegetables, sweets and biscuits. They all differ in form slightly but are all broken down into glucose because that is the only way the body can use carbohydrate.

The functions of carbohydrate are to provide energy for:

- the brain to function
- the liver to perform its functions
- muscular contractions at moderate to high intensities.

When carbohydrate foods are digested they are all broken down into glucose which is then absorbed in the small intestine and enters the bloodstream. From the bloodstream it can either be used immediately as energy or stored in the liver and muscles. Glucose is stored in the form of glycogen, which is bound to water (1 g of glucose needs 2.7 g of water) for storage. However, the glycogen molecule is bulky and difficult to store in large amounts. The body can store around 1600 kcals of glycogen, which would enable us to run for around two hours.

Key terms

Glucose: the smallest unit of a carbohydrate.

Glycogen: stored glucose in the muscles and liver attached to water molecules.

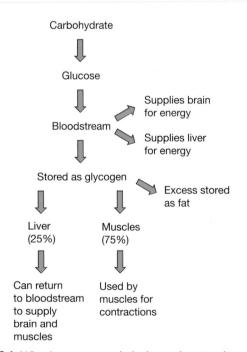

Fig 12.1 What happens to carbohydrate when it is digested

Forms of carbohydrate

Carbohydrates come in a variety of forms, but they are all made up of molecules of sugar. These molecules of sugar are called saccharides; they come in different forms depending upon the foods in which they are found. Eventually through the process of digestion they all become glucose. These saccharides are found as one of the following:

- monosaccharides
- disaccharides
- polysaccharides.

Monosaccharides are one saccharide molecule on its own. There are three types of monosaccharide:

- glucose – occurs naturally in most carbohydrate foods
- fructose – occurs in fruit and honey
- galactose – does not occur freely but is a component of the sugars found in milk products.

Disaccharides are two saccharide molecules joined together by a bond:

- sucrose = glucose + fructose – most commonly found as table sugar
- lactose = glucose + galactose – found in milk and milk products
- maltose = glucose + glucose – found in malt products, beers and cereals.

Mono- and disaccharides are commonly known as simple carbohydrates because they are in short simple chains – existing as individual molecules.

Polysaccharides are long, complex chains of glucose molecules containing ten or more molecules. Due to their complicated structures they are called 'complex carbohydrates'.

To digest polysaccharides, the bonds need to be broken down through the process of digestion so that they can become individual glucose molecules and be absorbed into the bloodstream. If a complex carbohydrate is processed or cooked in any way these bonds will start to be broken down before they enter the digestive system.

Polysaccharides or complex carbohydrates can come in either their natural or refined forms. Wheat and rice are naturally brown in colour due to their high levels of fibre, vitamins and minerals. Therefore, the brown varieties of bread, rice and pasta are of greater nutrient value than the white, refined varieties.

Good sources of polysaccharides:

- wholemeal, wholegrain or granary breads
- wholemeal pasta
- wholegrain rice
- potatoes
- sweet potatoes
- vegetables
- pulses.

Poorer choices of polysaccharides:

- white bread
- white pasta
- white rice
- rice cakes.

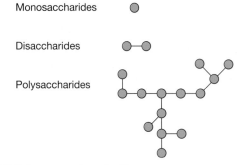

Fig 12.2 Structure of saccharides

Glycaemic index

The rate at which carbohydrate foods are broken down and how quickly they raise blood glucose levels is measured via the glycaemic index (GI). It is a ranking system that shows how quickly the carbohydrate is broken down and enters the blood as glucose in comparison with the speed at which glucose would enter the blood if consumed. Foods with a high glycaemic index break down quickly and rapidly increase blood glucose levels. Table sugar is a good example. Pasta would have a lower glycaemic index, breaking down into glucose more slowly. It would also have less of an immediate effect on blood glucose levels, causing a slower increase over a longer period.

The glycaemic index is one of the most important principles in nutrition currently. We deal best with foods of a low glycaemic index that release their energy slowly and over time. Foods of a high glycaemic index cause a rapid release of glucose into the bloodstream, followed by a rapid drop in blood glucose, causing hunger and fatigue. The person who eats high glycaemic index foods will experience fluctuating blood glucose levels and be tempted to overeat the wrong type of food. High glycaemic index foods, such as sweets, cakes, biscuits, fizzy drinks, white breads and sugary cereals, are linked to obesity and the development of type 2 diabetes. If a person eats low glycaemic index foods they will find that their stable blood glucose levels give them energy and enable them to concentrate throughout the day.

In the glycaemic index foods are either high, moderate or low.

High	Moderate	Low
Above 85	60–84	Below 60

Table 12.1 Glycaemic index for foods

209

The speed at which a food is broken down and enters the bloodstream is dependent on a range of factors. The following will lower the speed at which glucose enters the bloodstream:

- the presence of fibre in the food
- the presence of fat in the food
- the presence of protein in the food
- the type of saccharides present in the food
- the amount of carbohydrate eaten.

The following will increase the speed at which glucose enters the bloodstream:

- the length of the cooking process
- the amount the food has been refined or processed
- the riper the fruit has become.

Fig 12.3 Unrefined brown foods

Fibre

Dietary fibre is the part of a plant that is resistant to the body's digestive enzymes. It is defined as 'indigestible plant material', and although it is a carbohydrate and contains calories, the digestive system cannot unlock them from the plant. As a result, fibre moves through the gastrointestinal tract and ends up in the stool. The main benefit in eating fibre is that it retains water, resulting in softer and bulkier stools that prevent constipation and haemorrhoids. Research suggests that a high-fibre diet also reduces the risk of colon cancer. All fruits, vegetables and grains provide some fibre.

There are two types of fibre – soluble and insoluble – that perform slightly different functions.

Fig 12.4 Refined white foods

Soluble fibre dissolves into a gel in water and is found in the fleshy part of fruit and vegetables, oats, barley and rice. For example, when you make porridge the oats partly dissolve into a sticky gel and this is the soluble fibre.

Soluble fibre has two main roles to play:

- it slows down how quickly the stomach empties and how quickly glucose enters the bloodstream
- it binds to fat and blood cholesterol, thus decreasing the risk of heart disease.

Insoluble fibre will not dissolve in water and is found in the skin of fruit and vegetables, wheat, rye, seeds and pips of fruit. Insoluble fibre passes through the digestive system without being altered in any way. Its main roles are as follows:

- It adds bulk to faeces and speeds its passage through the large intestine.
- It helps to keep the large intestine clean and prevent bowel disease.
- It stretches the stomach and makes you feel full for longer.

● It slows down the release of glucose into the bloodstream.

It is recommended that we eat around 18 g of fibre a day. This can be done by eating foods in their natural form rather than in their processed or refined states.

Recommended daily intake of carbohydrate

A minimum recommended daily intake of at least 50 per cent of total kilocalories consumed should come from complex carbohydrate sources. The British Nutrition Foundation found that in Britain the average intake of carbohydrate is 272 g for men and 193 g for women, providing just over 43 per cent of the energy in the diet.

As with most nutrients, eating excess amounts can lead to problems. Excessive consumption of sugar (for example sucrose) can lead to tooth decay and is linked to a number of major diseases, such as diabetes, obesity and coronary heart disease. Excess carbohydrate in the diet will be converted to and stored as fat. Thus it is possible to gain body fat even on a low-fat diet.

Key learning points 1

● Carbohydrate provides energy for:
  – brain function
  – liver function and digestion
  – muscular contractions.
● Carbohydrates are made up of saccharides, of which there are three types:
  – monosaccharides – single units of saccharides known as 'simple sugars'
  – disaccharides – two units of saccharides joined by a bond called 'simple sugars'
  – polysaccharides – long chains of saccharides called 'complex carbohydrates'.
● Glycaemic index (GI) is the rate at which a carbohydrate food enters the bloodstream as glucose:
  – high GI = above 85
  – moderate GI = 60–85
  – low GI = less than 60.
● Fibre is 'indigestible plant material' which cannot be digested. It protects against heart disease and diseases of the colon by keeping the colon clean and the waste moving through quickly.

Q Quick quiz 1

Look at the list of carbohydrate-rich foods and put them into the appropriate column (some of them can go into more than one column).

Monosaccharide	Disaccharide	Polysaccharide	Fibre

Apple	Milk	Pasta
Cereal	Rice	All Bran
Bread	Cabbage	Banana
Honey	Potatoes	Cream
Sweetcorn	Beer	

Protein

The word 'protein' is derived from Greek and means 'prime importance'. Proteins are of prime importance because they are the building blocks that make up the structures of the body. Muscle, skin, bones, internal organs, cartilage and ligament all have a protein component. We gain our protein by eating protein-rich foods such as red meat, fish, chicken, eggs and dairy products.

The diet should consist of between 10 and 20 per cent protein depending upon the specific needs of the individual. Protein also provides a source of energy: 1 g of protein provides 4 kcals.

Amino acids

The smallest unit of a protein is an amino acid. Proteins are made up of long chains of amino acids which are formed into structures. Amino acids are the smallest unit of a protein and there are 20 amino acids in total. Amino acids can be seen to be like the alphabet. In the English language we have 26 letters from which we can make up millions of words. The protein alphabet has 20 amino acids from which can be produced approximately 50,000 different proteins present in the body. Just as different words are made up of different orders of letters, so different structures are made up of different orders of amino acids.

They can be split into essential and non-essential amino acids. An essential amino acid is one that must be gained through eating it in the diet, while a non-essential amino acid can be made in the liver if all essential amino acids are present. This means to produce all the structures of the body we must gain all the essential amino acids on a daily basis.

There are eight essential amino acids to be gained from the diet:

- isoleucine
- leucine
- lysine
- methionine
- phenylalanine
- threonine
- tryptophan
- valine.

There are 12 non-essential amino acids which are synthesised in the liver if all eight essential amino acids are gained from the diet:

- cystein
- yrosine
- histidine
- glutamine
- glutamic acid
- glycine
- alanine
- serine
- proline
- aspartic acid
- asparagine
- arginine.

Foods that contain all eight essential amino acids are described as being complete, while a food that is missing one or more essential amino acid is described as being incomplete. Table 12.2 shows sources of complete and incomplete proteins.

With the exception of the soya bean, the sources of complete protein are from animals, while incomplete proteins come from plant sources. To gain all eight essential amino acids from incomplete protein sources you need to eat a range of sources or combine protein sources. This is called 'complementary protein' and examples are:

- wheat and pulses (beans on toast)
- nuts and vegetables (nut roast)
- rice and lentils (vegetarian chilli).

All protein sources contain different amounts of amino acids. The greater the quantity of the essential amino acids in the food, the higher the biological value. Eggs have the highest quality or biological

Complete protein	Incomplete protein
Chicken	Wheat
Eggs	Oats
Fish	Rice
Red meat	Pulses
Dairy products	Nuts
Soya beans	Vegetables

Table 12.2 Complete and incomplete proteins

Fig 12.5 Complete protein

Fig 12.6 Incomplete protein

value of all foods and are given a protein rating of 100. All other proteins are compared with eggs in terms of their quality and quantity of amino acids. This is shown in Table 12.3.

Functions of protein

When we eat protein it is digested in the digestive system and then delivered to the liver as individual amino acids. The liver then rebuilds the amino acids into long chains to make up proteins. The proteins that the liver produces depend upon the needs of the body at that time. If we need to replace muscle the liver will produce the relevant proteins to replace muscle tissue.

Proteins have three specific roles in the body:

● to build structures (structural)
● to perform functions (functional)
● to provide fuel.

Protein forms a part of the following structures:

● muscle (skeletal, smooth and cardiac)
● bone
● internal organs (heart, kidneys, liver)
● connective tissue (tendons and ligaments)
● hair
● nails.

Protein forms part of the following structures which perform specific functions in the body:

● hormones (which send messages to cells – insulin and adrenaline)
● enzymes (biological catalysts which speed up reactions in cells)
● part of the immune system (white blood cells are made partly of protein)
● formation of lipoproteins (these help to transport fats around the body).

Protein is not the body's first choice of fuel but it can be used as energy. It is heavily used during endurance training and events, or at times of starvation.

Food	Protein rating
Eggs	100
Fish	70
Beef	69
Cow's milk	60
Brown rice	57
White rice	56
Soya beans	47
Wheat	44
Peanuts	43
Beans	34

Table 12.3 Protein ratings of different foods
Source: Adapted from McArdle *et al.* (2009)

Recommended intakes of protein

The average daily intake of protein in the UK is 85 g for men and 62 g for women. The recommended daily amount of protein for healthy adults is 0.8 g per kilogram of body weight, or about 15 per cent of total kilocalories. Protein needs are higher for children, infants and many athletes.

213

Key learning points 2

- Proteins are long chains of amino acids. There are 20 amino acids in total: eight are essential amino acids which need to be eaten in the diet, and 12 are non-essential amino acids which can be synthesised by the liver if all eight essential amino acids are present.
- Foods containing all eight essential amino acids are described as being complete protein. Foods missing one or more essential amino acid are described as being incomplete.
- Protein has the following main functions:
  - to build structures of the body
  - to perform specific functions
  - to provide fuel.

Q Quick quiz 2

Liver	Isoleucine	20	Nuts	8
Muscle	Aspartic acid	Soya bean	Eggs	Hormone

Choose the correct word or words to match the following descriptions.

1 This is an essential amino acid.

2 This is a complete protein.

3 This is an incomplete protein.

4 This body structure contains protein.

5 There are this number of amino acids in total.

6 There are this number of essential amino acids.

7 This is a non-essential amino acid.

8 This organ rebuilds amino acids into long chains.

9 This food has a very high protein rating.

10 Protein forms part of this structure.

Fats

Fats are often perceived as being bad or a part of the diet to be avoided. In fact, fats are vital to health and perform many important functions in the body. The intake of certain fats does need to be minimised and excess consumption of fats will lead to health problems.

The functions of fat are as follows:

- formation of the cell membrane
- formation of the myelin sheath which coats the nerves
- a component of the brain and nervous system
- protection of internal organs (brain, kidneys, liver)
- production of hormones (oestrogen and testosterone)
- transportation and storage of vitamins A, D, E and K
- constant source of energy
- store of energy
- heat production.

Fats and oils belong to a family called 'lipids' and they perform a variety of important roles in the body. Predominantly fats supply energy for everyday activities and movement. They are described as being 'energy-dense' because they contain a lot of energy per gram: 1 g of fat provides 9 kcals.

If we compare this figure to the 4 kcals which carbohydrates and protein provide (see Table 12.4) then we can see that it is significantly higher.

The difference between a fat and an oil is that a fat is solid at room temperature while an oil is liquid at room temperature.

The smallest unit of a fat is called a 'fatty acid'. There are different types of fatty acid present in the foods we ingest. In particular, a fatty acid can be

Macronutrient	Kcals per gram
Carbohydrate	4
Protein	4
Fat	9

Table 12.4 Kcalories per gram of macronutrients

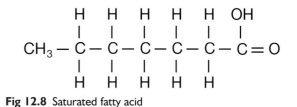

Fig 12.8 Saturated fatty acid

saturated or unsaturated; this is important because they will be shaped differently. In chemistry shape matters because it influences the function performed. Therefore, different fatty acids perform different functions in the body.

Triglycerides

Triglycerides are dietary fats in that they are how the fats we ingest are packaged. A triglyceride is defined as 'three fatty acids attached to a glycerol backbone'. Glycerol is actually a carbohydrate which the fatty acids attach to. During digestion the fatty acids are broken off from the glycerol backbone to be used by the body as required. The glycerol is used as all carbohydrates are used, to produce energy.

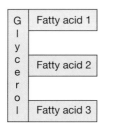

Fig 12.7 Structure of a triglyceride

Types of fatty acid

Fatty acids can be divided into:

- saturated fatty acids
- monounsaturated fatty acids
- polyunsaturated fatty acids.

A fatty acid consists of long chains of carbon atoms with an acid group (COOH) at one end and a methyl group (CH_3) at the other. The structure of the chains of fatty acids attached to the glycerol molecule determines whether the fat is classed as saturated, monounsaturated or polyunsaturated. If you think of different types of fats, such as butter, lard, sunflower oil and olive oil, you will notice that they differ in terms of their colour, texture and taste. This is because of the different types of fatty acids attached to the glycerol backbone.

A saturated fat is one where all the carbon atoms are attached to hydrogen molecules. The chain is said to be saturated with hydrogen.

We can see that the carbon atoms each have single bonds between them and each carbon atom has four bonds. The hydrogen atoms possess a very slight charge and gently push away from each other. This has the effect of making the chain straight in shape. In chemistry shape matters as it affects function and it also makes the saturated fat solid at room temperature. This is because the fatty acids can pack tightly together with little space between each one. Saturated fats are also described as being stable or inert. This means that their structure will not change when they are heated. They will melt but the structure of the fatty acid chain stays the same.

The majority of saturated fats come from animal sources (see Table 12.5).

Source	
Animal	**Plant**
Red meat	Coconut oil
Poultry	Palm oil
Eggs	
Dairy products	

Table 12.5 Sources of saturated fats

The Department of Health recommends a person should have a maximum of 10 per cent of daily kilocalories from saturated fat.

An unsaturated fat is one where there are hydrogen atoms missing from the carbon chain, causing the carbon atoms to attach to each other with double bonds. This is because carbon has to have four bonds and if there is no hydrogen present they will bond to each other. In this case the carbon chain is not saturated with hydrogen atoms and is therefore 'unsaturated'.

A monounsaturated fat is one where there is just one double bond in the carbon chain (see Figure 12.9).

Due to the slight charge the hydrogen atoms contain, they push each other away. Now that there are hydrogen atoms missing, it causes the chain to bend and become curved. The curved fatty acids cannot pack so tightly together, so their appearance

215

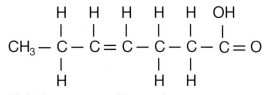

Fig 12.9 Monounsaturated fatty acid

changes and they will be in liquid or oil form. They will also be less stable or more reactive. This is because of the double bonds between the carbon atoms. Carbon attaches to itself only if there is nothing else to be attached to and it will take the opportunity to break off and attach to something else if it can. If monounsaturated fats are heated they change their structure.

Examples of monounsaturated fats are:

● olive oil
● peanut oil
● avocados
● rapeseed oil (canola oil)
● almond oil.

The Department of Health recommends a person should have a maximum of 12 per cent of daily kilocalories from monounsaturated fat.

A polyunsaturated fat is one where there are many double bonds in the carbon chain due to a shortage of hydrogen ions in the chain.

This has the effect of making the fatty acid even more curved and highly reactive in nature. They are also in oil or liquid form. Polyunsaturated fats are highly unstable when heated to high temperatures and will change their structure.

Examples of polyunsaturated fats are:

● sunflower oil
● safflower oil
● corn oil
● fish oils
● nuts
● seeds.

The Department of Health recommends a person should have a maximum of 10 per cent of daily kilocalories from these polyunsaturated fats.

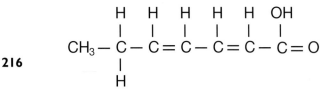

Fig 12.10 Polyunsaturated fatty acid

Saturated versus unsaturated fats

Saturated fats have always received bad press until recently when people realised that they have an important role in the diet. Due to their stable nature they always retain their structure. This is important because when they enter the fat cells, the cells will recognise them and know what to do with them. Saturated fats are always stored as fat in the fat cells.

Naturally occurring unsaturated fats, such as olive oil, have very beneficial effects when they are stored in fat cells – they improve circulation, lower cholesterol levels and improve the health of hair, skin and nails. The problem comes when unsaturated fats are heated or processed in any way because they then change their structure and start to look like saturated fats. They become 'hydrogenated' or altered structurally and when they enter the body they are accepted into the fat cells because they look like saturated fats. Once inside the fat cells, they start to cause damage to the cell and stop positive reactions occurring. The two most dangerous types of fats are:

● hydrogenated vegetable oil
● trans fats.

These have been linked to heart disease and cancer and are present in processed foods and deep-fat-fried foods.

Butter versus margarine?

In terms of fat content these two products are pretty similar. However, due to the margarine being an unsaturated fat (sunflower oil), it would appear to be beneficial to health. Sunflower oil is naturally a liquid and margarine is a solid product, which means it has been processed in some way and thus changed structurally.

The butter will not be changed structurally because it is predominantly saturated fat. For these reasons the butter is a better health choice because it is a more naturally occurring product. In particular, it is the cheap margarines that need to be avoided. If choosing a margarine, check the contents for hydrogenated vegetable oil and trans fats.

Essential fatty acids

The body can make all the fatty acids it needs except for two, the essential fatty acids (EFAs), which must be supplied in the diet. These fatty acids are omega 3 and omega 6.

Sources of omega 3 and 6 are as follows.

Omega 3 fatty acids:

● oily fish (e.g. salmon, mackerel, herring)
● flax oil

- walnuts
- soya beans.

Omega 6 fatty acids:

- sunflower oil
- pumkin seeds
- sesame seeds
- safflower oil.

Research into omega 3, and in particular fish oils, has shown that eating oily fish protects against heart disease. This is because the omega 3s may prevent the formation of blood clots on the artery walls and lower the levels of triglycerides circulating in the bloodstream.

The essential fatty acids are also thought to improve the function of the brain and promote learning as well as being beneficial for arthritics because they reduce swelling in the joints.

Cholesterol

Cholesterol can either be ingested or made in the body. It is found only in animal products and never in plants. It has some useful functions including building cell membranes and helping the function of various hormones.

There are two types of cholesterol: low-density lipoproteins (LDLs) and high-density lipoproteins (HDLs). LDLs are responsible for the deposits lining the walls of arteries and lead to an increased risk of coronary heart disease. HDLs actually reduce this risk by transporting cholesterol away to the liver and so are beneficial to health.

Recommended daily intake of fat

Fat intake should make up no more than 30 per cent of total kilocalories. Only 10 per cent of kilocalories should come from saturated fat. Dietary cholesterol should be limited to 300 mg or less per day.

There are many health problems related to eating an excess of fat, especially saturated fats. These include obesity, high blood pressure and coronary heart disease, although it is important to distinguish between the different types of fat eaten in a person's diet. Consumption of certain fatty acids (omega 3 fish oils found in tuna) is linked to a decreased risk of coronary heart disease.

As fat provides just over twice as much energy per gram as carbohydrate, a diet high in fat can make over-consumption more likely. It is thought that excess dietary fat may be more easily converted to body fat than excess carbohydrate or protein. Research suggests that more people are obese today than ever before. Obese people are more likely to suffer from a range of illnesses including coronary heart disease, adult-onset diabetes, gallstones, arthritis, high blood pressure and some types of cancer. However, most of the health problems associated with obesity are removed once the extra weight is lost.

Key learning points 3

- Fat performs some vital functions in the body:
  - formation of the cell membrane
  - formation of the myelin sheath which coats the nerves
  - a component of the brain and nervous system
  - protection of internal organs (brain, kidneys, liver)
  - production of hormones (oestrogen and testosterone)
  - transportation and storage of vitamins A, D, E and K
  - constant source of energy
  - store of energy
  - heat production.
- Saturated fats occur when all the carbon atoms are saturated with hydrogen. They are solid at room temperature, stable and unreactive. Examples of saturated fats include:
  - animal fats
  - fat of red meat and poultry
  - dairy products
  - eggs
  - coconut oil
  - palm oil.
- Unsaturated fats occur when there is a double bond in the carbon chain due to a shortage of hydrogen. They are liquid at room temperature, unstable and reactive. There are two types of unsaturated fats:
  - monounsaturated fats, which have one double bond in the chain and include olive oil and peanut oil
  - polyunsaturated fats, which have more than one double bond and include sunflower oil and fish oils.

1 Name three functions of fat.

2 What is the name of the family that fats and oils are in?

3 How many kcalories are there in 1g of fat?

4 What is the difference between fats and oils?

5 What is the smallest unit of a fat called?

6 What is a triglyceride?

7 Name the three categories that fatty acids can be placed in.

8 Describe the structure of an unsaturated fat.

9 What are the problems associated with saturated fats?

10 What is an essential fatty acid? Give three examples of one.

Vitamins

Vitamins are organic substances that the body requires in small amounts. The body is incapable of making vitamins for its overall needs, so they must be supplied regularly by the diet.

Vitamins are not related chemically and differ in their physiological actions. As vitamins were discovered, each was identified by a letter. Many of the vitamins consist of several closely related compounds of similar physiological properties.

Vitamins may be subdivided into:

● water soluble – C and B (complex)
● fat soluble – A, D, E and K.

The water-soluble vitamins cannot be stored in the body so they must be consumed on a regular basis. If excess quantities of these vitamins are consumed, the body will excrete them in the urine. Fat-soluble vitamins are stored in the body's fat so it is not necessary to consume these on such a regular basis. It is also possible to overdose on fat-soluble vitamins, which can be detrimental to health.

Varying amounts of each vitamin are required. The amount needed is referred to as the recommended daily allowance (RDA).

Fat-soluble vitamins

Vitamin A

● **Function:** to help maintain good vision, healthy skin, hair and mucous membranes, and to serve as an antioxidant; also needed for proper bone and tooth development

● **Source:** liver, mackerel and milk products
● **RDA:** 1.5 mg

Vitamin D (calciferol)

● **Function:** essential for calcium and phosphorus utilisation; promotes strong bones and teeth
● **Source:** sunlight, egg yolk, fish, fish oils and fortified cereals
● **RDA:** 0.01 mg

Vitamin E

● **Function:** antioxidant, helps prevent damage to cell membranes
● **Source:** wheat germ, nuts, whole grains and dark green leaf vegetables
● **RDA:** 15 mg

Vitamin K

● **Function:** used in the formation of blood clots
● **Source:** leafy green vegetables
● **RDA:** 70 mg

Water-soluble vitamins

B vitamins are not chemically related, but often occur in the same foodstuff. Their main function is to aid in the metabolism of food.

Vitamin B1 (thiamine)

● **Function:** helps convert food to energy and aids the nervous and cardiovascular systems
● **Source:** rice, bran, pork, beef, peas, beans, wheat germ, oatmeal and soya beans
● **RDA:** 1.5 mg

Vitamin B2 (riboflavin)

● **Function:** aids growth and reproduction, and helps to metabolise fats, carbohydrates and proteins; promotes healthy skin and nails
● **Source:** milk, liver, kidneys, yeast, cheese, leafy green vegetables, fish and eggs
● **RDA:** 1.7 mg

Vitamin B3 (niacin)

● **Function:** helps to keep the nervous system balanced and is also important for the synthesis of sex hormones, thyroxine, cortisone and insulin
● **Source:** poultry, fish, peanuts, yeast extract (for example Marmite), rice bran and wheat germ
● **RDA:** 20 mg

Vitamin B5 (pantothenic acid)

● **Function:** helps in cell building and maintaining normal growth and development of the central nervous system; helps form hormones and antibodies; also necessary for the conversion of fat and sugar to energy

- **Source:** wheatgerm, green vegetables, whole grains, mushrooms, fish, peanuts and yeast extract (for example, Marmite)
- **RDA:** 10 mg

Vitamin B6 (pyridoxine)

- **Function:** helps in the utilisation of proteins and the metabolism of fats; also needed for production of red blood cells and antibodies
- **Source:** chicken, beef, bananas, yeast extract (for example Marmite), eggs, brown rice, soya beans, oats, whole wheat, peanuts and walnuts
- **RDA:** 2 mg

Vitamin C (ascorbic acid)

- **Function:** essential for the formation of collagen; helps to strengthen tissues, acts as an antioxidant, helps in healing, production of red blood cells, fighting bacterial infections and regulating cholesterol; also helps the body to absorb iron
- **Source:** most fresh fruits and vegetables
- **RDA:** 60 mg

Folic acid (folacin)

- **Function:** helps the body form genetic material and red blood cells, and aids in protein metabolism; also acts as an antioxidant; research has shown that if folic acid is taken on a daily basis 30 days before conception, the fetus is less likely to suffer from birth defects such as spina bifida
- **Source:** green vegetables, kidney beans and orange juice
- **RDA:** 400 mg

Minerals

There are several minerals required to maintain a healthy body. Some are needed in moderate amounts, others in only very small amounts; the latter are referred to as trace minerals.

Calcium

- **Function:** needed to build strong bones and teeth, helps to calm nerves and plays a role in muscle contraction, blood clotting and cell membrane upkeep; correct quantities of calcium consumption have been shown to significantly lower the risk of osteoporosis
- **Source:** milk and milk products, whole grains and unrefined cereals, green vegetables and fish bones
- **RDA:** adults 1200 mg
- **Deficiency:** fragile bones, osteoporosis, rickets, tooth decay, irregular heartbeat and slowed nerve impulse response; vitamin D is essential for proper calcium absorption and utilisation

Magnesium

- **Function:** aids the production of proteins and helps regulate body temperature; helps lower blood pressure and assists with the proper functioning of nerves and muscles
- **Source:** whole grain foods, wheat bran, dark green leafy vegetables, soya beans, fish, oysters, shrimp, almonds and peanuts
- **RDA:** 350 mg
- **Deficiency:** decreased blood pressure and body temperature, nervousness, interference with the transmission of nerve and muscle impulses

Phosphorus

- **Function:** essential for metabolism of carbohydrates, fats and proteins; aids growth and cell repair, and is necessary for proper skeletal growth, tooth development, proper kidney function and the nervous system
- **Source:** meat, fish, poultry, milk, yoghurt, eggs, seeds, broccoli and nuts
- **RDA:** 800 mg
- **Deficiency:** bone pain, fatigue, irregular breathing and nervous disorders

Potassium

- **Function:** in conjunction with sodium helps to maintain fluid and electrolyte balance within cells; important for normal nerve and muscle function and aids proper maintenance of the blood's mineral balance; also helps to lower blood pressure
- **Source:** bananas, dried apricots, yoghurt, whole grains, sunflower seeds, potatoes, sweet potatoes and kidney beans
- **RDA:** 2500 mg
- **Deficiency:** decreased blood pressure, dry skin, salt retention and irregular heart beat

Sodium

- **Function:** works in conjunction with potassium to maintain fluid and electrolyte balance within cells
- **Source:** virtually all foods contain sodium, for example celery, cheese, eggs, meat, milk and milk products, processed foods, salt and seafood
- **RDA:** 2500 mg
- **Deficiency:** confusion, low blood sugar, dehydration, lethargy, heart palpitations and heart attack

Trace minerals

Copper

- **Function**: assists in the formation of haemoglobin and helps to maintain healthy bones, blood vessels and nerves
- **Source**: barley, potatoes, whole grains, mushrooms, cocoa, beans, almonds and most seafoods
- **RDA**: 2 mg
- **Deficiency**: fractures and bone deformities, anaemia, general weakness, impaired respiration and skin sores

Iron

- **Function**: required for the production of haemoglobin
- **Source**: liver, lean meats, eggs, baked potatoes, soya beans, kidney beans, whole grains and cereals, and dried fruits
- **RDA**: males 10 mg, females 18 mg
- **Deficiency**: dizziness, iron deficiency anaemia, constipation, sore or inflamed tongue

Selenium

- **Function**: a powerful antioxidant, aids normal body growth and fertility
- **Source**: seafood, offal, bran and wheat germ, broccoli, celery, cucumbers and mushrooms
- **RDA**: 1 mg
- **Deficiency**: heart disease, muscular pain and weakness

Zinc

- **Function**: necessary for healing and development of new cells; an antioxidant, plays an important part in helping to build a strong immune system
- **Source**: beef, lamb, seafood, eggs, yoghurt, yeast extract (for example Marmite), beans, nuts and seeds
- **RDA**: 15 mg
- **Deficiency**: decreased learning ability, delayed sexual maturity, eczema, fatigue, prolonged wound healing, retarded growth and white spots on nails

Water

One of the major chemicals essential to life is water, although it has no nutritional value in terms of energy. Water is used by the body to transport other chemicals. It also plays a major role in maintaining the body at a constant temperature. About 2.5 litres a day are needed to maintain normal functions in adults. This amount depends heavily on environmental conditions and on the amount of energy expenditure. In the heat a greater amount of water is needed, and exercise requires an increased intake of water due to the loss of fluid via sweating.

Only half of the body's water requirement comes in the form of liquid. The other half is supplied from food (especially fruit and vegetables) and metabolic reactions (the breakdown of food results in the formation of carbon dioxide and water).

Fig 12.11 Rehydration while performing

Key learning points 4

- Vitamins and minerals play key roles in sustaining life and the health of the body.
- Vitamins B and C are water soluble.
- Vitamins A, D, E and K are fat soluble.

Student activity 12.1　⏱ 60 minutes　P1

Nutrition and nutritional requirements

Good nutrition is important for every person and is even more important for athletes if they want to be able to perform at their optimal level.

Task 1

Design a poster that illustrates a person's normal nutritional requirements. These include:

- carbohydrates
- proteins – including essential and non-essential
- fats – including essential fatty acids

- vitamins
- minerals.

Task 2

Write a leaflet to go with your poster that describes nutrition and the nutritional requirements of people. Include in your leaflet the common terminology used to express how much of each type of macro- and micronutrient we should be consuming, for example RDA, and describe the meaning of each.

12.3 Digestion

P2

The digestive system is where foods are broken down into their individual nutrients, absorbed into the bloodstream and the waste excreted. It works through processes of mechanical and chemical digestion. Mechanical digestion starts before the food enters the mouth as we cook the food and then cut it up or mash it to make it more palatable. In the mouth we chew the food to tear it apart further, then digestive juices continue this process. The chemical digestion of foods occurs through the digestive enzymes which are present in the mouth and the organs the food passes through. Enzymes are defined as biological catalysts that break down the large molecules of the nutrients into smaller molecules which can be absorbed.

The aim of the digestive system is to break down the nutrients into their smallest units (see Table 12.6).

Nutrient	Smallest unit
Carbohydrate	Glucose
Protein	Amino acid
Fats	Fatty acid

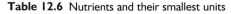

Table 12.6 Nutrients and their smallest units

The digestion, absorption and elimination of nutrients take place in the gastrointestinal tract, which is a long tube running from the mouth to the anus. It includes the mouth, oesophagus, stomach, small intestine and large intestine.

Mouth

The technical term for the mouth is the buccal cavity and this is where the food's journey begins. The teeth and jaw produce mechanical digestion through a process of grinding and mashing up the food. The jaw can produce forces of up to 90 kg on the food. Saliva acts to soften and moisten the food, making it easier to swallow and more like the internal environment. Saliva contains the digestive enzyme amylase, which starts the breakdown of carbohydrates. The tongue is also involved in helping to mix the food and then produce the swallowing action.

Oesophagus

When the food has been swallowed it enters the oesophagus, which delivers the food to the stomach through a process of gravity and peristalsis. Amylase continues to break down the carbohydrates.

Stomach

The stomach is situated in the upper left of the abdominal cavity and is behind the lower ribs. The stomach continues the process of chemical digestion, but no absorption of nutrients occurs in the stomach because the pieces are still too large. The only substance absorbed in the stomach is alcohol, which can enter the bloodstream here. The stomach is made up of three layers of smooth muscle which help to mix up the food. The parietal cells that line the inside of the stomach release hydrochloric acid which helps to dissolve the food and kill off the bacteria present. These cells also release another digestive enzyme, pepsinogen, which produces protein breakdown. The stomach takes around one to four hours to empty completely, depending upon the size of the

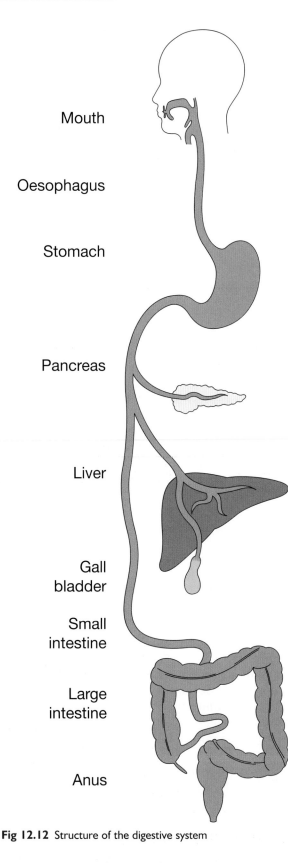

Mouth

Oesophagus

Stomach

Pancreas

Liver

Gall
bladder

Small
intestine

Large
intestine

Anus

Fig 12.12 Structure of the digestive system

meal. Carbohydrates leave the stomach most quickly, followed by proteins and then fats.

Small intestine

Around 90 per cent of digestion occurs in the upper two-thirds of the small intestine with help from the pancreas, liver and gall bladder. The small intestine is between five and six metres long and consists of three areas:

- the duodenum, the first 25 cm
- the jejunum, the next 2 m
- the ileum, around 3 to 4 m long.

The partly digested foods (called chime) move through the small intestine partly by gravity and mainly through the peristaltic action of the smooth muscle present in the intestine walls. The peristaltic action is also aided by the action of the villi and microvilli, which pushes the food along. These structures line the walls of the intestine and absorption of nutrients occurs between the villi. Any waste is passed into the large intestine.

Pancreas

The pancreas is an important organ in digestion because it secretes around 1.5 litres of a juice that contains three digestive enzymes. These are amylase to digest carbohydrates, lipase to digest fats and trypsin to digest protein.

Liver

The liver is bypassed by the food but it does secrete bile, which helps to emulsify and digest fats. Bile is synthesised in the liver and is stored in the gall bladder, which sits just below the liver.

Large intestine

The large intestine, or colon, performs the following functions:

- storage of waste before elimination
- absorption of any remaining water
- production of vitamins B and K
- breakdown of any toxins that might damage the colon.

The colon contains many millions of bacteria that work to keep the colon healthy through detoxifying the waste and producing vitamins. They are intestinal micro-flora and there are as many of these present in the colon as there are cells in the body. These can be supplemented by yoghurt drinks that promote and increase the number of friendly bacteria.

Anus

The anus is the end of the gastrointestinal tract and is the opening to allow the elimination of waste products of digestion.

Key learning points 5

- The aim of the digestive system is to produce the mechanical and chemical breakdown of the nutrients into their smallest units.
  - Carbohydrates are broken down into glucose.
  - Proteins are broken down into amino acids.
  - Fats are broken down into fatty acids.
- The main structures of the digestive tract are:
  - mouth
  - oesophagus
  - stomach
  - small intestine (duodenum, jejunum, ileum)
  - large intestine
  - anus.
- Other organs are vital in releasing digestive juices to aid in the chemical breakdown of foods.
  - The pancreas releases amylase to digest carbohydrates, lipase to digest fats and trypsin to digest proteins.
  - The liver produces bile to digest fats.

Student activity 12.2 — 30 minutes — P2

Digestion

In order for our body to use the foods that we have eaten, they need to be digested. The digestive system consists of many different parts.

Task 1

By hand, draw a diagram of the digestive system and include in your drawing:

- mouth
- oesophagus
- stomach
- small intestine
- pancreas
- liver
- large intestine
- anus.

Task 2

Write a paragraph that describes the structure and function for each part of the digestive system.

12.4 Energy intake and expenditure in sports performance

Energy intake and expenditure can be measured in either calories or joules. One calorie is defined as the amount of energy, or heat, needed to raise the temperature of one litre of water by 1°C.

A calorie should be referred to as a kilocalorie (kcal). Whereas in Britain we use calories, the international unit for energy is a joule or, more specifically, a kilojoule. To convert a kcalorie into a kjoule you need to use the following calculation: 1 kcal = 4.2 kjoules.

Energy value of food

To discover how much energy foods contain, a scientist in a laboratory would use a bomb calorimeter which is used to burn foods completely and see how much energy is liberated. We know that different nutrients provide different amounts of energy:

1 g of carbohydrate = 4 kcals
1 g of protein = 4 kcals
1 g of fat = 9 kcals

Energy produced by the body

The amount of energy produced by the body can be measured through direct and indirect calorimetry. Direct calorimetry involves having an athlete working in an airtight chamber or human calorimeter. There are coils in the ceiling that contain water circulating at a specific temperature. The athlete has a mouthpiece leading outside the chamber to enable them to breathe. As they work, the circulating water heats up, dependent on the amount of heat and energy the athlete gives off during their activity.

Indirect calorimetry is done by working out how much oxygen an athlete consumes. This works because all reactions in the body that produce energy need oxygen to be present.

Measuring body stores of energy

Our body stores any excess food that we consume as fat. This fat can be stored in and around our body organs and also just underneath the skin (subcutaneous fat). A store of too much body fat is not good for us and can lead to a variety of other health problems, including CHD, diabetes and cancer. In order to help determine whether a person has too much body fat there are different measuring techniques that can be used.

Skinfold analyses

The skinfold assessment test is done using skinfold callipers. It is done using the Durnin and Wormsley sites, as described below. It is carried out as follows:

1 Take the measurements on the left-hand side of the body.
2 Mark up the client accurately.
3 Pinch the skin 1 cm above the marked site.
4 Pull the fat away from the muscle.
5 Place the callipers halfway between the top and bottom of the skinfold.
6 Allow the callipers to settle for one or two seconds.
7 Take the reading and wait 15 seconds before repeating for accuracy.
8 Add up the total of the four measurements.
9 Calculate body fat percentage using the table on the opposite page.

Bioelectrical impedance

The bioelectrical impedance technique involves placing electrodes on one hand and one foot and then passing a very small electrical current through the body. The theory is that muscle will conduct the electricity while fat will resist the path of the electricity. Therefore, the more electricity that comes out of the body, the more muscle a person has; the less electricity that comes out, the more fat a person has.

This technique has benefits over skinfold measurement because it is easier to do and does not mean that the client has to remove or adjust any clothing. However, it has been shown to be not such an accurate measure of body fat percentage.

Hydro densitometry

Hydro densitometry or underwater weighing is a technique that is based on the Archimedes principle. It involves a person being weighed on land and then when fully submerged in water. Muscle and bone are denser than water while fat is less dense. A person with more bone and muscle will weigh more in water, have a higher body density and therefore less fat. Once the weight on land and weight in water are taken, a formula is used to work out percentage body fat.

This technique involves the use of a large pool of water and significant amounts of equipment. It is impractical for use outside a sport science laboratory.

Energy balance

Basal metabolic rate

Basal metabolic rate (BMR) is the minimal caloric requirement needed to sustain life in a resting individual. This is the amount of energy your body would burn if you slept all day or rested in bed for 24 hours. A variety of factors affects your basal metabolic rate. Some speed it up so you burn more kilocalories per day just to stay alive, whereas other factors slow down your metabolic rate so that you need to eat fewer kilocalories just to stay alive.

● Age: as you get older you start to lose more muscle tissue and replace it with fat tissue. The more muscle tissue a person has, the greater their BMR, and vice versa. Hence, as you get older this increased fat mass will have the effect of slowing down your BMR.
● Body size: taller, heavier people have higher BMRs. There is more of them so they require more energy.
● Growth: children and pregnant women have higher BMRs. In both cases the body is growing and needs more energy.

- Body composition: the more muscle tissue, the higher the BMR, and the more fat tissue, the lower the BMR.
- Fever: fevers can raise the BMR. This is because when a person has a fever, their body temperature is increased, which speeds up the rate of metabolic reactions (to help fight off an infection) and results in an increased BMR.
- Stress: stress hormones can raise the BMR.
- Environmental temperature: both heat and cold raise the BMR. When a person is too hot, their body tries to cool down, which requires energy. When a person is too cold they shiver, which again is a process that requires energy.
- Fasting: when a person is fasting, as in dieting, hormones are released which act to lower the BMR.
- Thyroxin: the thyroid hormone thyroxin is a key BMR regulator – the more thyroxin produced, the higher the BMR.

Student activity 12.3   ⏱ 30 minutes   P3

Working out your BMR

Task 1

Use the BMR calculations in the box below to estimate your BMR.

BMR Method 1

There is a very basic calculation that takes into account your body weight and gender. This calculation does not take physical activity or age into consideration.

Males: BMR = kg (body weight) × 24 = kcal/day

Females: BMR = kg (body weight) × 23 = kcal/day

BMR Method 2

This method is called the Harris–Benedict equation. It is a more accurate method of assessing a person's BMR because body size (weight and height) and age both affect your BMR.

Males: BMR = 66 + (13.7 × wt in kg) + (5 × ht in cm) − (6.8 × age in yrs)

Females: BMR = 655 + (9.6 × wt in kg) + (1.8 × ht in cm) − (4.7 × age in yrs)

BMR Method 3

This calculation takes into account a person's activity levels. The more active they are, the more calories they will burn on a daily basis.

Males

0–3 yrs (60.9 × wt) − 54

3–10 yrs (22.7 × wt) + 495

10–18 yrs (17.5 × wt) + 651

18–30 yrs (15.3 × wt) + 679

30–50 yrs (11.6 × wt) + 879

over 60 yrs (13.5 × wt) + 487

Females

0–3 yrs (61.0 × wt) − 51

3–10 yrs (22.5 × wt) + 499

10–18 yrs (10.2 × wt) + 746

18–30 yrs (14.7 × wt) + 496

30–60 yrs (8.7 × wt) + 829

over 60 yrs (10.5 × wt) + 596

To include exercise – multiply BMR by the appropriate activity factor:

Level type of activity factor

A Very light cooking, driving, ironing, painting, sewing, standing — 1.3 men, 1.3 women

B Light walking at 3 mph, electrical trades, sailing, golf, childcare, house-cleaning — 1.6 men, 1.3 women

C Moderate walking 3.5–4.0 mph, weeding, cycling, skiing, tennis, dance — 1.7 men, 1.6 women

D Heavy manual digging, basketball, climbing, football, soccer — 2.1 men, 1.9 women

E Exceptional training for professional athletic competition — 2.4 men, 2.2 women

Task 2

Which method do you think gives the most accurate estimate of your BMR and why?

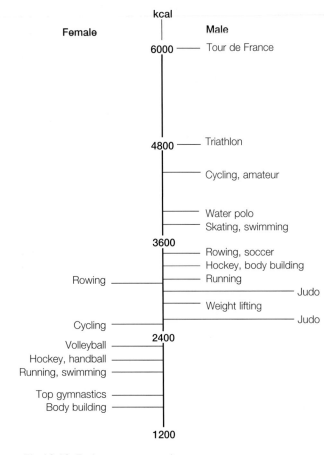

Figure 12.13 shows how differing athletes expend different amounts of energy. Here you can clearly see that a male cyclist on the Tour de France is expending by far and away more kcals than many other athletes. The reason behind this is that athletes on the Tour de France are exercising at high intensities for prolonged periods of time. Athletes who are body-building are at the bottom of this list as they exercise at very high intensity but for relatively short periods of time.

Key learning points 6

● Fat contains the most amount of energy per g compared with protein and carbohydrate.
● Direct calorimetry involves measuring the heat production of an athlete directly; indirect calorimetry involves working out how much oxygen a person consumes.
● Body fat stores can be measured by skin folds, bioelectric impedance and hydro densitometry.
● Basal metabolic rate can be affected by age, body size, body composition, fever, stress, environment, fasting and thyroxine.

Fig 12.13 Daily energy expenditure
(Source: van Erp-Baart *et al.*, 1989)

Q Quick quiz 4

Answer the following questions:

1   What is the definition of a calorie?
2   What is the international unit for energy?
3   Which macronutrient contains the most kcalories per gram?
4   Describe the process of direct calorimetry.
5   Name and describe factors that can affect a person's BMR.
6   Name three different methods of measuring a person's body fat.
7   Where is body fat stored?
8   What are the problems associated with having too much body fat?
9   Name five different types of sports where excess body fat does not affect performance.

Student activity 12.4   🕐 60–90 mins   P3   P4   M1   M2   D1

Energy intake and expenditure

In order to train and compete, most athletes need to make sure they are taking in sufficient amounts of energy, but not too much energy that they store excess as body fat.

Task 1

Prepare a written report that:

*   describes and explains energy intake
*   describes and explains energy expenditure.

Task 2

Describe and explain the importance of energy balance in relation to an athlete's sporting performance.

Task 3

Analyse the effects of energy balance on an athlete's sporting performance – for this task you may like to consider three different athletes who take part in different sports and how energy balance affects each of their sporting performances.

For example:

*   Usain Bolt – 100 m sprinter
*   Steve Backley – javelin thrower
*   Stefka Kostadinova – female high jump world record holder.

12.5 Hydration and its effect on sports performance

It is possible to survive for six or seven weeks without food because the body stores energy in the form of fat, protein and a small amount of carbohydrate. However, you could survive for only two or three days without drinking water. Every day we lose roughly two litres of water through breathing, sweating and urine production. This is increased if we train or compete as water is sweated out to control the heat produced as a waste product of energy production. Therefore, we need to drink at least two litres of water

a day – and more if we train or drink caffeinated or alcoholic drinks. The advice is that we should continually sip water throughout the day or take two or three mouthfuls of water every 15 minutes.

Dehydration

Dehydration is a condition that occurs when fluid loss exceeds fluid intake. The signs and symptoms of dehydration are:

*   thirst
*   dizziness
*   headaches
*   dry mouth
*   poor concentration
*   sticky oral mucus

- flushed red skin
- rapid heart rate.

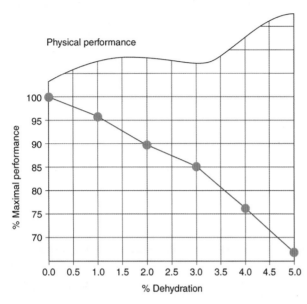

Fig 12.14 Dehydration index

Dehydration causes a significant loss of performance. This is because dehydration, also called hypo hydration, causes a loss of blood plasma affecting blood flow and the ability to sweat. Thus temperature starts to increase steadily. When we sweat it is predominantly blood plasma that is lost and thus cardiac output (the amount of the blood leaving the heart per minute) is reduced. Therefore, dehydration affects the circulation of the blood and the body's ability to control temperature.

Hyper hydration

Hyper hydration is when an athlete drinks extra water before exercising. This is done when they are exercising in a hot environment to prevent the negative effects of dehydration and to minimise the rise in body temperature. The advice is to increase fluid intake over the preceding 24 hours and then drink around 500 ml of water 20 minutes before the event starts. This does not replace the need to continually top up water levels during the competition.

Fluid intake

It is advised that an athlete continually takes on enough fluid to cover the 'cost' of their training or competition. This may involve them consuming around 2.5 to 3 litres of water a day. It should be taken on continually and then some extra taken on 20 minutes before the event. During the event they should top up their water levels when they have a chance. Finally, they should drink water steadily for around one to two hours after their performance, depending upon the demands of the event.

Choices of fluid intake

Water is a good choice, particularly bottled water served at room temperature. Chilled drinks, although refreshing, need to be warmed up in the stomach before they can leave the stomach to be absorbed in the small intestine. This slows down the speed of their absorption.

Sports drinks have a benefit over water in that they provide energy as well as fluid replacement.

Sports drinks are now a common sight at all sports grounds and there are three types of sport drink.

- Isotonic: these drinks have a similar concentration of dissolved solids as blood and as a result are absorbed very quickly. They contain 6 mg of carbohydrate per 100 ml of water and thus provide a good source of fuel as well as being good for hydration. These drinks are useful before, during and after performance, and are the most commonly used.
- Hypotonic: these drinks have a lower concentration of dissolved solids than blood and are absorbed even more quickly than isotonic drinks. With only 2 g of carbohydrate per 100 ml of water they are a relatively poor source of energy. They are used to hydrate after performance.
- Hypertonic: these drinks have a higher concentration of dissolved solids than blood and are absorbed relatively slowly. They contain 10 g of carbohydrate per 100 ml of water and are a very good source of energy but relatively poor for

Student activity 12.5   15 minutes   P5

Sports drinks

Task

Name as many different sports drinks as you can. Look through magazines, on the internet or in sports shops to help you. Note down the prices of these drinks and any claimed benefits of consuming them.

hydration. They are mostly used in endurance events of over an hour and a half.

These drinks also contain the correct amounts of the electrolytes, which ensure optimum speed of absorption. On the negative side, they often contain additives such as sweeteners and colourings which have a negative effect on health. They are also relatively expensive when compared with water.

An easy and cheaper alternative is to make your own sports drinks by taking 500 ml of unsweetened fruit juice, 500 ml of water and a pinch of salt to aid absorption. You will have made yourself an isotonic sports drink which is cheaper and without the additives.

Student activity 12.6   60 minutes   P5

Designing a sports drink

The aim of this practical is to make a sports drink. You need to decide which athletes you are making the drink for, and when it should be consumed (i.e. if you want to make an isotonic, hypertonic or hypotonic drink).

For this experiment, if you are using equipment taken from the science lab, it must have been thoroughly sterilised. You will need:

- measuring cylinders
- beakers
- weighing scales
- glucose
- sweeteners
- flavourings – your choice
- colourings – your choice
- tasting cups
- drinking water
- salt.

Method

Isotonic drink

- If you are designing an isotonic drink, you need to ensure that the carbohydrate content of your drink is between 6 and 8 per cent. To do this, for every 100 ml of water, you need to add between 6 and 8 g of glucose.
- You can then add other flavourings to your drink to make it taste better. These flavourings should not contain any carbohydrates, so use things that contain sweeteners, such as reduced-sugar squash.

Hypertonic drink

- If you are designing a hypertonic drink, it should contain at least 9 per cent carbohydrates. This means for every 100 ml of water, you need to add at least 9 g of glucose.

- You can then add other flavourings which can contain carbohydrates.

Hypotonic drink

- If you are designing a hypotonic drink, it should contain 5 per cent or fewer carbohydrates. To do this, to every 100 ml of water add 5 g of glucose or less.
- You can then add other flavourings, but these should not contain any carbohydrates, so you could use things that contain sweeteners.

Experiment with different flavours and quantities of flavour. Ensure that, each time, you write out exactly how much of each ingredient you use. When you have made a drink that you think tastes acceptable, place it in a beaker.

Results

Go around the class and sample other people's sports drinks. Do this by pouring their drink from the beaker into your own tasting cup. Ensure that you rinse out your cup after each tasting. Draw up a table for your findings.

Conclusion

In your conclusion answer the following questions:

1 Who was your drink designed for?
2 Did your drink taste acceptable?
3 Would people buy your drink?
4 What could you have done to improve the taste of your drink?
5 Out of the class tasting session, which drinks tasted the best and why?

Key learning points 7

● We need to drink at least 2 litres of water a day to keep hydrated, and 2.5 to 3 litres if we are active. It is best to regularly sip water, taking two or three mouthfuls every 15 minutes.
● There is a range of sports drinks available to provide fuel and rehydration:
  – Isotonic drinks are of the same concentration as blood and provide good fuel and good hydration.
  – Hypotonic drinks are less concentrated than blood and provide good hydration but will be a poor source of fuel.
  – Hypertonic drinks are more concentrated than blood and provide a good source of fuel but will be poor for hydration.

Q Quick quiz 5

Hypo hydration	2 litres	Dizziness
Hyper hydration	Hypotonic	Isotonic
Hypertonic	2.5–3 litres	Blood plasma

Select a word or words from the table to match the correct statement below:

1 This is how much water we lose per day through breathing, sweating and urine production.
2 This is a symptom of dehydration.
3 This is another name for dehydration.
4 This occurs when a person drinks excessive water.
5 An athlete should aim to drink this quantity of water per day.
6 This type of sports drink has similar concentration of dissolved solids as blood.
7 This type of sports drink has lower levels of dissolved solids than blood.
8 This type of sports drink has higher levels of dissolved solids than blood.
9 Sweat is produced from this.

Student activity 12.7 — 30 minutes — P5

Hydration and its effects on sports performance

As you now know, hydration levels are very important as dehydration can have a significant impact upon an athlete's performance.

Task 1

Design a leaflet that could be given to athletes that describes hydration and its importance in relation to sports performance.

12.6 Planning a diet for a selected sports activity

P6 **P7** **M3** **M4** **D2**

A balanced diet consists of the following quantities:

- 50–60 per cent of kcals from carbohydrates
- 10–20 per cent of kcals from proteins
- 30 per cent of kcals from fats
- a plentiful supply of vitamins and minerals from fruit and vegetables
- 2 litres of water.

For an athlete these percentages are slightly different:

- 65–70 per cent of kcals from carbohydrates
- 10–20 per cent of kcals from proteins
- 30 per cent of kcals from fats.

Fig 12.15 A body builder

When choosing foods there are some guidelines that will help you make a good choice:

- eat foods which are naturally occurring rather than processed
- eat foods that look as they occur in nature
- limit processed or take-away foods
- the best foods will not have a label containing ingredients
- avoid additives or E numbers
- eat organic foods where possible as they will contain more vitamins and minerals.

Basically what you eat will become a part of your body or affect the way your body functions, so be very particular about what you choose to eat.

When deciding upon a nutritional strategy for any person, you need to look at the physiological demands placed upon them and the effect these have on their body structures and fuel consumption. You may also have to make a decision about whether to use food alone or to combine food with supplements, protein shakes or multi-vitamins.

Student activity 12.8 ⏱ 60 minutes P6 M3

Components of a balanced diet

A balanced diet that includes carbohydrates, fats, proteins, water, fibre, vitamins and minerals is important for all people, athletes and non-athletes.

Task

Write a report that describes and explains the components of a balanced diet – you will need to include details on:

- carbohydrates
- fats
- proteins
- water
- fibre
- vitamins
- minerals.

Aerobic athletes

The physiological demands on the aerobic athlete are considerable and you will have to consider the following:

- replacing the energy lost during training
- maintaining high energy levels
- repairing any damage done to the body's structures during training
- the need for vitamins and minerals to ensure correct functioning of all the body's systems
- replacement and maintenance of fluid levels.

Anaerobic or power athletes

The physiological demands on the anaerobic athlete differ from the aerobic athlete and they will be:

- repairing the considerable damage occurring to the muscles and other structures of the body during training
- replacing the energy lost during training
- the need for vitamins and minerals to ensure correct functioning of all the body's systems
- replacement and maintenance of fluid levels.

Catabolism and anabolism

Catabolism refers to the breaking down of the structures of the body. Training, especially weight training, is catabolic in nature because it causes damage to the muscles being trained. We know this has occurred because we tend to feel sore and stiff the next day until the body has repaired itself. The process of catabolism releases energy.

Anabolism refers to the building up of the structures of the body. When the body is resting and recovering it will be in an anabolic state. Eating also promotes anabolism. While training is the stimulus to improving our fitness and strength of the body's structures, it is actually when we rest that the body builds up and becomes stronger. The process of anabolism requires energy.

When looking at different athletes' diets we need to give advice on two of the nutrients specifically. They are carbohydrate to replace the energy used and protein to repair the damage that has occurred to the structures. Each performer will still require around 30 per cent of kcals to come from fats, with 10 per cent from saturated fats, 10 per cent from monounsaturated and 10 per cent from polyunsaturated. They will each require at least five to nine portions of fruit and vegetables a day and enough water to replace their fluid loss.

Recommended protein intake

The amount of protein recommended is dependent upon the activity in which the individual is involved. Table 12.7 gives estimated recommended amounts.

Therefore, if you have a sedentary person of 70 kg you would work out their requirements in the following way:

70 × 0.8 = 56 g of protein

Or a body builder at 90 kg:

90 × 2.0 = 180 g of protein

Protein is best utilised if it is taken on in amounts of 30 to 35 g at a time. If any more is taken on it is

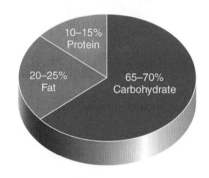

Fig 12.16 Pie chart showing how an athlete's calorie intake should be balanced

Activity	Grams of protein per kg of body weight
Sedentary adult	0.8 g
Recreational exerciser	0.8–1.5 g
Endurance athlete	1.2–1.6 g
Speed/power athlete	1.7–1.8 g
Adult building muscle (hypertrophy)	2 g

Table 12.7 Estimated recommended amounts of protein intake based on activity (Source: Adapted from Franklin, 2000)

either excreted in the urine or stored as body fat. A chicken breast, tin of tuna or a small steak gives 30 g of protein. The best advice for the body builder would be to consume six portions of 30 g of protein rather than three large protein meals.

Recommended carbohydrate intake

The amount of carbohydrate recommended is based on the activity level of the individual in terms of its length and intensity.

An endurance athlete would need 10 g a day, mainly from complex carbohydrate sources.

The continuum in Figure 12.14 shows an estimated calorie intake and clearly depends upon the size and weight of the individual.

Athlete group	Carbohydrate %	Protein %	Fat %	Kcals per kg of body weight
Triathlete:				
Male	66.2	11.6	21.2	62.0
Female	59.2	11.8	29	57.4
Cyclist:				
Male	54.3	13.5	31.7	46.2
Female	56.5	14.0	29.5	59.1
Swimmer:				
Male	50.3	15.0	34.7	45.5
Female	49.3	14.2	36.5	55.6
Runner:				
Male	48.0	14.0	38.0	42.2
Female	49.0	14.0	36.0	42.9
Basketball:				
Male	49.0	15.0	36.0	32.0
Female	45.3	160	34.7	45.6
Gymnast:				
Male	49.8	15.3	34.9	37.8
Female:	44.0	15.0	39.0	53.3
Dancer:				
Male	50.2	15.4	34.4	34.0
Female	38.4	16.5	45.1	51.7
Rower:				
Male	54.2	13.4	23.7	
Female	55.8	15.3	30.3	
Footballer:				
Male	47	14	39	
Weight lifter:				
Male	40.3	20.0	39.7	46.5
Marathon runner:				
Male	52	15	32	51

Table 12.8 Percentage of macronutrients needed by different types of athletes

233

Daily intake of carbohydrate, protein and fat

Table 12.8 shows a summary of the studies done into male and female athletes to show the percentage of macronutrients different types of athletes should be consuming in order to maximise their sporting performance.

Protein shakes

Recently there has been a boom in the use of protein shakes as a supplement to training. They are employed by athletes who want to lay down more muscle and need to gain more protein on a daily basis. Protein shakes are usually high in whey protein because it contains high levels of three essential amino acids: leucine, isoleucine and valine. These are important because they are the amino acids that are broken down most during training.

Protein shakes contain plentiful supplies of amino acids and are quick and convenient to use. However, there are several issues to consider:

● The human body has evolved to gain its protein from natural rather than processed sources (meats rather than powders).
● They often contain additives such as sweeteners, sugars and colourings.
● The process of drying the proteins into powder form damages the structure of the amino acids, making them unusable by the body.
● They are often very expensive.

Diet plans

If the amount of energy taken in (via food) equals the amount expended (physical activity and BMR) then a person will remain at the same weight. To lose weight, energy intake must be less than energy expenditure and to gain weight energy intake must exceed expenditure. Therefore, in order to lose weight a person needs to reduce intake (eat less) and increase expenditure (do more physical activity).

To lose one pound in body weight (approximately 0.45 kg) the energy deficit needs to be around 3500 kcals per week. If you expended 250 kcals per day and consumed 250 kcals less you would have a daily deficit of 500 kcal. In seven days you would have a deficit of 3500 kcals and hence you would have lost eleven pounds in body weight.

Weight loss

We have established that in order to lose weight it is necessary to consume fewer calories than your body needs. Athletes may not be overweight, but may need to lose excess weight to compete in a lower weight category. Excess weight in the form of fat usually acts to hinder a person's performance because a heavier body requires more energy for transport. Therefore, athletes may diet to get rid of any unessential fat. The best type of diet to help the person lose weight but still have enough energy to train seems to be a low-fat diet.

Low-fat diets

A low-fat diet recommends low-fat options whenever possible, plus regular consumption of complex carbohydrates like potatoes and brown bread. Low-fat diets are usually quite filling because they involve eating large amounts of complex carbohydrates, which include fibre. Weight loss is steady at about 1.5–2 pounds (0.5–1 kg) per week. Most experts agree that faster weight loss is not sustainable as the weight lost is from the glycogen stores and not from the fat stores of the body.

Here is an example of what you might eat on a low-fat diet.

A typical breakfast:

● glass of freshly squeezed orange
● large bowl of cereal with fat-free milk
● toast with no margarine, and yeast extract (for example Marmite) or jam
● tea/coffee.

A typical lunch:

● large brown bread sandwich with lean meat, and large salad with low-fat dressing
● low-fat yoghurt.

A typical dinner:

● 4 oz lean chicken with potatoes (no butter) and two helpings of vegetables
● chopped fruit topped with low-fat ice cream or low-fat fromage frais.

Typical snacks:

● fruit
● whole-wheat sandwiches
● low-fat yoghurts
● cereal.

Key learning points 8

- A typical athlete's diet should consist of:
  - 65–70 per cent of kcals from carbohydrates
  - 10–20 per cent of kcals from proteins
  - 30 per cent of kcals from fats.
- An aerobic athlete's diet should be designed to provide sufficient energy, repair damage and maintain fluid levels – these are usually high carbohydrate diets.
- An anaerobic athlete's diet should repair muscle damage, replace energy and maintain fluid levels – these are usually high protein diets.
- In order to lose weight a person needs to consume fewer calories than their body needs – this can be achieved through a low-fat diet.

Q Quick quiz 6

Answer the following questions.

1. What percentage of macronutrients should a typical athlete consume?
2. Describe catabolism and how it affects athletes.
3. Describe what anabolism is and how it affects athletes.
4. What is the main function of carbohydrates for athletes?
5. What is the main function of proteins for athletes?
6. Work out your recommended amount of protein per day.
7. Work out your recommended amount of carbohydrates per day.
8. What are the benefits of taking a protein shake?
9. Which athletes may benefit from protein shakes and why?
10. How many kcals are there in a pound of body fat?

Student activity 12.9   ⏱ 60–90 mins   P7 M4 D2

Planning a two-week diet plan for a sports performer

Select a sports person of your choice – they could be an aerobic or an anaerobic athlete.

Task 1

(a) Think about what sort of foods your athlete should consume and the percentages of each.

(b) Draw a spider diagram to show the different types of foods your athlete could consume, for example carbohydrates – rice, pasta, baked potato.

Task 2

Produce a two-week plan for your selected athlete of all the meals, snacks and drinks they should eat that meets with their dietary requirements.

Task 3

Write a report that explains and justifies your choice of foods and drinks in your two-week diet plan for your selected sports person.

References

Burke, L. and Deakin, V. (1994) *Clinical Sports Nutrition*, McGraw-Hill.

Clark, N. (2003) *Sports Nutrition Guidebook*, Human Kinetics.

Eisenman, P., Johnson, S. and Benson, J. (1990) *Coaches' Guide to Nutrition and Weight Control*, Leisure Press.

Franklin, B. (2000) American *College of Sport Medicine's (ACSM) Guidelines for Exercise Testing and Prescription*, 6th edn, Lippincott, Williams and Wilkins.

McArdle, W.D., Katch, F.I. and Katch, V.L. (1999) *Sports and Exercise Nutrition*, Williams & Wilkins.

McArdle, W.D., Katch, F.I. and Katch, V.L. (2001) *Exercise Physiology: Energy, Nutrition and Human Performance*, Williams & Wilkins.

van Erp-Baart, A., Saris, W., Binkhorst, R., Vos, J. and Elvers, J. (1989) nationwide survey on nutritional habits in elite athletes, *International Journal of Sports Medicine*, 10, 53.

Useful websites

www.ausport.gov.au/ais

Provides invaluable tips on nutrition for sports participants, including suitable recipes that can be downloaded easily.

www.netfit.co.uk/nutrition/nutrition/index.htm

Free useful food facts with the focus on health and fitness.

www.nutrition.org.uk/healthyliving/lifestyle/ eating-for-sport-and-exercise

Information from the British Nutrition Foundation on the best types of food to eat with specific sports in mind.

14: Instructing Physical Activity & Exercise

14.1 Introduction

The fitness industry continues to expand in a rapid manner and so does the demand for fitness trainers and instructors. The increasing competition has meant that customers are also looking for quality instructors who are knowledgeable and professional in their approach. This unit looks at the knowledge and technical skills that are required to become an effective instructor of physical activity and exercise.

By the end of this unit you should:

- know the principles of safe and effective exercise sessions
- be able to design an exercise programme
- be able to plan and lead an exercise session
- be able to review the design of an exercise programme and leading of an exercise session.

Assessment and grading criteria

To achieve a PASS grade the evidence must show that the learner is able to:	To achieve a MERIT grade the evidence must show that, in addition to the pass criteria, the learner is able to:	To achieve a DISTINCTION grade the evidence must show that, in addition to the pass and merit criteria, the learner is able to:
P1 describe the principles of fitness training	**M1** explain the health and safety considerations associated with exercise programmes and sessions	
P2 describe the health and safety considerations associated with exercise programmes and sessions		
P3 describe the importance of warm-up and cool-down in exercise programmes and sessions		
P4 design a six-week exercise programme for two selected contrasting clients	**M2** explain choice of activities for exercise programmes for selected clients	**D1** justify choice of activities for exercise programmes for selected clients, suggesting alternative activities
P5 plan a safe and effective exercise session	**M3** explain choice of activities for the planned exercise session	**D2** justify choice of activities for the planned exercise session and suggest alternative activities.
P6 deliver a safe and effective exercise session, with tutor support	**M4** independently deliver a safe and effective exercise session.	
P7 review own performance in the designing of exercise programmes and the planning and delivery of the exercise session, identifying strengths and areas for improvement.		

14.2 Principles of Safe and Effective Exercise Sessions

P1 P2 P3 M1

Components of Fitness

Fitness is a wide-reaching concept and the instructor needs to be able to answer one of the following questions: 'What does this client need to be fit for?' or 'What daily functions do they need to able to perform?'

Any of the following answers may apply:

● Lose a bit of weight to look and feel better
● Improve my endurance so I can play with my children
● Put on some muscle so I can do more tasks
● Improve my golf
● Stop feeling this back pain
● Be more effective at work
● Have more energy on a daily basis
● Be able to run a marathon.

Fig 14.2 Components of fitness

Fig 14.1 Playing with children

Each of these activities will involve a range of the components of fitness, which are the different aspects of fitness.

Aerobic Endurance

Also called cardiovascular fitness, this is the ability of the body to take in, transport and use oxygen. It depends upon the efficiency of the lungs in taking in oxygen, the heart in transporting oxygen and the working muscles in using oxygen. Examples of activities needing aerobic endurance fitness include long-distance running, swimming and cycling.

Flexibility

This is the range of movement available at a joint

or group of joints. Examples of activities needing flexibility include dancing, gymnastics, running and most everyday functions.

Strength

This is the maximum force that a muscle or group of muscles can produce. Examples of activities needing strength include weightlifting and scrummaging in rugby.

Muscular Endurance

This is the ability of a muscles or group of muscles to produce low-intensity forces repeatedly for long periods of time. Examples of activities needing

Fig 14.3 Running

239

muscular endurance include running, aerobics and carrying bags of shopping.

Body Composition

This is the make-up of the body in terms of how much of the body weight is fat and how much is not fat, which we call lean body weight (LBW). Many people would like to lose excess body fat and/or gain muscle bulk as they feel that this will make them look better.

Adaptations to Training

Our participant will start training because they are unhappy with their current position and they want to change something. They will be looking for 'training adaptations' or for their body's systems to adapt to the stimulus of training. Cardiovascular and resistance training will cause slightly different changes to occur.

Adaptations to Aerobic Endurance Training

Lungs:
- Respiratory muscles become stronger
- Lungs become more efficient
- Lungs are able to extract more oxygen from the air.

Heart:
- Heart muscle becomes larger
- Increase in the amount of blood pumped in each beat (stroke volume)
- Increase in amount of blood pumped per minute (cardiac output)
- Fall in resting heart rate.

Blood and blood vessels:
- Increase in number of capillaries (capillarisation)
- Increase in size of blood vessels
- Decrease in blood pressure
- Increase in blood volume and red blood cell count.

Muscles:
- Increase in number and size of mitochondria (energy-producing parts of cells)
- Increased tolerance to lactic acid
- Increased aerobic enzyme production (muscles will become better at producing energy using oxygen)
- Muscular endurance increases.

Bones:
- Bone density increases (if activity is weight bearing, like running).

Adaptations to Resistance Training

- Increase in muscle size (hypertrophy)
- Increase in strength of ligaments and tendons
- Increase in bone density
- Improved nervous system function
- Decreased body fat

- Improved body composition (ratio of muscle to fat)
- Increased resting metabolic rate
- Improved posture
- Less risk of injury.

Principles of Training

When designing an effective training programme you must take into account a range of factors to make sure that the programme is effective. These are called the 'principles of training'. When designing a training programme, these principles of training must always be applied.

Frequency: this means how often the participant will train. This may be three times a week.

Intensity: this means how hard the participant will be training. Intensity is usually stated in terms of what percentage of their maximum heart rate they will work at or by using the rate of perceived exertion.

Time: this means the length of each training session.

Type: this refers to the type of training they will be performing. For example, cardiovascular or resistance training.

Overload: this means applying intensity to the participant's training which is slightly higher than they are used to. The exact intensity of overload depends upon the individual's level of fitness and it can be produced by changing time, intensity or type.

Reversibility: this means that any adaptation which can be gained can also be lost if the training stops. It is commonly known as the 'use it or lose it' principle because if you don't use the fitness gain, you will quickly lose it.

Specificity: this means that any adaptations that occur will be specific to the training that has been performed. When designing a training programme every exercise must be specific to the needs of the individual, whether they are a golfer, a runner or want to lose some fat. If a programme is not specific the individual will not get the gains they require.

The principles of training spell the acronym FITTORS:

- **F**requency
- **I**ntensity
- **T**ime
- **T**ype
- **O**verload
- **R**eversibility
- **S**pecificity.

Health and Safety for Exercise Sessions

The health and safety of the individuals we are instructing in exercise environments is of paramount importance to a gym instructor. This is to ensure that they work within the law of the country and to ensure the safety of participants, themselves, colleagues, employers and employees. We are living in an increasingly litigious society where there is always blame to be apportioned.

Health and Safety at Work Act 1974

This Act is the basis of the British health and safety legislation and it clearly sets out the duties of employers and employees in implementing safety for themselves and the public. The Act says that employers must do everything that is 'reasonably practical' to ensure safety. This includes:

- Providing a safe working environment
- The safe use, storage and handling of dangerous substances
- Production of a written health and safety policy
- Maintaining a safe working environment, and appropriate health and safety equipment and facilities.

The Act also covers employees in the following ways:

- To take reasonable care of their own health and safety, and use the safety equipment provided
- To inform the employer of any potential risks to health
- To report any accidents and incidents.

Therefore, we need to minimise this risk by doing several things before training our participant.

- Fill out a detailed medical questionnaire and lifestyle form. This is called a PAR-Q or participation questionnaire and identifies any medical conditions and injuries a person may have; it helps us in our programme design.
- Fill out an informed consent form where the client is made to understand the risks of exercise and sign that they are willing to accept these risks.
- Check the training environment before every session to ensure all equipment is working properly and that there are no injury risks.
- Ensure the trainer is appropriately qualified and insured against personal injury.
- Check the client before every session to ensure they have no injuries and are dressed properly.
- Conduct a full warm-up and cool-down with the client.

Physical Activity Readiness Questionnaire (PAR-Q)
There is a range of questionnaires available but they all ask similar questions. An example is shown below in Fig 14.4.

The Exercise and Fitness Code of Ethics

The Exercise and Fitness Code of Ethics is a document produced by an organisation called the Register of Exercise Professionals (REPs). The code ensures that we deal with our clients in an appropriate manner and that we make their safety our priority. The code of ethics covers four main areas.

	Yes	No
1 Do you have a bone or joint problem which could be made worse by exercise?		
2 Has your doctor ever said that you have a heart condition?		
3 Do you experience chest pains on physical exertion?		
4 Do you experience light-headedness or dizziness on exertion?		
5 Do you experience shortness of breath on light exertion?		
6 Has your doctor ever said that you have a raised cholesterol level?		
7 Are you currently taking any prescription medication?		
8 Is there a history of coronary heart disease in your family?		
9 Do you smoke, and if so, how many?		
10 Do you drink more than 21 units of alcohol per week for a male, and 14 units for a female?		
11 Are you diabetic?		
12 Do you take physical activity less than three times a week?		
13 Are you pregnant?		
14 Are you asthmatic?		
15 Do you know of any other reason why you should not exercise?		

Fig 14.4 An example of a PAR-Q

Physical Activity Readiness Questionnaire (PAR-Q)

If you have answered yes to any questions, please give more details

_____

_____

If you have answered yes to one or more questions, you will have to consult with your doctor before taking part in a programme of physical exercise.

If you have answered no to all questions, you are ready to start a suitable exercise programme.

I have read, understood and answered all questions honestly and confirm that I am willing to engage in a programme of exercise that has been prescribed to me.

Name _____   Signature _____

Trainer's name _____   Trainer's signature _____   Date _____

Fig 14.4 _continued_

Principle 1 – Rights:
● Promote the rights of every individual to participate in exercise, and recognise that people should be treated as individuals
● Not condone or allow to go unchallenged any form of discrimination, nor to publicly criticise in demeaning descriptions of others.

Principle 2 – Relationships:
● Develop a relationship with customers based on openness, honesty, mutual trust and respect
● Ensure that physical contact is appropriate and necessary and is carried out within the recommended guidelines and with the participant's full consent and approval.

Principle 3 – Personal responsibilities:
● Demonstrate proper personal behaviour and conduct at all times
● Project an image of health, cleanliness and functional efficiency, and display high standards in use of language, manner, punctuality, preparation and presentation.

Principle 4 – Professional standards:
● Work towards attaining a high level of competence through qualifications and a commitment to ongoing training that ensures safe and correct practice, which will maximise benefits and minimise risks to the participant
● Promote the execution of safe and effective practice and plan all sessions so that they meet the needs of participants and are progressive and appropriate.

(Adapted from _The Code of Ethical Practice_ (2005), produced by the Register of Exercise Professionals)

Contraindications

A contraindication is any factor which will prevent a person from exercising or make an exercise unsafe. The aim of the PAR-Q and the initial consultation is to identify any potential contraindications and then decide what needs to be done about them to minimise their chances of being a risk.

Common contraindications to exercise are:

● Blood pressure higher than 160/100
● Body fat higher than 30 per cent for a male and 40 per cent for a female
● Diabetes mellitus
● Resting heart rate higher than 100
● Lung disorders
● Blood pressure medications and blood thinners
● Coronary heart disease
● Angina pectoris
● Joint conditions.

There are many more contraindications and the rule to follow is that if you are in doubt then refer the participant to a doctor prior to training.

Warm-Up

A warm-up is performed to make sure that the heart, lungs, muscles and joints are prepared for the activities which will follow. The warm-up also helps to activate the nervous system. A warm-up can be specific to the training session which is being performed or it can be more general.

A warm-up involves general body movements of the large muscle groups in a rhythmical, continuous manner. For example, you may use running or cycling to warm up the muscles for a weight training session. The limitation of this is that it does not prepare for the movements which are to follow and the neuromuscular pathways would not have been activated. This would be particularly dangerous for an athlete.

A specific warm-up involves the rehearsal of the exercises which are to follow. This may be through replicating the movement with dynamic stretches or using low-intensity resistance training exercises to prepare for the heavier weights to follow.

A warm-up can be summarised as having three main objectives:

● To raise the heart rate
● To increase the temperature of the body
● To mobilise the major joints of the body.

By gradually raising the temperature it will give the heart time to increase stroke volume and thus cardiac output. As the warm-up continues we start to experience a widening of the blood vessels within the muscles (vasodilation). The capillary beds within the muscles will open up and allow more oxygen and nutrients to flow through the muscles. Also, the warm-up should involve some of the movements that the person will perform in their main session. This gives the warm-up 'specificity' and acts as a rehearsal for the exercises to come.

A typical warm-up will involve the following components:

● A pulse raiser
● Joint mobility
● Dynamic stretching for muscles.

The **pulse raiser** involves rhythmical movements of the large muscle groups in a continuous manner. This would involve CV-type activity such as running, rowing or cycling. The pulse raiser should gradually increase in intensity as time goes on. A pulse raiser would typically last for around five minutes but may go on for ten minutes. At the end of the warm-up, the heart rate should be just below the rate that will be achieved during the main session. A person who is fitter is able to warm up more quickly as their body is used to it, while an unfit person will take longer and needs to warm up more gradually.

A warm-up for a run may involve one minute of walking, one minute of brisk walking, one minute of jogging, one minute of running and then one minute of fast running. An advanced performer could progress to running very quickly.

Joint mobility is used to enable the joints to become lubricated by releasing more synovial fluid on to the joints and then warming it up so it becomes more efficient. This means moving joints through their full range of movement. The movements will start off through a small range and slowly move through a larger range until the full range of movement is achieved. The joints that need to be mobilised are shoulders, elbows, spine, hips, knees and ankles. If a trainer is clever, they can use the pulse-raising movements to also mobilise the joints. For example, rowing will have the effect of raising the pulse and mobilising all the joints.

Dynamic stretching is a relatively recent introduction but is very important for the specific preparation of the muscles for the movements that are due to follow.

Static stretching, where a muscle is stretched and held, has been proved to be of limited value in a warm-up. The reasons being that static stretching causes a fall in heart rate and tends to relax the muscles. It can also act to desensitise the muscle spindles, which protect the muscle against injury. Static stretching has a role to play in a warm-up because a short, tight muscle may prevent the participant from performing some of the exercises in their main session with perfect technique. For example, tight hamstrings make squatting and bent-over rows very difficult to perform well.

The benefits of dynamic stretching are that it:

● Keeps the heart rate raised
● Stretches muscles specifically through the range of movements they will be doing
● Activates the nervous system and improves synchronisation between the nerves and muscles.

To perform dynamic stretching you need to copy the movements in the session you will perform. These movements are repeated in a steady and controlled fashion. In performing a set of ten repetitions you slowly speed up the movement as the set progresses. Figures 14.5, 14.6 and 14.7 show dynamic stretches.

Key term

Dynamic stretching: stretching the muscles through their full range of movement in a controlled manner.

Fig 14.5 Squat and press

Fig 14.6 Rear lunge with arm swing

Fig 14.7 Chest stretch

Main Component

Content

The content of the main component can vary and is specific to the needs of the client. It may involve some of the following:

- CV training
- Resistance training
- Aerobic training
- Mixture of CV training and resistance training.

The main component will last around 40 minutes dependent on the length of the warm-up and main session (a training session generally will last an hour).

Resistance Training

The participant should aim for around eight to ten exercises covering all muscle groups at least once. The larger muscle groups may be worked more than once. The design of a resistance training programme is covered later in this unit.

Aerobic Training

An aerobic session may last between 20 and 60 minutes, although it is agreed that 35 minutes is a good target to aim for. Designing aerobic training programmes is also covered later in this unit.

Methods of monitoring exertion

When you are training aerobically, it is important that the intensity worked at is closely monitored. This can be done by a number of methods:

- Heart rate training zones
- Rate of perceived exertion
- Karvonen formula.

Heart rate training zones: the intensity of exercise can be monitored by expressing it as a percentage of maximum heart rate. Your maximum heart rate is the maximum number of times your heart could beat. To find this out, you would have to work to your maximum intensity, which for most people would clearly be unsafe. Therefore, we estimate the maximum heart rate by using the following formula:

$$\text{Maximum heart rate} = 220 - \text{age}$$

For a 20 year old, their maximum heart rate would be $220 - 20 = 200$ b.p.m.

This is clearly a theoretical maximum heart rate because it is unlikely that every 20 year old in the country would have the same maximum heart rate. In reality, there will be a massive variation but it can be useful as a guideline.

To work out the heart rate training zone, we take percentages of heart rate maximum. If we work between 60 and 90 per cent, we would be working in the aerobic training zone, where the exercise we are performing is effective in improving aerobic fitness without being dangerous. It is still a wide range for a heart rate to be within, so we change the zone depending upon the fitness level of the participant.

Effective zones for different groups as percentage of maximum heart rate (MHR)	
Beginners	60–70% of MHR
Intermediate	70–80% of MHR
Advanced	80–90% of MHR

Rate of perceived exertion (RPE): this was developed by Gunnar Borg and is a scale which can be used by the participant to rate how hard they feel they are working between two extremes. Rather than monitoring heart rate, the participant is introduced to the scale and then asked during the aerobic session where they feel they are on the scale of 1–15 (see Table 14.1).

I	Rest
2	Extremely light
3	
4	Very light
5	
6	Light
7	
8	Somewhat hard
9	
10	Hard
11	
12	Very hard
13	
14	Very, very hard
15	Exhaustion

Table 14.1 Borg's 15-point scale

Borg's scale has been modified to a ten-point scale (see Table 14.2) because some participants have found working between 1 and 15 difficult.

I	Extremely light
2	Very light
3	Moderate
4	
5	Somewhat hard
6	
7	Hard
8	Very hard
9	Extremely hard
10	Maximal exertion

Table 14.2 Borg's modified RPE scale

To achieve aerobic fitness gains, the participant needs to be working around 12 to 15 on the 15-point scale and around 6 to 7 on the modified scale.

Karvonen formula: this is a more advanced way of working out a heart rate training zone. To find out the participant's heart rate training zone, you need to know the following information first:

- Age
- Resting heart rate
- Required exercise intensity (percentage of maximum intensity).

Age predicted maximum heart rate (APMHR) =
220 − age

Heart rate reserve (HRR) =
APMHR − resting heart rate (RHR)

Target heart rate (THR) =
HRR × exercise intensity + RHR

A participant, 20 years old, has a resting heart rate of 60 and wants to work at 70 to 80 per cent of their maximum intensity. They would have the following heart rate training zone:

APMHR = 220 − 20 = 200 b.p.m.

HRR = 200 − 60 = 140

Target heart rate reserve =
140 × 0.70 + 60 = 158 b.p.m.

Target heart rate reserve =
140 × 0.80 + 60 = 172 b.p.m.

We get a training zone of between 158 and 172 b.p.m. for this participant.

Cool-Down

A cool-down is performed to return the body to its pre-exercise state. Once you have finished training, your heart rate is still high and the blood is still being pumped to your working muscles, so you need to slowly bring the heart rate back to normal.

The cool-down has four main objectives:

- To return the heart to normal
- To get rid of any waste products built up during exercise
- To return muscles to their original pre-exercise length
- To prevent venous pooling.

The aim of the cool-down is opposite to the aim of the warm-up in that the pulse will lower slowly and waste products such as carbon dioxide and lactic acid are washed out of the muscles. Also, as the muscles work during the main session, they continually shorten to produce force and they end up in a shortened position. Therefore, they need to be stretched out so they do not remain shortened. Also, as the heart pumps blood around the body, circulation is assisted by the action of skeletal muscles. The skeletal muscles act as a 'muscle pump' to help return the blood to the heart against gravity. If the participant stops suddenly, the heart will keep pumping blood to the legs, but because the muscle pump has stopped, the blood will pool in the legs. This causes the participant to become light-headed and they may pass out.

The cool-down consists of the following activities:

- Lowering the heart rate
- Maintenance stretching on muscles worked
- Developmental stretching on short muscles.

Lowering the Heart Rate

To lower the heart rate you need to do the reverse of the pulse raiser. First, choose a CV-type exercise involving rhythmical movements and the large muscle groups. This time the intensity starts high and slowly drops to cause a drop in heart rate. This part should last around five minutes and an exercise bike is a good choice because it enables the client to sit down and relax as well. The gradual lowering of the intensity allows the muscle pump to work and avoid venous pooling. You want to ensure the pulse rate is around 100 to 110 b.p.m. at the end of the pulse lowerer.

Stretching

Two types of stretching can be used in the cool-down: maintenance and developmental. A maintenance stretch is used to return the muscles worked to their pre-exercise state. During training they will be continuously shortened and they need to be stretched out to prevent shortening. Stretching will also help eliminate waste products from the muscles and also prevent soreness the next day. A maintenance stretch is one where the muscle is stretched to the point of discomfort and then is held for around ten seconds or until the muscle relaxes and the stretch goes off. All muscles worked in the main session will need at least a maintenance stretch.

Developmental stretching is used on muscles which have become short and tight. They may be short because they have been overtrained or due to the positions adopted on a daily basis. If a person is sitting down all day, either in front of a computer or driving, they may develop shortened pectorals, hamstrings, hip flexors and adductors.

Developmental stretching involves stretching a muscle and then holding it for around ten seconds until it relaxes. Once it has relaxed, the stretch is increased and held for ten seconds; this is repeated three times.

Key learning points 1

- The components of fitness are aerobic endurance, flexibility, strength, muscular endurance and body composition.
- Frequency, intensity, time, type, overload, reversibility and specificity are the principles of training.
- All participants in exercise sessions should complete a PAR-Q to identify any contraindications to exercise.
- A warm-up will raise heart rate, increase the temperature of the body and mobilise the joints.
- The main component of a training session will contain CV work and resistance training.
- The cool-down will return the heart rate to normal and stretch muscles to their original length.

Q Quick quiz 1

Fill in the blanks in the following sentences regarding the adaptations to aerobic endurance training.

1 _____ muscles become stronger.
2 Lungs are able to extract more _____ from the air.
3 Increase in the amount of blood pumped in each beat (_____ _____).
4 Increase in the amount of blood pumped per _____ (cardiac output).
5 Decrease in blood _____.
6 Increase in blood _____ and ___ blood cell count.
7 Increase in the number and size of _____ (energy producing parts of cells).
8 Increase in muscle size (_____).
9 Bone _____ increases (if activity is weight bearing).

Student activity 14.1   ⏱ 20 minutes   P1

Match the descriptions to the principles of training in the table below.

Principle of training	Description
Frequency	How long the session lasts
Intensity	Working a system harder than it is used to
Time	How many times a week/month the participant will train
Type	Fitness gains can be lost as well as attained
Overload	Fitness gains will depend upon the type of training done
Reversibility	How hard a person works
Specificity	Description of the training performed

Student activity 14.2   ⏱ 45 minutes   P2   M1

A training session involves a trainer instructing a client in a training environment – each of these variables (trainer, client, environment) can pose a health and safety threat. For each variable, identify two health and safety considerations.

1 For P2, describe the health and safety consideration.
2 For M1, explain the health and safety consideration.

For example, the trainer may not be qualified and may instruct exercises incorrectly.

Student activity 14.3   ⏱ 30 minutes   P3

Complete the following table to show your understanding of the warm-up and cool-down.

Component	Content	Brief description of each part of the content	Describe its importance
Warm-up	Pulse raiser Mobiliser Dynamic stretches		
Cool-down	Pulse lowerer Developmental stretches Maintenance stretches		

14.3 Designing, Planning and Leading an Exercise Programme

P4 **P5** **M2** **M3** **D1**

D2

To ensure that participants are happy with their progress and will keep training, it is important that the trainer is able to design exercise programmes and session plans which are relevant to the specific needs of the participant. This section looks at the process you need to go through in order to write an effective training session for the participant.

Stage 1 – Gathering Information

To enable the trainer to design a specific exercise programme you need to carry out a comprehensive initial consultation. This will involve the participant filling out a questionnaire about their health, medical conditions, goals and lifestyle. This is followed up by a face-to-face discussion to find out more information about the participant. The trainer will be building up a detailed picture of this participant and their life so that the exercises they choose and the programme they design will have the best chance of succeeding.

Factors to Consider

When the trainer sits down to design the programme, they need to consider a range of factors to ensure that the programme is appropriate and that it will benefit the participant rather than harm them. The trainer will need to consider the following.

- PAR-Q responses – have any contraindications to exercise been identified?
- Medical history – do they have any conditions which may affect the training programme and choice of exercises?
- Current and previous exercise history – this will give an idea about the current fitness level of the client.
- Barriers to exercise – do they have constraints such as time, cost, family responsibilities or work commitments?
- Motives and goals – what is the participant aiming to achieve and what is their timescale?
- Occupation – hours worked and whether work is manual or office-based.
- Activity levels – amount of movement they do on a daily basis.
- Leisure time activities – whether these are active or inactive.
- Diet – what, how much and when they eat.

- Stress levels – either through work or their home life, and how they deal with it.
- Alcohol intake – how much they consume and how often.
- Smoking – whether they are a smoker or ex-smoker and the amount they smoke.
- Time available – the client needs to fit the training into their schedule and the trainer needs to be realistic when planning the programme.

Client Groups

Clients are the central focus of the fitness industry and it is essential that we understand the individual needs and goals of each one. Each person needs to be treated as an individual to ensure they remain on their training programme. Clients will come from a range of backgrounds, ages, fitness levels, shapes and sizes. You may see the following groups of people as clients:

- Varied ability levels – beginners, intermediates, advanced
- Varied fitness levels – low, moderate or high
- Elderly
- Juniors
- Athletes
- People with specific goals, such as running a marathon or weight loss
- Pregnant women
- People with medical conditions such as asthma or diabetes.

When you meet a new client it is important that you consider what this person is feeling and thinking.

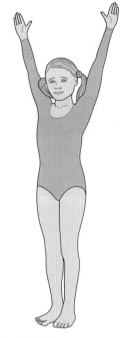

Fig 14.8 A young gymnast

You need to place yourself in their shoes to consider what it is they need. We call this 'walking a mile in their shoes'.

Activity Selection

When we have gathered information about the participant, we select an appropriate intervention in terms of the exercises we choose. You need to consider the following factors:

● Likes and dislikes – what is the participant comfortable doing? Why do they not like certain exercises?
● Accessibility – where can they get to for their training? This may be physical or limited by cost.
● Culture – are they limited by their culture in terms of expected roles and responsibilities, and also dress codes?
● Equipment available – are activities limited by the venue and what it has to offer? You may be training in a gym or maybe at the client's home or in a park.

Stage 2 – Establishing Objectives

To ensure the success of the programme it needs to be specific to the outcome a client wants. Therefore, it is important to find out exactly what this is. If you ask them what they want to achieve they will say that they want to get fit. You need to question them further and find out what this means to them. You may need to make suggestions as they may not know themselves. Their objectives could be any of the following:

● CV fitness
● Flexibility
● Weight loss
● Improved health
● Muscular strength
● Muscular size
● Muscle tone
● Power.

Once you have established the objectives, it is time to plan the programme.

Stage 3 – Planning the Programme

Programme design is an area of controversy, and different trainers have different ideas about what is right and wrong. Usually the programme will use the structure shown in Tables 14.3 and 14.4.

The training programme will usually last for one hour. The length of each component will depend upon the objectives of the client and the importance they place on each.

Warm-up	Raise pulse Mobilise joints Dynamic stretches	5–10 minutes
Resistance component	6–10 free weight or resistance machine exercises	30–45 minutes
CV component	Walking, running, cycling or rowing	20–60 minutes
Abdominal training	Abdominals and lower back	5 minutes
Cool-down	Lower the pulse Developmental stretches Maintenance stretches	5–15 minutes

Table 14.3 Programme structure

Objective:	Strength	Muscle size	Endurance	CV
Repetitions or duration	1–5	6–12	12–20	20 minutes +
Recovery period	3–5 minutes	1–2 minutes	30–60 seconds	N/A
Sets per exercise	2–6	3–6	2–3	1
Frequency per week	1–2 on each muscle group	1–2 on each muscle group	2–3 on each muscle group	3 sessions

Table 14.4 Meeting the objectives (adapted from Baechle and Earle, 2008)

Programme Design Rules

When designing the programme you need to follow rules and then check that you have done so.

Rule 1: Work muscles in pairs to keep them balanced

All muscles work in pairs and if they are not worked as pairs the body can become unbalanced. This means that joints will move out of their correct place, causing a change in posture and possibly pain. It also increases the chances of injury. The body works as a complete unit and it must be trained in this way too. Many gym programmes focus on a few muscle groups – usually the chest, arms and abdominals – as these are seen to make a person more attractive.

The main pairs of muscles are:

- Pectorals and trapezius
- Latissimus dorsi and deltoids
- Biceps and triceps
- Abdominals and erector spinae
- Quadriceps and hamstrings.

A check must be made to ensure that all muscle pairs have been worked equally.

Rule 2: Large muscle groups should be trained first

If you are training several muscles in one session it is important that the large muscle groups are trained first. The large muscles are the gluteus maximus, quadriceps and hamstrings, pectorals, latissimus dorsi and trapezius.

These muscles need to be worked first because they require the most effort to work and are best exercised when the client is feeling fresh. Second, if the smaller muscles become tired early on in the session it will be difficult to work the large muscles as hard.

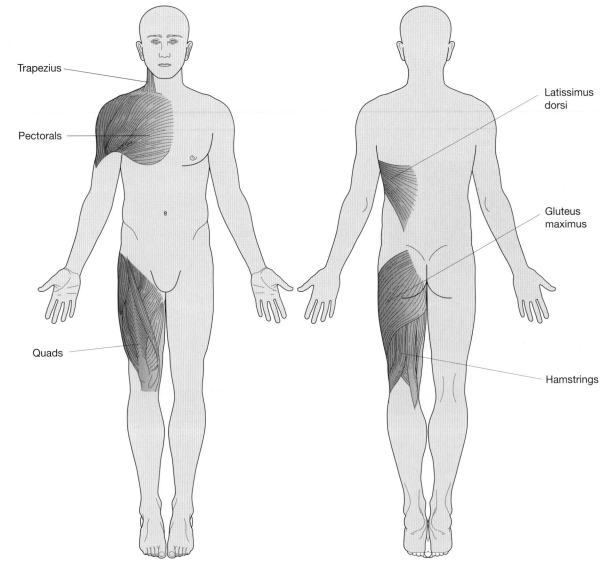

Fig 14.9 Large muscle groups

Rule 3: Do the difficult exercises first

Each exercise will have a difficulty rating and this depends upon two main issues: how many joints are moving and how much balance is needed. An exercise where only one joint moves can be seen as simple, while an exercise with two or more joints moving will be complex. Also, the more balance that is needed the more difficult an exercise becomes. The most difficult exercises need the most skill and should be done early on in the exercise session.

Rule 4: Work the abdominals and lower back at the end of the session

The abdominals and lower back are called the core muscles and these keep the body's posture correct. If they are tired out early on, it increases the risk of the spine becoming injured. They should be exercised after the resistance and CV work have been done.

Following these rules will make sure that the programme is performed in a safe and effective way.

Considerations for Aerobic Training

It is important to consider that not everyone will want to go to a gym to improve their fitness. You will need to be flexible in finding ways to make them more active in their daily lives. The Health Education Authority (HEA) has offered guidelines concerning health and fitness.

To improve cardiovascular fitness you need to train three times a week for between 20 and 60 minutes at 60 to 90 per cent of your maximum heart rate – jogging, running, swimming, cycling or rowing.

To improve health you need to be involved in an activity which makes you slightly warmer and slightly out of breath for 30 minutes between five and seven times a week.

This can involve activities such as brisk walking, gardening, mowing the lawn or recreational swimming. Also you can look at extra ways to increase activity levels, such as walking rather than taking the car, taking the stairs instead of the lift, getting off the bus at an earlier stop or parking the car in the furthest away parking spot!

Key learning points 2

There are a range of factors which will need to be considered when designing an exercise programme, including: medical history, exercise history, barriers, motives and goals, occupation, activity levels, leisure time activities, diet, stress levels, alcohol intake, smoking, time available, current and previous training history.

An exercise programme should have the following components:

● Warm-up
● Resistance component
● CV component
● Abdominal training
● Cool-down.

When designing an exercise programme you need to follow four rules.

Rule 1: Work muscles in pairs to keep muscles balanced.
Rule 2: Large muscle groups should be trained first.
Rule 3: Do the difficult exercises first.
Rule 4: Work the abdominals and lower back at the end of the session.

According to the HEA recommendations, to improve cardiovascular fitness you need to train three times a week for between 20 and 60 minutes at 60 to 90 per cent of your maximum heart rate. To improve health you need to be involved in an activity which makes you slightly warmer and slightly out of breath for 30 minutes between five and seven times a week.

Leading an Exercise Session

Preparation of the Session

When you take a participant through their exercise programme you need to follow a clear structure to ensure the training session is safe and that good customer care is applied.

Before the session starts you need to check the equipment and the environment:

● Availability of equipment
● Equipment is in working order
● All cables are strong
● Floor is clear of equipment and cables
● Temperature
● Ventilation.

251

Questions and Explanations

The session will start when you meet the participant. At this point you need to explain some safety issues and procedures. The following questions are appropriate to screen the participant prior to the session.

● Have you any illnesses or injuries I need to be aware of?
● Have you eaten today?
● Is your clothing appropriate and have you taken off your jewellery?

Then you need to explain some procedures:

● Fire exits and fire drill
● First-aid kit, first aider and nearest telephone
● Position of water.

Finally explain:

● The training programme and its demands
● The aims and objectives of the session
● The process of instruction.

Delivery of the Session

The aim of the exercise session is to get the participant working for as much time as possible in a safe and effective manner. It is important that the participant is supported and pushed to work as hard as they can within their limits.

The instructor will perform the following roles.

Communicate effectively

It is important that the client is able to understand you and respond in the way you would like them to. We communicate mainly through the words we use and also how we deliver these words and the body language we use. It is good practice to listen to your client and assess their level of knowledge before deciding how you will deliver your instructions. If a person is new to the gym you should keep things simple and use less technical language. The more experienced client will be able to communicate using more technical language.

Give instructions

An instruction is providing information on how to perform a technique. When providing instructions you must say what you want the client to do rather than what not to do. If you use the word 'don't' as in 'don't lock your knees', it increases the chances that they will actually do it!

Demonstrate

The instructor needs to give demonstrations to show the participant how to perform the technique. Once a demonstration has been give the instructor can explain the technique to the client and then let them practise to get the feel of the movement.

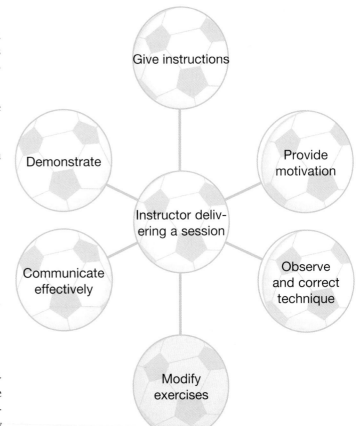

Fig 14.10 Instructor delivering a session

Provide motivation

The reason most people do not achieve the results they want is because their motivation is too low. They give up when the going gets tough. You will motivate them with what you say, how you say it and by using positive body language. This will push them to work as hard as they can within the limits of their fitness.

Observe and correct techniques

The instructor needs to observe the client's technique from a variety of positions by moving around the

Fig 14.11 Trainer and participant

252

client. Once they have observed for a short period, feedback needs to be given about what they are doing right and then what parts need to be corrected.

Modify exercises

If an exercise is too easy or too hard it can be modified in a variety of ways: changing the length of the lever used, getting them to stand up and resist the force of gravity, change the range of movement or the speed of movement (tempo).

End of Session

Once the session is finished you have two roles to perform.

● **Gain feedback**: it is important to ask the participant how they felt the session went and what they liked or did not like. Also, ask about the intensity of the session – whether it was too easy or too hard. This is vital when you reflect on your work and assess whether there are any changes that need to be made for next time to make your session even more effective.

● **Put equipment away and check for damage**: it is important to tidy up your equipment and leave the environment in a safe and acceptable state for the next person. Also, if any damage has occurred, it must be reported so that repairs can be made.

Key learning points 3

Before a session starts you need to check the environment, the client and tell them about the safety procedures.

During the session you need to be supporting the client in the following way:

● Communicate effectively
● Give instructions
● Demonstrate
● Provide motivation
● Observe and correct
● Respond to the client's needs.

At the end of the session ask your client for feedback about the session.

Q Quick quiz 2

Give short answers to the following questions:

1 Why should muscles be worked in pairs?

2 Why should the large muscles be worked first?

3 Why should the difficult exercises be done first?

4 Why should core muscles be worked at the end?

Match the main pairs of muscles that should be worked:

1 Pectorals and _____.

2 Latissimus dorsi and _____.

3 Biceps and _____.

4 Abdominals and _____.

5 Quadriceps and _____.

Choice of answers: triceps, hamstrings, deltoids, erector spinae and trapezius.

Student activity 14.4 ⏱ **120 minutes** | P4 | P5 | M2 | M3 | D1 | D2

1 (a) For P5, use the following template to plan a safe and effective training session.

Type of training	Exercises	Sets and reps
Warm-up – CV		
Stretching		
Resistance 1		
CV training		
Resistance 2		
CV training		
Core training		
Cool-down – CV		
Stretching		

(b) For M3, explain why you have chosen the exercises for this session.

(c) For D2, justify your choices of exercises for the planned session.

2 (a) For P4, plan a six-week exercise programme for two contrasting clients, showing how they will progress over the six-week period. Use the following template to show the progression.

Type of training	Week 1	Week 2	Week 3	Week 4	Week 5	Week 6	Alternative activities (D1)
Resistance 1							
CV 1							
Resistance 2							
CV 2							
Core training							

(b) For M2, explain your choices of activity for the two contrasting clients.

(c) For D1, justify your choice of activities for the two selected clients, including alternative activities.

14.4 Reviewing the Design of an Exercise Session and Leading of an Exercise Session

P6 | P7 | M4

The Purpose of Reviewing Sessions

To improve as a trainer and a person it is vital to regularly review your performance and identify any changes that need to be made. We can receive feedback from a range of sources and it is all useful.

Feedback is information about performance. It is neither good nor bad; it is just information. It allows us to improve our performance in the following ways.

● **Track progression**: we can assess whether our training is having the desired effect on the participant. This can be done through fitness testing or from their own perspective.

● **Adapt sessions**: if we are not achieving our aim or an exercise has had a negative response we can adapt the programme to achieve a different response.

● **Improve own performance**: we need to identify any weaknesses we may have as then we can improve how we work with our participants. Our strengths will always work for us but we will only improve if we address our weaknesses.

Codes of Practice

We must always be sure that what we do is ethical. Reflecting on how we act, talk and work with our clients will ensure we stay within accepted codes of behaviour.

Continued Professional Development

For a trainer to continue to improve their skills they need to be continually attending conferences and taking courses. This development should work on improving our weaknesses. It is also a requirement of the Register of Exercise Professionals (REPs) that each trainer who is a member of the Register must achieve 24 points for training per year.

Conducting a Review

The ideal time to conduct a review is as soon as you can after a session while the issues are still fresh in your own mind and your participant's. You may even be able to ask the participant some questions during the cool-down period, as the work is less intense and they will be starting to relax. You need to ask them specific questions regarding the session and its outcomes.

You could use a review form like the one shown below and cover the following detail.

Self-Evaluation

The client may not pick up things you see or feel yourself so you must ask yourself the same questions and answer them in an honest manner.

Particularly, you must assess yourself in terms of the safety of the session and then whether it was effective. Did it really meet the aims that you had set for your session?

The benefits of self-evaluation are as follows:

● You can plan future sessions to ensure they are enjoyable and effective
● Good evaluation is likely to increase the chances of the client sticking to their training programme
● The client will stay interested and motivated
● The client will keep progressing
● You are able to identify any training needs you may have
● You can set yourself goals for personal development and any training needs you may have.

Peer Evaluation

As part of your support group you may work with a colleague and observe each other's training sessions. This may give a third perspective on the training and highlight issues you would not have considered yourself.

Modifying an Exercise Programme

There are many ways to change a participant's training programme to ensure they continue to achieve overload and keep interested and motivated:

● Change a training principle
● Frequency – increase the number of times they train a week
● Intensity – make the programme harder by increasing speeds or resistance
● Time – make each session longer
● Type – change the training they do from aerobic to resistance training.

The body is expert at adapting and will only gain benefit from an exercise for a limited period. Therefore, if we change an exercise, we gain a new stimulus for the body to adapt to. So change from

Name:

1 Did you think the programme was effective in meeting your aims?

_____

2 What did you enjoy and not enjoy about the training session?

_____

3 To what extent did you feel safe?

_____

4 Could the session be improved in any way?

_____

Fig 14.12 An example of a review form

255

resistance machines to free weights or cable exercises and a change will occur.

You can also give the participant a new target each week to continue to push them – cycle 5 km in under ten minutes or run 5 km in 25 minutes.

SMART Targets

Regular evaluation can lead to improvements in performance. If you set yourself specific goals then you can monitor your actual performance. Achieving goals relies on effective goal setting using the SMART principle. This stands for:

- **S**pecific
- **M**easurable
- **A**chievable
- **R**ealistic
- **T**ime-constrained.

As you continue to evaluate yourself and improve your training skills, communication skills and motivation skills, you will see yourself become a more professional and effective trainer.

Student activity 14.5 ⏱ 45 minutes [P6] [P7] [M4]

1 Organise with your tutor a time when you can deliver your exercise session with a selected client. To achieve M4, you need to deliver the exercise session independently of tutor support.

2 Once you have delivered the session you need to review your own performance with regard to the design, planning and delivery of the session and then identify your strengths and weaknesses.

You could use the following template to help you think about areas you should be reviewing.

Categories to consider	Responses
Sources of feedback: 1. Your client 2. Your tutor 3. Yourself	
Design and planning: 1. Is it appropriate for the client? 2. Does it meet their goals and needs? 3. Is it varied and interesting?	
Delivery: 1 What did they enjoy about the session/not enjoy about the session? 2 What were your strengths and weaknesses with regard to: • your instructional skills • your motivational skills • your communication skills • your demonstrations • your explanations?	

Reference

Baechle, T. and Earle, R. (2008) *Essentials of Strength Training and Conditioning*, Champaign, IL: Human Kinetics.

Further reading

Ansell, M. (2008) *Personal Training*, Exeter: Learning Matters.

Baechle, T. and Earle, R. (2008) *Essentials of Strength Training and Conditioning*, Champaign, IL: Human Kinetics.

Coulson, M. (2007) *The Fitness Instructor's Handbook*, London: A&C Black.

Dalgleish, J. and Dollery, S. (2001) *The Health and Fitness Handbook*, Harlow: Longman.

Useful websites

www.netfit.co.uk/previous.htm
Extensive range of exercise and training techniques, some sports specific, others more general.

www.elitesoccerconditioning.com/FitnessTraining/FitnessTraining.htm
Drills, tips and ideas to help you maximise your footballing fitness and techniques.

www.sport-fitness-advisor.com/resistance-training.html
Excellent advice on how to design a resistance training programme for any sport in seven steps.

15: Sports Injuries

15.1 Introduction

While participation in sport and physical activity has a lot of positive aspects, such as improving fitness levels and being involved in a social group with common interests, it also has a negative aspect in the form of incurring physical injury. This unit will identify different types of sports injuries and how they can occur. It will consider both physiological and psychological responses to injury and then suggest some methods to prevent and treat sports injuries. Finally, this unit will outline a range of rehabilitation procedures that can be considered, together with important information on tracking and documenting injuries and their treatment.

By the end of this unit you should know:

- how common sports injuries can be prevented by the correct identification of risk factors
- about a range of sports injuries and their symptoms
- how to apply methods of treating sports injuries.

Assessment and grading criteria

To achieve a PASS grade the evidence must show that the learner is able to:	To achieve a MERIT grade the evidence must show that, in addition to the pass criteria, the learner is able to:	To achieve a DISTINCTION grade the evidence must show that, in addition to the pass and merit criteria, the learner is able to:
P1 describe extrinsic and intrinsic risk factors in relation to sports injuries	**M1** explain how risk factors can be minimised by utilisation of preventative measures	
P2 describe preventative measures that can be taken in order to prevent sports injuries occurring		
P3 describe the physiological responses common to most sports injuries	**M2** explain the physiological and psychological responses common to most sports injuries	**D1** analyse the physiological and psychological responses common to most sports injuries
P4 describe the psychological responses common to sports injuries		
P5 describe first aid and common treatments used for four different types of sports injuries		
P6 design a safe and appropriate treatment and rehabilitation programme for two common sports injuries, with tutor support.	**M3** independently design a safe and appropriate treatment and rehabilitation programme for two common sports injuries.	**D2** evaluate the treatment and rehabilitation programme designed, justifying choices and suggesting alternatives where appropriate.

15.2 The Prevention of Sports Injuries by the Correct Identification of Risk Factors

P1 P2 M1

Taking part in sport can result in injury to any part of the body. These injuries can be caused by a variety of factors which can be grouped into two categories:

- Extrinsic risk factors
- Intrinsic risk factors.

Extrinsic Risk Factors

An extrinsic risk factor is something external to the body that can cause an injury. These include:

- Inappropriate coaching or instruction
- Incorrect advice on technique
- Environmental conditions
- Other sports players
- Equipment, clothing and footwear issues.

Inappropriate Coaching or Instruction

Inappropriate instruction given by a coach or a trainer is an obvious way in which sports participants can easily become injured. It is vital that all instruction is given by someone who has an up-to-date and in-depth knowledge about the sport and is also able to communicate this appropriately and effectively. It is essential that the rules and regulations for the sport, as laid down by the specific governing body, have been correctly interpreted and are appropriately enforced. Likewise, during training activities, it is important that the information given by the coach/trainer is reliable. For this reason, many governing bodies have coaching schemes that are constantly reviewed so that coaching qualifications can be maintained at the highest and safest of standards.

Incorrect Advice on Technique

The technique of performing an action or specific sport skill is usually dictated by the guidance that the sports participant has received from the PE teacher, coach, trainer or instructor. This being the case, the above is particularly relevant. But it is very easy for individuals to start to slip from these standards if they are not reinforced at the right time. If correction does not occur the participant can soon start to adopt bad habits in terms of skill level and performance. This incorrect performance of skill can in turn lead to injury problems. An obvious example is weightlifting, where back injuries particularly occur due to incorrect and bad or poor technique.

Environmental Conditions

The environment in which we perform sports can also have a big impact on the likelihood of sustaining an injury. The environment encompasses the area in which a sport is played, so if you were playing basketball the environment would consist of the sports hall, and include the playing surface, the lighting and the temperature. If the lighting was poor, a player may be more likely to misjudge attacking or defensive moves and injure themselves or another player. If the surface was wet, a player would be more likely to slip over because the surface becomes much more dangerous when it is wet.

Other Sports Players

Some sports are obviously more susceptible to incurring sports injuries as the rules of the sport allow for tackles, scrums, etc. These are called contact sports. For instance, after a rugby game players will often come away with at least a few bruises from tackling or being tackled by other players. In non-contact games, players can also sustain sports injuries from other players from foul tackles or accidental collisions.

Equipment, Clothing and Footwear Issues

It is important to remember to always use the equipment needed to play a particular sport correctly or this too can increase the chances of injury to either the player themselves or to other players. For example, if a javelin, shot-put or a discus are not held and thrown correctly any improper use could cause serious damage to an individual.

The use of appropriate clothing can also be an issue. Certain sports require, as stipulated by the respective governing body of the sport, certain pieces of protective clothing, such as shin pads for football, and pads, gloves and helmets for cricket and hockey.

Other sports, by their very nature, need to have clothing which is very flexible and allows a full range of movement. For example, gymnasts wear clothing which allows them to perform complex movements on the floor and on specialised equipment. If restrictive clothing was worn this could greatly reduce the range of movement allowed and therefore cause injury.

Correct footwear for the correct surface that the sport is to be played on is a must. There is a phenomenal array of specialised footwear for all sports, including running, basketball, tennis, squash, gymnastics, football and rugby. All these specialised pieces of footwear are made to be supportive to the player and totally suitable for the surface required for the sport. Football has grass, artificial turf and sports hall floors as its main playing areas and there are specialised shoes and boots for each surface.

However, although a sports person may be wearing the correct footwear, certain types of footwear make a person more susceptible to injury. For instance, the studs on a footballer's or rugby player's boot can make the wearer more susceptible to leg injuries because the studs plant the foot in the ground, so if the person is turning on a planted foot they are more likely to twist their knee.

Incorrect footwear can also be a factor in causing a person to injure themselves while playing sport. For example, a marathon runner needs a lot of cushioning in their trainers to absorb the repeated impact of running. If they were to wear trainers with little padding they would be much more likely to sustain an overuse sport injury.

Intrinsic Risk Factors

An intrinsic risk factor is a physical aspect of the athlete's body that can cause an injury.

These include:

- Inadequate warm-up
- Muscle imbalance
- Poor preparation
- Postural defects
- Poor technique
- Overuse
- Age.

Inadequate Warm-Up

This is a very common cause of sports injury. The warm-up prepares both the body and the mind for the exercise that is to come by gradually taking the body from its non-active state to being ready for the exercise. How long it takes to warm up will vary from person to person, and will depend on their level of fitness. The environment will also affect the length of the warm-up. In cold surroundings it will be necessary to carry out a longer warm-up than in hot surroundings.

A warm-up should consist of three components:

- A pulse raiser to get the blood flowing more quickly around the body and so help to warm up the muscle tissues and make them more pliable
- A mobiliser, in which the joints are taken through their range of movement, such as arm circles, to mobilise the shoulder joint
- The main muscles that are going to be used in the sport should be stretched.

Muscle Imbalance

A muscle imbalance means that one muscle in an antagonistic pair is stronger than the other. This is often seen in footballers who have strong quadriceps muscles from extending their knee to kick the ball, but their hamstring muscles are not as strong. This can result in knee injuries because the hamstring muscles are not strong enough to put a brake on the kicking action of the knee. As a result, when a striker goes to score a goal they can over-kick, so that their knee hyperextends and gets injured.

Poor Preparation

This includes a player's fitness levels specific to the sport they are going to take part in. If a person is not fit to take part in a sport they are more likely to injure themselves because they are so tired that they develop a poor sports technique. A sports person must also acclimatise to the environment in which they are going to play. For example, if a marathon runner living in England wants to take part in a race in Australia in the summer time, they will have to train in hot conditions to get their body used to the heat.

Postural Defects

Most people are born with a slight postural defect, such as having one leg slightly longer than the other. If there is a large difference between the two legs, this can affect the person's running technique, which may then place more strain on one side of the body, which would make the person more likely to sustain injuries after long periods of exercising.

Poor Technique

If a person is not using the correct methods for exercising, they are more likely to sustain a sports injury. For example, if a swimmer continues to perform the front crawl stroke incorrectly with their arms, they may be prone to shoulder or elbow injuries. Note how this differs from the description of incorrect advice on technique in the extrinsic factors section. Poor technique is related to the individual's performance without the use of equipment as opposed to incorrect techniques related to the misuse of equipment to perform a movement.

Overuse

An overuse injury is caused because a sports person does not take time to recover after exercise. Every time we exercise we place our body under strain, which means the body has to repair itself afterwards. If a person does not allow their body to repair itself it will become weaker until eventually parts of the body become injured. Also, if we continue to use specific parts of the body over a long period of time the repair is sometimes difficult to manage. A runner puts a lot of pressure and strain through their body and particularly through the knees. Injuries to the knee joint can start to be a problem if a runner has trained or competed for a long period of time, even allowing for rest periods within training.

Age

The type of injury that is most common varies with the age of the subject and also the level of competition. In young children most injuries are due to falling. In older children injuries that result from collisions and violence are more common. In older age groups and in top-level sportsmen and women there are fewer acute injuries and more overuse injuries and those that are due to intrinsic factors.

Preventative Measures

Besides maintaining fitness and doing a warm-up, an important way to prevent sports injuries is to wear protective clothing. As already noted, some sports' governing bodies stipulate the use of protective equipment in order to minimise injury. Some sports do not require these but an individual may still consider protecting themselves with the use of certain items such as a gum shield or knee pads.

Suitable clothing minimises the risk of sustaining an injury in any sport. At the very least, people should wear loose-fitting or stretchy clothing and appropriate footwear. Jewellery should always be removed.

Supervision by a suitably qualified coach will also help to prevent injuries. Supervision should ensure that the sports performer is using the correct techniques for their sport. They will also be able to design training programmes that can adapt with the performer's needs. For example, if the sports performer is not training to the best of their ability, the coach may include more rest during one week of the training programme to ensure the person has recovered suitably from their training. A coach will also ensure that the equipment and environment is appropriate for training and, if not, they would ensure that either protective clothing or equipment is used or an alternative safe training session is carried out.

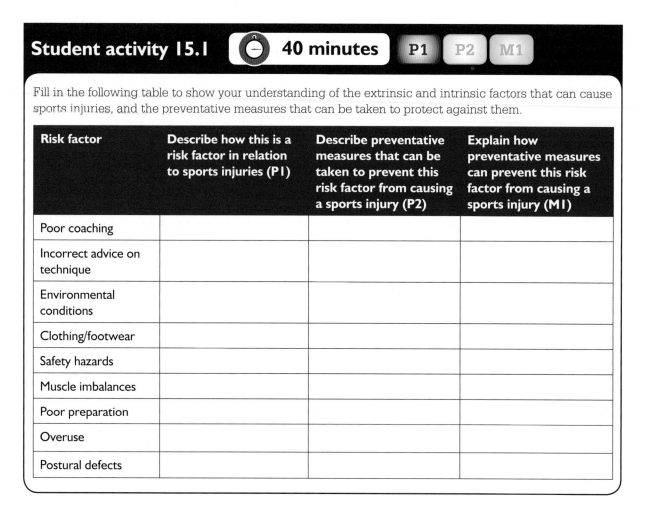

Student activity 15.1 ⏱ **40 minutes** P1 P2 M1

Fill in the following table to show your understanding of the extrinsic and intrinsic factors that can cause sports injuries, and the preventative measures that can be taken to protect against them.

Risk factor	Describe how this is a risk factor in relation to sports injuries (P1)	Describe preventative measures that can be taken to prevent this risk factor from causing a sports injury (P2)	Explain how preventative measures can prevent this risk factor from causing a sports injury (M1)
Poor coaching			
Incorrect advice on technique			
Environmental conditions			
Clothing/footwear			
Safety hazards			
Muscle imbalances			
Poor preparation			
Overuse			
Postural defects			

15.3 Sports Injuries and their Symptoms

The repair of injured soft tissue, such as muscle, actually commences within the first 24 hours following injury. One of the first signs that soft tissue is injured is the appearance of swelling. When the injured area starts to swell it will feel painful. This is due to the swelling creating pressure on the nerves surrounding the damaged tissue. The swelling occurs because the surrounding blood vessels are ruptured, allowing blood to bleed into the area and tissue fluid to gather around the injury site. The injured area will usually look red because the blood vessels surrounding the site dilate, which also has the effect of making the injured area feel hot. The injured area will show a reduced function or a total inability to function because of the pain and swelling.

The level of the above signs and symptoms will be directly related to the degree of the injury – the greater the degree of damage, the greater the effects of inflammation.

It is over a period of between 48 and 72 hours and up to 21 days that the repair is carried out with vigour by the body. The body's clotting mechanism seals the end of the torn blood vessels so that further blood plasma cannot escape into the surrounding tissues.

As the immediate effects of injury subside, the healing/repair process begins. This consists of:

● Absorption of swelling
● Removal of debris and blood clot
● Growth of new blood capillaries
● Development of initial fibrous scar tissue.

After 12 hours, and for the first four days, the cells become active and new capillary blood vessel buds form and gradually grow to establish a new circulation in the area. With the new blood supply the debris of dead cell tissues and the initial blood clot that was formed is cleared.

Scar Tissue

The damaged tissue is repaired by scar tissue. It is important to remember that scar tissue has 'plastic' properties.

Scar tissue is not elastic like muscle. It will form in a haphazard pattern of 'kinks and curls' and will contract or shorten if not carefully stretched daily for many months after the injury.

Fig 15.1 Scar tissue (bottom)

There is a great need for the new scar tissue to form in parallel 'lines' to give it strength. Correct 'stretching' causes the scar tissue to line up along the line of stress of the injured structure. Therefore, injured muscles or ligaments should be carefully mobilised and stretched daily (beginning five days after the initial injury).

The stretching will ensure that the scar is moulded to the desired length and improve the strength of the healed area (scar), and thus reduce a recurrence of damage to the scarred area and injured structure.

Muscular System

For a detailed discussion of skeletal muscular structure and function, read Unit 1: Anatomy for Sport and Exercise.

Ligaments and Tendons

Other tissues that are frequently damaged during sport are ligaments and tendons. These are also soft tissue and are primarily made out of collagen. Ligaments connect bone to bone and tendons connect muscles to bone. Ligaments and tendons can adapt to changes in their mechanical environment due to injury, disease or exercise. A ligament or tendon is made up of fascicles.

Each fascicle contains the basic fibril of the ligament or tendon and the fibroblasts, the cells that make the ligament or tendon.

Unlike normal ligaments, healed ligaments are partly made up of a different type of collagen, which has fibrils with a smaller diameter, and are therefore a mechanically inferior structure. As a result, the healed ligament often fails to provide adequate joint stability, which can then lead to re-injury or a chronically lax (permanently slightly unstable) joint.

For additional information on ligaments and tendons see Unit 1: Anatomy for Sport and Exercise.

Classification of Injuries

There are many ways in which we can classify the severity of an injury. One example is that there are three general stages of injury which can be applied to most sports injuries:

1   Acute stage (0 to 72 hours after injury).
2   Sub-acute stage (72 hours to 21 days after injury).
3   Chronic continuum (21 days after injury).

Note that the severity of the injury will dictate stages 2 and 3 of the above model – less severe will reach stage 3 some time before day 21; more severe may take longer than 21 days.

The following are examples of specific injuries and how they can be classified.

Haematomas

A haematoma is bleeding either into or around a muscle. If the bleeding is within the muscle, it is called an 'intramuscular' haematoma. This type of haematoma will lead to a pressure build-up within the muscle tissue as the blood is trapped within the muscle sheath. This will result in a marked decrease in strength of the injured muscle, a significant decrease in muscle stretch and a long recovery period.

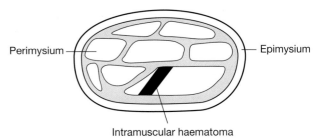

Fig 15.2 An intramuscular haematoma

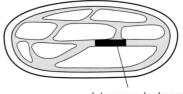

Fig 15.3 An intermuscular haematoma

Bleeding around the muscle tissue is called an intermuscular haematoma. This type of haematoma is much less severe than an intramuscular haematoma because the blood can escape from the damaged muscle and into the surrounding tissues, so there is less pressure in the area and the injury recovers much more quickly.

Sprained Ankle

Injuries to the ligaments of the ankle are usually graded into three categories.

● A first-degree sprain is the least severe. It is the result of some minor stretching of the ligaments, and is accompanied by mild pain, some swelling and joint stiffness. There is usually very little loss of joint stability.
● A second-degree sprain is the result of both stretching and some tearing of the ligaments. There is increased swelling and pain and a moderate loss of stability at the ankle joint.
● A third-degree sprain is the most severe of the three. It is the result of a complete tear or rupture of one or more of the ligaments that make up the ankle joint. A third-degree sprain will result in massive swelling, severe pain and gross instability. With a third-degree sprain, shortly after the injury most of the localised pain will disappear. This is a result of the nerve endings being severed, which causes a lack of feeling at the injury site.

From the explanations above, you can see that pain and swelling are the two most common symptoms associated with an ankle sprain. You can also expect some bruising to occur at the injury site. The associated swelling and bruising are the result of ruptured blood vessels and this in turn will produce heat or inflammation.

Psychological Responses to Injury

The response to injury varies from individual to individual. It may vary within an individual alone, dependent on when the injury occurs – at the start of a training session, middle of a season or during a major competition.

The reaction initially is negative in the main but positive attitudes can be formed. For example, it may give an individual more personal time to spend with family and friends, or time to develop new skills such as coaching, or to work on other aspects of their performance. Generally, though, the reaction is negative.

In reality, while some individuals struggle with the negative feelings that they experience, most cope without great difficulty, particularly if the injury is not so severe.

Various theoretical models have been proposed to explain the response to injury. These all include as early reactions:

● Shock
● Disbelief
● Denial.

These are followed by possible further responses:

● Anger
● Depression
● Tension
● Helplessness
● Acceptance
● Adaptation
● Reorganisation.

After the initial shock is over, many athletes tend to play down the significance of the injury. However, as the injury becomes more apparent, shock is often replaced by anger directed towards themselves or towards other people. The responses can vary in intensity depending on situational and personal factors but can be especially strong in individuals whose self-concept and personal identity are based on being 'an athlete/a player/a competitor'. The loss of this identity due to the inability to perform can cause much distress.

Following anger, the injured athlete might try bargaining or rationalising to avoid the reality of the situation. A runner may promise to train extra hard on return to training. By confronting reality, and realising and understanding the consequences of the injury, an individual can become depressed at the uncertainty of the future. An injured individual who belongs to a team may start to feel isolated from the 'group' and this in turn can lead to depression. It must be noted, however, that depression is not inevitable and has not always been observed during the grief reaction in research studies.

Tension and helplessness are then generated as the individual becomes frustrated at not being able to continue as normal with training or playing. Again, the isolation that injury causes, from a normal routine or from being with 'the team', can be difficult for some people to accept.

Finally, the individual starts to move towards an acceptance of the injury and adaptation of lifestyle while injured. The focus is then turned to rehabilitation and a return to sports activity. This stage tends to mark the transition from an emotional stage to a problem-coping stage as the individual realises what needs to be done to aid recovery. The timescale for progression through these stages can vary considerably depending on the individual and the severity of the injury, and setbacks during rehabilitation can lead to further emotional disturbance. In cases of very serious injury and ones in which the emotional reactions are prolonged, the skills of a clinical psychologist might be required.

It must be stressed that this process may not be a linear one for all individuals who experience some of these feelings.

Motivations and goal-setting strategies have been shown to help some people. It is possible as a coach, trainer or parent to help an injured individual recover sensibly, effectively and more positively by encouraging them to follow professional advice relating to physical rehabilitation. You can also reassure them that the feelings they are experiencing are not uncommon.

The channelling of a positive attitude can ease the rehabilitation for not just the injured player but also those around them!

Key learning points 2

- Physiological responses to injury – how the body reacts to an injury immediately after its occurrence and how it adapts over a period of time.
- Physical signs of injury may include swelling, bleeding, damaged tissue, discoloration and abnormal alignment of a limb or joint.
- Non-physical signs may include pain and heat (inflammation).
- Adaptation over time will include:
  - absorption of swelling
  - removal of debris and blood clots
  - growth of new blood capillaries
  - development of initial fibrous scar tissue.
- Psychological responses to injury – how the sports person mentally reacts and copes with the physical injury. This response can vary from individual to individual; can be determined by the severity of the injury; can be different dependent on when the injury occurs, e.g. start of the playing season; and can change within an individual during the course of rehabilitation.

Q Quick quiz 2

Fill the blanks in the following sentences.

1 A soft tissue injury, such as an injury to _____, will cause _____, which is painful due to increased pressure on _____.

2 There are three stages of injury: the _____ stage occurs 0 to 72 hours after the injury; then from 72 hours to 21 days comes the _____ stage, after which the _____ is entered.

3 A _____ is a description of bleeding into or around a muscle. The bleeding is called _____ if it is within the muscle, and _____ if it is around the muscle.

Student activity 15.2   ⏱ 60 minutes   P3 P4 M2 D1

Read the case study and then answer the questions below.

1 From your reading of the case study and knowledge of muscle injuries, what physiological responses will Carly be experiencing? (P3)

2 From your reading of the case study, describe the psychological responses Carly is experiencing. (P4)

3 Explain the physiological and psychological responses that Carly will be experiencing. (M2)

4 Analyse the physiological and psychological responses that Carly will be experiencing. (D1)

Carly is a talented 17-year-old long jumper who has just competed in the school's county championships. However, during her second jump, she felt a sharp pain down the back of her left hamstring. She thinks she may have heard a small 'pop' as well. She had to pull out of the jump and hobbled through the sand. She was not able to take any further part in the competition. When she goes to see a physiotherapist the next day, she feels pain and tenderness as he presses on the back of her left hamstring; there is also some bruising around the site of the injury. She finds that it is very painful when she bends her knee and also her hip. She is still a bit shaken up by the injury and feels very upset about getting injured, particularly as she has a national event coming up in a month's time in which she is desperate to compete. She asks the physiotherapist if she will be fit in time and he says he cannot answer that. She starts to get very worried and secretly thinks that she will rest for a couple of days and then start training again. But when she starts to think about jumping again, it makes her feel anxious.

15.4 Methods of Treating Sports Injuries

Injuries can be categorised into soft tissue and hard tissue injuries. Soft tissue refers to the muscles, tendons, ligaments and skin, whereas hard tissue refers to the skeleton, including joints, bones and cartilage.

Hard Tissue Injuries

Dislocation

Dislocation is the displacement of a joint from its normal location. It occurs when a joint is over-stressed, which makes the bones that meet at that joint disconnect. This usually causes the joint capsule to tear, together with the ligaments holding the joint in place. Most dislocations are caused by a blow or a fall. If a person has dislocated a joint then it will usually look out of place, discoloured and/or misshapen. Movement is limited, and there is usually swelling and intense pain.

Subluxation

A subluxation is when one or more of the bones of the spine moves out of position and creates pressure on, or irritates, the spinal nerves. This interferes with the signals travelling along these spinal nerves, which means some parts of the body will not be working properly.

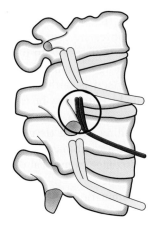

Fig 15.4 A subluxation

Cartilage Damage

Normal synovial joint function requires a smooth-gliding cartilage surface on the ends of the bones. This cartilage also acts to distribute force during repetitive pounding movements, such as running or jumping. Cartilage injury can result in locking, localised pain and swelling around the affected area. It appears as a hole in the cartilage surface. As cartilage has minimal ability to repair itself, it needs treatment in order to minimise the deterioration to the joint surface.

Haemarthrosis

Haemarthrosis is where there is bleeding into the joint. It is a serious injury, and swelling of the injury site occurs very rapidly. The swelling works to protect the joint structures by limiting or preventing movement of the injured joint.

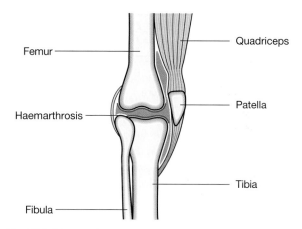

Fig 15.5 Haemarthrosis

Fractures

A fracture is the technical term for a broken bone. They result whenever a bone is hit with enough force to make it break, creating either a small crack or, in a serious fracture, a complete break. There are five main types of fracture.

- **Transverse fractures** are usually the result of a direct blow or force being applied at a sideways angle to the bone. The resultant shape of the bone ends helps transverse fractures stay in alignment more easily than those of other fractures, where the resultant ends do not line up so readily.

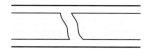

Fig 15.6 A transverse fracture

- **Spiral fractures** are also known as **oblique fractures**. They usually occur as a result of a twisting movement being applied about the long axis of the bone – for example, the foot being held trapped by football boot studs while the leg twists around it.

267

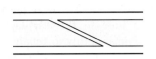

Fig 15.7 A spiral fracture

● A **comminuted fracture** is where there is splintering of the bone so that the bone is broken into a number of pieces. This type of fracture can take longer than others to heal, and is usually caused by direct trauma.

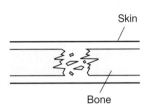

Fig 15.8 A comminuted fracture

● A **stress fracture** is an overuse injury. It occurs when muscles become fatigued and are unable to absorb added shock. Eventually, the fatigued muscle transfers the overload of stress to the bone, causing a tiny crack called a stress fracture. Stress fractures usually occur because of a rapid increase in the amount or intensity of training. The impact of an unfamiliar surface or incorrect trainers can also cause stress fractures.

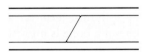

Fig 15.9 A stress fracture

● An **open fracture** is also called a **compound fracture**. It is generally a more serious type of injury because the bone breaks through the skin. The break causes considerable damage to surrounding tissue and can cause serious bleeding if a large artery is ruptured. It also exposes the broken bone to the possibility of infection, which can interfere with healing.

Fig 15.10 An open fracture

268 Soft Tissue Injuries

Strains

A strain is a twist, pull and/or tear to a muscle or tendon, and is often caused by overuse, force or over-stretching. If a tear in the muscle occurs, surgical repair may be necessary. Muscle strains can be classified into three categories.

First-degree strains commonly exhibit the following symptoms:

● Few muscle fibres are torn
● Mild pain
● Little swelling
● Some muscle stiffness.

Second-degree strains commonly exhibit the following symptoms:

● Minimal to moderate tearing of the muscle fibres
● Moderate to severe pain
● Swelling and stiffness.

Third-degree strains commonly exhibit the following symptoms:

● Total rupture of the muscle
● Severe pain
● Severe swelling.

Sprains

A sprain is a stretch and/or tear to a ligament and is often caused by a trauma that knocks a joint out of position, and over-stretches or ruptures the supporting ligaments. Sprains often affect the ankles, knees or wrists.

Muscle contusions or **haematomas** occur due to direct trauma, commonly a blow to the outer part of the thigh or back of the calf; this injury is commonly referred to as a 'dead leg' – it is a bruising of muscle tissue caused by the muscle being squashed between the object causing the impact and the underlying bone. The muscle fibres are squashed and associated capillaries are torn. This results in bleeding into the area with resultant haematoma formation. Usually the haematoma formed is fairly small. But in some circumstances the bleeding may be extensive and can cause a 'pressure problem'.

Oedema is swelling in the tissue due to trauma. The swelling may be a combination of tissue fluid and blood. The blood comes from local damage to capillaries at the injury site.

Bursitis is inflammation or irritation of a bursa. Bursae are small sacs of fluid that are located between bone and other moving structures such as muscles, skin or tendons. The bursa allows smooth gliding between these structures. If the bursa becomes inflamed it will feel painful and restrict movement within that area. Bursitis is an injury that usually results from overuse.

Tendonitis is inflammation or irritation of a tendon. It causes pain and stiffness around the inflamed tendon, which is made worse by movement.

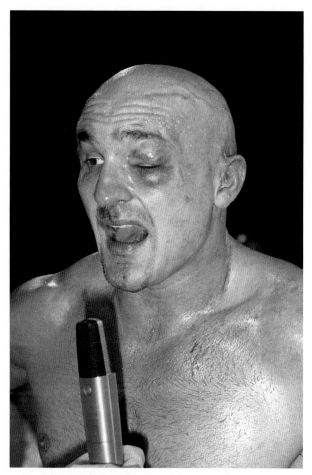

Fig 15.11 Oedema (swelling)

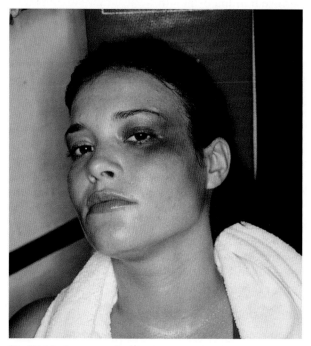

Fig 15.12 Contusion (bruising)

Almost any tendon can be affected with tendonitis, but those located around a joint tend to be more prone to inflammation. Tendonitis usually results from overuse.

A **contusion** is the technical term for a bruise. Contusions are often produced by a blunt force such as a kick, fall or blow. The result will be pain, swelling and discoloration.

An **abrasion** is when the surface of the skin is grazed so that the top layer is scraped off, leaving a raw, tender area. This type of injury often occurs as a result of a sliding fall.

First Aid

First aid is the immediate treatment given to an injured person. When a suitably qualified person arrives on the scene they then take over the care of the person. Anyone with some knowledge of first aid can have a huge impact on the health of an injured person, so it is always useful to know some basics. By completing a recognised first-aid qualification you will gain a very good basic knowledge of what to do in an emergency situation. It is not in the scope of this book to cover all aspects of first aid because practical work is required to complement the theoretical principles of first aid. Therefore, this section will cover only some very basic aspects of first aid.

Immediate Treatments

It is necessary to establish what is wrong with the person. If they are lying on the ground, you should follow the guidelines below.

1 Assess the situation – identify any risks to yourself and to the casualty.
2 Make the area safe, such as turning off an electric switch.
3 Assess the casualty and give first aid if appropriate. Establish if the person is conscious and then check their ABC. This would be thoroughly covered in a first-aid course:
   (a) **A**irway – they have an open airway
   (b) **B**reathing – they are breathing
   (c) **C**irculation – check their circulation by assessing if they have a pulse.
4 Try to get help as soon as possible.
5 Deal with the aftermath – complete an accident or incident report.

If you follow a first-aid course you will be taught how to:

● Check the ABC
● Open a person's airway
● Deal with them if they are not breathing by performing artificial resuscitation

269

● Check if a person has a pulse and how to administer cardiac compressions if they do not.

Calling for an Ambulance

If a person is injured and you believe the injury requires professional attention, you must ensure that someone calls for an ambulance. If you are dealing with a casualty by yourself, minimise the risk to them by taking any vital action first (check their airway, breathing and circulation), then make a short but accurate call.

● Dial 999 and ask for an ambulance.
● Give your exact location.
● Give clear details of the accident and the severity of the injuries your casualty has sustained.
● Give the telephone number you are calling from and the sex and approximate age of the casualty.

If you get someone else to make the call, always ask them to report back to you to confirm that the call has been made.

When the paramedics arrive, tell them as much as possible about how the casualty has behaved, such as if they are unconscious, if they needed artificial resuscitation, and so on.

Contents of a First-Aid Box

A first-aid box should contain a number of items in order for a person to effectively administer first aid. The contents of a first-aid box for a workplace or leisure centre must conform to legal requirements and must also be clearly marked and readily accessible. Below is a list of materials that *most* first-aid kits contain:

● Sterile adhesive dressings (plasters) – there should be a range of sizes for dressing minor wounds
● Sterile eye pads – a sterile pad with a bandage attached to it to cover the eye following eye injuries
● Triangular bandages – these can be used as a pad to stop bleeding, or to make slings, or used as a sterile covering for large injuries such as burns
● Large and medium wound dressings – a sterile, non-medicated dressing pad with a bandage attached to it
● Disposable gloves – these should be worn at all times when dealing with blood or body fluids
● Face shield for resuscitation – this may be used to prevent contamination by the casualty's vomit, blood or other body fluids.

Bleeding

A person may suffer from external bleeding, which is usually obvious to the first-aider as blood flows out from the site of injury. Internal bleeding, however, is not so obvious – it is not visible as the blood is flowing out of the injury site into the body. The first-aider should ensure they are adequately protected when dealing with a casualty who is bleeding to ensure that they do not expose themselves to any blood-borne viruses such as HIV.

External bleeding should be treated in the following manner:

● Lay casualty down
● Apply direct pressure with a gloved hand or finger to the site of bleeding and, as soon as possible, place a clean dressing over the wound
● Elevate and rest the injured part when possible
● Seek medical assistance.

Internal bleeding is difficult to diagnose, but some of the potential signs and symptoms are:

● Coughing up red frothy blood
● Vomiting blood
● Faintness or dizziness
● Weak, rapid pulse
● Cold, clammy skin
● Rapid, gasping breathing.

The treatment for a person you suspect has internal bleeding is as follows:

● Lay the casualty down
● Raise the legs or bend the knees
● Loosen tight clothing
● Urgently seek medical assistance
● Give nothing by mouth
● Reassure the casualty.

Shock

When a person is suffering from shock, there is not enough blood going to the major organs of the body. Shock can be caused by a number of things, including burns, electric shock, allergic shock or severe injuries. A person suffering from shock will usually have cool, moist skin, a weak, rapid pulse and shallow breathing. Other symptoms may include nausea, vomiting or trembling. The treatment for a conscious casualty suffering from shock is to reassure them, then try to find and treat the cause of shock, such as control any bleeding. Keep the casualty lying down and check for neck, spine, head or abdomen injuries. If none of these injuries is apparent then the casualty's feet should be raised so that they are higher than their head.

Unconscious Adult Casualty

If you see a person lying on the ground, talk to them first to see if they respond – they may just be asleep! If they do not respond, speak to them with a louder voice, asking them if they are all right. If you still receive no response, gently shake them. If the person is not injured but is unconscious, they should be placed in the recovery position (see Figure 15.13). This position helps a semi-conscious or unconscious person breathe and allows fluids to drain from the nose and throat so that they do not choke. The casualty should not be moved into the recovery position if you suspect that they have a major injury, such as a back or neck injury.

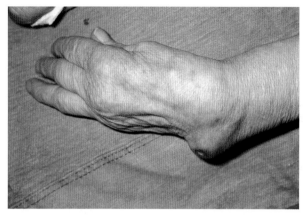

Fig 15.14 A fracture

Fig 15.13 The recovery position

Fractures

There are five different types of fracture. All the closed fractures can be treated in a similar manner, but an open fracture needs special attention. A person can be diagnosed as having a fracture if the injured area looks deformed or is tender, if there is swelling in the area, if the casualty cannot move the injured part, or if there is a protruding bone, bleeding or discoloured skin at the injury site. A sharp pain when the individual attempts to move the injured body part is also a sign of a fracture. The casualty should be told firmly not to move the injured part, since such movement could cause further damage to surrounding tissues and make the casualty go into shock.

A fracture should be immobilised in order to prevent the sharp edges of the bone from moving and cutting tissue, muscle, blood vessels and nerves. The injured body part can be immobilised using splints or slings. If a casualty has an open fracture, the first-aider should never attempt to push the bones back under the skin. A dressing should be applied to the injury site to protect the area and pressure should be applied in order to try to limit the external bleeding. A splint can be applied, but should not be placed over the protruding bone.

SALTAPS

The sooner an injury is treated, the greater the chances of a complete recovery and the faster the rehabilitation. The immediate treatment can be summarised by the acronym SALTAPS:

- **S**ee the injury occur and the mechanism of injury
- **A**sk the casualty what is wrong and where they have pain
- **L**ook for signs of bleeding, deformity of limbs, inflammation, swelling and redness
- **T**ouch the injury or close to the injury for signs of heat, tenderness, loss or change of sensation and pain
- **A**ctive movement – ask the casualty to move the injured area; if they are able to, ask them to move it through its full range of movements
- **P**assive movement – try to move the injured site only if a good range of movement is available
- **S**trength – if the casualty has been taken through the steps above with no pain, use resisted movements to assess loss of function; for example, with an injured ankle you would assist the casualty to their feet, then ask them to stand unaided, then progress the test to walking and running.

This process will determine the extent and severity of the injury, although it may be obvious. Treatment at this stage should consist of protect, rest, ice, compression, elevation and diagnosis by a professional (PRICED), which is described below.

In minor injuries, all stages of SALTAPS can usually be completed. But if a person sustains a serious sports injury, such as a fracture or dislocation, the assessment should not be completed because further injury may occur.

PRICED

If a person has suffered from a soft tissue injury such as a strain or a sprain, ensuring that they follow the **PRICED** regime will help to limit the severity of their injury:

- **P**rotect the injured body part from further injury
- **R**est – as soon as a person has injured themselves they should be told to discontinue their activity; further activity could cause further injury, delay healing, increase pain and stimulate bleeding
- **I**ce – an ice pack or cold compress should be applied to the injured area; this will help to reduce the swelling and pain of the injury
- **C**ompression – gentle pressure should be applied to the injury site by surrounding the area with padding, a compressive bandage or a cloth; compressing the injured area will reduce blood flowing to the injury site and also help to control swelling by decreasing fluid seeping into the injured area from adjacent tissue; after applying a compression bandage, the casualty's circulation should be checked by squeezing the nail beds of the injured limb; if blood is seen to return to the nail bed on release, the compression bandage is not too tight; the compression bandage should be reapplied after 24 hours in order to maintain compression over the injury site
- **E**levation – the injured area should be supported in a raised position above the level of the heart in order to reduce the blood flow to the injury, which will further help to minimise swelling and bruising at the injury site
- **D**iagnosis by a professional – the injured person should be examined as soon as possible by a professional, such as a sports therapist or a physiotherapist, so that the injury can be accurately diagnosed.

Cold Application

Cooling an injured body part to minimise the swelling and bruising of an injured area and to reduce pain is essential. When a person sustains a soft tissue injury, blood vessels are torn and blood cells and fluid escape into the spaces among the muscle fibres. By cooling the injury site, the local blood vessels are constricted, so blood flow to the area is reduced. The application of something that is cold to the injured area not only has the effect of decreasing the flow of this fluid into the tissues but also helps to slow the release of chemicals that cause pain and inflammation. Cold also decreases the feeling of pain by reducing the ability of the nerve endings to conduct impulses.

Because cold reduces bleeding and swelling within injured tissue, it is best used immediately after injury has occurred, and for up to 48 to 72 hours after an injury.

Ice bags (plastic bags with ice cubes in, a bag of frozen vegetables or chemical cold packs) can be used. Never apply ice directly on to the skin. The injured area should be covered with a cloth towel in order to prevent direct contact of the ice with the skin, which could cause a blister or 'ice burn'. The cold application should be applied to the injured area for no more than ten minutes. During this time, the person's skin will pass through four stages of sensation:

1 Cold.
2 Burning.
3 Aching.
4 Numbness – as soon as the skin feels numb the cold therapy should be stopped.

The cooling procedure should be repeated every two waking hours. There are a number of methods of cold treatments (cryotherapy) on the market, including ice and gel packs, ice bath immersion and cans of spray.

Heat Treatments

The application of heat to an injury site will act to dilate the local blood vessels, thus increasing the blood flow to the area. This type of treatment should only be given in the sub-acute stage in order to aid in the healing process. The increased blood supply will have the effect of absorbing the swelling and removing the dead cells from the injury site. It will also help to increase the growth of new blood vessels in the area and help scar tissue to form. The application of heat to muscles allows them to relax and aids in pain relief. Heat treatment would not be suitable during the early stages of injury, on an open wound or where tissues are very sensitive, such as the genital region.

Contrast Bathing

Contrast bathing is the process by which alternating treatments of both hot and cold therapy are applied to the injury site and should be used during the sub-acute phase. The application of a hot treatment will increase the blood flow to the area and, when this is followed by a cold treatment, the blood flow to the area will decrease and take with it the debris from the injury site. The injured site should be immersed in alternating hot and cold water for periods ranging from one to four minutes, with increased time initially in the cold water.

Support Mechanisms

In order to help protect and support some injuries,

it is possible to use a variety of products that are readily available at chemists, sports retailers and via the internet, including tubigrip, tape and neoprene support.

Bandaging and taping can be carried out in order to prevent injury, or to treat or rehabilitate an injured joint. Both are performed in order to increase the stability of a joint when there has been an injury to the ligaments that normally support it. They limit unwanted joint movement, support the injury site during strengthening exercises and protect the injury site from further damage.

Taping involves the use of adhesive tape (e.g. zinc oxide tape), whereas bandaging uses strips of cotton and/or specialised pressure bandages. Their purpose is to restrict the joint movement to within safe limits. Taping should not be carried out if the joint is swollen or painful, or if there are any lesions around the taping area. The person who applies the taping/bandaging should be careful to ensure that they do not bind the injury site too tightly so that circulation is affected.

It should also be noted that some individuals have an allergic reaction to some types of tape, such as zinc oxide. Ideally, they should be asked about this possibility before application of the tape. If there is any uncertainty, an underwrap can be applied to provide a protective barrier between the skin and the tape. Unfortunately, this can impair the tape's performance as tape also provides a proprioceptive response mechanism by having its contact directly with the skin. It reminds the individual that it is there to protect and maintain a joint within a range of movement.

The use of tape may well provide support and comfort for a sports person, but the benefits of use over approximately 20 minutes are diminished due to the material properties. This said, it is often used for time periods well beyond the 20-minute mark and its proprioceptive response declines after this amount of time. The psychological value of tape is valuable for a lot of players at all levels of competition, to the extent that it may even be applied to an injury that has fully recovered because the player still feels 'comforted' by the application of the tape!

Bandaging can be used to create pressure around the injury site in order to restrict swelling.

Key learning points 3

- Soft tissue injury – injury to muscles, tendons, ligaments and skin.
- Hard tissue injury – injury to the skeleton, i.e. bones, joints and cartilage.
- First aid – the immediate treatment given to an injured person, preferably by a qualified first-aider.
- SALTAPS – See, Ask, Look, Touch, Active movement, Passive movement, Strength.
- PRICED – Protect, Rest, Ice, Compression, Elevation, Diagnosis.

Q Quick quiz 3

Decide whether each of these statements is true or false.

1 Cartilage has the ability to heal itself quickly.
2 Haemarthrosis is defined as bleeding into a joint.
3 A second-degree strain is when a few muscle fibres are torn.
4 A sprain is an injury suffered by a ligament.
5 Oedema is a description of increased swelling in tissue.
6 Heat treatment is used to restrict the flow of blood to an injury site.

Student activity 15.3   ⏱ 40 minutes   P5

Complete the following table to show your knowledge of first aid and other treatments for four different types of sports injury.

Type of sports injury	First-aid treatment	Other common treatments
Sports injury 1		
Sports injury 2		
Sports injury 3		
Sports injury 4		

You might choose from the following injuries: fractures, ligament injuries, muscle injuries, tendonitis, haematoma, burns.

15.5 Planning and Constructing Treatment and Rehabilitation Programmes

Rehabilitation is the restoration of the ability to function in a normal or near-normal manner following an injury. It usually involves reducing pain and swelling, restoring range of motion and increasing strength with the use of manual therapy (massage and manipulation), therapeutic methods such as ultrasound and an exercise programme.

If a sports person does not rehabilitate their injury effectively, they are much more likely to sustain another injury to the same area.

It should be taken into consideration that, as well as the physical rehabilitation of the player, the psychological rehabilitation may also need to be considered. The trauma of the injury itself and the resulting exclusion from training/coaching sessions, competitions, matches and after-competition social events can be very difficult for some individuals to come to terms with. In some cases, this alone can force injured players to try to start playing again much too soon.

Physical Rehabilitation Process

For rehabilitation to occur, an accurate and immediate diagnosis is needed to help establish effective treatment and rehabilitation management of an injury. Therefore, it is essential that an appropriately qualified person diagnoses the injury as early as possible. This may include a sports therapist, a physiotherapist, a doctor or some other suitably qualified person.

The diagnosis relies on accurate information given by either the injured person or someone who saw the injury happen. The smallest of details can make a difference to how accurate a diagnosis can be. So all information, including information regarding the environment, previous injury history, as well as the actual injury event is very important to communicate.

Post-Injury Treatment and Rehabilitation

There are numerous ways in which to classify injury and its management. The following is a commonly accepted role model. This is called the 'stepladder approach' to rehabilitation.

Phase 1

The aim of treatment at this stage is to:

- Prevent as much of the initial swelling as is possible (e.g. if you are dealing with a sprained ankle injury, do not remove footwear at this stage – it will help with compression)
- Protect the injured part from any further damage (e.g. remove from field of play)
- Control any bleeding (apply cover and add pressure)
- Help to relieve the pain (help support or position the injured part in a comfortable position – non-weight-bearing).

So the use of cold compression, elevation and rest are vital.

Phase 2

The aim of treatment at this stage is to:

- Control any bleeding and swelling (maintain sterile cover and cold compress, elevate)
- Relieve pain (cold compress and elevation)
- Protect from further damage (advise to refrain from using as much as possible)
- Give advice for home treatment (do not wear compression bandages throughout the night, correct use of ice, PRICED, etc.).

Phase 3

During this stage, the injury should be in the early stages of recovery:

- Absorption of swelling
- Removal of debris/dead cells from the area
- Growth of new blood vessels
- Development of scar tissue.

The use of treatments such as contrast bathing, elevation and massage, and passive exercises, such as non-weight-bearing exercises, will help to disperse the products of inflammation. The joint should be moved through its pain-free range in order to increase the range of movement, help to strengthen and lengthen the muscles around the injury, and also to help the scar tissue to form in alignment. Throughout these exercises, the person should feel no pain.

Contrast bathing as well as the use of heat packs may also aid the healing process. It may be necessary to use walking aids to protect from further injury or bandages for added support. The use of strengthening exercises specific to the injured area will help the tone of muscle and encourage stability around a joint. Attention to scar tissue development is essential during this stage.

Phase 4

Before starting active rehabilitation, it is important to make sure that the following applies to the injured part:

- There is no significant inflammation
- There is no significant swelling
- While there may be some joint stiffness, there is some range of movement free from pain
- There is the ability to undertake some weight-bearing.

Initially the range of movement needs to be improved as there may have been some weakening of muscles through injury. For every week of immobilisation, a person may lose up to 20 per cent of their muscle strength. Therefore, it is important to start to encourage movement first through non-weight-bearing exercises and then to progress to weight-bearing activities.

The use of supports may still be necessary in the early part of this stage. Prolonged immobilisation will lead to stiffness of the joints in the injured area and a decrease in ligament strength. However, if the injured area is mobilised early on in the rehabilitation process, regrowth of the damaged tissues is encouraged and sports ability and skills are maintained.

A selection of exercises used for the injured part should be encouraged on a regular basis as well as continuing to exercise the rest of the body without undue pressure on the injury. Care should be taken to avoid over-exercising, which may result in more damage and therefore a delay in rehabilitation.

The two main types of exercises that should be used throughout this stage are:

- Mobilisation activities to improve the range of movement and reduce joint stiffness
- Strengthening activities that will help stability of joints and strengthen the weakened muscles.

Phase 5

The aim of treatment at this stage is to:

- Improve balance and movement coordination
- Restore specific skills and movement patterns to pre-injury level
- Provide psychological reassurance of function.

Progression to a functional phase is dependent on the ability to repeatedly perform a task at the level below.

Here are some examples of exercises in the stepladder approach.

Phase 1: play/exercise should cease as soon as injury occurs. 'Playing on through the pain' is not the best advice. Immediate treatment should be given as specified earlier.

Phase 2: very little exercise should be performed during this stage as the aim of the treatment is to control the bleeding and swelling, and protect the injured body part from further damage. PRICED is recommended at this stage for up to 72 hours.

Phase 3: contrast bathing and massage are used during this phase along with stretching. Stretching the injured body part is very important in order to help ensure that the new tissue is laid down in the correct orientation. If there are any signs that the injured body part is not ready to commence this stage, such as heat or swelling around the injury, then stretching should not be started. When stretching, the person should have their injured body part made as warm as possible. This can be done through the use of a thermal heat pack or soaking in a hot bath. Stretches should be held (static stretches) to the onset of discomfort for 15 to 20 seconds. However, a person should never stretch to the extent that they are in pain. Stretching should be performed for short periods of time and frequently throughout the day.

Phase 4: the strengthening exercises that can be used start with isometric exercises. This is where the muscle contracts but no joint movement occurs. Once these have been carried out and no pain has been felt, concentric muscle contractions can be introduced. This is where the muscle shortens – for example, the biceps shortening in a biceps curl.

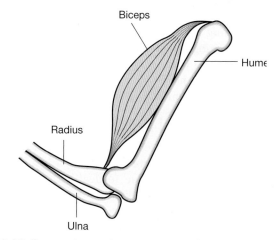

Fig 15.15 Concentric muscle contraction in a biceps curl

Once this type of muscle contraction can be carried out with no pain, eccentric muscle contractions can be performed. This involves the muscle lengthening under tension. An example of this is the quadriceps muscle lengthening as the knee flexes into the sitting position.

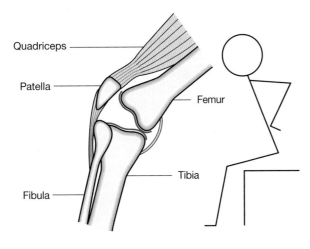

Fig 15.16 The quadriceps muscle demonstrates an eccentric muscle contraction when getting into a sitting position

If the person has injured their leg(s), initially all the strength-training exercises should be carried out in a non-weight-bearing position, so the injured body part should not take the weight of the body. Instead, the person should be sitting down, lying down or standing on their good leg. The next stage is partial weight-bearing, where the arms are used to help support the body weight. Lastly, the exercises can be carried out with the full body weight on the injured body part.

Phase 5: initially this stage should involve the very basic elements of the sports person's usual sport. For example, a footballer would start with running on the spot or in a straight line. Then they would progress to running up and down hills, then on a diagonal and changing direction. This would then progress to skill training. Once they are able to complete these exercises with no problems, they can commence full training and eventually be ready for competitive play.

Psychological Rehabilitation

Alongside the injured player's physical rehabilitation programme, there should run a psychological rehabilitation programme to deal with the feelings and emotions of the individual during the altering stages and phases of recovery to full fitness.

Frequently athletes react to injuries with a wide range of emotions, including denial, anger and even depression. An injury often seems unfair to anyone who has been physically active and otherwise healthy. Although these feelings are real, it is important to move beyond the negative and find more positive strategies to cope with this setback. In many cases, dealing positively with an injury will make for a more focused, flexible and resilient athlete/player.

The following are some suggestions that can help form a psychological coping strategy alongside the physical rehabilitation of an injury.

Learn about the Injury

The individual should learn as much as possible about the cause, treatment and prevention of their injury. Not fully understanding an injury can cause fear or anxiety. The professional treating the individual should be aware of this, but if the nature of the injury is not explained, there will be some uncertainty about the recovery as far as the injured player is concerned. Identification of the facts is a good starting point in the psychological rehabilitation process.

At the start of the physical rehabilitation process, diagnosis is key. If the individual knows *and* understands the answers to some of the following questions, a lot of uncertainty can be removed before the related feelings have time to develop.

- What is the diagnosis (what type of injury is it)?
- How long will recovery take?
- What type of treatment is available?
- What is the purpose of the treatment?
- What should be expected during rehabilitation?
- Can alternative exercise help?
- What are the warning signs that rehabilitation is not progressing?

By understanding the injury and knowing what to expect during the rehabilitation process, an individual will feel less anxious and may also feel that they have a greater sense of control over their recovery.

Responsibility for the Injury

This does not mean that the individual should blame themselves or anyone else for the injury that they have sustained. What it means is that they accept that they *have* an injury and that they can be in control of their own recovery. By taking on responsibility for the recovery process, individuals tend to find a greater sense of control and some go through the process quickly, rather than dwelling on the past or blaming the injury on an outside factor.

Monitor Attitude

Just as the person dealing with the physical rehabilitation will keep records on the progress of the individual, it is also important that the psychological aspects are considered and recorded. If an individual has accepted their injury and is positive at the start of rehabilitation, it does not mean that they will stay like this, feeling exactly the same over a period of time. Particularly if the recovery does not go as planned, it can be very easy for an individual to become disillusioned.

Using Support

A common response after an injury is to feel isolated and to withdraw from being around teammates, coaches and friends. It is important to maintain contact with others during recovery from an injury. Teammates, friends and coaches need to be good at listening when there is emotion to vent, or able to offer advice or encouragement. Simply realising that other people care and are willing to help so that the injury does not have to be faced alone can also be a tremendous comfort to an injured person. So, it might be that the injured player is encouraged to go along to training, to matches, remain around the gym and the weight room, or be visible and included by being an active member of the group – for example, scoring or compiling data, such as the number of tackles, etc.

Set Goals

When not injured, most sports people set themselves targets and goals to achieve, perhaps in training, or in a match, or by the end of a season. Injury does not mean that this should stop. Planning or setting goals can be a very positive focus. Rather than viewing the injury as a crisis, it can be seen as another training challenge. The goal is now focused on recovery rather than performance. This will help keep the individual motivated. By monitoring these goals, it becomes easier to notice small improvements in the rehabilitation of the injury. This in turn encourages confidence in the recovery process. It is important that realistic goals and targets are set so this should always be done in conjunction with the person in charge of the physical rehabilitation process. Most athletes have a tendency to try to speed up their recovery by doing too much too soon. It is important that the injury is accepted and that the individual takes professional advice and knows their own limits.

Training to Stay Fit

Depending upon the type of injury incurred, it may be possible to continue training to some extent and maintain cardiovascular conditioning or strength. This is vitally important to how quickly someone can go back to playing after the injury. If their overall fitness has dropped during the rehabilitation phase while the injury has been dealt with, the individual is not at an appropriate level of fitness to return to playing. A good alternative training programme should be devised between the coach/trainer, the therapist and the injured player to ensure appropriateness throughout.

With the right knowledge, support and patience, an injury can be overcome without it being a totally negative experience. By taking things slowly, setting realistic goals and maintaining a positive, focused approach, most athletes can overcome minor injuries quickly and major injuries in time.

Recording data

With any accident or incident resulting in a person being injured, it is important to keep accurate and up-to-date records to help prevent, where possible, the injury happening again.

This information will normally be maintained by a coach, a teacher or a sports centre, or wherever the injury took place. This information is necessary to protect individuals from being sued for malpractice but also helps to highlight issues which may prevent other similar injuries.

It may help to make sports environments safer, and more importantly, for the coach/trainer, it can help to log the process of injury–treatment–rehabilitation. This can become an accurate record to be used as a template for similar injuries on other players or to identify the recurrence in the same player, which may lead to taking into account why the injury is happening regularly. This could be down to inappropriate training regimes, inappropriate fitness levels and/or insufficient time to rehabilitate through the differing phases.

Key learning points 4

- Rehabilitation is the restoration of normal function following an injury.
- The stepladder approach to rehabilitation passes through five phases.
- It is important to offer support to address the psychological aspects of an injury.

Student activity 15.4 ⏱ 90 minutes   P6   M3   D2

Use the following template to decide upon a treatment and rehabilitation programme for Carly, the long jumper from Student Activity 15.2, and another individual of your choice.

Name:
Description of injury:
Aims of rehabilitation:

	Range of motion methods	Strengthening methods	Coordination methods
Stage 1			
Stage 2			
Stage 3			

To achieve M3, this programme needs to be designed independently. To achieve D2, you need to evaluate your training programme, justify why you have chosen each method of treatment and suggest alternatives where it is appropriate.

Further reading

Cash, M. (1996) *Sport and Remedial Massage Therapy*, London: Ebury Press.

Crossman, J. (2001) *Coping with Sports Injuries: Psychological Strategies for Rehabilitation*, Oxford: Oxford University Press.

Peterson, L. and Renstrom, P. (2001) *Sports Injuries: Their Prevention & Treatment*, 3rd edn, London: Taylor and Francis.

Sports Coach UK (1999) *Sports Injury: Prevention and First Aid Management*, Leeds: Coachwise Solutions.

Useful websites

www.physioroom.com
Provides an A–Z guide of sports injuries and suggested treatments

www.injuryupdate.com.au
Contains a wide range of resources for sports injuries and access to journal articles

www.sportsinjuryclinic.net
Described as a virtual sports injury clinic, this site contains information on a wide range of injuries and conditions

16: Sports coaching

16.1 Introduction

Sports coaches are vital to the success of a number of programmes across a range of sports. They are at the heart of participation and performer development. Whether the coach of an after-school club or a top international coach with support staff, coaches are at the very centre of the development of sport.

This unit will assist those starting on the coaching ladder to learn the rules and responsibilities, the qualities and characteristics of sports coaches. It will provide an understanding of the role of the coach in promoting a positive coaching experience.

By the end of this unit you should:

● know the roles, responsibilities and skills of sports coaches
● know the techniques used by coaches to improve the performance of athletes
● be able to plan a sports coaching session
● be able to deliver and review a sports coaching session.

Assessment and grading criteria		
To achieve a PASS grade the evidence must show that the learner is able to:	To achieve a MERIT grade the evidence must show that, in addition to the pass criteria, the learner is able to:	To achieve a DISTINCTION grade the evidence must show that, in addition to the pass and merit criteria, the learner is able to:
P1 describe four roles and four responsibilities of sports coaches, using examples of coaches from different sports	**M1** explain four roles and four responsibilities of sports coaches, using examples of coaches from different sports	**D1** compare and contrast the roles, responsibilities and skills of successful coaches from different sports
P2 describe three skills common to successful sports coaches, using examples of coaches from different sports	**M2** explain three skills common to successful sports coaches, using examples of coaches from different sports	
P3 describe three different techniques that are used by coaches to improve the performance of athletes	**M3** explain three different techniques that are used by coaches to improve the performance of athletes	**D2** evaluate three different techniques that are used by coaches to improve the performance of athletes
P4 plan a sports coaching session		
P5 deliver a sports coaching session, with tutor support	**M4** independently deliver a sports coaching session	
P6 carry out a review of the planning and delivery of a sports coaching session, identifying strengths and areas for improvement.	**M5** evaluate the planning and delivery of a sports coaching session, suggesting how improvements could be reached in the identified areas.	**D3** justify suggestions made in relation to the development plan.

16.2 The roles, responsibilities and skills of sports coaches

P1 **P2** **M1** **M2** **D1**

Effective coaches tend to find new ways of improving existing practices or theories. Some adapt the way in which they practise, others deal with how to play specific strategies in differing situations. Other coaches integrate new developments or technologies to improve performance. Consider the trampoline coach who adapts a harness that supports a performer for use while learning somersaults, allowing them the freedom to twist at the same time and add to the range of skills and techniques achievable. Performers who work with innovative coaches speak about how they are never bored and always trying something new.

Trainer, educator and instructor

The difference between a teacher, educator and instructor is hard to discern. Teaching implies a

Fig 16.1 A tennis coach and player

transfer of learning through demonstration, modelling or instruction. Coaches can also teach emotional and social skills. Young performers in particular can be encouraged to increase their social awareness, learn to cope with losing and winning, and develop self-confidence. Good coaches will be aware that people learn in different ways. They then adapt and use a range of techniques to ensure that learning takes place.

In some cultures trainers and coaches are taken to mean the same thing. Since all sport requires some kind of physical exertion, it is important that these physical demands are recognised and that allowance for these demands is incorporated into coaching programmes.

A sound knowledge of anatomy, physiology and fitness theory is essential for coaches. In the role of trainer, you might expect to design and implement training programmes for your performers.

Motivator

Motivation can come merely by providing a stable environment in which to learn, in a positive and safe atmosphere. Performers who constantly find negativity are certain at some point to become despondent and suffer a reduction in self-confidence and improvement.

Evidence suggests that performers who receive praise and positive feedback are likely to get more from their performances. When providing feedback to performers you would employ the following technique: KISS, KICK, KISS.

This technique would be applied in providing feedback such as in skill learning. When communicating with performers, the emphasis with this technique would be to start your feedback with a positive comment. There is nearly always something that is positive in any performance. Second, a corrective comment can be presented in as positive a manner as possible. Finally, leave the interaction with a positive comment and possibly an action plan. Consider a tennis player struggling to make a particular shot:

KISS – 'Good positioning prior to the shot and you watched the ball well.'
KICK – 'You should consider how you back-lift the racket; you could prepare your grip earlier.'
KISS – 'If you practise these changes you will almost certainly improve.'

Role model

In almost every coaching situation players will look mostly, if not entirely, to the coach as their source of inspiration and knowledge, never more so than when working with children. Children often imitate the behaviour and manner of their coach. For this reason it is vital that coaching is safe and responsible, and that behaviour is considered good practice.

The coach can influence player development in a number of ways.

● Social – sport offers a code of acceptable social behaviour, teamwork, citizenship, cooperation and fair play.
● Personal – players can be encouraged to learn life skills, promote their self-esteem, manage personal matters like careers or socialising, and develop a value system including good manners, politeness and self-discipline.
● Psychological – coaches can create environments that help performers control emotions and develop their own identities. Confidence, mental toughness, visualisation and a positive outlook on life can be developed or improved.
● Health – in taking care to design coaching or training sessions to include sufficient physical exercise, good health and healthy habits can be established and maintained.

The responsibilities of a coach

Many expectations are put upon a coach. Some of these responsibilities are clear-cut, others less so. Coaching and playing sport should always be enjoyable, and to that end coaches should not be overburdened by expectation. Common sense and a good knowledge of safety and ethics will provide the basis of a responsible coach.

As coaching is now considered a profession, so coaches will increasingly be measured and assessed, whether paid or voluntary, and increasingly expected to work to a code of practice.

A coaching code of practice

So that performers achieve their potential, coaches should:

● remain within the bounds of adopted codes of practice
● maintain safe and secure coaching environments
● make best use of all facilities and resources
● establish good working relationships with all involved
● control the behaviour of participants where possible.

Many sports governing bodies and sports coach UK have established a code of conduct for sports coaches, which includes the following sections.

● Rights – coaches must respect and champion the right of every individual to participate in sport. Coaches should ensure that everyone has an equal opportunity to participate, regardless of age, gender, race, ability, faith or sexual orientation.
For example, you would organise sessions in a place that has childcare arrangements, and you would be sensitive to religious festivals of all denominations and make allowances for the absences of performers on notable religious dates.
Coaches also have a responsibility to ensure that no discriminating behaviour occurs during their working sessions. Every member of the coaching group should have the right to feel part of the group, free from prejudice.
● Relationships – coaches need to establish relationships with performers that are based on openness, trust and mutual respect. This is not just about effective communication. Good coaches understand how their performers think and what is best for them. Performers will also learn better in an atmosphere of trust and respect for their coach. Involving performers in the decision-making process is an excellent way of establishing an effective relationship with a performer. When deciding what is best for a performer or group of performers, an example could be a situation where the coach presents the performers with information about their performance, such as a particular phase of play in a tennis competition. Having supplied that information and perhaps offering their opinion, the coach could present the performer with a range of options that relates to the best course of action – how to improve on the last period of play. The performer who has an input into the decision in this process will come to appreciate the knowledge and analytical skills of the coach and over time their relationship will develop based on trust and respect.

Coaches should also anticipate and deal with potential relationship problems such as:

● dealing with parents
● dropping players from squads
● assuming control as a carer.

Personal standards

Coaches should demonstrate model behaviour at all times. Their influence should always be positive and would usually mean working to a code.

Professional conduct

It is not enough to achieve a coaching qualification. Coaches should have a commitment to continual and ongoing learning or professional development. This could include:

- attaining higher-grade qualifications
- attending workshops and seminars
- being aware of changes to their sport.

Skills of sports coaches

The essential skills required of a sports coach are illustrated in Figure 16.2.

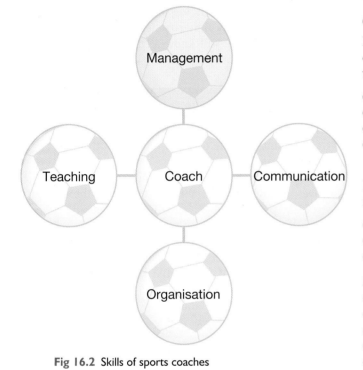

Fig 16.2 Skills of sports coaches

Management

The key ways to demonstrate good leadership in coaching are:

- checking that participants are well prepared and organised
- checking that participants and appropriate others are well deployed
- safe management and coordination of equipment and facilities
- safe and well-delivered sessions
- maintaining support and guidance to participants
- establishing and maintaining effective communication with appropriate others within the coaching environment.

It is important that coaches motivate participants by ensuring that they remain interested and challenged. Coaches will get the best from their sport if they are self-motivated and working in an atmosphere that allows them to:

- enjoy their coaching sessions

- share their experiences with others and socialise with peers and friends
- compete in a safe and non-threatening environment
- achieve negotiated goals
- remain fit and healthy
- achieve success or reward
- please others and receive praise
- create a positive self-image.

Organisation

Planning and organisation are critical to the success of coaching. When planning a session there is much to consider, but the main points are to:

- have identified a set of goals for the session
- have an awareness of the resources available
- have enough information about the participants
- have developed a plan that allows participants to achieve.

During a session coaches need to be constantly making judgements about the following:

- Is the practice working?
- What could be adapted and how?
- Are the facilities being used to full advantage?

Many coaches now keep records, usually in the form of logbooks. Many coaching qualifications require candidates to complete logbooks as part of the formal assessment process. Few coaches have the privilege of just turning up, coaching and going home. Often coaches are also involved in booking facilities, arranging equipment or contacting participants,

Role	Responsibilities
Coach	Team selection
Assistant coach	Warm-up, cool-down & general preparation
Player 1	Calling players to arrange meeting place for away fixtures
Player 2	Washing & looking after kit
Player 3	Contacting officials prior to games
Player 4	Maintaining website & making travel arrangements
Player 5	All communication with league
Player 6	Introducing new players & schools liaison
Player 7	Seeking sponsorship

Table 16.1 Responsibilities and roles within a senior women's volleyball team

which involves a great deal of organisation. Some coaches delegate these responsibilities as in the example for a senior women's volleyball team shown in Table 16.1.

In some clubs such as this, some or all of these responsibilities and others are undertaken by appropriate others, usually with the coach in control of exactly who is capable and most responsible for the task.

Communication

Perhaps the single most valuable skill is the ability to convey your thoughts and ideas in such a way as to be easily understood. It is not enough to just present your opinions: you must be able to send effective messages – these are mostly non-verbal signals. Consider the body language of a coach in a variety of scenarios. The main feedback a performer receives in almost every sport is non-verbal body language from their coaches.

Talking too much can lead to confusion. The pace, tone and volume of the spoken word will all have a marked effect on participants. The coach who spends most of their time shouting abuse will quickly lose the respect of their participants and will be less likely to be successful.

You must also be able to receive incoming messages. This particular skill is concerned with understanding and interpreting the signs and signals of other players, officials, etc. You must also listen to opinions from players regarding tactical decisions, drills in practice or perhaps even concerning opponents.

You must also be able to check message reception. Good coaches will question their players and check their understanding. If an instruction is not understood, this is the fault of either the performer lacking concentration or the coach in the quality of the message. One way of ensuring understanding is to ask players to explain a concept in their own words.

Teaching

One of the key processes of teaching is an understanding of how people learn. Drills and practices need to be designed in a way that allows participants to progress at an appropriate pace. As a rule of good practice, the following model is useful when teaching skills:

- introduce and explain the technique
- demonstrate the technique
- practise (allow performers to experience the technique)
- observe and analyse the participants
- identify and correct errors.

It is vital that learning is achieved in simple, short and logical steps. The most valuable knowledge that a coach can gain is through learned experience, judging for themselves and from their performers what is effective and what is not.

Coaching is a continuous process which lends itself to self-reflection and evaluation. Since the knowledge and skills required to be a successful coach are constantly changing and developing with the sport, it is unlikely that coaches will ever reach the point where they will know all that there is to know!

Key learning points I

- The roles of a sports coach are many and varied, and include teacher, trainer, motivator and instructor.
- Coaches can have a direct influence on the lives of their performers in terms of their social, psychological, personal and health development.
- Most coaches in the UK work to a code of conduct or practice that is established to set the parameters of acceptable behaviour and effective coaching.
- The essential skills toolkit of a successful sports coach includes:
  - management
  - communication
  - teaching
  - organisation.

Q Quick quiz I

Fill in the blanks in the following paragraph.

Coaches will perform many different roles as they work with their performers. They will act as a _____ as they demonstrate and model skills. They will need to have a good knowledge base, including _____ and _____ . Coaches will need to pick out the good points so that performers remain motivated and also act as a _____ _____ so they influence performers in a positive way.

Student activity 16.1 · 60 minutes · P1 · P2 · M1 · M2 · D1

Roles and responsibilities of a sports coach

Part 1

Investigate the roles, responsibilities and skills of the sports coach by filling in the following table.

Role/Responsibility	Describe each of the roles/responsibilities, using examples of coaches from different sports	Describe each of the roles/responsibilities, using examples of coaches from different sports	Compare and contrast the roles, responsibilities and skills of successful coaches from different sports
Role 1: Trainer			
Role 2: Educator			
Role 3: Role model			
Role 4: Motivator			
Responsibility 1: Working within a code of practice			
Responsibility 2: Maintain a safe and secure environment			
Responsibility 3: Equal opportunities			
Responsibility 4: Professional conduct			

Part 2

Take three coaches of your choice:

(a) Describe how they use the skills of communication, organisation and analysis to improve the performance of athletes:

Coach	Communication	Organisation	Analysis
Coach 1:			
Coach 2:			
Coach 3:			

(b) To achieve a merit you need to explain these three techniques.

(c) To achieve a distinction you need to evaluate the effectiveness of each of the three techniques.

16.3 Techniques used by coaches to improve performance

Coaches in all sports have a number of techniques at their disposal that they can use to improve the performance of their athletes.

Coaching diaries/logbooks

Diaries come in different sizes, paper or electronic. They can be used to record personal thoughts, make appointments or log training sessions. Diaries can be useful in aiding self-reflection, planning and evaluation of coaching sessions.

Guidelines for getting the most from your diary are as follows:

- Complete the diary soon after the coaching session.
- Write down what happened in order.
- Focus on what went well first.
- Describe what needs improvement.
- Action plan to develop what needs to be improved.

The benefits of diaries are that they can show progress over a period of time and are usually honest and describe how you felt about a situation at that time.

Performance profiles

If a trampolinist is not performing a somersault correctly or is not coping with the physical demands of the sport, the coach or trainer can design a suitable exercise or coaching programme. But what if the trampolinist has trouble with their nerves before the start of the competition, or they have some kind of mental block that stops them from executing a skill?

Although not always obvious, the following psychological factors can affect sporting performance:

- confidence: belief in yourself and your abilities
- concentration: the ability to attend to relevant cues, not being distracted
- control: the extent to which you feel able to influence events
- commitment: the level to which you apply yourself
- re-focusing after errors: the ability to adjust to negative outcomes in a positive way
- enjoyment: the amount of fun that you can have.

To use a performance profile you would talk with the performer and ask them to tell you how they feel about their sport. Do they ever feel anxious, and if so, when? Do they understand the terms above and if so, how do they rate them?

In Table 16.2, a performer has been asked to rate out of ten the importance of each of the factors and then rate their own proficiency in that factor.

It seems that the performer's main emphasis for any intervention should be focused on the areas that they identify as a weakness, in this case re-focusing after errors and concentration.

Key term

Intervention: an interruption that brings about change (in sporting performance).

In the same way, coaches can adapt this approach and apply it to their own coaching (as in the example below).

Observation and analysis

It is possible to be observed and analysed by your team or club mates, your coach and yourself, particularly if you have access to a video of your performance.

Interviews

It is possible to get a great deal of information from an interview. You could ask a performer about what

Performance factors	Importance to performer	Self-assessment
Confidence	9	9
Commitment	10	10
Concentration	9	6
Control	9	8
Re-focusing after error	10	6
Enjoyment	7	9

Table 16.2 Factors and proficiency

Strengths	Weaknesses
A good relaxed swing Excellent body positioning in relation to the ball A low-risk safety-first approach	Not accurate with driving clubs Putting is inconsistent Poor technique in short iron game (head up too early)
Opportunities	Threats
Short game practice has improved in recent weeks Has learned how to mentally rehearse Opponent has no knowledge of the course	Can be prone to getting annoyed easily and letting it spoil their game Environment – windy day Opponent is a better player

Table 16.3 SWOT analysis of a golfer

they consider to be their strengths and weaknesses, or you could ask them about what tactics they might use against a particular opponent.

SWOT analysis

This is a subjective analysis of a performance or a performer's ability. Table 16.3 shows an example of a SWOT analysis carried out on a golfer.

Simulation or conditioned practice

This is about artificially creating a competition-like situation in a practice session, or a particular condition that may be likely to happen in a competitive situation. A basketball coach might consider the merits of initially removing defenders, or outnumbering them in a practice situation that is aimed at improving a particular attacking focus. Defenders

Coaching factors	Importance to coach	Self-assessment
Planning & preparation	9	9
Needs of participants considered	10	10
Technical progression & sequencing	9	6
Health & safety observed	9	8
Goals defined at start of session	10	6
Technically accurate instructions/demonstrations	7	9
Appropriate content & structure		
Variety of drills		
Monitored progress		
Skills related to game situation		
Errors identified & corrected		
Control & behaviour of group		
Time management		
De-brief & feedback to participants		
Checked player understanding		
Stopped & brought group together		
Evaluated against objectives set		
Made provisions for future planning		

Table 16.4 Assessment of factors for coaching

can be added when the techniques are well practised. Or, conversely, extra defenders could be added so that the attacking technique could be practised under greater pressure. Similarly, defenders in these practices could be asked to take one of three roles according to the conditions required by the coach:

- passive, offering little resistance other than presence
- active, playing under normal conditions, tempo, intensity
- pressure, playing with extra intensity.

Conditioned games are used when a coach wants to create a situation that is likely to happen in a game, such as practising defending free kicks in football. Or simply adding a condition that emphasises a teaching point, such as choosing a target area on a tennis court with a chalk circle or hoop where the player is expected to return the balls in a practice drill.

Video analysis

Video gives the person who watches it an objective record of a performance. The greatest benefit of video is the playback feature, including slow motion, which can be used to demonstrate skill execution, tactical efficiency or a more general generic performance evaluation.

Here are some guidelines on the use of video analysis in sport:

- Do not try to film your performers and coach them at the same time. Ask someone reliable to do the filming and brief them on what you want – follow the player or the ball, try to capture tactics or specific techniques, etc.
- Try to pick up all of the sound as it can provide useful feedback.
- Start the recording before the action and end it well after, judging players' body language before and after performance.
- Label and date the film immediately, to keep a record.

Notation

Notation is a way of collecting data and can be done by hand or with a computer. Hand notation is a system of recording detailed analysis of a sport and literally noting the data on a sheet of paper using a predefined set of symbols. Systems like this exist for many sports, such as tennis, archery and football.

The advantage of these systems is that they are inexpensive and, if completed by a skilful recorder, will produce quick information in real time, so that the coach or performer can have instant access to detailed information. The main disadvantages of this system are that it is open to human error, can be difficult to interpret and can be difficult in certain conditions such as bad weather.

On the next page there is an example of a match analysis sheet for a team sport. This could be filled in by the performer, a peer or a neutral observer, scoring 1 to 10 for both achieved and target scores.

Key learning points 2

- Coaches can make good use of reflective diaries in order to improve their coaching performance.
- Performance profiles can be used for performers and coaches alike.
- Coaches are expected to make interventions to improve performance, having identified areas for development.
- Coaches can condition games to facilitate the teaching of a specific skill or tactic.

Q Quick quiz 2

Which coaching techniques are the following sentences a description of?

(a) Watching the individual performing skills.

(b) Identifying strengths and weaknesses.

(c) Recording data about performance by hand or using a computer package.

(d) Getting a performer to rate different aspects of their performance out of 10.

(e) Creating similar conditions to those of competition.

Possible answers:

SWOT analysis, performance profiling, observation, simulation, notational analysis.

Student activity 16.2 — 45 minutes — P3 M3 D2

Techniques used by a sports coach

Fill out the following table to show your understanding of different techniques used by coaches.

Coaching technique	Describe the techniques used by coaches to improve the performance of athletes	Explain the techniques used by coaches to improve the performance of athletes	Evaluate the techniques used by coaches to improve the performance of athletes
Observation analysis			
Performance profiling			
Coaching diaries			

16.4 Plan a coaching session

P4

Planning can be separated into the following stages:

- collecting and reviewing relevant information
- identifying participant needs
- goal setting
- identifying appropriate resources
- identifying appropriate activities to enable goals to be achieved
- planning coaching sessions and/or programmes.

Before you coach any session you need to answer the following questions:

- What is the starting point, what are their skill levels, who are they?
- Where do they want to be and what do they want from you?
- How will you achieve this?
- What will you need to do this – facilities, equipment, etc.?
- How will you/they know if they have improved?

To plan an effective coaching session or programme of sessions, the coach needs to establish:

- the number of participants, as this will affect the kinds of practices that the coach can employ
- the age of participants, as this will affect the kinds of practices that the coach can use, and even how they might approach coaching that group
- the level of experience and ability of the participants
- whether the participants have any special

requirements relating to diet, health, culture or language.

An example of a session planner is reproduced in Table 16.5.

Setting SMART goals

It is a good idea to use the SMART principle when planning your sessions or season.

Key terms

Specific: this means that the session meets what you want it to meet, and is specific to the sport. For example, you could focus a cricket batting session on dealing with short-pitched, fast deliveries, thus being explicit and specific.

Measurable: this is the way in which you measure your results. If you have identified that you want to improve a basketball player's jump shooting, then you might measure this by counting how many shots are successful in a training or game situation and then measure again after the training programme.

Achievable: what you set out to improve must be possible. It would not be fair to ask a beginner in trampolining to complete a complicated routine with multiple somersaults.

Realistic: it must be possible and realistic to achieve what you intend to achieve.

Time-constrained: there should be a reasonable amount of time to achieve the learning goal. Some goals will be short term in nature and established to be achieved in the next session, others more long term and established for the entire season.

Session planner	
Date	Venue
Time	Duration
Group	No. of participants
Equipment required	Aims of session
Safety checks required	
TIME	CONTENT
	Warm-up
	Fitness work
	Main technical skills work
	Game play/tactical work
	Cool-down
Injuries/issues arising	
Evaluation of session	

Table 16.5 Example of a session planner

Health and safety

The health and safety of all involved in sport should be the most important of the coach's considerations. In most cases it is necessary to ensure that facilities and equipment are safe and well maintained, and that performers are adequately aware of key health and safety issues, particularly relating to their own safety and the safety of others.

Coaches should consider the following as a checklist, though it is by no means exhaustive.

- The context in which the sport will take place – the facilities and equipment. Does the provider have a normal operating procedure and emergency action plan? This should cover number of players allowed, coach:learner ratio, conduct and supervision, hazardous behaviours, fire and evacuation procedures.
- The nature of the sport, for playing and training:
  - what to do when rules are not observed
  - what to do with injured players
  - not teaching activities beyond the capabilities of the performers
  - in competitive situations, matching performers where appropriate by size, maturity or age.
- The players:
  - are you aware of any special individual medical

needs, and the types of injuries common to the sport?
  - safety education – informing players of inherent risks and establishing a code of behaviour
  - teammates and opponents to be aware of their responsibilities to each other
  - players should be discouraged from participating with an existing injury.
- The coach:
  - safe practices
  - safe numbers for the area
  - arranging appropriate insurance
  - dealing with and reporting accidents
  - being aware of emergency actions.

Risk assessments

Risk assessments are not just forms to fill out. A risk assessment is a skill that helps prevent accidents or serious events. You need to consider what could go wrong and how likely it is.

Risk assessments should be kept and logged, and stored in a safe place. Examples of risk assessments for sporting activities are wide ranging and will depend upon who they are prepared for, the nature of the sport and the competence of the person making the assessment.

Contingency planning

Nothing ever goes completely to plan and for that reason it is good practice to plan for the unexpected so that everyone remains safe and continues to learn. Consider the following as examples of what can happen and what you could plan for.

- Weather threatens your outside session.
- You fall ill and are no longer able to continue as coach.
- There are not enough participants for the session.
- The facility is double-booked when you arrive for the session.
- The group is not responding to your style of coaching or the practices that you have chosen.

The components of a session

While the demands of the structure of sessions for different sports are quite different, the general rules for the layout of sessions are common to all sports.

Student activity 16.3　　45 minutes　P4

Planning a coaching session

Using the session planner provided, plan a sports coaching session for a group or individual of your choice.

16.5 Deliver a coaching session

P5　P6　M4　M5　D3

This is concerned with the actual 'doing' part of coaching, and will help with the principles of coaching sessions.

Like the planning of a session, delivering a session follows a logical path.

- Ensure the session plan fits all.
- Identify any risks to the delivery of the session.
- Introduce and start planned activities.
- Manage the behaviour of all involved.
- Monitor and adapt the session as it progresses.
- Summarise and conclude the coaching session.

Once the session is under way, the coach should work to maintain what is going well, and the role of the coach changes to become more of a manager/supervisor.

Skills should be introduced, followed by an explanation which could help performers understand their relevance and when they could be used in a competitive situation.

A competent demonstration should follow, which could be from the coach or with the aid of a video model. This must be a technically correct example and should be thorough, without too much expla-nation. There should be a balance between verbal instruction and visual demonstration. There will also need to be a balance between activity, instruction and discussion depending on the age, experience and maturity of performers. It is essential for the coach to note the differing rates of learning of individuals.

Performers will then need time to practise the skill or technique. Coaches can use questions to check understanding. The role of the coach changes again to become one of observer/analyst, and it is here that the coach will be looking to assist learners and correct any faults.

To improve performance the coach must have highly developed awareness relating to how to identify errors, compare to a perfect model example and, most importantly, knowledge of how to bridge the gap using feedback, observation and application of a range of suitable techniques.

There is no substitute for practice at this stage. A session that is continually interrupted by a coach for whatever reason is less likely to be successful. It is also important that a coach does not attempt too much in one session.

Most coaches enjoy this part of the coaching process the most, but it is too easy to forget what the aims of the session are and how to keep track of achievement.

Reviewing a session

It is important to consider that coaching does not finish at the end of a session when everyone has cooled down or even gone home. Coaching is a continuous process, and the best coaches reflect on what happened and, more importantly, how to improve. A well-considered evaluation should aid the improvement of subsequent sessions.

The process is as follows:

- Collect, analyse and review – information about the session from feedback, self-reflection and from others.
- Session effectiveness – identify the effectiveness of the session in achieving objectives.
- Review key aspects – drills or practices.
- Identify development needs and take steps to action them.

When evaluating a session a coach should consider the following:

- Performance against pre-set goals: effective coaches will be familiar with the goals for the season, both long and short term. There should be an opportunity to decide to what extent, if at all,

the session objectives were met and to what extent this matched the other goals.
- Participants' progress: the review will enable coaches to monitor the performer's progress over a period of time, and help plan for future sessions. Typical review questions could be:
  - How well did the performers learn the skills or techniques introduced to them?
  - What performance developments were evident for each participant?
  - Are the performers ready to progress to the next session?
- Coaching ability: this is the part where the coach can review their own performance:
  - What went well?
  - What went less well?
  - How did the performers respond?
  - Were the performers bored or restless?
  - Did the coach behave acceptably?
- Future targets: this is all about planning for future goals and objectives based on achievements and progress made by participants.

Tools for the review process

There are a number of tools that coaches can use.

- Videos – an excellent way of improving your coaching effectiveness. Videos can be used to judge coaching actions, interaction with your performers, facial expressions and gestures, as well as what you say.
- Critical analysis and self-reflection – self-reflection allows you to explore your perceptions, decisions and subsequent actions to work out ways in which performers can improve technical, tactical or physical ability.
- A mentor – a mentor coach can help provide you with a role-model figure who can offer you practical solutions, work as a sounding board and generally provide you with a range of support.
- Coaching diaries – these can act as a permanent source of information to record your thoughts and feelings, and serve as a true account of what happened and when. Diaries or logs can certainly help with self-reflection and form the basis of action plans for improvement.

Formative and summative reviews

A formative review occurs during the process of coaching and changes can be made immediately. A summative review is done at the end of the coaching session as you reflect on the process overall.

Student activity 16.4 ⏱ 45 minutes P5 P6 M4 M5 D3

Delivering a sports session

Part 1

Once you have planned your session, arrange with your tutor when you are going to deliver your session.

Part 2

When you have delivered your coaching, you need to carry out a review of the planning and delivery of the session in the following manner:

1 Gain as much feedback/information as you can about the planning and delivery of your session by asking open questions to:

- the participants in your session
- your tutor
- other people who were observing your session.

You want to find out what was good and what was not so good about your session.

Then think deeply about your session and the parts that you thought were good and not so good.

2 What will you ask them about? The more specific you can be in your questioning, the better information you will receive and the more you will learn.

First, ask them:

- whether the aims and objectives of the session were met

- what parts went particularly well
- what parts went particularly badly.

Then, ask them about the skills you used to coach during the session:

- communication
- organisation
- observation
- decision-making
- time management.

3 Once you have gained the information to achieve a pass you need to identify the strengths and weaknesses of your session.

To achieve a merit you need to dig a bit deeper and think about what it was about each of these factors that made it a strength or a weakness. For example, if you felt your communication was good, what was it about your communication that was good? Did you use the right tone of voice, did you explain things well, did you use language that was appropriate? When you have evaluated all your strengths and weaknesses, you can then make suggestions about how you could improve your performance for the next session.

To achieve a distinction you need to justify the improvements you have suggested and say how they will improve the skills that you felt needed improving.

Further reading

Crisfield, P. (2001) *Analysing Your Coaching*, Coachwise.

Gordon, D.A. (2009) *Coaching Science*, Exeter: Learning Matters.

Martens, R. (2004) *Successful Coaching*, Human Kinetics.

Miles, A. (2004) *Coaching Practice*, Coachwise.

Useful websites

www.brianmac.co.uk/
Contain many resources for coaching a wide variety of sports

www.sportscoachuk.org
Provides resources such as details of vacancies, teaching tips and research articles specifically for sports coaches; free registration necessary for full access

17 & 18: Practical Individual & Team Sports

17.1 Introduction

Sport and sports participation are on the increase in the UK. Sport has many purposes: to improve health, for enjoyment and the natural human urge to compete among others. There are many different types of sports, and this unit includes details of how to improve your performance in sport and your knowledge of the rules and regulations, as well as the ways in which you can measure and assess performance.

By the end of this unit you should:

- be able to use a range of skills, techniques and tactics in selected team and/or individual sports
- understand the rules and regulations of selected team and/or individual sports
- be able to assess your own performance in selected team and/or individual sports
- be able to assess the performance of a team in two selected team sports or other individuals in selected individual sports
- be able to use a range of skills, techniques and tactics in selected team and individual sports.

This unit combines units 17 & 18 as per the Edexcel specification.

Assessment and grading criteria		
To achieve a PASS grade the evidence must show that the learner is able to:	**To achieve a MERIT grade the evidence must show that, in addition to the pass criteria, the learner is able to:**	**To achieve a DISTINCTION grade the evidence must show that, in addition to the pass and merit criteria, the learner is able to:**
P1 describe skills, techniques and tactics required in two different team/individual sports	**M1** explain skills, techniques and tactics required in two different team/individual sports	
P2 describe the rules and regulations of two different team/individual sports, and apply them to three different situations for each sport	**M2** explain the application of the rules and regulations, of two different team/individual sports, in three different situations for each sport	
P3 demonstrate appropriate skills, techniques and tactics in two different team/individual sports		
P4 carry out a self-analysis using two different methods of assessment, identifying strengths and areas for improvement in two different team/individual sports	**M3** explain identified strengths and areas for improvement in two different team/individual sports, and make suggestions relating to personal development	**D1** analyse identified strengths and areas for improvement in two different team/individual sports, and justify suggestions made
P5 carry out a performance analysis using two different methods of assessment, identifying strengths and areas for improvement in the development of a team/an individual in a team/individual sport.	**M4** explain identified strengths and areas for improvement in the development of a team/an individual in a team/individual sport, and make suggestions relating to development of a team.	**D2** analyse identified strengths and areas for improvement in the development of a team/an individual in a team/individual sport, and justify suggestions made.

17.2 Team and Individual Sports

P1 **P3** **M1**

Team sports are those in which two or more players compete together with a single aim. They include sports such as football, rugby, netball and lacrosse.

Individual sports are those in which the competitor usually competes on their own and is solely responsible for their own actions. These include sports such as gymnastics, judo, trampolining and golf.

Sports can be further classified as follows:

● **Invasion sports**: games such as football, netball, basketball and rugby, where the object of the sport is to invade the opponent's territory

Fig 17.1 Netball is an example of an invasion sport

● **Court sports**: non-contact sports because opponents are normally on opposite sides of a net, such as badminton, volleyball and tennis
● **Target sports**: involve the use of marksmanship and include golf and archery
● **Striking/fielding**: games with a batting and a fielding team, and include cricket and rounders
● **Martial arts**: these come from different ancient fighting methods, many of which originated in the Far East, such as judo, taekwon do and karate
● **Water sports**: activities undertaken on or in water, including swimming, sailing and water polo
● **Athletic sports**: take place on track or field
● **Field sports**: hunting sports associated with the outdoors, such as shooting and fishing.

Fig 17.2 Taekwon do – an example of a martial art

Skills and Techniques in Team and Individual Sports

A skill is the ability to do something well and requires lots of practice. Technique is a way of undertaking a particular skill. If a basketball player is able to perform a jump-shot well, it is said that they have a good technique in playing the shot.

There are many shared skills in different team sports, and having the awareness and ability to undertake them will be an advantage to your team. They include:

● Passing – moving the ball around your teammates
● Receiving – being able to receive a pass from a teammate
● Shooting – aiming at a specific target, such as a goal or a basket
● Dribbling – moving around with the ball
● Throwing – there are many ways of throwing an object, normally specific to the sport being played
● Intercepting – this is where a player stops the ball from reaching its intended place; this could be through a block or a tackle
● Creating space – this means moving away from opponents so that you are in a position in which you can receive a pass or create a shooting opportunity.

In addition to the skills and techniques required of a sport, players may also be judged on other criteria, such as their performance over the duration of a game.

All sports are made up of a range of specific skills. In tennis there are a number of different shots that you can play at different times during a game. Playing these effectively will allow you to win points. They include:

● Forehand drive with spin variation
● Forehand volley
● Service
● Lob
● Smash
● Return of service.

Tactics

Tactics in sport are usually focused directly or indirectly on winning. Tactics can depend on the opposition, players of the other team or opponents, the importance of the competition and maybe the weather. Tactics can be:

● Pre-event tactics – a particular plan before the event
● In-event tactics – a plan implemented during the game, such as switching from man-to-man to zone defence in basketball.

Tactics can fail if the opposition work them out too easily, if the tactic is employed too late or if the player or players are simply not able to understand or execute the necessary tactic(s).

Consider the range of options that a tennis player has at their disposal. First, where should they stand while waiting for their opponent's return? If the ball is likely to come over the net in the middle and low, then the player might consider standing close to the net to make a volley. In this way, the player has selected a tactical position and shot selection. The same player might also consider serving the ball to the forehand or backhand of their opponent, some with spin, some without and some faster than others. This is known as variation.

If the conditions of the match are that the player is losing, that player might start to play defensive shots in an attempt to prevent them from falling further behind.

Tactics can include playing precise formations against specific opponents. Football teams may play more defensively away from home and opt to play with more defending players rather than strikers. In certain sports, opposing players may be marked to stop them having a positive effect for their team.

Other tactics may include working on specific set plays, such as line-outs in rugby, and corners and free kicks in football.

In order to improve your performance, it is a good idea to actually watch yourself perform the skill. Ask a friend or coach to video you while you perform a set skill. You can then analyse your performance and see what you are doing. You may be surprised and realise your body is not doing what you thought it was! You will then need to amend the skill, practise it and video yourself again, to check that you are now performing the skill properly.

Key learning points 1

● Sports can be classified as:
  – Invasion games
  – Court sports
  – Target sports
  – Striking/fielding
  – Martial arts
  – Water sports
  – Field sports.
● A skill is the ability to perform something well.
● Techniques are a way of undertaking a particular skill.
● A tactic is a plan of action to achieve a goal.
● Team and individual sports are different, not just in terms of numbers, but also in terms of the skills and techniques to be developed and assessed.

Quick quiz 1

1 Place the following sports into their correct classification:
  (a) Tennis.
  (b) Judo.
  (c) Clay-pigeon shooting.
  (d) Windsurfing.
  (e) 400 m running.
  (f) Shot put.
  (g) Squash.
  (h) Lacrosse.
  (i) Curling.
  (j) Mountain biking.

2 What skills do you need to perform well for your favourite sport?

3 Name three different tactics used in your favourite sport.

Student activity 17.1 — 60 minutes — P1 M1

Select two individual or two team sports for the following tasks.

Task 1

Draw a spidergram for two sports which illustrates the skills, techniques and tactics required for each.

Task 2

Write a report that describes and explains the skills, techniques and tactics for each of your two selected sports.

Task 3

Take part in your two selected sports and demonstrate appropriate skills, techniques and tactics in each sport.

17.3. Rules and Regulations

P2 M2

The rules and regulations of any sport are normally set and amended by its national governing body (NGB) and international sports federations (ISFs). These are set to ensure that the sport is played fairly and that the opponents are aware of how to win.

International sports federations and national governing bodies may change the rules and regulations periodically, as they look to improve the sport. For example, FIBA, the international governing body for basketball, meets every four years at a world congress, with a view to changing or clarifying rules to the benefit of the sport.

Time

Many team sports have time constraints and are split into periods of play:

● Ice hockey has three periods of 20 minutes.
● Basketball has four periods of 10 minutes.
● Rugby union has two halves of 40 minutes.

Usually the team with the most points or goals is declared the winner, and if the scores are tied, the game is normally declared a draw. For sports like rugby and football, the timing is described as real time, since the start and finish times are exact (except for added time), whereas basketball and ice hockey are played in artificial time, because the game clock is stopped on a regular basis for a variety of reasons, meaning that the whole of the running game time is spent on the court/field of play.

In some sports, a winner can be declared before the allocated time has elapsed. Often in test match cricket, a team will have bowled out a team twice and

scored the required number of runs before the five days are completed.

Few individual sports are constrained by time, the outcome of the event usually being determined by the success of the competition, and usually by accruing points to a critical point.

Scoring

Each sport has a different scoring system, with the team or individual with the most points usually being declared the winner. An exception to this is golf, where the player who has taken the fewest strokes is the winner. Scoring may include putting the ball into a goal in football and handball.

Facilities and Equipment

Specific sports require certain facilities to enable play to take place. Different surfaces can be used for different sports, and often sports are played on a range of surfaces. Tennis is a good example, as it can be played on grass, clay and hard surfaces, and can be played inside or outdoors. Occasionally, rules may be adapted for sports played on different surfaces.

Many sports require the participants to wear or use specialist equipment. In football, the laws of the game insist that all players must wear shin guards to protect their lower legs. In sports such as hockey, rugby and cricket, players may wear specific equipment to reduce the risk of injury. This could include arm guards, helmets and padding.

You can find the rules and regulations of each sport via its national governing body. The NGB looks after many aspects of a sport, including organising major competitions, running coaching schemes and dealing with the development of the sport at all levels.

Unwritten Rules and Etiquette

Unwritten rules cover those situations in sports where the normal rules of the sport are unclear or require the discretion or cooperation of the competitors. Examples include the following:

- **Football**: when a player appears to be injured, the opposition often put the ball out of play, and in an act of fair play the other team returns the ball to its generous opponents.
- **Fencing**: points in fencing are scored when an opponent strikes another. In a fast-moving sport, the electronic scoring apparatus can misinterpret an inaccurate contact, such as the blade contacting the floor. Sporting opponents often either concede the point or suggest that the contact was not eligible for scoring.
- **Cricket**: a batsman can choose to 'walk' on appeal. In other words, if a fielder appeals for a dismissal decision, the batsman can choose to walk from the field of play, effectively admitting that they were out.
- **Golf**: players can 'give' competitors shots, usually when their opponent's ball is very close to the hole. In doing so, they allow them to score that shot without actually playing it.

Officials

Officials in sport have wide-ranging roles and duties, including football fourth officials, trampoline judges, athletics markers, cycle marshals, netball umpires and cricket third umpires. The role of these officials varies in terms of their physical nature, their proximity to the event and the support that they receive from their co-officials.

Playing Surfaces

The amount and type of surfaces played on in sports are many and varied. While some surfaces can be used for a variety of sports, others are more specialised. The level of competition can also have a bearing. Artificial surfaces come in many varieties – with rubber crumbs or sand drainage.

Fig 17.4 Playing tennis on clay

Situations

Rules and regulations are often used to describe what should be done in certain situations, such as what to do if a player handles the ball in football, or when a ball is out of bounds in golf. Where rules are broken, officials have a predetermined course of action and a penalty may follow.

Football Rules

Football rules are known as the 'laws of the game'. There are 17 laws, which have changed marginally over the years. The international sports federation, FIFA, adapts them as it considers necessary. Recent examples of this include changing the offside law to encourage more attacking football.

The following is a summary of the 17 laws:

- **Field of play**: this law looks at the surface, dimensions, layout and markings of the football pitch.
- **Ball**: the shape and dimensions of the football are covered, as well as replacing the ball should it burst during a match.

Fig 17.3 A cricket umpire indicating a leg bye during a match

- **Number of players**: there should be 11 players at the start of a match, including a designated goalkeeper; the use of substitutions is also looked at.
- **Players' equipment**: the health and safety considerations of what players wear is mentioned. No jewellery should be worn and all players must wear shin guards. The goalkeeper must also wear a top that distinguishes him from the other players.
- **Referee**: this law looks at the responsibilities of the referee, which include enforcing the laws, taking responsibility for the safety of the players, acting as a timekeeper, punishing serious offences and providing a match report to the relevant authority.
- **Assistant referees**: assistant referees assist the referee to control the game, signalling when the ball goes out of play and any offences that the referee may miss.
- **Duration of the match**: a football match is played over two equal periods of 45 minutes. This time may be reduced for youth football. Time can be added for substitutions, injuries and time wasting, at the referee's discretion.
- **Start & restart of play**: the team that wins the toss of a coin can choose which goal they want to attack. The game starts with a kick-off, where all players must be in their own half of the pitch; this method is also used after a goal has been scored.
- **Ball in & out of play**: the ball is out of play when the whole ball crosses one of the perimeter lines or when the referee blows his whistle to stop play.
- **Method of scoring**: the rule states that a goal is scored when the ball crosses the line between the posts and under the crossbar. The team with the most goals wins.
- **Offside**: a player is offside if 'he is nearer to his opponent's goal line than both the ball and the second last opponent' and receives a pass from one of his teammates. The player also needs to be in his opponent's half and interfering with the game. However, you cannot be offside if you receive the pass from a goal kick or throw-in.
- **Fouls & misconduct**: fouls and misconduct are penalised by either a direct or indirect free kick. There are ten offences that result in a direct free kick, including kicking, tripping or pushing an opponent. Indirect free kicks are given for infringements such as a goalkeeper picking up a back pass or throw-in, or for impeding an opponent. Direct free kicks are given for offences that are committed by a player in their own penalty box and are awarded as a penalty kick.
- **Free kicks**: following a foul, a free kick is awarded, which will be either direct or indirect. Opponents

must be a minimum of ten yards away from the ball. A direct free kick shot directly into the opponent's goal will be awarded a goal, while a goal can be scored from an indirect free kick only if it has touched another player before going into the goal. A referee will signal an indirect free kick by raising one arm into the air above their head.

- **Penalty kick**: awarded when an offence is committed by a player in their own penalty area. The goalkeeper must remain on their line until the ball has been kicked. A penalty taker cannot touch the ball until it has touched another player if they miss.
- **Throw-in**: the ball is thrown back on to the pitch when the ball goes out of play on either side of the pitch. A throw-in is taken with two hands on the ball and the ball must be released from behind the player's head.
- **Goal kick**: the ball is kicked back into play from within the goal area when the ball crosses the goal line and was last touched by an attacking player. The ball must leave the penalty area before it can be played again.
- **Corner kick**: a corner is awarded when the ball crosses the goal line and was last touched by a defending player. The kick is taken from within the corner arc. A goal can be scored direct from a corner kick.

The FA has set a number of regulations to help the running of football in England. Regulations are rules controlled by the organising bodies. The FA has included regulations on:

- The control of youth football
- The doping control programme
- Disciplinary procedures.

Key learning points 2

- Rules are established and controlled by national governing bodies (NGBs), such as the Rugby Football Union (RFU).
- Sports can be played in real time, like one-day cricket, or in artificial time, like basketball.
- Unwritten rules are situations that can occur when players and officials can choose to demonstrate fair play.
- Governing bodies are responsible for any necessary changes to rules or changes to interpretations of rules.

Student activity 17.2   60–90 mins   P2   M2

Select two team or two individual sports of your choice to carry out the following:

- List the rules and regulations of each of your selected sports.
- Describe and explain the rules and their application for each of your two selected sports.

- Demonstrate your ability to apply these rules in three different situations for each of your selected sports.

Q Quick quiz 2

1 Name three sports that take more than one day to complete.
2 Name three sports that can be completed in two hours.
3 Describe why sports need rules.
4 Give four examples of where you have witnessed fair play.
5 Name six different types of playing surfaces.
6 Give the name for the leading official(s) in the following sports (e.g. for football, it is referee).
   (a) Tennis.
   (b) Netball.
   (c) Athletics.
   (d) Gymnastics.

17.4 Assessing Own and Other People's Performance in a Team or Individual Sport

P4   P5   M3   M4   D1

D2

Performance Assessment

Performances can all be assessed. Assessment should always be conducted with a view to improve future performances.

Some assessors try to correct errors in performance by simply shouting instructions, like 'You are not trying hard enough' or 'Get more aim on your shot' in basketball. These instructions give the sportsperson an idea of what they should be doing, but not how to achieve this. To analyse techniques from a coach's viewpoint, it is important to:

- Sort the effective techniques from the less effective
- Break down complete movements into simple parts
- Concentrate on the techniques that need the most improvement, in the right order.

There are many different factors to consider when evaluating a team's or individual's performance:

- How well do they perform specific skills?
- Are they using the correct techniques?
- Are they using appropriate tactics?
- Are they successful at employing these tactics?

There are several ways in which to assess performance:

- Assessment can be completed by the individual, known as self-assessment.
- Peer assessment is the assessment of an individual or a group of individuals on performance.
- Other observers could be teachers, coaches or judges.

Here are some key terms in assessing performance:

- **Observation** – watching sporting performances
- **Analysis** – deciding what has happened
- **Evaluation** – the end-product of observation and analysis, where decisions are made and feedback is given to the performer
- **Qualitative analysis** – largely subjective, meaning that it is open to personal interpretation and is therefore subject to bias or error; the more knowledge the observer has, the more valid the observations
- **Quantitative analysis** – more involved and scientific, and involves the direct measurement of a performance or technique; match statistics recorded while the game is in progress are called 'real-time', while match statistics recorded after the events are called 'lapsed-time' analysis.

There are a number of methods of assessment that can be used to assess performance.

Video Analysis

Video gives the person who watches it an objective record of a performance. The greatest benefit of video is the playback feature, including slow motion, which can be used to demonstrate skill execution, tactical efficiency or a more general generic performance evaluation.

Here are some guidelines on the use of video analysis:

● Do not try to film your performers and coach them at the same time. Ask someone reliable to do the filming, and brief them on what you want – follow the player or the ball, try to capture tactics or specific techniques, and so on.
● Try to pick up all the sound, as it can provide useful feedback.
● Start the recording before the action and end it well after, judging players' body language before and after performance.
● Label and date the film immediately to keep a record.

Table 17.1 is an example of a match analysis sheet for a team sport. This could be filled in by the performer, a peer or a neutral observer, scoring 1 to 10 for both achieved and target scores.

Notation

Notation is a way of collecting data and can be done by hand or with a computer.

Hand notation is a system of recording detailed analysis of a sport and literally noting the data on a sheet of paper using a predefined set of symbols.

Systems like this exist for many sports, such as tennis, archery and football.

The advantage of these systems is that they are inexpensive and, if completed by a skilful recorder, produce quick information in real time, so that the coach or performer can have instant access to detailed information. The main disadvantages of this system are that it is open to human error, can be difficult to interpret and can be difficult in certain conditions, such as bad weather.

Figure 17.5 gives an example of a profile of a hockey player's skills and techniques. The darker column is the assessment of the level of performance by the performer, and the lighter column is the assessment of the level of performance as identified by the coach.

If you look at the results, it is clear that there are differences in opinion as to level of performance. It is important that, if there are such differences, the coach and performer discuss the issues and decide on what needs development in practice and game situations and how that can be achieved.

Technology in Performance Analysis

As video and sound technology improve, new software packages have been developed that can analyse all physical activities. Packages such as Kandle and Dartfish are capable of producing a range of exciting analysis tools, including:

● Video delay systems
● Distance and angle measurement
● Overlays and comparators that compare other performances
● Multi-frame sequencing that breaks down complex skills
● Drawing and annotation tools.

Date	Opponent	Result	
		Mark	**Target**
Analysis area			
Positional play			
Tactical awareness/decision-making			
Fitness levels			
Skills/techniques			
Cooperation/teamwork			
Concentration/psychological factors			
Diet/nutrition			

Table 17.1 Match analysis of an individual sport

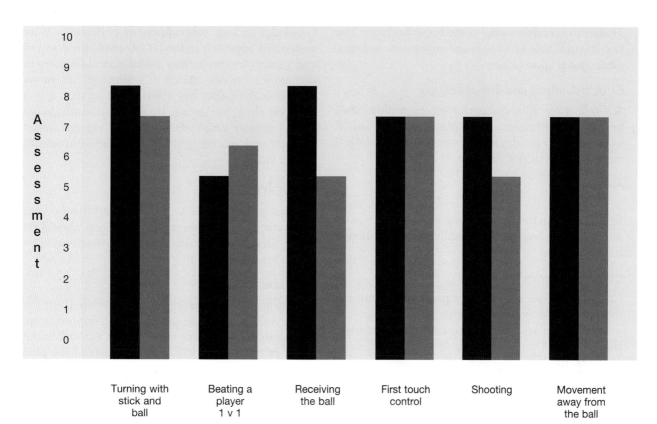

Fig 17.5 Profile of hockey player's skills & techniques

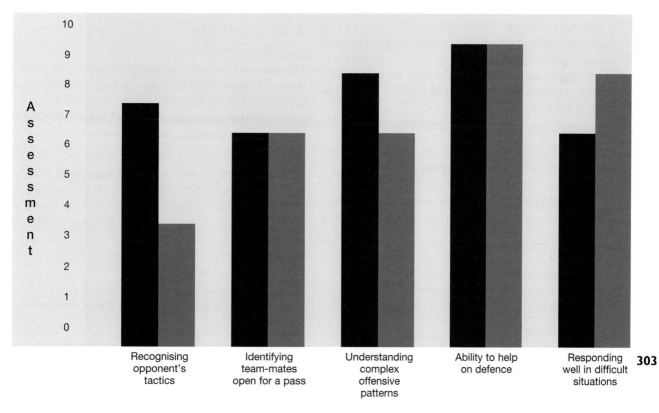

Fig 17.6 Profile of basketball player's skills & techniques

Thanks to ever decreasing costs, these packages have become available in schools and colleges, as well as at professional sports clubs.

Critical Analysis and Self-reflection

Self-reflection allows a performer to explore their perceptions, decisions and subsequent actions, to work out ways in which they can improve technical, tactical or physical ability.

A Mentor

A mentor should be someone who is a role-model figure, who can help provide practical solutions, work as a sounding board and generally provide a range of support.

Coaching Diaries

Coaching diaries can act as a permanent source of information to record thoughts and feelings, and serve as a true account of what happened and when. Diaries or logs can certainly help with self-reflection and form the basis of action plans for improvement.

SWOT Analysis

An example of a SWOT analysis carried out on a golfer is shown in Table 17.2.

Performance Profiling

Performance profiling is a method that can be used by a performer or, more typically, applied by a coach or observer. Put simply, it is an inventory of attributes, skills and techniques that form the basis of an assessment grading model.

Performance profiling can be used to analyse and record technical or tactical factors as well as psychological attributes.

Scouting

This is a process where an expert observer can identify either a talented individual or produce a report about an opponent. In the first case it could result in bringing a new player to a team to strengthen the existing squad. The second aspect – gaining knowledge of how your opponent performs – is an underused approach in the UK. A simple observation and a few notes can be very useful in deciding how to prepare for the next match. If a tennis player knows that their opponent has a fast, hard service, but is poor on their backhand, their preparation should have a greater emphasis on service returns under pressure and returning the ball to their opponent's weaker side.

Development

The last stage is what to do once performance has been assessed. In other words, what you should do about what you have discovered, be it strengths or points for improvement.

Aims and Objectives

Following analysis, it is important to collate the information relating to the performance improvement. Having done this, there needs to be an established set of priorities that will form the basis of the plan of action. These aims or objectives need to be the foundation of the targets to be set.

It is a good idea to use the SMART principle in designing an action plan. SMART stands for:

- **S**pecific
- **M**easurable
- **A**chievable
- **R**ealistic
- **T**ime-constrained.

Specific

This means that the action plan meets what you want it to meet. For example, instead of saying that attacking play is a technical weakness in football, you could say that running off the ball, pass completion and beating a defender are weaknesses.

Measurable

This is the way in which you measure your results. If you have identified that you want to improve a basketball player's jump-shooting, you might measure this by counting how many shots are successful in a

Strengths	Weaknesses
A good relaxed swing	Not accurate with driving clubs
Excellent body positioning in relation to the ball	Putting is inconsistent
A low-risk safety-first approach	Poor technique in short iron game (head up too early)
Opportunities	**Threats**
Short game practice has been improved recently	Can be prone to getting annoyed easily and letting it spoil their game
Has learnt how to mentally rehearse	Environment – windy day
Opponent has no knowledge of the course	Opponent is a better player

Table 17.2 An example of a SWOT analysis

training or game situation, and then measure again after additional training sessions.

Achievable

What you set out to improve must be possible. It would not be fair to ask a beginner in trampolining to complete a complicated routine with multiple somersaults.

Realistic

It must be possible and realistic to achieve what we intend to achieve.

Time-constrained

There should be a reasonable amount of time to complete an action plan or achieve a goal.

Key learning points 3

● Performances can be analysed by the performer themselves, their peers and observers such as coaches.
● Video capture and analysis is a very effective performance assessment tool, especially features like slow motion, freeze frame and video playback.
● SMART goals should be used to establish action points for the improvement of performance.

Student activity 17.3   90–120 mins   P4   P5   M3   M4

D1   D2

Task 1

Select two different methods of self-analysis, then carry out this self-analysis for two different individual or team sports of your choice.

Task 2

Write a report based on your self-analysis that identifies, explains and analyses identified strengths and areas for improvement. Where possible, try to make justified suggestions on your own personal development.

Task 3

Select two different methods of performance analysis, then carry out this analysis for an individual who is taking part in either two team or two individual sports.

Task 4

Write a report based on your performance analyses that identifies, explains and analyses identified strengths and areas for improvement. Where possible, try to make justified suggestions on the individual's personal development.

Further reading

Crisfield, P. (2001) *Analysing your Coaching*, Coachwise.

Galligan, F., Crawford, D. and Maskery, C. (2002) *Advanced PE for Edexcel, Teacher's Resource File*, Oxford: Heinemann.

Miles, A. (2004) *Coaching Practice*, Coachwise.

Stafford-Brown, J., Rea, S., Janaway, L. and Manley, C. (2006) *BTEC First Sport*, London: Hodder Arnold.

Useful websites

www.kidsexercise.co.uk/TeamSports.html
Online article that explains the benefits of playing team sports; also links to wider site that offers advice such as sports nutrition and free exercises (downloadable) for young people

http://news.bbc.co.uk/sport1/hi/academy/default.stm
Access to information and resources on a wide range of sports and sports skills

www.netfit.co.uk/previous.htm
Extensive range of exercise and training techniques, some sports specific, others more general

19: Outdoor & Adventurous Sports

19.1 Introduction

Outdoor and adventurous activities are very popular these days. Many of these activities require people to work as a team, which helps them to learn social skills and leadership skills.

The aim of this unit is to introduce outdoor and adventurous activities and to give tips for developing skills and techniques in these activities. The unit explores the organisation and range of provision for outdoor activities, including governing bodies and the places in which these sports can take place. As most outdoor and adventurous activities do involve an element of risk, safety considerations are also covered. The effect of these activities on the environment is also explored so that outdoor pursuits participants can be made aware of how to protect the environment and still enjoy their activities.

By the end of this unit you should:

- know about the organisation and provision of outdoor and adventurous activities
- know the safety and environmental considerations associated with outdoor and adventurous activities
- be able to participate in outdoor and adventurous activities
- be able to review own performance in outdoor and adventurous activities.

Assessment and grading criteria		
To achieve a PASS grade the evidence must show that the learner is able to:	To achieve a MERIT grade the evidence must show that, in addition to the pass criteria, the learner is able to:	To achieve a DISTINCTION grade the evidence must show that, in addition to the pass and merit criteria, the learner is able to:
P1 describe four different outdoor and adventurous activities, including their organisation and provision		
P2 describe safety considerations associated with four different outdoor and adventurous activities	**M1** explain safety considerations associated with four different outdoor and adventurous activities	
P3 describe environmental considerations associated with four different outdoor and adventurous activities	**M2** explain environmental considerations associated with four different outdoor and adventurous activities	**D1** evaluate the safety and environmental considerations associated with four different outdoor and adventurous activities
P4 demonstrate appropriate skills and techniques in two different outdoor and adventurous activities, with tutor support	**M3** independently demonstrate appropriate skills and techniques in two different outdoor and adventurous activities	
P5 carry out a review of own performance in outdoor and adventurous activities, identifying strengths and areas for improvement		
P6 design a development plan for improving own performance in outdoor and adventurous activities.	**M4** explain identified strengths and areas for improvement in own performance in outdoor and adventurous activities, and explain suggestions relating to development.	**D2** justify suggestions made relating to the development plan.

307

19.2 The Organisation and Provision of Outdoor and Adventurous Activities

Types of Outdoor and Adventurous Activities

Outdoor and adventurous activities normally take place in an outdoor rural environment and often contain an element of danger or risk. These activities can be placed into two main categories: land based and water based.

Land-Based Activities

As the name suggests, these types of outdoor and adventurous activities take place on land. Examples include the following:

- **Rock climbing**: this involves using a range of methods to climb vertical rock faces. Climbers use harnesses, ropes and safety equipment to help them climb.
- **Mountain walking**: this is the practice of hiking and navigating mountains. In Britain, the classification of a mountain is that it has to be 2,000 ft above sea level.

- **Caving**: caving involves exploring caves. It may involve some potholing, whereby the person has to manoeuvre their body through small passageways.
- **Orienteering**: this sport uses a map and compass to determine the correct travel route. It is often performed competitively, whereby people have to navigate across challenging terrain from point to point aiming to arrive at the finish first.
- **Mountain biking**: this is basically off-road cycling which uses specially designed mountain bikes. It can be performed recreationally or competitively.

Water-Based Activities

These sports are carried out in or on water. Types of water include the sea, rivers, canals and lakes. Activities include the following:

- **Canoeing**: people often mistake kayaking for canoeing. A canoe is an open-top boat and is usually paddled by kneeling up and using a single paddle.
- **Kayaking**: a kayak is similar to a canoe, except the paddler is fully enclosed, and uses a double-bladed paddle from a sitting position.
- **Windsurfing**: this is more correctly known as sailboarding. Windsurfing uses a small board and is powered by wind acting on a single sail, which is connected to the board via a flexible joint.
- **Sailing**: this is done in a wind-propelled boat. A rudder helps to steer the boat and a sail is used to harness the wind and propel the boat across the water.

Fig 19.1 Mountain biking

Fig 19.2 Kayaking

Student activity 19.1 ⏱ **30–40 mins** P1

Carry out research and investigate different types of land-based and water-based outdoor and adventurous activities. Make a list of five land-based and five water-based outdoor and adventurous activities that you would like to take part in and explain why.

National Governing Bodies

There are many providers of outdoor and adventurous activities in the UK. Most activities have their own governing bodies that are responsible for the activity in Great Britain.

The governing bodies promote their activity, liaise with other agencies to try to improve the access and availability of their activity and also offer personal development and coaching qualifications. Many governing bodies provide job opportunities either through coaching and educating or in administration.

The British Orienteering Federation

The British Orienteering Federation (BOF) is the official governing body for orienteering in the UK. Its responsibilities include overseeing development and coordinating a range of orienteering events.

The BOF has a national badge scheme, which awards badges on the basis of performance over a series of events. It also runs five coaching awards, which specialise in teaching orienteering in a range of different environments, and caters for beginners through to experts.

The British Canoe Union

Canoeing is the most popular water sport in the UK. The British Canoe Union (BCU) is the governing body for canoeing and kayaking in the UK, with a membership of 60,000. Its prime aim is to encourage and provide opportunities for people to participate in canoeing. The BCU is currently working on improving access to more rivers in England and Wales.

The BCU operates a widespread range of coaching and education courses. These courses are designed to ensure that coaches and participants are sufficiently prepared to take part in the sport and that the coaches have the relevant qualifications to instruct participants in all aspects of technique, skills and safety.

The Royal Yachting Association

The Royal Yachting Association (RYA) is Britain's national association for all forms of recreational and competitive boating. This includes sailing, motor cruising, sports boats, sailboarding, inland boating, powerboat racing and personal watercraft.

It helps to organise competitions and offers a range of training schemes. Around 185,000 people per year complete RYA training courses in 20 different countries. Other aims of the RYA include:

- To increase boating participation
- To promote safety while afloat
- To protect boaters' rights to enjoy their activity in a responsible way
- To achieve international competitive success.

Mountain Leader Training UK

Mountain Leader Training UK (MLTUK) is the coordinating body responsible for improving the nation's education and training in the skills required for leadership and instruction for safe rural walking, hill and mountain walking, rock and ice climbing, and other associated activities that take place in cliff and mountainous environments.

Where appropriate, MLTUK works in conjunction with other bodies to help their cause. MLTUK is the coordinating body for all mountain training schemes in Great Britain. It oversees the training and assessment of approximately 6,000 leaders, instructors and guides, and is the awarding body of the Mountaineering Instructor Award (summer), Mountaineering Instructor Certificate and European Mountain Leader Awards. MLTUK also has direct links with the mountaineering councils (the British Mountaineering Council, Mountaineering Council of Ireland and Mountaineering Council of Scotland), enabling the training schemes to support the needs of the sport as a whole.

The British Caving Association

The British Caving Association (BCA) is the governing body for underground exploration in the UK. It represents people with either a sporting interest or a scientific interest in caves. Some of its aims are to:

- Maintain and seek to improve access to caves and sites of special interest
- Seek to achieve a better public understanding of all matters to do with caves and caving
- Promote and advise on training, equipment, science and safety
- Promote and administer caver training
- Provide necessary services and information on behalf of cavers in general
- Organise and/or support meetings and events, including training, conservation, science and education.

Statutory Bodies

There are many organisations that have an effect on the running of outdoor and adventurous activities. Examples of these include the Countryside Agency, which is responsible for looking after the British countryside and running England's national parks.

National Parks

There are currently 12 national parks in England and Wales:

- The New Forest
- The Norfolk Broads
- Snowdonia

309

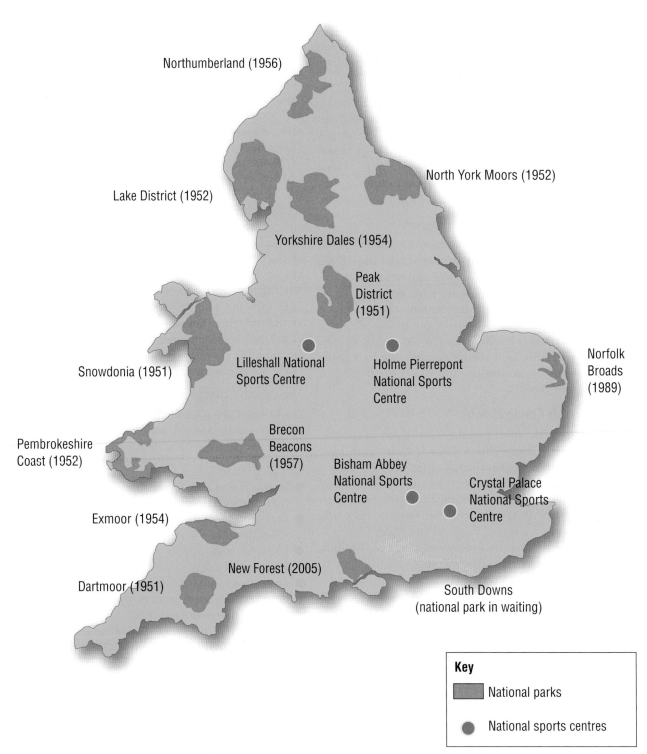

Northumberland (1956)

North York Moors (1952)

Lake District (1952)

Yorkshire Dales (1954)

Peak District (1951)

Lilleshall National Sports Centre

Holme Pierrepont National Sports Centre

Norfolk Broads (1989)

Snowdonia (1951)

Brecon Beacons (1957)

Pembrokeshire Coast (1952)

Bisham Abbey National Sports Centre

Crystal Palace National Sports Centre

Exmoor (1954)

New Forest (2005)

Dartmoor (1951)

South Downs (national park in waiting)

Key

National parks

National sports centres

Fig 19.3 National parks and national sports centres

310

- The Pembrokeshire Coast
- The Brecon Beacons
- Dartmoor
- Exmoor
- Northumberland
- The Peak District

- The Lake District
- The North York Moors
- The Yorkshire Dales.

These national parks all provide excellent opportunities to participate in a range of outdoor and adventurous activities.

National sports centres also exist to provide top-level participants with the opportunity to train and prepare for competition. Holme Pierrepont in Nottingham is the National Water Sports Centre, and has a regatta lake and slalom course amongst its facilities. Plas y Brenin is the National Mountain Centre and is located near Snowdonia in North Wales. Its location means that it can offer some of the best places to participate in mountaineering, climbing and canoeing. It also has a climbing practice wall, ski slope and indoor canoe pool.

Voluntary Bodies

The Ramblers' Association is Britain's biggest charity working to promote walking and improve conditions for all walkers. It has 143,000 members in the UK and has been in place for 70 years. Its aims are to:

● Safeguard Britain's network of public paths
● Provide information to help plan walks and enjoy them in safety and comfort
● Increase access for walkers – its work helps to establish statutory rights of access to the outdoors
● Protect the countryside and green spaces from unsightly and polluting developments
● Educate the public about their rights and responsibilities, and the health and environmental benefits of walking.

Urban Outdoor Pursuit Centres

Due to the increase in the number of people living in more urban areas (built-up towns and cities), there has been an increase in the number of facilities offering alternative opportunities to participate. Somebody who participates in rock-climbing and lives in London will find it difficult to get to natural rocks regularly to practise.

As technology has advanced, there have been many man-made facilities created that replicate natural resources. Indoor climbing walls and man-made lakes have meant that more people gain the opportunity to participate in a wider range of activities. An example of modern technology is seeing artificial ski slopes being replaced by real-snow indoor skiing facilities. Xscape, in Milton Keynes and Castleford, near Leeds, is a company that has built indoor skiing arenas, with slopes containing real snow.

Therefore, the construction of man-made facilities has increased participation in many activities, which otherwise would not be easily accessible to some people.

Key learning points 1

● There is a range of different organisations that provide facilities for outdoor and adventurous activities to take place. These include the Countryside Agency and national sports centres.
● A national governing body is the organisation responsible for the running of an activity in this country (e.g. British Canoe Union). Most activities have their own specific national governing body and provide details of where people can go to take part in their sport.

Student activity 19.2　　⏱ 60 minutes　　P1

Think about the different types of outdoor and adventurous activities that you like to take part in. Select four of these activities and carry out the following tasks.

Task 1

Using the internet, find out who the governing bodies are for all four of your selected outdoor and adventurous activities. Find out where you can take part in each of your selected activities in both your local area and further afield.

Task 2

Design a poster to show the organisation and provision of each of your four selected activities, which also includes a written description of the organisation and provision for each.

19.3 Safety Considerations

P2   M1

Taking part in outdoor activities can be immensely beneficial, as well as great fun. You can often find yourself miles away from the roads, shops and other people. But this isolation could prove to be very dangerous without the correct safety awareness, should you or a member of your team get into difficulty. You should follow safety precautions to help keep you and your party safe.

The Adventure Activities Licensing Authority

The Adventure Activities Licensing Authority (AALA) is an independent, government-funded organisation responsible for inspecting activity centres and other outdoor and adventurous activity providers on behalf of the Department for Children, Schools and Families. If the Adventure Activities Licensing Authority is satisfied that the provider meets nationally accepted standards of good practice, then they will issue a licence. This helps provide the public with assurances that the activities do not entail unnecessary danger or risks of injury.

The AALA also provides guidance and advice on running educational trips and reporting accidents. It has links with many of the governing bodies for outdoor and adventurous activities, such as the British Canoe Union (BCU), the Royal Yachting Association (RYA) and Mountain Leading Training UK (MLTUK).

Health and Safety Executive

The Department for Education and Skills (now the Department for Children, Schools and Families) created the Health and Safety Executive, who are responsible for the regulation of all risks to health and safety. They have produced guidelines on arranging and undertaking risk assessments for outdoor activities and educational visits.

Most governing bodies for outdoor adventurous activities also provide support, advice and guidelines on health and safety matters relevant to their activity.

Risk Assessments

A risk assessment is a procedure used to help prevent any potential accidents and injuries. This process is usually performed by the manager or instructors working in the outdoor pursuit centre. The assessment allows people to take time to consider what could go wrong when taking part in their activity. The risk assessment examines the possible hazards that may occur, the risks involved, the likelihood of them happening and how the hazards are being prevented. Risk assessments should be logged, kept and reviewed regularly to see if they are up-to-date and none of the details has changed.

Two examples of hazards are:

● A strong current in the sea, used for windsurfing
● Ice on a footpath.

Key terms

Hazard: a potential source of danger which has the potential to affect someone's safety or cause an injury.

Risk: the possibility of something bad happening.

A risk is linked to the chance of somebody being harmed by the potential hazard. Risks are often categorised into how likely they are to happen, and how serious they are likely to be if they do happen. Something that is a low risk means that the likelihood of it happening is low, whereas something that is high risk means that it is likely to happen. Examples of risks include:

● Slipping on ice and twisting your ankle
● The boom hitting your head while sailing
● Capsizing while kayaking.

Control measures are the measures taken to control (i.e. manage) the risks (see below).

Undertaking a Risk Assessment

Once you have highlighted a hazard, the easiest way to assess it is to use the following formula to assess any potential problems that may arise:

Likelihood × severity

Likelihood – is it likely to happen?

1 Unlikely.
2 Quite likely.
3 Very likely.

Severity – how badly someone could be injured.

1 No injury/minor incident.
2 Injury requiring medical assistance.
3 Major injury or fatality.

Table 19.1 shows an example for capsizing in a kayak.

Likelihood of happening	Severity
2 Quite likely	1 No injury

Table 19.1 Capsizing in a kayak

By multiplying the likelihood against the severity you will be able to draw up a chart that looks at the potential problems and make a decision on whether you want to take the risk or whether it is too much of a hazard. The example in Table 19.1 would be $2 \times 1 = 2$.

An example of a risk assessment form is shown below as Fig 19.4.

Likelihood × severity	Is the risk worth taking?
1	Yes, with caution
2	Yes, possibly, with caution
3	Yes, possibly, with extreme caution
4	Yes, possibly, with extreme caution
6	No
9	No

Table 19.2 Is the risk worth taking?

Risk Assessment

Location of risk assessment: _____

Risk assessor's name: _____

Date: _____

Hazard	People at risk	Likelihood	Severity	Level of risk	Control measures

Fig 19.4 An example of a risk assessment form

An example of a risk assessment for kayaking is shown as Fig 19.5.

Control Measures

Control measures reduce the likelihood of an accident happening. This could include using specialist protective equipment to help minimise the risk of injury.

- Mountain bikers wear helmets in case they fall off their bike.
- Safety ropes are used in climbing to minimise the risk of falling.
- Hiking boots are worn when mountain walking to minimise the risk of slipping and twisting an ankle.
- Life jackets or buoyancy aids are worn for most water sports to minimise the risk of drowning.

Risk Assessment

Activity: Kayaking
Location: Lake Coniston, Lake District
Risk assessor's name: Steve Paddle
Date: 25ᵗʰ October 2010

Hazard	Risk	People at risk	Likelihood	Severity	Level of risk	Control Measures
Water	Drowning	All participants	1	3	High	All participants to wear buoyancy aids to reduce the risk of drowning.
Cold water and weather	Participants suffering from hypothermia	All participants	1–2	3	High	All participants to wear wetsuits and wind-proof cagoules to protect them from the cold.
Rocks	Injuries to head from capsizing	All participants	2	2–3	High	All participants to wear helmets.

Fig 19.5 A risk assessment form for Kayaking

Student activity 19.3 ⏱ 30–40 mins P2 M1

Make a list of four outdoor and adventurous activities. For each outdoor and adventurous activity, identify the following:

- Four hazards
- Four risks associated with each hazard
- Four control measures that could be used to minimise these risks.

Contingency Plans

A contingency plan is about expecting the unexpected. It is planning for any event that might happen. In this way, it is possible to imagine and then calculate what you would do in any given situation. You or your instructor should have devised a contingency plan for every activity so that they know what to do should such a situation arise.

When planning an activity you could ask yourself a series of 'What would I do if . . .' questions:

- What would I do if someone became seriously injured?
- What would I do if the minibus broke down?
- What would I do if the weather became really bad?
- What would I do if a participant got lost?
- What would I do if we ran out of food and drink?
- What would I do if the leader was unable to continue?

Emergency Procedures

When an emergency occurs it is important that you remain calm. If there are casualties it is important to summon assistance as soon as possible. Use either a mobile or public phone to dial 999 and ask for an ambulance (and possibly the mountain rescue team, depending on where you are located). You will need to give them the following details:

- The name and age of the casualty, and a description of their injuries
- The exact location of the injured person – grid references and the map sheet number
- The time and nature of the accident
- The weather conditions.

You should then stay on the phone until you are met by the emergency services.

If the injury is life-threatening, a rescue helicopter

may have to be brought in. If this is the case, there are a few precautions that you will need to follow before and during its arrival:

- Secure all loose equipment; this can be done with stones or rucksacks
- Raise your arms in a V shape as the helicopter approaches; this will signal to the helicopter that you are the casualty group – do not wave to the helicopter as this is the signal for everything is OK
- Shelter the injured person from the rotor downdraught
- Do not approach the helicopter unless directed.

If you do not have a mobile phone or there is no signal, you would have to send a distress signal. If you have a whistle with you, give a series of six loud blasts followed by one minute's silence. Continue this process until you receive a response. If you are in an area where it may be difficult for other people to hear this sound, you should use a visual signal. Smoke from a fire gives a good visual signal. If you hear or see an aircraft, you should try to attract its attention with a mirror, glass or any other shiny object. You should also try to spread out any bright clothing you have on the floor which will help draw attention to yourselves.

At night you should use a torch to signal the code SOS. This is done by giving three short flashes, three long flashes, followed by another three short flashes.

Student activity 19.4 ⏱ **40 minutes** P2 M1

In groups of four, imagine one of you has been injured on a mountain. Two people should carry out a role play to determine how they will get help. The fourth person should observe and give feedback to the group on what they did well and how they could improve.

Safety Equipment

You should always carry a basic first-aid kit with you on any outdoor activities. If you are taking part in water-based activities, make sure the following pieces of safety equipment are kept in a sealed watertight container:

- Ten plasters in various sizes
- Two large sterile dressings for management of severe bleeding
- A medium sterile dressing for care of larger wounds
- Four triangular bandages to support suspected broken bones, dislocations or sprains
- An eye pad in case of a cut to the eye
- Four safety pins to secure dressings
- Disposable gloves.

You should also carry the following:

- A survival bag – a large heavy-duty bag that you can climb into to keep you insulated against the cold
- A torch and spare batteries in your rucksack so that you can see where you are going and give distress signals if required
- A whistle in your pocket or on a string around your neck so that you can give distress signals

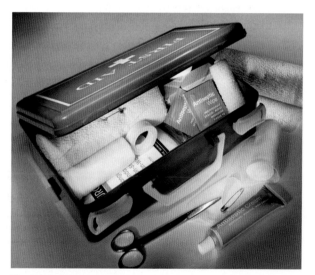

Fig 19.6 A first-aid kit

- Enough food for your journey as well as emergency rations (energy-dense foods, such as Kendal mint cake or a Mars bar) just in case you find yourself trapped or having to spend longer out on the activity than you intended.

Key learning points 2

- A hazard is something that has the potential to cause injury or compromise safety.
- A risk is the likelihood of something happening.
- A risk assessment is a list of possible hazards that states the likelihood of them happening, and ways of controlling them.
- The level of risk is worked out by multiplying likelihood of risk by severity. A risk level of 6 or more means that either more safety precautions should be introduced or the activity should not take place.
- Distress signals: six loud blasts on the whistle followed by one minute of silence, to be repeated until help arrives.
- Torchlight flashes: three short flashes, three long flashes, three short flashes, break and repeat.

Q Quick quiz 1

Contingency plan	Adventure Activities Licensing Authority	Risk assessment	Survival bag	Kendal mint cake
Control measures	SOS	Eye pad	Health and Safety Executive	Wave

Answer the following questions using the word or words from the table above:

1 This organisation is an independent, government-funded organisation responsible for inspecting activity centres and other outdoor and adventurous activity providers.

2 This organisation is responsible for the regulation of all risks to health and safety.

3 This is carried out to try to help prevent any potential accidents and injuries.

4 These are procedures taken to control risks.

5 This is something that is done so you can plan for any event that might happen.

6 This distress signal is performed with a torch by giving three short flashes, three long flashes, followed by another three short flashes.

7 This should be in every first-aid kit.

8 This should be carried with your equipment in case of emergencies.

9 This is an energy-dense food that should be carried in case of emergencies.

10 You should not do this to a rescue helicopter as this is the signal for everything is OK.

Student activity 19.5 ⏱ 60 minutes P2 M1 D1

Taking part in outdoor activities can be immensely beneficial, as well as great fun; however, most of these types of activities do carry an element of risk. You should therefore follow safety precautions to help keep yourself and other participants safe.

Task 1

Select four different outdoor and adventurous activities and draw a spider diagram to show the safety considerations required for each.

Task 2

Write a report that examines each of your four outdoor and adventurous activities and then describe, explain and evaluate the safety considerations associated with each.

19.4. Environmental Considerations

Areas of Outstanding Natural Beauty and National Nature Reserves

When enjoying walking in the outdoors it is essential that you respect the environment to preserve its beauty. Some of the areas you choose to explore may be subject to special protection, such as Areas of Outstanding Natural Beauty (AONBs). An area of natural beauty is an area with a greatly valued landscape that should be preserved. There are 41 AONB in England and Wales, and they include coastlines, meadows and moors.

There are also National Nature Reserves (NNRs), which are places designated to putting wildlife first. They help to protect, preserve and study wildlife and their habitat. Nearly every rural county has an NNR. The majority of NNRs have access for visitors.

The Countryside Rights of Way Act

The Countryside Rights of Way Act 2000 (known as CRoW) was put in place in order to increase the public's ability to enjoy the countryside. It allows the public access to open country and registered common land, whereas before some people restricted access. It aims to modernise the rights of way system, provide better management for AONBs and strengthen wildlife enforcement legislation. Wherever you walk in the countryside, you should always adhere to the Countryside Code.

● Always close and secure gates after yourself.
● Leave property as you find it.
● Protect plants and animals – do not damage or move plants, trees or rocks from their natural habitat.
● Do not leave litter of any type – take it home with you and dispose of it properly.
● Keep dogs under close control.
● Consider other people – do not make too much noise and do not block entrances and driveways with your vehicle.

Participating in outdoor and adventurous activities usually does cause some impact on the natural environment. It is therefore important that participants are aware of how they can preserve the environment, so that people can continue to enjoy it.

If an activity or our own mistreatment continues to damage these areas, then authorities will use control measures to reduce the impact.

The Countryside Agency is the government's advisory body responsible for all aspects of the countryside. It is responsible for improving and conserving the countryside and looking at the social and economic impact it has on people.

There are many ways in which participants can help look after these environments, and the national governing bodies all prioritise looking after the countryside, and set recommendations to follow, to help avoid impacting on the environment.

Types of Environmental Impact

Erosion

Erosion is a major factor in the outdoors, so what is it and what does it affect?

Erosion affects paths and tracks. It is a natural process where soil wears away due to heavy exposure to rain and wind. Because of the slope on hills, the soil moves down the slope towards the streams and rivers. Human activity can also increase the rate of erosion. Many major paths have been formed over the years and many have been treated to combat the effects of erosion. Sometimes paths will be closed as they are treated.

There are often dry-stone walls in the countryside, which act as boundaries and markers. Walkers should ensure that they use the gates and stiles rather than trying to climb over these because dry-stone walls are easily damaged and difficult to put back together. It is also important to close all gates after use, so that livestock cannot escape from their allocated space.

Pollution

Pollution is another factor that has increased in the countryside. This has come mainly from the increase in cars visiting the areas. There is often limited car parking, so parking should be considered before travelling. There has also been an increase in the number of motorised activities taking place in rural settings (e.g. quad bikes). Many countryside users have complained about the noise and pollution that these activities cause. The Countryside Agency is monitoring this closely and has clamped down on groups doing these types of activities in public spaces.

Rubbish and litter should be taken home with you and not dumped in the countryside. Not only does rubbish look untidy, but it is also harmful to livestock and wildlife. Rubbish can also attract scavengers, which can displace the species of the area.

Human Disturbance

Both plants and wildlife are easily disturbed by human behaviour. Humans should not touch wildlife or pick plants, as many are rare and even protected. It is important that dogs are also kept on leads, as they may worry animals. Rare species of birds often leave their nests through fright and do not return to hatch their eggs.

Often competitions are in conservation areas and involve getting off the main paths to find specific checkpoints, therefore trampling plants and disturbing the wildlife.

The British Orienteering Federation (BOF) is committed to preserving the environment, as research has shown that orienteering has a low impact on the environment. The BOF has responded to some criticism by:

● Its members declaring a high commitment to conservation principles
● Using a qualified environmental scientist as their Environmental Officer
● Commissioning independent scientific researchers to look at the environmental impact of orienteering.

Key learning points 3

● Environmental impact is anything that can affect the natural environment.
● All people visiting the countryside should adhere to the Countryside Code.
● Participants in outdoor and adventurous activities should try to reduce their environmental impact as much as possible.

Quick quiz 2

Answer the following statements with true or false:

1 Pollution is a natural process where soil wears away due to heavy exposure to rain and wind.
2 Rubbish and litter should be taken home with you and not dumped in the countryside.
3 Walkers can climb over dry-stone walls rather than using the gates and stiles.
4 An Area of Outstanding Natural Beauty is not subject to protection.
5 It is OK to pick plants and flowers while out walking in the countryside.
6 It is OK to drop waste products on the ground if they are biodegradable.
7 The Countryside Agency is the government's advisory body responsible for all aspects of the countryside.
8 There are 45 Areas of Outstanding Natural Beauty in England and Wales.
9 The Countryside Rights of Way Act 2000 prevents people from accessing country footpaths.
10 The Countryside Code states that you should always close and secure gates after you.

Student activity 19.6   45–60 mins   P3 M2 D1

Outdoor and adventurous activities can have some negative impacts on the environment; however, once people are aware of these, they can try to reduce this impact.

Task 1

Select four different outdoor and adventurous activities (it would be a good idea to choose those that you selected for Student Activity 19.5).

Task 2

Design four leaflets, one for each of your chosen activities, that can be given to people who take part in those activities. Your leaflet should describe, explain and evaluate environmental considerations associated with each outdoor and adventurous activity.

19.5 Participate in Outdoor and Adventurous Activities

Skills and Techniques

There is a host of skills and techniques required for each outdoor activity you choose to take part in. As there is not enough room in this book to detail every skill and technique required for each activity we will explore only map reading, navigation and route planning, as these skills are required for a number of outdoor and adventurous activities.

Maps

Maps give an accurate representation of the ground as seen from above. They are then scaled down to different sizes. Most maps you will use are Ordnance Survey (OS) maps, with a scale of 1:25,000. This means one unit of length represents 25,000 units on the ground. So, if one unit was 1 cm, 1 cm would cover 250 m on the ground. Maps contain different symbols to show different landmarks on the ground. They also contain the following useful information:

- Map title – the area of ground that the map covers
- Key to the symbols
- The year the map was made
- The sheet number – the whole of the UK is covered by 203 sheets
- Adjoining sheet numbers
- Grid numbers
- A scale line to measure distances.

Measuring Distance

There are two main methods you can use to measure the distance of your route. The cheapest method uses only a piece of string. Take a piece of string and place it along the exact route on the map. Place the string on the scale line and count the distance it covers. This should give you an idea of the route you are planning. You could also use a commercially made map measurer, which you run along your route and it will tell you the distance covered.

Navigation

Key term

Navigation: the process of plotting and following a route from one place to another.

There are a number of different methods you can use to navigate your journey. The best one to use will be determined by the lay of the land, the weather and the time of day or night. No matter what type of navigation you use, you will always need a map.

Across an OS map, you will see a series of lines going up and across the map, dividing it into 1 km block squares. These lines are blue; the ones that run across the map are known as Eastings and those that run up and down the map are Northings. The lines are numbered and allow you to pinpoint your exact location on a map. When giving a grid reference you should always give the Eastings first. A good way to remember this is to think 'Go along the corridor and then up the stairs.'

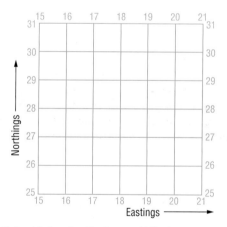

Fig 19.7 A grid showing Eastings and Northings

Student activity 19.7   ⏱ 30 minutes   P4   M3

- Look at an OS map and plan a route from an area that contains water or forest to another area that contains a building of some sort. Work out the distance using a piece of string and the scale line on your map.

- If you have one available, carry out the same exercise using a map measurer.
- Compare the distances you get and try to explain why there may be any differences.

Student activity 19.8   ⏱ **20 minutes**   P4   M3

Look at a map and choose three features. Give the grid references of these three different features.

Most areas that you plan to walk through will not be totally flat. Therefore, contour lines are drawn on to maps to show the height of the land above sea level. The height between contour lines on OS maps is 10 m. The height is written into some of these lines. The numbers are written with the top of the number facing uphill.

Contour lines also give you a good impression of the shape of the land. Areas of the map that contain lots of closely packed contour lines show that the land has a steep slope. Valleys and ridges can also be shown by these lines.

Fig 19.9 Contour lines showing valleys and ridges

Fig 19.8 Contour lines

Student activity 19.9   ⏱ **20 minutes**   P4   M3

Look at a map and choose an area with contours. Now try to draw the formation of the land in relation to the contours.

Setting the Map

Setting the map is a method of placing the map in a position so that all the features are lined up and your location is at the central point. So, if you were to look to your left, you would see the same features on the ground as you would on the map, and the same would be true for looking ahead or to your right. You may find the writing on the map is upside down when you have set it.

This process can be carried out without any problems if there is good visibility. Look for a prominent feature on the map such as a church, a hill or a village then turn the map so that the features on the ground are in line with you at the central point. If visibility is poor – fog or night-time – you will have

to use your compass to set the map. The compass will show you where magnetic north is. Then you will need to line up north on the map with north on the compass. While you are walking, ensure that you keep the map set (i.e. change its position) as you change direction so, if you turn right, turn the map in the same direction so that it remains set.

Using a Compass

You need to carry your compass in such a way that it is accessible at all times and you are able to move it in any direction. You must also be able to let it go without losing it. The best method of carrying a compass is to attach a long cord to it and carry it over one shoulder.

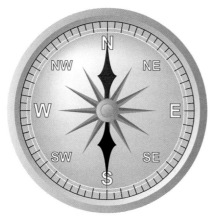

Fig 19.10 A compass

Taking a Bearing

Key term

Bearing: a direction of travel, between 0 and 360 degrees from north in a clockwise direction.

When you are walking in poor visibility you will need to take bearings from your map and walk on a bearing.

Place the compass on the map so that the arrow is pointing in the direction you wish to travel. Then line up the baseplate with where you want to travel to. Then turn the compass housing so that the north arrow is pointing to the north on the map. Ensure the lines within the compass housing are running parallel to the grid lines running northwards.

Now you need to convert the bearing to a magnetic bearing by adding magnetic variation, which is 5 degrees. Hold the compass horizontally in front of you. Change your direction until the red end of the compass needle is over the orienteering arrow and parallel to the lines in the bottom of the housing. Look in the direction of the travel arrow to see if you can see a feature on the landscape that it lines up with. You can then walk towards this feature. When you have reached the feature, stop and repeat the process until you have reached your desired location. If you do not see a feature to walk towards, hold the compass in front of you and keep walking in the direction of the travel arrow.

Fig 19.11 Taking a bearing

Measuring Distance Travelled

There are two methods of estimating the distance you have covered: timing and pacing.

Timing

This process works on the principle of estimating your walking speed and knowing how long you have been walking for. The speed that you walk at will vary depending on whether you are walking uphill or on flat terrain. Most fit people walk at a speed of about 5 km per hour on flat ground. You then need to add ten minutes for every 100 m of height gained or one minute for every 10 m gained (Naismith's rule). Walking down steep hills will take longer than walking

Student activity 19.10   ⏱ 15 minutes   P4   P3

Work out your own paces by counting how many double steps you take when walking along a 100 m athletics track.

on the flat, so you should add 1 minute for every 30 m descent.

Pacing

This process uses the principle of counting the number of steps you have taken and estimating the distance covered from these steps. It takes an average-sized male about 60 double steps to cover 100 m. From this you can then work out how far you have travelled. You need to be aware that the size of your pace will vary depending on whether you are travelling uphill or downhill.

Planning your Route

This process should be thought through carefully and planned properly. If you do not give it full attention you may find yourself walking up some very steep mountains or having to walk through boggy ground when you really just wanted to have a fairly easy walk. Think about what you want to accomplish on your expedition and the features you would like to see, such as lakes or forests. Think about how far you would like to walk and the time it will take you, or if you are in a group, how long it will take your slowest walker.

You will also need to factor in meal breaks. You may wish to aim to eat lunch at a certain place by a river or in a cafe. If you are planning an overnight expedition, make sure you have given yourself enough time to reach your campsite or have chosen an appropriate place to pitch your tent for the night. You should then prepare a route card and make sure you leave a copy of it with someone, preferably a police officer at the nearest police station to your route or a person at the nearest mountain centre. This is very important as it will not only aid your navigation, but if you get into difficulty, this route card can be used to locate and rescue you.

An example of a route card is shown in Table 19.3.

Use of Equipment

The equipment used for taking part in outdoor activities is often very specialised and specific to the activity. There are, however, some generic items that are worn for both water-based and land-based activities.

Water-Based Activities

For most water-based activities, you will usually need to wear either a wetsuit or a drysuit and a buoyancy aid.

Wetsuits are used to try to protect your body from the cold water and are used during the warmer seasons – late spring, summer and early autumn.

Fig 19.12 A life jacket in use

Team leader: R. Ambler		Starting point: GR 328800					ETD: 0800	
Date: 26.10.10		Finishing point: GR 337621					ETA: 1800	

Leg	From	From	To	To	Bearing	Bearing	Distance	Remarks, hazards etc.
	Location	GR	Location	GR	Grid	Mag		
1	River	327645	Stile	337644	342	347	500 m	Cairns
2	Stile	337644	Xroads	341044	54	59	1,700 m	Steep slope

Table 19.3 Route card

Fig 19.13 A buoyancy aid

A buoyancy aid is different from a life jacket. A buoyancy aid will help to keep you afloat if you fall into the water, whereas a life jacket will not only help to keep you afloat, but is designed to help keep your head up and out of the water should you fall unconscious during your time submerged. Buoyancy aids are usually worn for windsurfing, kayaking and small dinghy sailing because they allow greater mobility than life jackets. Life jackets are usually worn on larger sailing boats as these tend to be used for sailing further out into the water and further away from help and rescue.

Land-Based Activities

For most land-based activities, one of the most important pieces of equipment you will buy is your footwear. If you choose the wrong type or if they do not fit you properly it could mean your activity has to be ended prematurely due to blisters or injury. Both hiking boots and shoes are available. Boots give ankle support, which helps prevent twisting ankles on uneven ground. The top of the boot or shoe should be waterproof or water repellent. The soles should be able to give good grip on all walking surfaces you may face. The soles should also provide some cushioning from the impact of walking.

They use your own body heat to keep you warm by trapping air, and then the neoprene of the wetsuit helps to keep you warm by acting as an insulator for your body heat. When you fall in the water or capsize, you will feel cold for a short while as your body heat warms up the layer of water trapped in the wetsuit. For a wetsuit to work effectively, it is essential that it fits the wearer snugly.

An alternative to wetsuits are drysuits. These are worn during the colder seasons, such as late autumn, winter and early spring. They are designed to keep the wearer dry, even when the person is totally submerged in water. Underneath the drysuit, a person usually wears thermal clothing to keep them warm. A drysuit does not need to fit as snugly as a wetsuit because it is airtight so it sucks the suit closer to your body.

Key learning points 4

Ensure you can demonstrate an understanding of the following:

- Know how to read and set a map
- Ensure you are able to read and give grid references
- Know how to use a compass
- Know how to take and follow bearings
- Know how to write a route card.

The equipment you use for your outdoor activity is necessary to ensure your safety and enjoyment. Always find out exactly what you need to wear and take with you. Research the different types of equipment available and then determine what is best for you, based on the time of year and the location of your activity.

Student activity 19.11   30 mins   P4   M3

Time: 1–6 weeks for practice, 30 minutes for observation

Practise the appropriate skills and techniques for two outdoor and adventurous activities of you choice. Ensure you are able to carry out the skills and techniques to perform each activity appropriately and safely.

With your tutor/teacher or supervisor watching you, demonstrate the skills and techniques that you have practised for two different outdoor and adventurous activities. The amount of tutor support you receive during each demonstration will affect the grade that you can receive.

19.6 Review Performance in Outdoor and Adventurous Activities

P5   P6   M4   D2

Having completed an activity, it is important to gain some feedback on how to improve performance. Feedback can come from a number of sources.

● From yourself: a log book, how the activity felt, did you complete the skill effectively, etc.
● From your peers: verbal feedback, comparison of ability, how well you work as a team, etc.
● An assessor: did you achieve the set target?
● An instructor: verbal feedback, video footage.

Strengths and Areas for Development

Information about strengths and weaknesses provides us with a template for improvement. You should be able to learn something new about your abilities after every activity session. Examples of development feedback could be:

● Poor or ineffective stroke (canoeing or kayaking)
● Ineffective/unsafe knots used (climbing)
● Ineffective communication with the group
● Inaccurate pacing technique (hiking).

All of the above can be improved. You should develop your own self-assessment techniques, paying particular attention to what needs to be improved and in what order.

Target Setting

Once a decision has been made about your areas of development, it is an appropriate time to think about setting targets. Remember that you may not be able to achieve your desired skill levels immediately and while these remain your long-term goal it is important to set realistic short-term targets to lay the pathway to achieving your skills. When you have identified areas for development, it is good practice to apply the SMART principle. This stands for the following:

● **S**pecific
● **M**easurable
● **A**chievable
● **R**ealistic
● **T**ime-constrained.

Specific: the target must be specific to what you want to achieve. For example, you may need to improve your paddle position in order to complete an Eskimo roll.

Measurable: targets must be stated in a way that is measurable, so they need to include figures. For example, 'I want to be able to hike 15 km in eight hours.'

Achievable: it must be possible to actually achieve the target.

Realistic: we need to be realistic in our setting and look at what factors may stop us achieving the target.

Time-constrained: there must be a timescale or deadline on the target. This means you can review your success. It is best to state a date by which you wish to achieve the goal.

From this information, you can then determine your aims and objectives. Do you want to be able to complete certain awards for your chosen outdoor activity? If this is the case, you will have to investigate whether there are any clubs in your area that run the activity or perhaps you could go on a residential course at an outdoor pursuits centre. From this information you will be able to continue developing your skills and techniques in your chosen outdoor activities and possibly eventually take on instructing qualifications and pursue a career in these sports.

Student activity 19.12 ⏱ 30–40 mins P6 M4 D2

Select two outdoor activities that you have taken part in. Find out:

- The nearest clubs that cater for these activities
- The award scheme for each activity
- What you need to be able to do to achieve your first or next qualification in this activity.

Student activity 19.13 ⏱ 60 minutes P5 P6 M4 D2

Using the feedback you have received from your tutor/teacher or supervisor and other participants, as well as your self-assessment, carry out the following tasks.

Task 1

Write a review of your own performance in both of your selected outdoor and adventurous activities. In your review, you should identify and explain your strengths and any areas that you think you could improve upon.

Task 2

Produce a development plan to show how you can improve your own performance in each of your selected outdoor and adventurous activities. Things that you may like to consider include: local clubs, NGB proficiency awards, etc. Explain and justify these suggestions, explaining how you will carry them out and overcome any barriers that may be in your way.

Key learning points 5

You should review your performance in your selected outdoor and adventurous activities by examining your strengths and areas for improvement in order to improve your skills and techniques.

Try to set SMART targets to help you to make these improvements. SMART stands for

- **S**pecific
- **M**easurable
- **A**chievable
- **R**ealistic
- **T**ime-constrained.

Further reading

Cox, D. (2002) *The Sailing Handbook*, New Holland Publishers.

Hanson, J. and Hanson, R. (1997) *Ragged Mountain Press Guide to Outdoor Sports*, McGraw-Hill.

Lockren, I. (1998) *Outdoor Pursuits*, Nelson Thornes.

Long, S. (2003, revised 2004) *Hill Walking*, Mountain Leader Training UK.

Rowe, R. (1989) *Canoeing Handbook, Official Handbook of the British Canoe Union*, Chameleon Press.

Useful websites

www.bcu.org.uk

Provides information on canoeing provision and coaching opportunities

www.thebmc.co.uk

Offers details of intructing opportunities and information on equipment, safety and forthcoming events for climbers, mountaineers and hill walkers in the UK

www.ramblers.org.uk

Provides information, such as walking routes and appropriate equipment

www.rya.org

Provides information on sailing and windsurfing provision, equipment, tides, courses and instructing opportunities

325

26: Laboratory and Experimental Methods in Sport & Exercise Sciences

26.1 Introduction

This unit provides an introduction to laboratory and experimental methods in kinanthropometry. Kinanthropometry is the study of the relationship between the structure and function of the human body and is used in a number of different sport and exercise sciences disciplines including biomechanics, nutrition and exercise physiology.

The unit starts by examining the health and safety issues associated with carrying out sport and exercise experiments in a laboratory and related ethical issues. There follows a section on alternative anthropometric methods for the prediction of the percentage of body fat of an individual. Validity and reliability issues will be covered in relation to the different types of tests and the testing procedures used.

The anthropometric somatotype is then explored in ways in which a person can investigate the anthropometric somatotype of an individual and interpret the results in relation to sports performance.

The final part of the unit explores experimental methods used to estimate the aerobic fitness of an individual using a range of different methods and how to interpret the results.

By the end of this unit you should be able to:

- Understand health, safety and ethical issues associated with laboratory and experimental methods in sport and exercise sciences
- Estimate percentage body fat using anthropometric methods
- Measure and interpret the anthropometric somatotype
- Use experimental methods to predict maximum oxygen uptake.

Assessment and grading criteria		
To achieve a PASS grade the evidence must show that the learner is able to:	To achieve a MERIT grade the evidence must show that, in addition to the pass criteria, the learner is able to:	To achieve a DISTINCTION grade the evidence must show that, in addition to the pass and merit criteria, the learner is able to:
P1 explain health and safety issues associated with laboratory and experimental methods in sport and exercise sciences		
P2 evaluate ethical issues associated with laboratory and experimental methods in sport and exercise sciences		
P3 follow test guidelines for the prediction of percentage body fat of an individual using two alternative anthropometric methods		
P4 describe validity and reliability issues of the two selected anthropometric methods	**M1** explain validity and reliability issues of the two selected anthropometric methods	**D1** analyse validity and reliability issues of the two selected anthropometric methods
P5 carry out calculations for the prediction of percentage body fat of an individual using two alternative anthropometric methods, interpret results and describe the strengths and areas for improvement	**M2** carry out calculations for the prediction of percentage body fat of an individual using two alternative anthropometric methods, explaining the results and the strengths and areas for improvement	
P6 carry out an assessment of the anthropometric somatotype of an individual, describing the results	**M3** carry out an assessment of the anthropometric somatotype of an individual, explaining the results	**D2** carry out an assessment of the anthropometric somatotype of an individual, analysing the results
P7 follow two different experimental methods to predict the maximum oxygen uptake of an individual, describing the results.	**M4** follow two different experimental methods to predict the maximum oxygen uptake of an individual, explaining the results.	**D3** follow two different experimental methods to predict the maximum oxygen uptake of an individual, analysing the results.

26.2 Health, Safety and Ethical Issues Associated with Laboratory and Experimental Methods in Sport and Exercise Sciences

In sport and exercise sciences, experimental tests are carried out on people. Therefore, as a tester it is very important that you are fully aware of all of the health, safety and ethical issues involved so that you can be sure to adhere to these and thus help to protect the health and well-being of the people that you are testing. People that you use in your testing procedures are called 'subjects' and will be referred to as such throughout the rest of this unit.

Health & Safety

It is very important to ensure the health and safety of subjects in your investigation and also to consider the legal implication of your actions. You must ensure that your testing procedures meet certain considerations deemed necessary to minimise any risks to the subject. This will involve following strict procedures which are usually outlined in the protocol that you are following. Also, you will have carried out a risk assessment prior to any testing. Where risks have been identified, ways to eliminate or reduce the risk to the subject should be included, such as having a medically trained person being present during the testing process.

Health Screening

Before you start to conduct any sport and exercise sciences-related tests you will need to carry out health-screening tests to ensure that the subject is fit and able to take part in the tests without their health being negatively affected. The subject can complete a health-screening questionnaire which covers areas such as medical conditions, illnesses and injuries, as well as past history of exercise and lifestyle factors. An example of a health screening questionnaire is in Figure 26.1.

Section 1 – Personal Details

Name _____

Address _____

_____

_____

_____

_____

Telephone Home _____

Mobile _____

Email _____

Occupation _____

Date of Birth _____

Doctor's name & address _____

_____

_____

Emergency contact name _____

Address _____

_____

Section 2 – About your lifestyle

1 How many units of alcohol do you drink in a typical week? _____

2 Do you smoke? _____ If 'yes', how many a day? _____

3 Do you experience stress on a daily basis? _____

4 If 'yes', what causes you stress (if you were to know) _____

5 What techniques do you use to deal with your stress?_____

_____

Section 3– About your physical health

1 Do you experience any of the following?

☐ Back pain or injury
☐ Knee pain or injury
☐ Ankle pain or injury
☐ Swollen joints
☐ Shoulder pain or injury
☐ Hip or pelvic pain or injury
☐ Nerve damage
☐ Head injuries

2 If 'yes', please give details

_____

_____

_____

_____

3 Are any of these injuries made worse by exercise _____

4 If 'yes', what movements in particular will cause pain? _____

_____

_____

5 Are you currently receiving any treatment for any injuries? _____

Section 4 – Medical history

1 Do you or have you had any of the following medical conditions?

☐ Asthma
☐ Bronchitis
☐ Heart problems
☐ Chest pains
☐ Diabetes
☐ High blood pressure
☐ Epilepsy
☐ Other

2 Are you taking any medication (If 'yes', state what, how much and why) _____

_____

Participant's Name: ....

Participant's Signature: ....

Tester's name:...

Tester's signature:...

Date: ....

Fig 26.1 An example of a health screening questionnaire

Pre-test procedures

When testing people it is important that the tests are safe for the subject. Also, that the conditions the tests are performed in are consistent and stable. To reduce the risk of something going wrong the following should be taken into consideration:

The **subject** should:

● have medical clearance for any health conditions
● be free of injuries
● be wearing appropriate clothing
● not have had a heavy meal three hours before any strenuous testing
● have avoided stimulants such as tea, coffee or nicotine two hours before the test.

The **environment** of the testing area should be:

● at room temperature (around 18°C)
● well ventilated
● clean and dust free

Test sequence

The order in which tests are conducted must be considered because this may change the accuracy of the results you produce. You may even have to do different tests on different days to produce the best results.

Our knowledge of sport science can help to decide which tests should be done first and for how long the subject will need to rest between tests in order to obtain reliable results. For example, a test that requires effort over a long period of time will require 1 to 2 hours for recovery. Also, tests requiring a high level of skill or coordination should be attempted. This is because our skills level person decreases when we are tired. Therefore, the correct order of tests to follow would be:

1 Sedentary tests (i.e. height, weight, body composition, flexibility)
2 Agility tests
3 Maximum power and strength tests
4 Sprint tests
5 Muscular endurance test
6 Aerobic endurance tests.

First Aid procedures

Your testing area should have access to basic first aid equipment and there should be methods of communicating with a first aider or emergency services such as a telephone within easy reach of the testing area. For some testing such as maximal tests, you may be required to have nearby a suitably qualified person to act as an observer to the testing procedure and who can advise you to terminate the test if the subject is over-exerting and likely to put their health at risk.

Reasons for terminating a test

Your subject should be fully aware of the fact that they may terminate the test at any point. However, there will be occasions where it becomes unsafe to continue with a test due to physiological changes within the subject. The following is a list of specific situations when a test should be stopped:

● Chest pains or angina-like symptoms
● Excessive increase in blood pressure (250/115)
● Shortness of breath and wheezing
● Leg cramps or pain
● Light-headedness, nausea or pale, clammy skin
● Heart rate that does not rise with exercise intensity
● Irregular heart beat
● Client requests to stop
● Signs and symptoms of severe exhaustion
● Equipment fails.

Ethical considerations

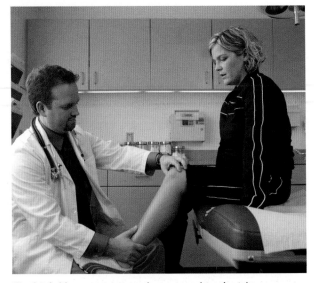

Fig 26.2 You must ensure that your subject's rights are not violated during physiological tests

Ethical considerations respect the rights of subjects involved in the investigation in order to ensure the subjects are not negatively affected by your tests.

As most of the studies in sport and exercise sciences involve carrying out tests on humans, it is necessary for the researcher to ensure that the research setting or activity does not frighten, embarrass or negatively affect the participants. (Tuckman, 1978)

Your testing should allow subjects to take part voluntarily and are not harmed in the process of the investigation, participant results are anonymous and kept confidential. (De Vaus, 1996).

Your subjects should be made aware of their right to withdraw from a test or programme of exercise at any time during the study. The decision to undertake a test or exercise programme rests with the individual; if they decide they do not want to continue, you must stop the test. You should explain the full procedures and programmes that any individual will be following, give them details of the group (if any) they will be in, and tell them who will be testing them. This is an important part of testing, as it allows you to be sure that the subject is clear about what they are doing. You do not want the results to be affected by a lack of understanding on the subject's part.

Gaining Permission

An informed consent form should be produced and signed by the subjects involved in the investigation. An informed consent form should contain the following information:

- A fair explanation of the procedures that the participant will be expected to follow
- A description of the possible discomforts and risks to the participant
- A description of the benefits to be expected from carrying out the research
- An offer to answer any enquiries concerning the procedures
- An instruction that the participant is free to withdraw consent at any time and terminate the testing process.

Anonymity

Participants should be referred to by a method which ensures that they remain anonymous so that other people who have not directly been involved in the investigation will not know exactly who the subjects were or their experimental results.

Anonymity can be preserved by giving each subject an identification number which is used instead of their name.

Confidentiality

The Data Protection Act (1998) states that any information collected from a subject must be kept

---

1. Explanation of the tests
You will perform a series of tests which will vary in their demands on your body. Your progress will be observed during the tests and stopped if you show signs of undue fatigue. You may stop the test at any time if you feel unduly uncomfortable.

2. Risks of exercise testing
During exercise certain changes will occur such as the rising of blood pressure, fainting, and raised heart rate and, in rare cases, heart attacks or even death. Every effort is made through screening to minimise the risk of these occurring during testing. Emergency equipment and relevantly trained personnel are available to deal with any extreme situation which might occur.

3. Responsibility of the participant
You must disclose all information in your possession regarding the state of your health or previous experiences of exercise as this will affect the safety of the tests. If you experience any discomfort or unusual sensations it is your responsibility to inform your trainer.

4. Freedom of consent
Your participation in these tests is voluntary and you are free to deny consent or stop a test at any point.

I have read this form and understand what is expected of me and the tests I will perform. I give my consent to participate.

Participant's signature..
Print name ....
Date...

Tester's signature...
Print name ....
Date...

Fig 26.3 An example of an informed consent form

confidential. Therefore, where information is kept, only authorised people should be able to access it. For example, you should use password-protected computer programmes and locked storage facilities etc. When reporting results to people not directly involved in the investigation, personal details of the subjects should be omitted. However, it is possible to allow third parties to information relating to the general background information of the subjects such as age, gender, ability level, etc, so that they can determine the demographics of the population that the information refers to.

You must also ensure that you have permission to carry out the testing from the centre in which you are carrying out the investigation. Your tutor will have gained approval from your Ethical Advisory Committee to allow you to carry out the physiological tests that will take place in this unit.

Key learning points I

- All tests on people are subject to health and safety regulations to protect the health and well-being of participants.
- All subjects should be fully health-screened prior to testing.
- Subjects should have full knowledge of the tests and complete an informed consent form to verify that they have understood the testing protocol.
- Ethical considerations need to be carried out prior to any subject testing.
- Subject's anonymity should be maintained and data records of test results kept confidential.

Student activity 26.1   1–2 hours   P1   P2

As virtually all testing in sport and exercise sciences takes place on people, it is very important that health, safety and ethical guidelines are understood and adhered to before, during and after the testing processes.

Task

Prepare a written report that:

- **explains** health and safety issues associated with laboratory and experimental methods in sport and exercise sciences.

- **evaluates** the ethical issues associated with laboratory and experimental methods in sport and exercise sciences.

26.3 Estimating percentage body fat using anthropometric methods

In very simple terms, a person's body weight or mass can be split into two categories: **fat mass** and **lean body weight** (i.e. all that is not fat). Table 26.1 shows Behnke & Wilmore's (1974) 'reference man' and 'reference woman', giving the breakdown of the components of fat mass and lean body and the respective contributions of each type for tissue to overall body mass.

You can lose weight by reducing any of the components of the body; however, lean body weight could be seen as healthy weight, as it contributes to the

performance of the body (muscles contractions, etc.). Fat weight in excess would be unhealthy weight because it would cause a loss in performance as it requires oxygen without giving anything back to the body in terms of performance.

It is necessary to take a body fat measurement to show that the weight loss is through loss of fat and not loss of muscle.

It is impossible to turn muscle into fat or fat into muscle. This is because they are completely different types of tissue in the body. A good training programme will produce a loss of fat or excess fat and a gain in muscle tissue. So while it may look like one is turning into the other, this is not the case. It is important to use measures of body composition assessment to see where the weight gain is coming from (fat mass or lean body mass) as only then can you see whether the actions the individual is taking are achieving the goals that they desire.

Body composition can be assessed in many ways. In this unit we will examine the following methods:

Reference man	Reference female
Age = 20-24 Height = 174 cm Mass = 70 kg	Age = 20-24 Height = 164 cm Mass = 56.7 kg
Total Fat mass = 10.g kg (15%) *of which:* Storage fat = 8.4 kg (12%) Essential fat = 2.1 kg (3%)	Total Fat mass = 15.3 kg (27%) *of which:* Storage fat = 8.5 kg (15%) Essential fat = 6.8 kg (12%)
Lean body mass = 61.7kg *of which:* Muscle = 31.3 kg (44.8%) Bone = 10.4 kg (14.9%) Other (organs, water, connective tissue) = 17.6 kg (26.3%)	Lean body mass = 48.5 kg *of which:* Muscle = 20.4 kg (36%) Bone = 6.8 kg (12%) Other (organs, water, connective tissue) = 14.1 kg (25%)

Table 26.1 Behnke & Wilmore's (1974) theoretical model for reference man and reference female

- Skinfold methods
- Bioelectrical impedance
- Hydrodensitometry
- Circumferential analyses

However, before testing it is important to follow some pre-test guidelines

Test guidelines

Firstly, you must be properly trained to carry out the test and have gained the permission of your subject to carry out to the test. They should have signed an informed consent form. You will need to explain exactly what is involved in each test and what they can expect to feel; this will put them at ease. Before undertaking a body fat percentage test the tester must make sure that the subject follows these guidelines:

- Is well hydrated
- Has avoided drinking alcohol on the day of the test (and to excess the day before)
- Has avoided large amounts of caffeinated drinks
- Has avoided exercise or any form of strenuous physical activity on the day of the test

Anthropometric methods

Durnin & Wormsley skinfold method

The skinfold assessment test is carried out using skinfold callipers and using the Durnin & Wormsley (1974) sites described in Table 26.2.

1. Take the measurements on the left-hand side of the body.
2. Mark the client up accurately.
3. Pinch the skin 1 cm above the marked site.
4. Pull the fat away from the muscle.
5. Place the calipers halfway between the top and bottom of the skinfold.
6. Allow the calipers to settle for one or two seconds.
7. Take the reading and wait 15 seconds before repeating for accuracy.
8. Add up the total of the four measurements.
   Triceps =
   Biceps =
   Subscapular =
   Suprailiac =
   Total =
9. Calculate body fat percentage using the table provided.

Area	Description of site
Triceps	Is a vertical pinch taken halfway between the shoulder and elbow on the back of the arm
Biceps	Is a vertical pinch taken 1 cm above the site for the triceps on the front of the arm
Subscapular	Taken at a 45-degree angle 2 cm below the lowest point of the shoulder blade
Suprailiac	Taken just above the iliac crest (hip bone), directly below the front of the shoulder

Table 26.2 Description of four sites for measuring body composition

1. **Triceps brachii**
   With the client's arm hanging loosely, a vertical fold is raised at the back of the arm, midway along a line connecting the acromion (shoulder) and olecranon (elbow) processes.

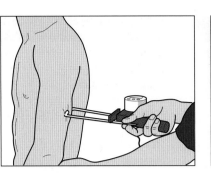

2. **Biceps brachii**
   A vertical fold is raised at the front of the arm, opposite to the triceps site. This should be directly above the centre of the cubital fossa (fold of the elbow).

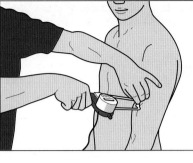

3. **Subscapular**
   A fold is raised just beneath the inferior angle of the scapula (bottom of the shoulder-blade). This fold should be at an angle of 45 degrees downwards and outwards.

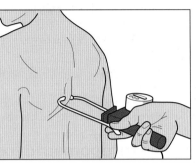

4. **Anterior suprailiac**
   A fold is raised 5–7 cm above the spinale (pelvis), at a point in line with the anterior axillary border (armpit). The fold should be in line with the natural folds downwards and inwards at up to 45 degrees.

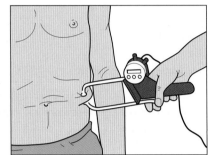

Fig 26.4 Body fat measurement

Jackson & Pollock's (1978) Body Density Equations

An alternative method of calculating percentage body fat is by using Jackson and Pollock's (1978) body density equation that are specific to males and females. Body fat percentage is calculated based on three skinfold methods from different sites for male and females. The sites on the body from which to take skinfold measurements are described in Tables 26.3 and 26.4.

Area	Description of site [Col hdg]
Pectoral (chest)	A skinfold taken at 45° along the border of the pectoralis major half-way between the anterior axillary fold and the nipple
Abdominal	A vertical skinfold taken 2 cm from the umbilicus
Mid thigh	A vertical skinfold taken on the anterior aspect of the thigh halfway between the inguinal crease and the proximal border of the patella. The knee should be flexed to 90 degrees with the subject seated

Table 26.3 Location of skinfold measurements for men

Area	Description of site
Suprailium	A horizontal fold above the iliac crest directly below the anterior axillary border. It is slightly in front of the iliac crest
Triceps	A vertical skinfold on the posterior aspect of the triceps exactly halfway between the olecranon process and the acromiom process with the hand in the supinated position
Mid-thigh	A vertical skinfold taken on the anterior aspect of the thigh halfway between the inguinal crease and the proximal border of the patella. The knee should be flexed to 90 degrees with the subject seated

Table 26.4 Location of skinfold measurements for females

Equations to measure body density and body fat percentage

In order to work out the body fat percentage, initially you must work out body density by using the following equations:

Males

Body density = 1.10938 – (0.0008267 × sum of chest, abdomen and thigh skinfolds in mm) + (0.0000016 × square of the sum of chest, abdomen and thigh) – (0.0002574 × age)

Source: Jackson & Pollock, 1978, based on a sample aged 18-61

Females

Body density = 1.0994921 – (0.0009929 × sum of triceps, thigh and suprailiac skinfolds + (0.0000023 × square of the sum of triceps, thigh and suprailiac skinfolds in mm – 0.0001392 × age in years)

Source: Jackson, Pollock & Ward, 1980, based on a sample aged 18–55

Once you have reached this figure for body density you can then work out body fat percentage by using the following Siri equation for men and women:

Percentage body fat = (495/body density) – 450

Validity & reliability

Skinfold methods are a popular and practical method for measuring skinfolds and they can be reliable if the tester is appropriately trained and skilled at differentiating between lean tissue and fat tissue. To be fully valid and reliable the person being tested must adhere to the pre-test procedures and, in particular, must be well-hydrated. The equipment that is being used must be of good quality, well maintained and correctly calibrated. It is vital for the test protocol and to ensure reliability that the skinfolds are taken at least twice with a gap of fifteen seconds between measurements on the same site. One drawback with skinfold testing is that some people find the method to be invasive to their privacy and they feel uncomfortable having their skinfolds measured. This is a problem that can be overcome by the next method of assessing body composition.

Bioelectrical Impedance Analysis (BIA)

This measures the resistance (or impedance) of the tissues of the body. BIA involves the passing of a small and harmless current through the body, usually from the feet to the hands, and the measurement of how much of the current has been conducted and

how much has been impeded. The current will pass unimpeded more quickly through fat-free tissue due to its higher water content than through fat tissue as this has a lower water content. In simple terms, lean tissue will conduct electricity and fat tissue will resist or impede electricity.

Formulae are then used to convert the reading for impedance into the measurement of body composition. This is usually done by the machine itself or by computer software, and it is necessary to enter height, weight, age and activity level of the subject so that the body fat percentage is calculated accurately.

The accuracy of this test is dependent on the individual being well hydrated as dehydration can cause inaccurate results. Dehydration is the result of loss of water from the body. Thus, impedance will be increased and a higher reading for body fat percentage will occur. The subject should also avoid eating for 4-5 hours before a test as a large meal can also increase impedance and produce a higher reading.

Hydrodensitometry

This method is commonly known as underwater weighing and is an application of Archimedes' principle to measure body volume. Body volume is calculated as the difference between body mass measured on land and body weight measured underwater. Body weight is the correct term here as body mass remains unchanged under water.

The test is carried out in the following way. The subject is placed on a chair that is suspended from a weighing scale and is hanging over water. The first measurement is made in the air with an adjustment for the weight of the seat. Then the subject is submerged and the weight of the subject is measured after a full exhalation followed by the subject holding their breath for 5-8 seconds. It is recommended that the test is repeated 8 to 12 times to gain a dependable score and increase the score's reliability.

Hydrodensitometry is regarded as the gold standard for assessing body fat percentage. However, it requires highly specialist equipment and access to a sport science laboratory. It is rarely used with the general public due to its invasive nature and lack of portability.

Circumferential analyses

Circumferential or girth measurements are useful because they are quick and easy to take and need skill to take. There are formulae that can be used to convert circumferential measurements to body composition but these have not proved to be accurate. Having taken girths you can use them to monitor either fat loss or muscle gain dependent upon the aims of the

subject and the type of training they are involved in. Thus, they could be used for a person training for fat loss or a person training for muscle development.

In order to take circumferential measurements you need to follow this protocol:

● Take the measurements under clothing (or record details of clothing)
● Mark up the exact location of the measurement site
● Hold the tape measure lightly on the skin to avoid compression
● Take each reading three times and then take the average of the three scores.

The sites for measurement are as follows in Table 26.5

Q Quick quiz I

1 Summarise why it is important to take body composition measurements rather than rely on body mass index.
2 What factors influence the reliability of skinfold measurement to assess body composition?
3 What are the benefits and drawbacks of using bioelectrical impedance and hydrodensitometry to assess body composition?

Fig 26.5 Underwater weighing

Name of site	Description of location of site
Biceps	With the arm straight and extended in front of the body the measurement is take halfway between the shoulder (acromiom process) and the elbow (olecranon process)
Forearm	With the arm extended in front of the body the measurement is taken at the widest point of the forearm
Abdomen	Taken one inch above the umbilicus
Gluteals	Standing with the heels together the widest point is taken around the buttocks
Right thigh	The widest point of the right thigh just below the buttock
Right calf	Widest point of the calf midway between the ankle and the knee

Table 26.5
Source: adapted from McArdle, Katch & Katch, 2007

Key learning points 2

- A person's body mass is made up of total fat mass and lean body mass
- Before a body composition test the subject must be well hydrated and have avoided alcoholic and caffeinated drinks as well as strenuous physical activity
- Durnin & Wormsley (1974) skinfolds are taken at biceps, triceps, subscapular and suprailiac
- Jackson & Pollock (1978) skinfolds are taken in different places for males (pectoral, abdominal, mid-thigh) and females (suprailium, triceps and mid-thigh)
- Validity and reliability are dependent upon the skill of the tester, the accuracy of the calipers and the preparation of the subject
- Bioelectrical impedance is based on the ability of lean tissue to conduct an electrical impulse and fat tissue to impede it
- Hydrodensitometry is based on Archimedes' principle and is viewed as one of the most accurate measures of body composition.

Student activity 26.2   120 minutes   P3   P4   P5   M1

Task 1
M2   D1

Assess an individual's body fat percentage following the appropriate guidelines using two anthropometric methods

Task 2

Use the following table to demonstrate an understanding of the validity and reliability of two anthropometric methods.

Name of method	Describe validity and reliability issues of the two methods P4	Explain validity and reliability issues of the two methods M1	Analyse validity and reliability issues of the two methods D1
1.			
2.			

Task 3

Carry out calculations to predict body fat percentage using two different methods of anthropometric assessment, interpret the results and describe the individual's strengths and areas for improvement (P5). Note: to achieve M2 you need to explain the results and the strengths and areas for improvement.

26.4 Be able to measure and interpret the anthropometric somatotype

P6 **M3** **D2**

Somatotyping is used to assess the individual's body shape and composition. The Heath-Carter

Anthropometric Somatotype is the most commonly used somatotyping method. To calculate somatotype it is necessary to take 10 body measurements that are taken at least twice to ensure reliability. In the Heath-Carter Anthropometric somatotype a person can be described by three numbers representing three different components. These are described in Table 26.6.

Component	Component name	Component description
1	Endomorphy	The relative roundness or fatness of a person, especially in relation to their height
2	Mesomorphy	The relative musculoskeletal development or muscularity of a person
3	Ectomorphy	The relative thinness or linearity of a person's physique

Table 26.6 Description of the three components of the Heath-Carter Anthropometric somatotype

(c)

(b)

(a)

Fig 26.6 (a) Endomorph, (b) Mesomorph, (c) Ectomorph

Each of these components is rated on a score of 1–7 in the following way:

Endomorphy Lean 1-2-3-4-5-6-7 Fat

Mesomorphy Slender 1-2-3-4-5-6-7 Muscular

Ectomorphy Heavy 1-2-3-4-5-6-7 Light

However, an individual is rated on all three components and their somatotype can be entered on the somatotype chart (Figure 26.7).

Their body shape will be described by the component that scores highest. For example, a person who scores 5-3-2 (point A on Figure 26.8) will be described as an endomorph; a score of 2-6-1 (point B on Figure 26.8) would be described as a mesomorph and 2-3-6 (point C on Figure 26.8) would be described as an ectomorph. It is possible to have two scores quite close together. For example, a score of 4-5-1 would have elements of endomorphy and mesomorphy, but would predominantly be a mesomorph. They are described as an endomorphic mesomorph.

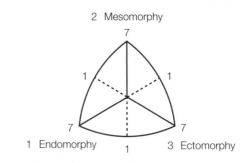

Fig 26.7 Somatochart

Figure 26.11 shows examples of endomorph, mesomorph and ectomorph.

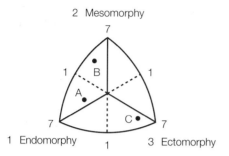

Fig 26.8 Measuring with the somatochart

Measuring & calculating each component of the somatotype

In order to assess an individual's somatotype you will need to take 10 measurements:

1 **Triceps skinfold:** with the subject's arm hanging in the anatomical position take the measurement half-way between the shoulder (acromiom process) and elbow (olecranon process).
2 **Subscapular skinfold:** 1-2cm below the inferior angle of scapula (its lowest point) at a 45° angle.
3 **Suprailiac skinfold:** 5-7cm above the anterior superior iliac spine directly below the axillary line (front of the armpit); taken horizontally.
4 **Medial calf:** taken on the medial (inside) side of the calf at the point of widest girth.
5 **Height** measured in both centimetres and millimeters.
6 **Bone breadth 1:** the humeral epicondylar (width of the elbow) between the medial and lateral epicondyles of the humerus with the elbow flexed.
7 **Bone breadth 2:** the femoral epicondylar (width of the knee) between the medial and lateral epicondyles with the knee flexed.
8 **Circumferential measurement 1:** the biceps muscle with the elbow flexed and the muscle tensed taken at the widest girth.
9 **Circumferential measurement 2:** the calf muscle taken from a standing position at the point of the widest girth.
10 **Weight:** mass measured in kilograms and taken on scales.

The calculation for each component of the somatotype is done using the following equations.

Endomorphy

Add the skinfolds at the *triceps, subscapular* and *suprailiac* sites
Multiply this sum by 170.18 / height
This total (in mm) is "X" in the following calculation:

$$\text{Endomorphy} = 0.7182 + 0.145X - 0.00068X2 + 0.0000014X3$$

Mesomorphy

Record height (H), humerus breadth (HB) and femur breadth (FB), maximum calf girth and maximum upper arm girth, with the arm flexed to 45° and tensed.
Calculate corrected arm (AG) and calf girth (CG) by subtracting triceps and medial calf skinfolds from the respective girths.
Substitute these values in the following equation:

$$\text{Mesomorphy} = 0.858HB + 0.601FB + 0.188AG + 0.161CG) - (0.131H) + 4.5$$

Ectomorphy

Record height in cm and weight in kg
Divide the height by the cube root of weight to calculate the reciprocal of the ponderal index or RPI. The magnitude of the RPI determines which formula is used to calculate ectomorphy.

If RPI > 40.74, Ectomorphy = 0.732RPI − 28.58
If 39.65 < RPI < 40.74, Ectomorphy = 0.463RPI − 17.615
If RPI < 39.65, Ectomorphy = 0.5

Once the three components of the somatotype have been calculated, the results can be plotted on the somatochart.

Key learning points 3

- Somatotyping assesses an individual's body shape
- Endomorphy is a description of the fatness of a person
- Mesomorphy is a description of the muscularity of a person
- Ectomorphy is a description of the leanness of a person
- To assess somatotype ten measurements need to be taken

339

Student activity 26.3   ⏱ 90 minutes

Using the following chart carry out an assessment of the anthropometric somatotype of an individual and describe the results (P6). Note: to achieve M3 you need to explain the results; to achieve D2 you will need to analyse the results.

1   Triceps skinfold
2   Subscapular
3   Suprailiac skinfold
4   Medial calf
5   Height measured in cm and mm

6   Bone breadth 1 – the humeral epicondylar
7   Bone breadth 2 – the femoral epicondylar
8   Circumferential measurement 1 (biceps muscle)
9   Circumferential measurement 2 (calf muscle)
10   Weight in kg:

Endomorph score =

Mesomorph score =

Ectomorph score =

26.5 Experimental Methods to Predict Maximum Oxygen Uptake

P7   M4   **D3**

Maximum Oxygen Uptake (MOU) is a method used to measure a person's aerobic capacity. Aerobic capacity is determined by the body's ability to take in and use oxygen and use it effectively and efficiently to produce energy for carrying out aerobic activities.

There are a range of tests available designed to predict a person's aerobic capacity and these can be placed into one of two categories:

1   Maximal.
2   Sub-maximal.

Maximal tests require the subject to exercise to exhaustion, which means that they are putting themselves under a great deal of stress and discomfort. If a person has any underlying health issues then a maximal test may pose a risk to their health, in which case sub-maximal tests should be carried out. However, a maximal test does produce more accurate predictions of VO_2 compared to sub-maximal tests. A sub-maximal VO_2max test provide less reliable and less valid predictions of VO_2 max. However, they usually require less equipment and are more suitable for some subjects for whom over-exertion is not medically appropriate. Also, they can usually be carried out without the need for supervision by a medically qualified person.

There are also **direct** and **indirect tests**. A direct test is named because it directly measure the amount of oxygen the subject breathes in and out during the test. In an indirect test other variables such as heart rate are measured to estimate VO_2max.

The reliability and validity of each test is important and will be discussed for each test in order to help you to determine the strengths and weaknesses for each test.

If a test produces consistent and reproducible results

Key term

Reliability: quality which makes something reliable; trustworthy; if a test is reliable, it will give the same results when repeated.

over time it would be deemed to be reliable. For example, if you were to administer the same VO_2max test on the same person under the same conditions, you would expect to see the same VO_2max score. However, if the test results differ significantly, then the test would be deemed to be unreliable.

Key term

Validity: this examines if a test actually measures what it is supposed to measure.

A range of fitness tests are available that state that they predict a person's VO_2max. However, some tests are better predictors than others and will, therefore, be a more valid test.

VO_2max results

VO_2 max can be expressed in one of two ways:

● Absolute
● Relative.

Absolute is measured as $L.min^{-1}$ and does not take into account a person's body size. **Relative** is expressed as $ml.kg^{-1}.min^{-1}$ –, which allows you to compare people of different body sizes meaningfully.

Pre-test procedures

Prior to any testing procedures, you will need to ensure that you have completed the full pre- test procedures outlined at the start of this unit to ensure the health and safety of the subject. These include:

- gaining permission to test
- completion of an informed consent form
- appropriate health screening.

Maximal Tests

Maximal tests usually produce more valid and reliable predictions of a person's maximum oxygen uptake, but these tests should not be carried out if:

- the subject is ill
- you are unsure of the test
- you are on your own.

VO₂max direct test

The direct VO_2max test is the most accurate method of assessing a person's aerobic capacity. However, the testing equipment can be expensive and it does require the subject to exercise to exhaustion. Also, a person with suitable medical qualifications should be present.

In order to attain valid and reliable VO_2max test scores, subjects should exercise on a piece of exercise equipment that matches the subject's main sport as closely as possible. Therefore, if the subject is a runner, then a treadmill would be best suited to them; for a rower, a rowing ergometer would be more suitable; for a cyclist, a cycle ergometer.

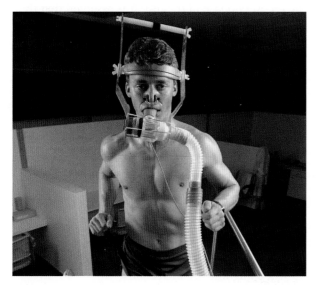

Fig 26.9 Testing a person's aerobic capacity

There are a range of different protocols available for a direct measurement of VO_2max test, which follow the procedure of increasing workload so that there is a gradual increment from moderate to maximal intensity. On line gas analysers or Douglas bags are used to calculate the oxygen uptake from oxygen and carbon dioxide in the expired air and minute ventilation, and the maximal level is determined at or near the completion of the test.

When a person has attained their VO_2max you should see some or all of the following indicators:

- a plateau in the oxygen uptake/exercise intensity relationship
- A final respiratory exchange ratio of 1.15 or above
- Final heart rate within 10 $b.min^{-1}$ of age predicted max

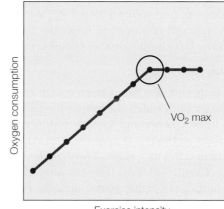

Fig 26.10

Validity & Reliability

A direct VO_2max test is the most reliable and valid indicator of a person's aerobic capacity.

Multi-stage fitness test

This test was developed at Loughborough University and allows a number of subjects to carry out the test at one time with minimal equipment.

This test is also known as the 'bleep' test because subjects have to run between timed bleeps. The time between recorded beeps decrease between each level with the initial running velocity at 8.5 km/hr increasing by 0.5 km/hr each minute.

The multi-stage fitness test requires participants to be motivated and they will usually need to be encouraged to exercise to exhaustion.

You will need a pre-recorded CD or tape and a flat area of 20 metres with a cone at either end. The protocol is as follows:

1   Mark out a length of 20m with cones.

341

2 Start the tape and the athletes will run when the first bleep sounds. They will run the 20m before the second bleep sounds.

3 When this bleep sounds they will turn around and run back.

4 They continue to do this and the time between the bleeps gets shorter and shorter so they have to run faster and faster.

5 If the subject fails to get to the other end before the bleep on three consecutive occasions then they are out.

6 Record at what point the athlete dropped out.

7 Work out the subject's score, which is the level and number of shuttles reached before they were unable to keep up with the bleeps.

Results

Refer to the tables provided in the multi-stage fitness test package to find your predicted VO_2 max. To work this out, you will just need to know the level of the test and the last shuttle number that you completed.

Validity & Reliability

Results from this test have shown a high correlation to VO_2max scores, which shows that the test has high validity values. Leger and Lamber found the correlation values for this test as a predictor for VO_2max to be greater then 0.9, which shows a very good correlation.

The reliability of this test can vary depending upon whether the subjects did actually exercise to exhaustion or 'give up' prior to working at maximal levels.

Cooper 12-minute Run Test

This test allows a number of subjects to carry out the test at one time and requires minimal equipment. The subject is required to run as far as possible around an athletics track within a 12-minute period.

You will need an athletics track and a stop-watch, whistle and cones.

1 Place the cones at 50m intervals around the track.

2 Start the subject and stop-watch off. The subject should run or walk for 12 minutes, trying to cover as much distance as possible in this time.

3 Once the 12 minutes is up, a whistle is blown to instruct the participant to stop. The total distance they cover is measured.

Results

To predict your subject's VO_2 max, use the following equation:

$$VO_{2max} \text{ (in ml/kg/min)} = (35.97 \times miles) - 11.29.$$

Validity & Reliability

Validity is quite high for this test, Cooper reported a correlation of 0.90. However, other tests have found a correlation of around 0.65. The reliability of this test can be affected by the motivation of the subject and also the amount of practice that they have had in carrying out this test.

Sub-maximal tests

Step Tests

In the following two step tests, the recovery heart rate is recorded and prediction equations are used to estimate VO_2max. The basic principal here relies on the fact that there is virtually a linear relationship between heart rate and oxygen uptake during exercise.

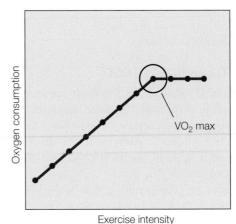

Fig 26.11

Therefore, if a person has a lower heart rate during the recovery phase of the test, it is assumed that they would have a higher VO_2max compared to a person with a higher heart rate.

Both tests allow a number of subjects to carry out the test at one time and require minimal equipment.

Harvard Step Test

This test requires the subject to step up onto a low platform of a specified height, and then down to the floor, repeating this action for five minutes. For this test you will need a step or platform that is 50.8 cm high, a stopwatch, a metronome or cadence tape.

1 The subject steps up and down on the step for a period of five minutes.

2 The subject may stop stepping before this five-minute period if they are unable to maintain the stepping rate for 15 seconds

3 The subject immediately sits down on completion

of the test, and their heart beats are counted for 1 to 1.5, 2 to 2.5, and 3 to 3.5 minutes.

Results

This test does not actually produce VO_2max results. However, it does produce scores that are representative of a person's aerobic capacity.

The results are determined by the following equation:

Results = (100 × test duration in seconds) divided by 2 × (total heartbeats in the recovery periods).

Scores are as follows:

Excellent	>90
Good	80–89
High average	65–79
Low average	55–64
Poor	<55

Queen's College Step Test

This is an adapted form of the Harvard Step test where the step used is 41.3 cm in height, which is slightly lower than the one used in the Harvard Step test.

1 Males step up and down from the platform at a rate of 24 steps per minute; females at a rate of 22 steps per minute for 3 minutes.
2 Five seconds after finishing the test the subject's heart rate is counted for fifteen seconds.

Results

VO_2max is predicted using the following equations:
For men:

VO_2max (ml/kg/min) = 111.33 – 0.42 × heart rate (bpm)

For women:

VO_2max (ml/kg/min) = 65.81 – 0.1847 × heart rate (bpm)

Validity & Reliability

For both of these sub-maximal step tests, correlation to VO_{2max} has been reported between 0.6 to 0.8. The reliability of these tests can vary if the stepping rate is not kept constant or the subject is not appropriately motivated. Provided that the stepping rate is constant and the motivation of the subject is maintained, the reliability levels of these tests can be high.

Astrand Cycle Ergometer Test

This test does require some specalised equipment and only allows one person to be tested at a time.

1 For this test you will need a cycle ergometer, a heart rate monitor and a stop-watch.
2 Ensure that subject is seated at the height appropriate for them; if necessary, adjust the handle bars to meet your subject's requirements.
3 Add the correct load for your subject based on Table 26.6. If your subject is fit then they should be given a load that is towards the top weighting in their particular age and gender category.
4 Your subject should pedal at a cadence of 60 rpm for a period of six minutes.
5 Take heart rate recordings every minute.
6 After two minutes, your subject's heart rate should be between 130–160 bpm. If it is higher than this, the load needs to be reduced by 25W; if heart rate is lower, the load needs to be increased by 25W.
7 After six minutes record heart rate and load wattage.

Results

To predict VO_2max you will need to use the Astrand-Ryhiming Nomogram, which is a recorded table of results and the recorded heart rate.

Results

Using Table 26.7 draw a line between pulse rate to the work rate in Watts, and where the line crosses the VO_2max it will give you the predicted value for VO_2max L min-1.

Reliability & Validity

Most reports for this test show high levels of correlation to predict a person's VO_2max. Macsween (2001) found this test to have a high level of correlation with values of over 0.9 to predict a person VO_2max.

Normative Data for VO^2max

You will notice that there are different tables for males and females to take into account the physiological differences between the two genders' VO_2max. Compare the results that your subject has scored on the normative tables (see Tables 26.8 & 26.9).

Age in years	Load for Males	Load for Females
Under 35	100–150	100–125
35–55	100–125	75–100
Over 55	75–100	

Table 26.7 Astrand Test Loading Wattages

Age	Very Poor	Poor	Fair	Good	Excellent	Superior
13–19	<26.0	26.0 – 30.9	31.0 – 34.9	35.0 – 38.9	39.0 – 41.9	>41.9
20–29	<23.6	23.6 – 28.9	29.0 – 32.9	33.0 – 36.9	37.0 – 41.0	>41.0
30–39	<22.8	22.8 – 26.9	27.0 – 31.4	31.5 – 35.6	35.7 – 40.0	>40.0
40–49	<21.0	21.0 – 24.4	24.5 – 28.9	29.0 – 32.8	32.9 – 36.9	>36.9
50–59	<20.2	20.2 – 22.7	22.8 – 26.9	27.0 – 31.4	31.5 – 35.7	>35.7
60+	<17.5	17.5 – 20.1	20.2 – 24.4	24.5 – 30.2	30.3 – 31.4	>31.4

Table 26.8 VO_2max for female ml/kg/min

Age	Very Poor	Poor	Fair	Good	Excellent	Superior
13–19	<35.0	35.0 – 38.3	38.4 – 45.1	45.2 – 50.9	51.0 – 55.9	>55.9
20–29	<33.0	33.0 – 36.4	36.5 – 42.4	42.5 – 46.4	46.5 – 52.4	>52.4
30–39	<31.5	31.5 – 35.4	35.5 – 40.9	41.0 – 44.9	45.0 – 49.4	>49.4
40–49	<30.2	30.2 – 33.5	33.6 – 38.9	39.0 – 43.7	43.8 – 48.0	>48.0
50–59	<26.1	26.1 – 30.9	31.0 – 35.7	35.8 – 40.9	41.0 – 45.3	>45.3
60+	<20.5	20.5 – 26.0	26.1 – 32.2	32.3 – 36.4	36.5 – 44.2	>44.2

Table 26.9 Male ml/kg/min
Source: Heyward (1998)

Work out how your subject's VO_2max results compare to the normative data results.

Elite male endurance athletes have average VO_2max recordings of around 70 ml/kg/min. Lance Armstrong, the Tour de France cyclist and race winner, has a reported VO_2max of 85 ml/kg/min.

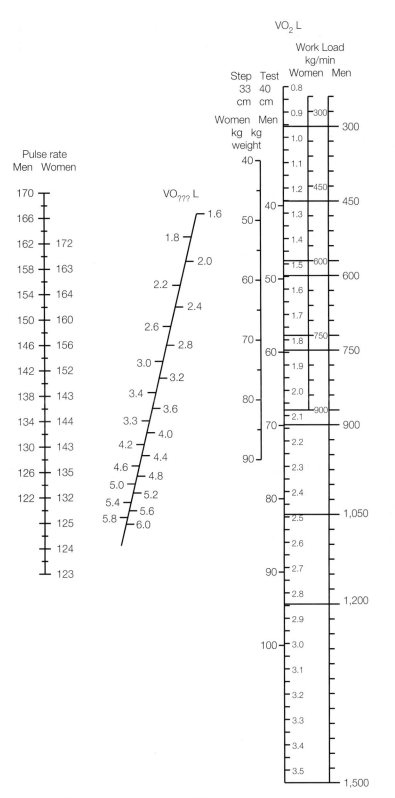

Fig 26.12 Astrand Nomogram to help to work out a person's VO₂ max

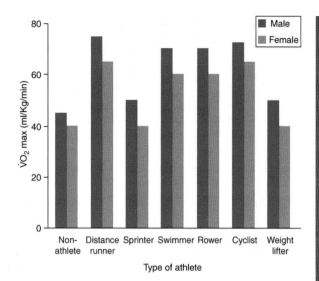

Fig 26.13 Approximated values of VO$_2$max for a range of sports

Key learning points 4

- All subjects taking part in aerobic capacity tests should be properly screened prior to participation and prepared appropriately for the test.
- Prediction of a person's aerobic capacity can be carried out through maximal and sub-maximal tests.
- Direct and indirect methods can be used to predict a person's aerobic capacity: **direct** tests measure the differences in oxygen uptake and output during exercise; **indirect** measurements rely on other testing other physiological variables, such as heart rate.
- The VO$_2$max test is the most reliable and valid method of predicting a person's VO$_2$max.
- The test should be as sport specific to the subject's selected sport in order for the VO$_2$max results to be valid.
- Maximal aerobic capacity tests include VO$_2$max and the multi-stage fitness test.
- Sub-maximal tests include Harvard step test, Queen's college step test and the Astrand cycle ergometer test.

Student activity 26.4 — 3–4 hours — P7 M4 D3

There are a range of methods available to help predict a person's VO$_2$max, choice is usually determined by the subject that is being tested and the availabilty of equipment to carry out the test.

Task 1

Select two different methods of predicting maximal oxygen uptake.

Task 2

Carry out and follow to different experimental methods to predict maximum oxygen uptake or an individual.

Task 3

Write a report that describes, explains and analyses your results from both sets of experiments.

References

Abernethy, B., S. J. Hanrahan, V. Kippers, L. T. MacKinnon & M.G. Pandy (2005) *The Biophysical Foundations of Human Movement*, Human Kinetics.

Astrand, P-O & K. Rodahl (1986) *The Textbook of Work Physiology: Physiological Bases of Exercise (3rd ed.).* New York: McGraw-Hill

Behnke, A. R. & J.H Wilmore (1974) *Evaluation and Regulation of Body Build and Composition.* Prentice-Hall.

Cooper, K. H. (1968) 'A means of assessing maximal oxygen uptake', Journal of the American Medical Association, 203:pp. 201-204.

Durnin, J.V. & J., Wormersley (1974) 'ody fat assessed from total body density and its estimation from skinfold thickness: measurement on 481 men and women aged 16 to 72 years', *British Journal of Nutrition*, 32, pp. 77-92.

Heyward, V. H. (1998) *Advance Fitness Assessment & Exercise Prescription*, 3rd edition,

Jackson, A. S. & M. L. Pollock (1978) 'Generalized equations for predicting body density of men', *British Journal of Nutrition*, 40, pp. 497-504.

Jackson, A. S., M. L. Pollock & A Ward (1980) 'Generalized equations for predicting body density of women', *Medicine & Science in Sports and Exercise*, 12, pp. 175-182.

Leger, A. & J. Lamber (1982) European Journal of Applied Physiology & Occupational Physiology, **49**, (1) June, p. 1-12.

Macsween, A. (2001) *Journal of Sports Medicine & Physical Fitness*, 41(3): pp. 312-317.

McArdle, W.D., F. I. Katch, & V. L. Katch (2007) *Exercise Physiology: Energy, Nutrition and Human Performance,* Lippincott, Williams and Wilkins.

Wilmore, J.H. & D.L. Costill (2005) *Physiology of Sport and Exercise:* 3rd edition. Champaign, IL: Human Kinetics

Useful websites

www.acsm.org

Contains up-to-date information on guidelines and protocols for fitness testing.

www.bases.org.uk

Offers lots of information on fitness testing procedures, ethics and health and safety in laboratory testing.

www.topendsports.com

Provides excellent resources for body composition assessment techniques, including visual presentations of assessment sites.

www.somatotype.org

Contains excellent resources on somatotyping and it assessment, including a full pdf on instructions on how to assess somatotype using the Heath-Carter method.

Index

trigger points 203
triglycerides 6, 131–2, 215
Type A/B (personality theories) 56

unconsciousness 270–1
unsaturated fats 215, 216
urban outdoor pursuit centres 311

Valsalva manoeuvre 35–6
variability measures 92–3
vector 120
veins/venules 21
vertebrae 5–6
vertical jump test 154–5
vibration (massage technique) 203
video analysis 288, 302

vitamins 136, 218–19
VO$_2$max tests 48, 152–3, 341–3, 344
    normative data for 343–6
voluntary bodies 311

warm-ups 179, 242–3, 261
waste products: effects of 44–5
water 208, 220: *see also* hydration
water-based activities 308, 322–3
water-soluble vitamins 218–19
water sports 296
weight loss 234
Weiner's attribution theory of motivation 57
white blood cells 23
windsurfing 308
Wingate test 155–6